D0934556

THE ASSASSINATION
OF LUMUMBA

THE ASSASSINATION
OF LUMUMBA

◆

LUDO DE WITTE

Translated by

ANN WRIGHT and **RENÉE FENBY**

VERSO

London · New York

To Jacquie

First published by Verso 2001
This edition © Verso 2001
Translation © Ann Wright and Renée Fenby 2001
First published as *De Moord op Lumumba* by Editions Uitgeverij van Halewyck 1999
© Ludo De Witte 1999
All rights reserved

The moral rights of the author and the translators have been asserted

Verso
UK: 6 Meard Street, London W1F 0EG
USA: 180 Varick Street, New York, NY 10014–4606

Verso is the imprint of New Left Books

ISBN 1–85984–618–1

British Library Cataloguing in Publication Data
A catalogue record for this book is available from the British Library

Library of Congress Cataloging-in-Publication Data
A catalog record for this book is available from the Library of Congress

Typeset by M Rules
Printed by Biddles Ltd, Guildford and King's Lynn

"The Gods are not all powerful, they cannot erase the past."

Agathon

"How can a beret coloured blue erase, just like that, the preju-
dices of conservative officers from Sweden, Canada or Britain?
How does a blue armband vaccinate against the racism and
paternalism of people whose only vision of Africa is lion hunt-
ing, slave markets and colonial conquest; people for whom the
history of civilisation is built on the possession of colonies?
Naturally they would understand the Belgians. They have the
same past, the same history, the same lust for our wealth."

Patrice Lumumba

CONTENTS

Translators' note
xi

Acknowledgements
xiii

Preface to the English-language edition
xv

Introduction
xxi

Map of the Congo in 1960
xxvii

Who's Who on 17 January 1961
xxviii

The International Actors
xxx

1 PREPARING THE GALLOWS

A "nigger" upstart (30 June 1960) · Belgian troops and the Blue Berets in Katanga (July–August 1960) · The elimination of Lumumba's government (August–September 1960) · In the steps of the CIA: Operation Barracuda

1

2 UNITED AGAINST "SATAN"

Mobutu's appearance on the political scene · The copper state, an "oasis of peace" · The offended King Baudouin · The Belgian government

27

3 THE DEATH CELL

d'Aspremont Lynden and Loos in Africa. Lumumba delivered to Mobutu by the UN (2 December 1960) · Camp Hardy at Thysville · The Belgians wait in Katanga · Tshombe saved again by the UN

46

4 THE GREEN LIGHT FROM BRUSSELS

Colonel Vandewalle's new mission · Patrice Lumumba must die · Mutiny in Thysville, panic in Leopoldville and Brussels (12–14 January 1961) · Bakwanga or Elisabethville? (14–17 January 1961) · d'Aspremont Lynden orders Lumumba's transfer to Katanga (16 January 1961)

67

5 LUMUMBA'S LAST DAY

From Thysville to Lukala, then to Moanda · From Moanda to Elisabethville in the DC-4 · Arrival in Katanga · At the Brouwez house · "No blood on our hands" · Tshombe celebrates · Back at the Brouwez house · Lumumba's last hour

93

6 OPERATION "COVER-UP"

Anxiety or celebration? · Masquerade in Katanga · "No blood on our hands" (encore) · Masquerade in Brussels and New York · To the depths of hell · The world is informed

125

7 A RIVER OF BLOOD

The martyrdom of Jean-Pierre Finant at Bakwanga (9 February 1961) · Cover-up in New York and Brussels · The price of blood · Colonel Vandewalle and Leopold II

153

8 *DANSE MACABRE* IN GBADOLITE

Guy Weber's confession · *Danse macabre* in Gbadolite (1985) · Lumumba's nationalism: a provisional evaluation

165

Conclusion: Lumumba's political testament
184

Notes
186

Bibliography
204

Chronology
211

Index
215

TRANSLATORS' NOTE

A few terms have been left in the original French to avoid any risk of misinterpretation. They are *élimination définitive,* the crucial two words from the important 5/6 October 1960 telegram which can be rendered in English alternatively as "to eliminate/dispose of/get rid of once and for all"; *Gendarmerie,* the army of seceded Katanga, and the Bureau Conseil, the Belgian advisory committee in Katanga.

We have, wherever possible, retained the exact titles and ranks of the people detailed in the narrative (though have not always used such titles on second and subsequent mentions). The equivalent of the Commandant rank in the Belgian army and *Gendarmerie* (Major in the English army) is styled *Major* to avoid confusion with the specific and separate rank of Major in the Belgian army and *Gendarmerie*, which remains Major.

The term *casques bleus* which is used for the UN peacekeeping forces in the original French text has been rendered as Blue Berets, although this English term was not apparently used until the 1970s. All quotes from the United Nations' correspondence in English are the original texts; some are ungrammatical (not having been written by native English speakers) and some include in-house abbreviation. The name of Kasa Vubu, often rendered in the original UN documents as Kasavubu, is here styled throughout as Kasa Vubu to avoid possible confusion.

ACKNOWLEDGEMENTS

I would like to express my gratitude to all who helped me with this book: Marilla B. Guptil (United Nations Archives, New York); Professors François Houtart (Louvain-la-Neuve), Benoît Verhaegen (Kinshasa) and Herbert Weiss (New York); the staff of the Institut Africain (ASDOC/CEDAF, Brussels); the depositaries of the A.E. De Schryver Archives; Bert Govaerts (VRT, Flemish television) whom I advised on his documentary about Lumumba's assassination; Angèle Vandewalle-Saive, depositary of Colonel Frédéric Vandewalle's Archives; the staff at the Albertine Library (Brussels) and at the Louvain University Central Library; the lawyer Jules Raskin, who let me have his correspondence with Lumumba; Patricia Van Schuylenbergh from the Musée Royal de l'Afrique Centrale; the officials at the Archives Department of the Joseph Jacquemotte Foundation (Brussels); Jacques Brassinne, who let me read his doctoral thesis on Lumumba's assassination; and Françoise Peemans and Claudine Dekais at the Belgian Foreign Ministry Archives Service (Brussels).

Albert de Coninck, Father Jacques Steffen and Professor Benoît Verhaegen shared their memories with me; they either witnessed or participated in these historical events. Jules Gérard-Libois (Founder-director of CRISP, the Centre de Recherches et d'Informations Socio-Politiques) gave me his time for a very interesting exchange of ideas on the subject. Erik Kennes (Institut Africain) and Jean Van Lierde gave me documents and specific information or ideas for further research.

Several people helped me in the final stage of this book: Professor Jan Blommaert (Ghent), Jacqueline Dever, Bert Govaerts (VRT), Mputu Tshimanga Chantal, Olela Odimba Raphaël, Walter Roelants, Daouda Sanon, Geert Seynaeve, Tshimanga Ilunga Jean, Jean Van Lierde, Professor Benoît Verhaegen (Kinshasa) and Eric Wils. Although I take full responsibility for this book, their comments were an important addition to the final version of this work.

PREFACE TO THE ENGLISH-LANGUAGE EDITION

When this book first appeared in Dutch, the press duly concentrated on its main conclusion: that the Belgian government was primarily responsible for the murder of the Congolese prime minister Patrice Lumumba. It is obvious to the reader, however, that other parties were equally guilty. True, the Belgians and the Congolese actually killed Lumumba, but without the steps taken by Washington and the United Nations during the preceding months, the assassination could never have been carried out. In July 1960, after Belgium intervened in the Congo and after the rich copper state of Katanga seceded, the United States went into action. The Western super-power supported intervention by the United Nations to stop Lumumba calling on friendly African armies or the Soviet Union to help him combat Belgian–Katangese aggression. Dag Hammarskjöld, the UN Secretary General, deployed an impressive array of military force. The Blue Berets protected Katanga and played a decisive role in overthrowing the Congolese government. Meanwhile, US President Dwight Eisenhower had instructed his aides to liquidate Lumumba and a top secret CIA unit was given the task of eliminating him. Brussels wholeheartedly agreed with this objective and also sent out a commando operation.

While the US and Belgium were plotting murder, other Western powers were equally convinced that Lumumba represented a big danger to their neo-colonial enterprise in Africa. On 19 September 1960, the American president and the British foreign minister Lord Home discussed the Congo crisis. The minutes of that meeting suggest that London could have known of Washington's plan to assassinate Lumumba who had, in the mean time, been removed from office: "The president expressed his wish that Lumumba would fall into a river full of crocodiles; Lord Home said regretfully that we have lost many of the techniques of old-fashioned diplomacy." A week later, President Eisenhower and British prime minister Harold Macmillan met, accompanied by their respective foreign ministers. The record of this meeting leaves little to the imagination as far as London's intentions were concerned: "Lord Home raised the question why we are not getting rid of Lumumba at the present time. If he were to come back to power, there would be immediate stress on the Katanga issue, which would get us into all sorts of legalistic differences. He stressed that now is the time to get rid of Lumumba." Meanwhile, on the other side of the Atlantic, high-ranking British civil servants and the Lord Privy Seal Edward Heath (who would later become prime minister) were in consultation. Was it just coincidence that the opportunity for an assassination was on the agenda?[1]

A few months later, the Belgian minister for African affairs and his representatives in the Congo set the scene for the murder. Lumumba's transfer to Katanga, delivering him into the hands of his worst enemies, was done with the full knowledge of Lawrence Devlin, the CIA station chief in the capital. He must have been relieved, because only a few days earlier he had cabled Washington to note that only "drastic steps" would prevent Lumumba's return to power. Devlin's superiors and their NATO allies must also have been relieved: in the weeks leading up to Lumumba's transfer, intense negotiations between the US, Belgium, France, the UK-controlled Rhodesian Federation, Portugal, Mobutu and Tshombe in the Congo, to discuss various secret actions to fight the Congolese nationalists, had taken place.[2]

A good number of the writers examining Washington's role have analysed the Congo crisis in terms of the Cold War. Their discussions are based on the argument put forward by Washington and London at the time to justify Western intervention – that Soviet expansion needed to be checked. But does this argument stand up to the facts? It is true that the year 1960 surely marked a climax in the East–West conflict. On 1 May 1960, a U2 spy plane was brought down in Soviet air space, although Eisenhower totally denied the existence of aerial espionage. At a summit meeting in Paris, the Soviet leader Nikita Krushchev called Eisenhower a liar. The summit was cancelled. The Congo crisis turned into a war of words. Washington, London and Brussels accused Moscow of wanting to get its hands on central Africa. Lumumba was called a "Communist", a "crypto-Communist" or at the very least a politician who was willing to open the door to Soviet intervention. During the UN General Assembly in the autumn of that same year, Krushchev replied vehemently, accusing Hammarskjöld of being an agent of imperialism, intent on safeguarding the UN's interests in the Congo.

On closer inspection, however, the Congo crisis was not really a war between East and West with hegemony in central Africa at stake. Moscow was certainly not opposed to extending its influence in the world nor to having more control, but Stalin's heirs were even more interested in stability and peaceful coexistence with Washington. The latter was a critical factor in their policies towards Africa, which after all was part of the Western hemisphere. The Kremlin had neither the political will nor the means to threaten the West's supremacy in the Congo and this was clear to most observers at the time. The Kremlin certainly did not want to support Lumumba unconditionally during the Congo crisis; it was more interested in a propaganda victory: Krushchev denounced Western intervention to reinforce his diplomatic position in the Afro-Asian world. The destruction of Congolese nationalism was a devastating blow to those struggling for liberation throughout Africa, but it did not worry the blinkered conservative bureaucrats of the Kremlin: for them, Lumumba and African nationalism were throwaway items. Krushchev told the US ambassador in Moscow off the record that "he was sorry for him [Lumumba] as a person when he was in prison but that his imprisonment actually served Soviet interests". For Moscow, Lumumba's defeat was no more than a propaganda coup. "With respect to Congo 'K' said what had happened there and particularly the murder of Lumumba had helped communism." On the whole, Moscow's support for the Congolese nationalists was only ever a symbolic gesture. Was it not significant that the US ambassador in the Congo, who inundated Washington with messages about the Soviet danger in central Africa, recognised during a (behind closed doors) interview with a US Senate commission that the Kremlin's support for the Lumumbists was never more than a "trickle"?[3]

Congolese independence was primarily an expression of the anti-colonial revolution which pitted the colonialist North against the colonised South. Since World War II, millions of people had thrown off the yoke of colonialism through strikes, civil disobedience movements and full-scale wars: India in 1947, China in 1949, Vietnam in 1954. A war of liberation had been raging in Algeria since 1954, the second war in Indochina broke out in 1957, and the Cuban people had overthrown Batista's semi-colonial regime in 1959. Sub-Saharan Africa was no exception. In 1953, four African states were members of the UN; by the end of 1960 there were twenty-six member-states. The UN declared 1960 the Year of Africa; no less than sixteen states on the black continent gained their independence that year, and the largest and potentially richest of them was the Congo. To counter the obstacle that independence presented, the West had to change its policy of overt domination for one of indirect control, and new national leaders had to learn to respect the neo-colonial order.

Lumumba barred the way to this goal, because he advocated a complete decolonisation that would benefit the population as a whole. He had, therefore, to be stopped. In order to get public opinion on their side, Western strategists invoked a series of noble objectives. Just as the Belgian king Leopold II had legitimised the conquest of the Congo by presenting it as liberating Africans from the hands of Arab slave traders, and colonial exploitation had been justified as a civilising enterprise, so in 1960 the nationalists were destroyed in the name of protecting Africa from Soviet imperialism. "Saving Africa from the Cold War" or "containing Soviet influence in the process of de-colonisation" were the coded phrases used by the West.

Lumumba was not a communist. He was a nationalist, prepared to accept help from any quarter provided that it was unconditional help which did not compromise sovereignty. The comparisons between Lumumba and Castro quoted in the Western press of the time were grossly exaggerated: the scale of anti-imperialist mobilisation, the degree of organisation of the people and the ability and depth of the ruling cadre were much less developed in the Congo than in Cuba. However, the comparison was not completely inappropriate. Under pressure from the people, Nasser in 1956 had reclaimed from the West the national heritage which had been stolen from the Egyptians. What had happened in Egypt could happen under Lumumba, turning the anti-colonial struggle into a broader fight for national liberation which would qualitatively weaken imperialism's hold in the Congo. The imminence of this process of radicalisation explained why the Congolese leader was seen as a mortal enemy by the Belgian establishment, Wall Street and the City of London.

The public has recently become familiar with several of the Belgian protagonists and witnesses in this drama. Jacques Bartelous, Jacques Brassinne, Jean Cordy, Louis Marlière, Gerard Soete and Armand Verdickt have appeared in a television documentary; some of them have given radio or television interviews and made statements to the press. These witnesses confirm, directly or indirectly, the main arguments of this book which, apart from a few minor adaptations, reproduces the Dutch original.

The interviews with former police commissioner Gerard Soete caused an outcry. Soete, who got rid of Lumumba's, Mpolo's and Okito's bodies, showed journalists two of Patrice Lumumba's teeth and a bullet taken from his skull. Later he said he had thrown them into the North Sea. Elsewhere he said he "may have" kept one of Lumumba's phalanx bones. The part of his book which recounts his exploits is reproduced in Chapter 6 of this book under the heading "The Depths of Hell" and should be read as authentic testimony.

The most interesting "confession", however, comes from Colonel Louis Marlière, a key figure and a leading witness to what we can now call one of the twentieth century's most important political assassinations. In Chapter 3 I write: "On October 6, Major Loos, military adviser to [Belgian minister] d'Aspremont Lynden, leaves Brussels for a brief mission to Pointe-Noire, Congo-Brazzaville. He has discreet contacts with Colonel Marlière, who is busy preparing for Operation Barracuda [code name for the Belgian plot to dispose of Lumumba]. We can guess the purpose of their discussions: the day Loos leaves for Africa, d'Aspremont Lynden's telegram to Mistebel calls for Lumumba's *élimination définitive*."[4] Recently, various apologists for Belgian policy at the time have stressed that the word *élimination* should not be taken as meaning Lumumba's physical elimination, merely his political elimination. However, Marlière's recent confession confirms my argument that Brussels did want to eliminate Lumumba physically. Confronted with documents from the Foreign Ministry archives, Colonel Marlière admitted that Major Loos, the minister for African affairs' right-hand man, had offered him "a crocodile hunter to bump off Lumumba".[5]

Following the revelations in my book and their repercussions in the media, the Belgian parliament set up a Commission of Inquiry into Belgian responsibility for Lumumba's assassination. The commission will submit its conclusions to parliament in autumn 2001. Hitherto, too many archives have remained closed and too many of those implicated have kept silent. If the Commission succeeds in opening the archives and questioning those implicated under oath, new revelations will surely come to light on the martyrdom of the Congolese prime minister, whose fate was sealed by message 64 of 15/16 January 1961 from the Belgian Minister for African Affairs d'Aspremont Lynden, in which he ordered Lumumba be transferred to Katanga. Needless to say, it is in the interests of many influential forces that this should not happen.[6]

Ludo De Witte
April 2001

INTRODUCTION

Few events in recent history have been the target of such a ferocious campaign of disinformation as the war waged by the Belgian establishment against the first Congolese government of Patrice Lumumba. Foreign intervention began shortly after the Belgian colony gained its independence on 30 June 1960; first Belgian soldiers landed in the Congo, then the Blue Berets. Brussels and the other Western powers, operating under cover of the United Nations, were determined to overthrow Lumumba's nationalist government and install a neo-colonial regime, thereby putting the country at the mercy of the trusts and holding companies which had controlled it for decades. The West soon obtained its first success. In September 1960, the Congolese government and parliament which supported Lumumba were swept aside by Colonel Joseph-Désiré Mobutu. The war against the Congolese nationalists came provisorily to a head when, on 17 January 1961, Lumumba and two of his closest associates were assassinated in Katanga, which was then being propped up by Belgian military and government personnel.

This dark episode was suppressed for almost forty years, hidden from the history books. For fear of losing prestige, funding and other facilities, nobody has dared undertake a serious analysis and describe the Congo crisis as it really happened. No politician has taken the initiative of subjecting Belgium's Foreign Ministry archives to careful scrutiny, or requested a debate or parliamentary inquiry on the subject. On the contrary – once Lumumba's government was ousted, an attempt was made to deprive the Africans of the true story of his overthrow: not only had Lumumba been physically eliminated, his life and work were not to become a source of inspiration for the peoples of Africa either. His vision of creating a unified nation state and an economy serving the needs of the people were to be wiped out. In an attempt to prevent another Lumumba ever appearing again, his ideas and his struggle against colonial and neo-colonial domination had to be purged from collective memory.

What was true for the destabilisation and overthrow of the Congolese government was even more true for the culminating event of that work of
destruction: the assassination of the former Congolese prime minister.
Lumumba's corpse was barely cold when *La Libre Belgique*, the Brussels daily
paper and mouthpiece of the former colonial power, explained away the murder
by ascribing it to the political immaturity of the Congolese: "What it demonstrates, alas, is that in Africa and in certain countries with the same level of
development, access to democracy is still a murderous affair".[1] With a slight shift
of emphasis, the same argument still survives today. The assassination is portrayed as a Congolese affair, a settling of scores "among Bantus", which had
nothing to do with the West.

The aim of this book is to turn this argument on its head. In *Crisis in Kongo*
(1996) (Crisis in the Congo), I told the story of Lumumba's overthrow through
the important international players who engineered intervention in the Congo
from the outset: the Eyskens government, US Presidents Eisenhower and
Kennedy, and senior United Nations officials headed by Dag Hammarskjöld.
Crisis in Kongo is based primarily on an examination of the United Nations
archives in New York which deal with the UN intervention in the Congo
(1960–64). They show quite clearly that the United Nations leaders supported
the war the Western powers were waging against Lumumba's government and
that, at certain times, the UN was the willing tool of Western interference.
Most of the conclusions reached in *Crisis in Kongo* are taken up in *The Assassination
of Lumumba*. However, I do not wish merely to present a simple analysis of
Western strategies, troop deployments, diplomatic intrigues, state visits and the
rhetoric of the media in those days. I also want to concentrate on the last days,
the last hours, of Patrice Lumumba, on the suffering of the world's then most
famous prisoner.

The Assassination of Lumumba contains, therefore, a second account which in a
sense complements the story described in *Crisis in Kongo*. The geo-political history conceived in Western drawing rooms becomes real, tangible, flesh and
blood. The violation of Congolese democracy is expressed in Lumumba's
imprisonment; UN complicity is demonstrated by the help given to Mobutu's
soldiers in capturing Lumumba; the Belgian attack on Congolese sovereignty is
proved by the Barracuda plot and the actions of white officers in Katanga. And
finally, surely Lumumba's assassination encapsulates the essence of the Congo
crisis – a crisis which, as Lumumba's comrade Antoine Gizenga put it, was in
fact a colonial reconquest.[2]

My account relies heavily on the archives of the Belgian Foreign Ministry and
on "Enquête sur la mort de Patrice Lumumba" (Inquiry into the Death of Patrice
Lumumba), the unpublished doctoral dissertation that Jacques Brassinne
defended at the Université Libre de Bruxelles (ULB) in 1991. Brassinne's work
is a vast and detailed document dealing with the murder; it relates numerous
hitherto unknown facts and contains remarkable testimonies. However, at the

same time, it applauds Belgian actions during that period and represents the most sophisticated attempt possible to put Lumumba's assassination down to a purely internal Congolese conflict. Only one expert, Professor Benoît Verhaegen, has taken the trouble to do a serious critique of the dissertation and of the popular version of it entitled *Qui a tué Patrice Lumumba?* (Who Killed Patrice Lumumba?) published by Jacques Brassinne and Jean Kestergat in 1991.[3]

The non-scientific premises of the dissertation which was so praised by the academic world and the Belgian press are glaringly obvious.[4] Brassinne collaborated with the Katangan regime which he himself recognises was guilty of the assassination. On 17 January 1971 he took part in a meeting of Belgians who could have taken the decision to save Lumumba's life, had they really wanted to. The results of his research, which is based essentially on interviews with witnesses who are directly implicated, are therefore slanted in their very nature. These witnesses knew perfectly well that Brassinne was implicated. Any revelation could be used not only against the witness but also against the investigator. Moreover, Brassinne is extremely influential in Belgian political circles. He was knighted by King Baudouin in 1988 while he was working on his dissertation. His witnesses were not free to express themselves because he – their questioner – was involved up to his neck in the crime, as also was the ruling class of which he is a member. The rules of objectivity which are essential for the collection of scientific data were not respected.

In his "Enquête" there is no objective analysis of the activities of the Belgian government and its collaborators in the Congo and Katanga. Officially, power was held by Africans in secessionist Katanga. In fact, Belgians were pulling all the strings. Brassinne makes no effort to analyse how power was exercised. Katanga's real nerve centre, the Belgian Bureau Conseil, is simply left out of his account. The Belgians who kept Katanga going are presented as isolated advisers, working with no coordination, vision or master plan. And, he continues, the small group of Belgians who actually did the dirty work were subject to *force majeure*, at the mercy of the Katangans. He says in his dissertation that the Belgians who took part in the assassination of Lumumba were "disciplined subalterns" of the Katangan government. He concludes: "They bear no responsibility for what happened." The Katangan ministers, he continues, were likewise subject to *force majeure*. He presents the Katangans as the instruments of "Bantu tradition" which made the crime inevitable. He quotes a witness statement: "The Bantu of Katanga believed that if a member of a given tribe met an enemy and had the opportunity to kill him but did not do so, he was disgraced in the eyes of the rest of his tribe."

The truth is very different from that which Brassinne would have us believe. As a first step, the reader must jettison a good number of established canons on the subject. Most of the studies on the Congo crisis allege that Lumumba was assassinated by the Congolese. A few sophisticated versions mention help from the CIA. Hence, Manu Ruys, a very influential Belgian political commentator, maintains in his book *Achter de maskerade* (1996) (Behind the Masquerade) that the CIA backed Lumumba's elimination. In his article on *Crisis in Kongo,* this man who claims he wants to unveil the power brokers' masquerade, although he helped to keep their masks in place for decades, sticks to this position without providing the slightest proof.[5]

It is in fact no more than a persistent myth. It is an obvious tactic by those who want to shield Brussels from being implicated; or perhaps it is an a posteriori interpretation of events put forward by certain well-meaning commentators who have been misled by the support the United States gave Mobutu and his Second Republic between 1965 and 1990, and by a superficial reading of the Church Report published in 1975 by the United States Senate Select Committee on Washington's involvement in attempts on the lives of Rafael Trujillo, Ngo Dinh Diem, Fidel Castro and Patrice Lumumba. The fact is that the CIA had already abandoned its action against Lumumba by the beginning of December 1960. It was Belgian advice, Belgian orders and finally Belgian hands that killed Lumumba on that 17 January 1961. Political assassinations are not only the prerogative of American, French and British governments: the Belgian government of Gaston Eyskens is directly responsible for the assassination of the Congolese prime minister.

Can we call *The Assassination of Lumumba* a committed book? It may well make readers feel indignant, indeed angry, especially since the victim of this crime was not only a legally elected prime minister but also the leader of an incipient nationalist movement which, had the West not won, could have influenced the course of history in Africa for the better. Lumumba's political career, which was short and dazzling, has inspired a good number of political writers. He was, in the words of Jean-Paul Sartre, "a meteor in the African firmament". But did Lumumba disappear as quickly as he appeared? Has he really disappeared? In politics, time takes on a different meaning. For many Africans, the figure of Lumumba is still a source of political inspiration: in fact, the task which Lumumba saw himself facing forty years ago is for the most part still waiting to be carried out today.

The book can also be seen as the counterpart to Brassinne's dissertation. When organising the public defence of the dissertation, lecturers at the ULB held an imaginary trial in which Brassinne was invited by Lumumba's murderers to play the role of defence counsel. *The Assassination of Lumumba* can be read as the public prosecutor's closing address in the courtroom. Supported by facts, documents and witnesses, it wants to convince the jurors. Patrice Lumumba's assassination is not, therefore, treated as a "faction thriller". The machinations of the protagonists in Brussels are reconstructed as objectively and conscientiously as possible. It was never my intention to paint a black and white picture of the principal actors in this drama: the "baddies", the murderers (Brussels and collaborators), on the one hand, and the "goodies", the victim (Patrice Lumumba), on the other. It is clear that what I call "Brussels", a term referring to the Belgian ruling class (with, at its nerve centre, the Belgian government, the Société Générale bank and the monarchy), cannot be defined as a monolithic bloc. Inside this network, between junctions and ramifications, there is friction and tension. Furthermore, not everyone favoured "strong measures" against Lumumba, to echo Jacques Brassinne's euphemism. For his part, Lumumba was not a saint, but a human being. He certainly made political mistakes, and so did his assistants and supporters. But the fact remains that he was the legally elected prime minister who was assassinated with the backing of Brussels and its appendages. This book concentrates on this dirty *Belgian* affair, on the process by which Brussels and its emissaries in Africa finally took that risky decision, with such serious consequences, to assassinate Lumumba. A preliminary attempt to analyse Lumumba's life and work is given in the section "Lumumba's nationalism: a provisional evaluation", in Chapter 8.

Finally, this drama is much more than an old story, dead and gone. It is a staggering example of what the Western ruling classes are capable of when their vital interests are threatened. Assassination then becomes a useful measure, a possible solution. The murders of Lumumba, Rosa Luxemburg, Félix Moumié and Malcolm X, as well as the massacres at Guernica, Buchenwald, Dresden, Hiroshima and My Lai, are the expressions of a system which turns men into beasts. In his famous play *The Threepenny Opera*, Bertolt Brecht puts these words into the mouth of Macheath, who is active in the banking business: "What's a jemmy compared with a share certificate? What's breaking into a bank compared with founding a bank? What's murdering a man compared to employing a man?"

The inquiry into the assassination is just as topical when viewed from another angle. This murder has affected the history of Africa. The overthrow of the Congo's first government, the elimination of Lumumba, the bloody repression of the popular resistance to the neo-colonial regimes of Joseph Kasa Vubu, Mobutu and Moïse Tshombe and finally the creation of the Second Republic in this vast strategic country: the repercussions of all these events have had disastrous consequences throughout Africa as a whole. Lumumba and the Congolese government appeared just when the anti-colonial revolution was at its peak worldwide. Lumumba was the product of these favourable power relationships, but at the same time his downfall was a sign that a neo-colonial counter-offensive was already gaining ground. The neo-colonial victory in the Congo indicated that the tide had turned for the anti-colonial movement in Africa. The change of direction became clear with Portugal's success in delaying decolonisation in its overseas territories; with the temporary halt of the anti-apartheid movement in South Africa; with the temporary reprieve for Ian Smith's "settler" regime in Rhodesia, and finally with the overthrow of Ben Bella in Algeria in 1965. If Africa was a revolver and the Congo its trigger, to borrow Frantz Fanon's analogy, the assassination of Lumumba and tens of thousands of other Congolese nationalists, from 1960 to 1965, was the West's ultimate attempt to destroy the continent's authentic independent development.

But this story is not only made up of sadness, treachery, defeat and death. The courage of the central protagonist, true to his principles to the last, and despite his increasingly difficult circumstances, also sheds light on events happening today. In fact, several threads link the murdered leader with Pierre Mulele and his rebels who rose up against the neo-colonial regime in Léopoldville in 1964. In the early 1960s, the young nationalist leader Laurent-Désiré Kabila was fighting the disastrous regime the West wanted to establish in the Congo. That same Kabila played a key role in bringing down Mobutu in May 1997. And although Congolese sovereignty has been badly damaged over the past decades, the current situation there offers an opportunity for going back over the past and remodelling it for the present day on the basis of an authentically nationalist programme.

The crushing weight of the dictatorship has been shaken off. The time has in fact come to take up the ideas that Lumumba tried to embody before being removed from history and the history books. If this book can in some way keep Lumumba's memory alive in the collective consciousness and help all those men and women who are fighting for greater justice in the world and for the emancipation of Africa, I will have more than won the day.

THE CONGO IN 1960

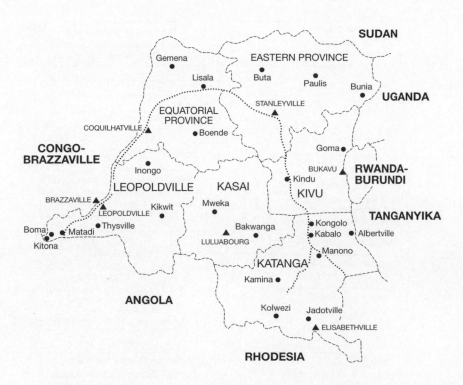

Key

COUNTRY

PROVINCE

PROVINCIAL CAPITAL

Town

·········· Railway line

Name changes

Congo 1960	/	Congo 2001
Albertville	=	Kalemie
Bakwanga	=	Mbuji-Mayi
Coquilhatville	=	Mbandaka
Elisabethville	=	Lubumbashi
Jadotville	=	Likasi
Katanga	=	Shaba
Léopoldville	=	Kinshasa
Luluabourg	=	Kananga
Paulis	=	Isoro
Stanleyville	=	Kisangani
Thysville	=	Mbanza-Ngungu

WHO'S WHO ON
17 JANUARY 1961

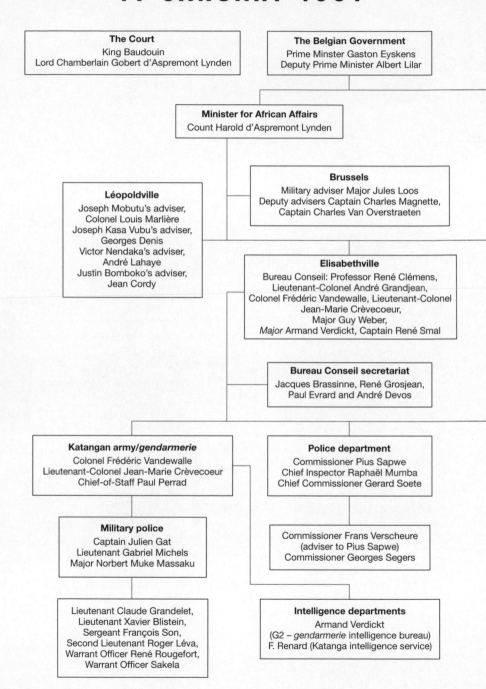

The Court
King Baudouin
Lord Chamberlain Gobert d'Aspremont Lynden

The Belgian Government
Prime Minster Gaston Eyskens
Deputy Prime Minister Albert Lilar

Minister for African Affairs
Count Harold d'Aspremont Lynden

Brussels
Military adviser Major Jules Loos
Deputy advisers Captain Charles Magnette,
Captain Charles Van Overstraeten

Léopoldville
Joseph Mobutu's adviser,
Colonel Louis Marlière
Joseph Kasa Vubu's adviser,
Georges Denis
Victor Nendaka's adviser,
André Lahaye
Justin Bomboko's adviser,
Jean Cordy

Elisabethville
Bureau Conseil: Professor René Clémens,
Lieutenant-Colonel André Grandjean,
Colonel Frédéric Vandewalle, Lieutenant-Colonel
Jean-Marie Crèvecoeur,
Major Guy Weber,
Major Armand Verdickt, Captain René Smal

Bureau Conseil secretariat
Jacques Brassinne, René Grosjean,
Paul Evrard and André Devos

Katangan army/*gendarmerie*
Colonel Frédéric Vandewalle
Lieutenant-Colonel Jean-Marie Crèvecoeur
Chief-of-Staff Paul Perrad

Police department
Commissioner Pius Sapwe
Chief Inspector Raphaël Mumba
Chief Commissioner Gerard Soete

Military police
Captain Julien Gat
Lieutenant Gabriel Michels
Major Norbert Muke Massaku

Commissioner Frans Verscheure
(adviser to Pius Sapwe)
Commissioner Georges Segers

Lieutenant Claude Grandelet,
Lieutenant Xavier Blistein,
Sergeant François Son,
Second Lieutenant Roger Léva,
Warrant Officer René Rougefort,
Warrant Officer Sakela

Intelligence departments
Armand Verdickt
(G2 – *gendarmerie* intelligence bureau)
F. Renard (Katanga intelligence service)

Société Générale
Governor P. Gillet
Union Minière's director, Jules Cousin

Foreign Affairs Minister
Pierre Wigny

Brussels
Ambassador Robert Rothschild
Cabinet attaché Etienne Davignon
Assistants A. Lebrun et A. Carlier,
Chargé d'affaires J. Westhof

Bakwanga
Commanding officer Jules Crèvecoeur
Major Noël Dedeken,
Hubert Bondroit

Elisabethville
Consul General
Henri Créner
Assistant
Jan R. Vanden Bloock
Major Jules Loos's contact
Albert Liégeois

Brazzaville
Ambassador Marcel Dupret
Security Commissioner
Jean-Baptiste Crokart

President Moïse Tshombe's political secretariat
Major Guy Weber, Jacques Bartelous, Xavier Grandjean,
François Thomas

Interior Minister Godefroid Munongo's private secretary
Victor Tignée
Defence Secretary Joseph Yav's cabinet:
Lieutenant-Colonel André Grandjean and Carlo Huyghé

THE INTERNATIONAL
ACTORS

The United States
President Dwight D. Eisenhower
(from 20 January 1961 John F. Kennedy)
Secretary of State Christian A. Herter
CIA director Allen Dulles

The United Nations
Secretary General Dag Hammarskjöld
Aides: Ralph J. Bunche, Andrew W. Cordier,
Indar Jit Rikhye, Heinrich Wieschhoff
US Ambassador to the UN James J. Wadsworth
Belgian Ambassador to the UN Walter Loridan

United Kingdom
Prime Minister Harold Macmillan
Foreign Secretary Lord Home

France
President Charles de Gaulle
Minister of Foreign Affairs
Maurice Couve de Murville

Congo

Léopoldville
President Joseph Kasa Vubu
Army chief Joseph-Désiré Mobutu
President of the College of Commissioners
Justin Bomboko
Chief of Intelligence Services Victor Nendaka
Chief of UN operations in the Congo
Rajeshwar Dayal
US Ambassador Clare H. Timberlake
CIA station chief Lawrence Devlin
UK Ambassador Ian Scott

Stanleyville
Acting Prime Minister of the
nationalist government
Antoine Gizenga

Soviet Union

President Leonid Brezhnev
First Secretary of the Communist Party and
Prime Minister Nikita S. Khrushchev
Foreign Minister Andrei Gromyko

Afro-Asia

Congo (Brazzaville): President Fulbert Youlou
Ghana: President Kwame Nkrumah
Guinea: President Sékou Touré
India: Prime Minister Jawaharlal Nehru
Morocco: King Mohammed V
Tunisia: President Habib Bourguiba
United Arab Republic (Egypt/Syria):
President Gamal Abdel Nasser

Bakwanga

President of the autonomous
state of South Kasai
Albert Kalonji

Elisabethville

President of Katanga Moïse Tshombe
Ministers Jean-Baptiste Kibwe, Evariste Kimba,
Godefroid Munongo, Gabriel Kitenge
UN Representative in Katanga Ian E. Berendsen
Commander of the Blue Berets in Katanga
Colonel H.W. Byrne
US Consul William C. Canup
UK Consul A.G. Evans

1

PREPARING THE GALLOWS

A "NIGGER" UPSTART (30 JUNE 1960)

On independence day in the Congo, 30 June 1960, the Palais de la Nation in Léopoldville is packed with Congolese and foreign dignitaries. The bronze statue of Léopold II, founder of the independent state of the Congo, still dominates the front entrance by way of a welcome, as if the handover of political power is going to change nothing. The newly elected Congolese politicians – members of parliament, senators and ministers – are gathered in a semicircle, as are the national and international press, and all the great and the good of Belgium.

At first, the solemn handover of sovereignty goes smoothly for Brussels. In a speech heavy with paternalism, King Baudouin paints a glowing picture of colonisation and an equally promising neo-colonial future. "The independence of the Congo is the result of the undertaking conceived by the genius of King Léopold II," he says, later adding

> Don't compromise the future with hasty reforms, and don't replace the structures that Belgium hands over to you until you are sure you can do better. . . . Don't be afraid to come to us. We will remain by your side, give you advice, train with you the technical experts and administrators you will need.[1]

After the Belgian king, it is the turn of Joseph Kasa Vubu, the Congo's first president, to speak. He gives a perfectly innocuous speech, conforming exactly to what the former masters expect from the new African elite: the Africans, he implies, will be ministers, will drive luxury cars and live in beautiful houses but, behind the scenes, will allow the Europeans to continue pulling all the strings without fear of being contradicted. The idyllic image of the colonial period evoked by the king contrasts painfully with the memory of colonial misdeeds and the crimes engraved in the collective consciousness of Africans. But who, in Brussels, cares to express those concerns? For decades, the law of silence covering colonial misdeeds has been respected: the Congo is known as the "empire of silence", a phrase coined by the *France-Soir* journalist O.P. Gilbert, and colonial repression is a taboo subject.

Immediately after Kasa Vubu's few words, the president of the House of Representatives, Joseph Kasongo, invites Prime Minister Patrice Lumumba to speak. Baudouin and the Belgian Prime Minister Gaston Eyskens are flabbergasted. The programme makes no mention of a third speech and Infor Congo has not provided them with an advance copy of Lumumba's text, although it has been circulated to the assembled press. The content of the speech makes their blood run cold. The prime minister does not address himself to his former masters, but to "Congolese men and women, fighters for independence, who are today victorious". Suddenly, the foreign dignitaries disappear from the centre of the political stage and become spectators at the celebration of a nationalist movement and its first victory. They listen in astonishment as the nationalist leader addresses the Congolese people and responds to the king, who meanwhile has turned a deathly pale. Talking directly to the people over the heads of the assembled diplomatic corps, he explains that the granting of independence is not a generous gift offered by Brussels, as King Baudouin maintains. Independence has been proclaimed in agreement with Belgium, but: "no Congolese worthy of the name can ever forget that it is by struggle that we have won [our independence], a struggle waged each and every day, a passionate idealistic struggle, a struggle in which no effort, privation, suffering, or drop of our blood was spared."

Lumumba describes in the frankest of terms the colonial system that Baudouin had glorified as his great-uncle's chef-d'œuvre and condemns it as "the humiliating slavery that was imposed on us by force". He goes on:

We have known sarcasm and insults, endured blows morning, noon and night, because we were "niggers". Who will forget that a Black was addressed in the familiar *tu*, not as a friend, but because the polite *vous* was reserved for Whites only? We have seen our lands despoiled under the terms of what was supposedly the law of the land but which only recognised the right of the strongest. We have seen that this law was quite different for a White than for a Black: accommodating for the former, cruel and inhuman for the latter. We have seen the terrible suffering of those banished to remote regions because of their political opinions or religious beliefs; exiled within their own country, their fate was truly worse than death itself. . . . And, finally, who can forget the volleys of gunfire in which so many of our brothers perished, the cells where the authorities threw those who would not submit to a rule where justice meant oppression and exploitation.

Lumumba puts the role played by Brussels in the process of decolonisation into perspective: "Belgium, finally understanding the march of history, has not tried to oppose our independence."

Lumumba's speech is interrupted eight times by sustained applause from all the Congolese present and honoured by a veritable ovation at the end. In no time, the thousands following the festivities on the radio have spread the news of the bombshell to the four corners of the Congo. Lumumba has spoken in a language the Congolese thought impossible in the presence of a European, and those few moments of truth feel like a reward for eighty years of domination. For the first time in the history of the country, a Congolese has addressed the nation and set the stage for the reconstruction of Congolese history. By this one act, Lumumba has reinforced the Congolese people's sense of dignity and self-confidence.

The representatives of defunct colonialism are stunned. Brussels is suddenly facing the anti-colonial revolution it feared. The colonial enterprise, so highly praised by the king, has been depicted as humiliating slavery in front of the Europeans themselves. And all this is the work of Patrice Lumumba, the man who, only a few weeks earlier, after his electoral victory, was described in the Belgian press as an illiterate thief, an upstart, a Black parachuted to the top!

At the back of the room among the lower-ranking Congolese officials, Colonel Frédéric Vandewalle is listening attentively to Lumumba's speech. He is standing, having given his seat to Pétillon, the former governor general and former minister for colonial affairs, whom protocol had forgotten. The colonel, aged forty-eight, is the head of the colonial intelligence services which, after 30 June 1960, will be renamed the Sûreté congolaise, the Congolese intelligence service. He is wearing a suit for the occasion "because he felt the days of uniforms and shiny braid were over". The colonel surveys with suspicion the inauguration of the democracy put in place by "generous Utopians". In his view, Brussels has put "no restrictions" on the transfer of power. He does not like the content of Lumumba's impromptu speech, although he has the intellectual honesty to recognise that it is what Africans expect of their leaders: "That release of pent-up emotions, incongruous and offensive to the Belgians, was an act of revenge for many Congolese. It was an instant success with those attending the ceremony uninvited. Their applause was echoed by the crowd outside."[2]

Vandewalle is an acute observer, despite being a dyed-in-the-wool colonialist. In his *Mille et quatre jours* (A Thousand and Four Days), he describes how the Congolese masses wanted to make independence a reality and see it reflected in jobs, promotions and wage increases:

During the military parade [after the ceremony at the Palais de la Nation], if you watched carefully, you saw the African crowd reserve special applause for the Blacks wearing the silver star of a warrant officer. It represented the first breach in the armour of military tradition in the Congo, the Africanisation of the officer class, unreasonable according to Belgian criteria, but desired by the majority of Congolese.[3]

Who is this man who will play such a decisive role in the outcome of the Congo crisis? At first Vandewalle appears reserved. He has no wish to be in the limelight. Moving to the intelligence services has given him the taste for working without too much show, "between the wallpaper and the wall", as a comrade in arms puts it. But behind this grey bureaucratic façade is a man with a strong personality, perfectly qualified for his role of *éminence grise*. Guy Weber, who saw him on the job in Katanga in early 1961, described him as "devilishly intelligent" and said that he greatly impressed Moïse Tshombe and his entourage.

Vandewalle is no less racist than the other colonials, and an implacable enemy of Congolese nationalism. But this does not prevent him from refusing to accept the half-truths and downright lies his colleagues used in their campaign against Lumumba. Hence, he rejected the Eyskens government's conspiracy theory when it accused Lumumba of using the soldiers' revolt of July 1960 as a pretext for expelling all Belgians: "No proof of any plot has ever been supplied. . . . it was a put-up job by M. Eyskens, aided by the intelligence services of Colonel Margot."[4]

Mille et quatre jours is one of the few works of reference about the recent history of the Congo. In it Vandewalle shows a strategic vision, experience of the terrain and a very frank view of neo-colonial scheming. There is a reason for this frankness. At the beginning of the 1970s, when Vandewalle was working on his book, the neo-colonial victory in Central Africa appeared complete. Mobutu was firmly in the saddle and Congolese nationalism appeared to have been totally eradicated. In these conditions, the author thought he was entitled to consummate his African career with documents and thoughts, with the assurance, indeed the arrogance, of the victor.

When, shortly after independence, the Congo crisis broke out and Colonel Vandewalle was recalled to Brussels, his career in the tropics appeared to be at an end. But the colonel re-emerged on the scene and left his mark on events with his customary rigour. Brussels was to use all means at its disposal to eliminate the upstart "nigger". In the light of this objective, the intelligence and experience of the former head of the colonial Sûreté rendered excellent service.

BELGIAN TROOPS AND THE BLUE BERETS IN KATANGA (JULY–AUGUST 1960)

For Patrice Emery Lumumba, then aged thirty-five, 1960 was a year of great political victories, but also of terrible defeats. At the beginning of the year, the leader of the Congolese National Movement (MNC) was still languishing in jail in Jadotville, Katanga. In May he won the elections and the following month he became prime minister. By the end of the year he was back in prison, in what turned out to be his death cell.

Lumumba was arrested for the first time in early November 1959, when the massive anti-colonial demonstrations in Stanleyville, his political stronghold, ended in bloody battles with the forces of order. But imprisoning him proved to be merely a rearguard action, an act of desperation by a moribund colonial regime. When Lumumba's incarceration won him prestige among a broad cross-section of the population, Brussels did a political about-turn. Aware of the irresistible advance of the anti-colonial movement, the Belgian government, the monarchy and the colonial trusts opted for accelerated decolonisation, in an attempt to stave off the radicalisation of the Congolese masses and keep tabs on the nationalist leaders' growing prestige. They counted on being able to keep control behind the scenes once political power was in the hands of inexperienced Congolese politicians. In January 1960, the government of Gaston Eyskens, a coalition of Christian Democrats and Liberals, bowed before the anti-colonial movement and set 30 June as the official date for granting independence to the Congo.

The result of the May 1960 elections, however, surprised Brussels, as the electoral contest was won by radical nationalists like Patrice Lumumba, Christophe Gbenye, Antoine Gizenga, Anicet Kashamura and Pierre Mulele. The Belgian government was unable to prevent the appointment of Lumumba as prime minister and of Joseph Kasa Vubu, the veteran Congolese nationalist, to the more or less honorary function of president. This first Congolese government represented the culmination of the work of the nationalist movement which in barely eighteen months had overcome all colonial obstacles. Lumumba's government intended to claim its rightful independence immediately and set out to combat all vestiges of colonialism and all forms of neo-colonialism; he hoped to persuade the Congolese peoples to build a unified nation in a democratic state within the rule of law. This national-democratic programme was intended as a mobilising force, an invitation to the Congolese masses to grasp the political helm themselves. However, it went against the interests of the colonial trusts, the missions and the colonial bureaucracy newly handed over to the infant state. These pillars of colonialism had expected to hold on to their privileged position in an independent Congo, albeit with an African façade.

Only Katanga, the copper-producing province and fiefdom of the Union Minière, delivered a success for Brussels in the elections. When in mid-June 1960, barely a few weeks before independence, a government headed by Lumumba appeared to be inevitable, the Belgian parliament unilaterally modified the provisional Congolese constitution, the Basic Law. Initially it had provided for control of the provincial governments to be decided on a proportional basis.

Tshombe, the Katangan leader, and the Belgian community that had designated him their man of straw, were unable to form a provincial government because the nationalists challenged the result of the elections. But Brussels ignored their protests and simply abolished the proportional rule. Suddenly the way was open for Tshombe to form a homogeneous provincial government. Professor Van Bilsen called this a "legal *coup d'état*". During a debate in the Belgian parliament prior to the vote, Gaston Moulin, a Communist Party deputy, uttered these prophetic words: "It is proposed that they legislate under the threat of a party [Tshombe's] which says it is ready to secede from the Congo. . . . We have no guarantee that those separatists who threaten to secede immediately will not do it tomorrow with the legal assistance we will have given them."[5]

Lumumba's speech at the independence ceremony was a glaring confirmation that the new government took its right to independence very seriously. He warned that the end of colonisation in no way meant the end of the struggle: "We will make sure that our country's land truly benefits its children. We will review all previous laws, and make new ones which will be just and noble." This commitment to the Congolese people, who had been dispossessed of millions of acres under the colonial administration, showed that Lumumba intended to jettison the dead weight of colonial heritage and combat any neo-colonial designs on the country. It was clear that this nationalist discourse was much more than simple electoral rhetoric; it would become the central plank of his policy.

Brussels' trump card in controlling Lumumba's government was the Congolese army's Belgian officer corps. This corps was a legacy of the colonial army, the Force Publique. It had developed an extremely conservative caste mentality, totally consistent with its major *raison d'être*: not to defend national territory against a possible outside aggressor but to repress the enemy within. The Force Publique was established in 1886 as an army of conquerors, under the pretext of fighting slavery and preventing tribal wars. In reality its job was to establish a colony in the heart of Africa for Léopold II. Once the territory was conquered, it became an occupation force whose main task was to subjugate the Congolese people.

On 5 July 1960, General Janssens, the reactionary commander-in-chief of the Congolese army, let it be known unilaterally that there was no question of Africanising the army. He wrote the following provocative equation on the board: "Before Independence = After Independence". The Congolese soldiers rebelled immediately. This was not a mutiny in the traditional sense, whatever certain writers may think; in other words, it was not an uprising against the legal government but a revolt against the Belgian officer class, a revolt with social demands or, as Lumumba put it, "a strike". The Congolese government took the side of the soldiers. Janssens was relieved of his duties and the soldiers were invited to appoint black officers. Victor Lundula became the commander-in-chief of the Armée Nationale Congolaise (Congolese National Army, ANC),

Joseph Mobutu became colonel and chief-of-staff. Most of the Belgian officers were retained as advisers to the Congolese officers. The Africanised garrisons returned to normal. Vandewalle admitted with a great deal of lucidity: "Removing the top level from the Force Publique and the measures taken by the officers [the Congolese government's Africanisation measures], which General Janssens condemned, restored order to the two main garrisons: Léopoldville and Thysville."[6]

A hard core of Belgian officers, however, regrouped in Elisabethville, the capital of the province of Katanga. Supported by Tshombe, who feared the nationalist soldiers, they rejected the government's Africanisation measures. Meanwhile, rumours of the rape of European women by a small group of soldiers caused a mass exodus to Belgium on 8 July. Brussels made no effort to persuade Belgian officers to support the Congolese government's decision. On the contrary, Eyskens used the European exodus as an excuse to intervene. During the morning of 9 July, after consulting King Baudouin and the board of the Société Générale, the Belgian government took the decision to intervene in Katanga despite the fact that no serious incident had been reported there. The intervention took place during the night of 9 to 10 July, when black soldiers in Elisabethville rebelled against officers who wanted to stop Africanisation. At 5.50 a.m., four planes left their base at Kamina in Katanga, with men of the infantry battalion *Libération* and a platoon of paratroopers on board. The troops landed at 6.20 a.m. The Congo crisis had begun.[7]

Once the Congolese soldiers in Katanga had been disarmed, the way was open for Tshombe, under the protection of Belgian soldiers, to disregard the authority of Léopoldville and proclaim the province's independence. Colonel Vandewalle recognises that the decision to support the secessionists in Katanga and to fight Africanisation in the Katangese garrisons was a political one, based on "mistrust between the authorities in Brussels and Lumumba. They had all heard the 30 June speech." Like most analysts, Vandewalle claims that the mistrust began with Lumumba's speech. But this is wrong. What tipped the balance for Brussels was the fact that Lumumba followed up his words with actions, supporting the soldiers' movement and proclaiming the Africanisation of the army. In so doing he broke the army's colonial backbone. Lumumba had shown that his speeches were not just empty rhetoric, but words which led to action. Vandewalle sums up the outcome of events in a single sentence: "On 11 July, having got rid of the Congolese army, Katanga proclaimed its independence."[8]

The peace-making effect of the Africanisation measure, the integration of white officers as advisers in the army and the goodwill existing between the Congolese authorities and Belgian officials (on 11 July, Kasa Vubu, Lumumba and the Belgian vice-consul at Luluabourg drew up a preliminary agreement to station Belgian soldiers in the province to reassure the Europeans there) – all were wiped out by the secession of Katanga and Belgian reconquest operations. The news of the Belgian intervention unsettled the Congolese soldiers; this in turn became another reason for intervening. The Belgian attack on Matadi, carried out on 11 July, despite the departure of almost all the Europeans, was a failure; but Luluabourg was occupied on 10 July, Léopoldville on the 13th, Bakwanga on the 15th, Coquilhatville on the 16th and Kindu and Boende on the 17th. The attack on the sovereignty of the Congo took a dramatic turn on 12 July, when the Belgo-Katangan lobby denied a plane carrying Kasa Vubu and Lumumba access to the secessionist province.

Intervention meant preventing the Africanisation of the ANC spilling into Katanga and depriving the Belgian government of the jewel in the colonial crown. A second objective soon took shape in Brussels. By Africanising the ANC and raising wages by 30 per cent, Lumumba's government not only kept faith with its nationalist ideals, it was also inviting the public employees and the black proletariat in the mines and factories to follow the soldiers' lead and consolidate independence with social demands. On 12 and 13 July, the capital witnessed a wave of strikes in the private sector. Ralph Bunche, a UN official living in Léopoldville, observed in a telegram to the secretary general: "Strikes continue and spread, encouraged and triggered originally by successful tactics of army." This pre-revolutionary dynamic had to be destroyed at all costs since it was preventing the restoration of neo-colonialism. The Belgian Ambassador Jean Van den Bosch in Léopoldville immediately set about looking for candidates to replace Lumumba. On 13 July, he sent a telegram to Brussels: "I received Bomboko at midnight . . . I criticised the attitude of the prime minister and certain dubious members of the cabinet and I did not hide our hope of seeing him leading the army or the country. He understands our position and deplores his government's weaknesses."

Throughout the Congo crisis, Justin Bomboko kept in touch with Belgian emissaries.[9]

On 12 July, the day after the secession of Katanga, the Congolese authorities sent a telegram to the UN urgently requesting "military aid . . . against the present external aggression". This request to the UN from the Congolese leaders was the opposite of what the UN secretary general had indicated a few days earlier would be the only type of intervention possible, that is a Security Council session to approve Belgian intervention. On 9 July, when the significance of the events had become clear in New York, Secretary General Dag Hammarskjöld, alias "H", sent Bunche this message: "Possibility that situation will develop where European military intervention becomes a psychological necessity . . . I can see Security Council pass resolutions but not what contribution they could make beyond possibly legalising an operation." The Security Council resolution of 14 July decided, however, to provide the Congolese government with military aid until the Congolese armed forces were in a position to "fulfil their tasks properly". Operation "United Nations Organisation in the Congo" (UNOC) was born. Brussels was requested to withdraw its troops. But Belgian intervention, which attacked Congolese sovereignty and violated the United Nations' Charter, was not condemned. No date was set for Belgian withdrawal. And by reducing the crisis to a question of maintaining law and order, the UN adopted the Belgian argument – protection of life and liberty in a context of chaos – thereby giving it some legitimacy. Eight countries voted in favour of the resolution, none against. China, France and Britain abstained. The enormous pressure exerted by the Africans in favour of intervention finally forced the Soviet Union to vote for the resolution, despite its previous plea for the debates to be adjourned.[10]

The last Belgian soldier left Léopoldville on 23 July. The Blue Berets set up camp throughout the Congo, except in Katanga. While Brussels strengthened Tshombe's regime in Katanga unhindered, the UN kept the legal Congolese government on a tight rein. Hammarskjöld rejected all bilateral aid to Léopoldville from Moscow, Ghana, Guinea or any other country, stating that any aid to the Congo had to go through the United Nations. When Lumumba was told that aid would not be channelled through the Congolese government, his Deputy Prime Minister Gizenga declared:

> The people of the Congo do not understand why we, the victims of aggression, we who are in our own land . . . are systematically and methodically disarmed while the aggressors, the Belgians, who are in our conquered country, still have their arms and all their firepower. . . . The UN forces allow Katanga to consolidate secession and let the Belgians behave as if they were in an occupied country under the smokescreen of a phoney Katanga provincial government that we, the legitimate government of the Congo, have declared illegal.[11]

However, pressure from the Congolese government and African public opinion was forcing "H" to seek a solution to the Katangan impasse. On 26 July, he indicated in a confidential document addressed to his assistants that he would probably negotiate with Tshombe "to give him some kind of assurance that he does not risk his personal political future or the legitimate aims for which he stands by accepting UN troops". What aims did he mean? Count Harold d'Aspremont Lynden, former assistant private secretary to Prime Minister Eyskens, was the Belgian representative in Katanga and head of the Belgian technical mission, the real centre of power in Elisabethville. Brussels would not formally recognise the copper state as Eyskens's government hoped to rebuild the former Belgian Congo around an all-powerful conservative Katanga. Manu Ruys defended this option in an editorial in the Belgian daily paper *De Standaard*:

> Certain circles in Brussels propose revoking the declaration of independence [of the Congo] and establishing a military regime. However, this policy seems to be a dead end. Will public opinion accept a guerrilla war in the Congo

where hundreds and perhaps thousands of our boys will be massacred? . . .
The only ray of hope in all this chaos is Katanga. . . . A strong Katanga, linked
to Belgium, constitutes an element of order and prosperity in central Africa,
around which a larger confederation could be built. . . . This is the policy
Belgium must duly adopt.[12]

The political class shared this vision. Henri Rolin later told the Senate on behalf
of the Social Democrat opposition:

> As far as Katanga is concerned, the entire Senate, like everybody in Belgium,
> was overjoyed in July 1960 to learn that order had been restored to
> Elisabethville after a few days. While the rest of the Congo gradually fell prey
> to anarchy, industrial, agricultural and commercial activity continues
> throughout most of the southern province. We are delighted, because we
> have important interests there and a large number of settlers.

In a speech on 21 July, Baudouin expressed the same wish, with harsh words for
Lumumba and praise for Tshombe: "Entire ethnic groups, led by men of honesty
and courage, have pledged their friendship and begged us to help them build
their independence in the midst of the chaos in what used to be the Belgian
Congo. It is our duty to respond to all those who loyally ask for our help."[13]

Baudouin was certainly not the only player in this particular Congolese game.
In his letter to Tshombe dated 25 July 1960 Eyskens confirmed his wish to use
Katanga as a lever against Lumumba's Congo. The tone of his letter recalls King
Baudouin's 21 July speech:

> Belgium notes that the Congolese no longer agree with the structures set out
> in the provisional Basic Law passed by the Belgian chambers in May 1960. . . .
> I add that the Belgian government takes great satisfaction in the fact that,
> thanks to your wisdom and energy, Katanga has not been drawn into the
> chaos and that our compatriots have quickly been able to return to their
> peaceful occupations.

Later Vandewalle remarked: "The prime minister did not add 'and lucrative'."
The Church also had a word to say on the subject. Cardinal Van Roey,
Archbishop of Mechelen, wrote in a pastoral letter: "The Congolese people,
who cannot be identified with a minority of rebel soldiers or troublesome elements, will for us never be foreign."

On 26 July, Pierre Wigny, Belgian foreign minister, sent a telex to
Elisabethville, stating: "Any sign of other Congolese provinces siding with
Katanga is to be encouraged." On 25 July, while Lumumba was abroad,
Tshombe had suggested to Kasa Vubu that they organise a summit to consider "a
system of Congolese states grouped within an association or federation". The

main target of this strategy was Léopoldville, where it was hoped that a neo-colonial government would be established.[14]

The Belgian and international press shamelessly supported this bellicose stance. An editorial on 13 July in the prestigious London daily *The Times* clearly described the main planks of the West's strategy: "Recognition of Katanga would be premature for the moment, but it should not be dismissed as a possibility if Mr. Tshombe succeeds in consolidating his regime. Later, when passions have cooled, it might realign itself in some looser federal relationship with the rest of Congo."

Writing in *De Standaard* of 16 July Manu Ruys described Lumumba as "a revolutionary demagogue" who aimed only to "create disorder and chaos". Katanga, on the other hand, where "order and tranquillity reign", relied on the West:

It is the duty of the Belgian government to draw the UN's attention to the special case of Katanga, which has decided its own destiny and refuses to submit to Lumumba's revolutionary policies. We highly recommend that the UN puts the Belgian troops stationed in Katanga in charge of maintaining order. If not, we fear that the Lumumba government's harmful influence will spread to Elisabethville.

In *De Standaard* of 26 July, he was even more forceful.

The Congo now only has one chance of escaping total collapse: moderate forces . . . must take charge. This enormous country must become a feder-ation; each state could, depending on its possibilities and degree of development and based on renewed cooperation (no longer colonial) between Black and White, achieve order, well-being and freedom. . . . If Lumumba stays in power and maintains his anti-Belgian stance, the Congo will have a troubled future.

The press campaign against Lumumba's government reached its most scurrilous in *La Libre Belgique*. An article on 19 July about Lumumba's stay at Blair House, the official residence for foreign heads of state visiting the United States, reported: "At Blair House, an old lady looks after the guests. She is white. Let us hope nothing happens to her." Marcel de Corte, a lecturer in moral philoso-phy, made a thinly veiled public appeal to end Lumumba's life. In the 27 July editorial, he wrote: "Look at Lumumba. . . . He's a barbarian. . . . Officers [Belgian officers on the Ndjili plain] cry with rage because a manly act from them would have delivered the planet from his bloody cheek." Not without cause *La Gauche* commented on 4 March 1961: "The press probably did not treat Hitler with as much rage and virulence as they did Patrice Lumumba."

In a confidential letter of 28 July, Baudouin demanded that the UN secretary general reject any claim to sovereignty over Katanga by the Congolese government after the arrival of the Blue Berets. According to the king, Léopoldville must at all costs be prevented from establishing an "arbitrary judicial organisation" there. Hammarskjöld reassured the king: in a report of 6 August, he observed that in his eyes, Lumumba, the legitimate prime minister, and Tshombe, leader of a coup, had the same constitutional rights:

> The problem [of UN troops entering Katanga is not caused by] a desire on the part of the authorities of the province to secede from the Republic of Congo. . . . They consider this seriously to jeopardize their possibility to work for other constitutional solutions than a strictly unitarian one . . . This is an internal political problem to which the United Nations as an organization obviously cannot be a party.

The United Nations had no intention, therefore, of touching Tshombe's power in Katanga. *La Libre Belgique* of 8 August was delighted to see a serious challenge to the Congolese constitution: "M. Tshombe's success at the United Nations vigorously reinforces federalist arguments in the Congo. . . . The Abako [Kasa Vubu's party supported by the Bakongo, the people of Léopoldville and its environs] . . . now supports Tshombe's argument. So does M. Kalonji's MNC, which controls the Baluba regions of the Kasai."

On 9 August, Albert Kalonji proclaimed the independence of South Kasai. His state was dubbed the République de la Forminière, after the subsidiary company of the Société Générale which controlled diamond extraction there.

Faced with unconstitutional secessions which eroded the very foundations of the state, Lumumba's government found itself forced to take measures against the press organs that openly sided with the coup leaders. The Belgian press took this as an opportunity to launch even harsher attacks on the Congolese government. From Léopoldville, Manu Ruys entitled an article: "Lumumba Restricts Press Freedom". News blended imperceptibly into a call to arms against the Congolese government: "Prime Minister Lumumba's brutal condemnation of federalism [in fact of secessions!] . . . We are in a police state where the future is no longer secure."[15]

On 12 August, the UN secretary general arrived in Elisabethville to negotiate with Tshombe. The Katangan minister Godefroid Munongo, assured of Western support, was brutally frank about the concerns of the secessionist regime: "The UN troops who replace them [Belgian troops] . . . must . . . allow us to stop central government interfering in the affairs of Katanga in any way". In answer to the question as to what the UN would do if Léopoldville attacked Katanga, Hammerskjöld replied: "In that case, UN troops could not remain indifferent and your position would seem to me stronger than M. Lumumba's."

Referring to Kamina, a base set up on Katangan soil and of prime strategic military importance for the entire south-eastern Congo, he said: "Be thankful that the base will not serve as a haven and jumping-off point for M. Lumumba against Katanga and that the two bases [Kamina and Kitona] will be used exclusively by the UN who will be totally responsible for them." It was, therefore, hardly surprising that a few months later, when Tshombe was unhappy with the difficulty the UN troops were having in putting down the Baluba revolt against his regime, he threatened to publish the typescript of these conversations.[16]

On 13 and 14 August, the first Blue Berets took over from Belgian troops in Elisabethville. From that moment on, the UN acted as a political but also a military buffer between the Congolese government and Tshombe. Moreover, contemptuous of Léopoldville's sovereignty, UN leaders condoned the fact that Belgian administrators and advisers were staying on to build Tshombe's state. Belgian soldiers also had the right to stay: changing into African uniforms, they would create a Katangan army.

Brussels and Elisabethville were satisfied with this settlement which made the Blue Berets an obstacle to the re-establishment of territorial integrity; this meant consolidating the secession, and eventually and inevitably ensured Tshombe's triumphant return to a unitary framework. The journalist Pierre Davister described Elisabethville's reactions to the agreement with the UN:

The d'Aspremont Lynden–Rothschild team couldn't believe their ears! . . . Until now the whole Katanga solution has relied on a wonderful bluff which allowed something sensational and unique in the history of the world to happen. Have we not actually seen the UN secretary general agree to enter into official negotiations with an unrecognised state? . . . Lumumba has clearly lost the match.

In a telegram to Brussels, d'Aspremont Lynden and Robert Rothschild gloated that Hammarskjöld

is . . . preserving the *de facto* territorial integrity of Katanga . . . from now on we can be optimistic about the way the general situation in Katanga will evolve. Barring new accidents, the Katangan structures will be protected by UN troops and, in the not too distant future, by Katangan troops under the command of Belgian officers, instead of on an extremely precarious basis by Belgian troops.

Satisfied, the Belgian foreign minister told the House of Representatives: "Thanks to his perseverance, and I can also say thanks to our diplomatic prudence, Monsieur Tshombe has gained recognition".[17]

How can the UN's respect for Tshombe be explained? Hammarskjöld was well aware of the artificial nature of the copper state. Bunche, his assistant, made it very clear in his telegrams that Tshombe was "a puppet manoeuvred by the Belgians, that he took no decision that was not inspired by the Belgians, that no official meeting was held without the presence of a Belgian and that without the Belgians, he would never have come to power". But the UN leadership shared the West's strategy: to use secession as an instrument to destroy the Congolese government. In his confidential message of 26 July, Hammarskjöld talked of Tshombe's "legitimate aims". A telegram sent by "H" on 1 August reveals that the UN leaders were convinced of the need to break Lumumba's nationalist government. The secretary general was in Léopoldville at the time:

> After a number of meetings here with the Cabinet and members of the Cabinet, I have a fairly clear picture of the internal dynamics of politics in the Central Government. The two or three men who may be characterized as moderates and who at all events are men of real integrity, intelligence and sense of national responsibility understand, I believe, fully my approach. . . . However, the vast and vocal majority have a highly emotional and intransigent attitude. . . . Until the Katanga problem is in hand . . ., there will, I am sure, be a continued drift towards extremism in the Cabinet and a continued weakening of those on whom, in my view, Congo's political future if at all possible has to be built.[18]

In the light of developments, the Congolese nationalists could draw only one conclusion, one that Colonel Vandewalle much later formulated as follows: "Until the final drafting of the Congolese constitution and its approval by Katanga, the status quo would be based on the Katangan constitution. . . . This arrangement . . . consolidates the Katanga regime. It was to have dire consequences for Lumumba."[19]

THE ELIMINATION OF LUMUMBA'S GOVERNMENT (AUGUST–SEPTEMBER 1960)

A furious exchange of correspondence occurred on 14 and 15 August between Lumumba and Hammarskjöld, who was in the Congolese capital. For Lumumba, it was clear that, in view of the 14 July resolution, "the UN is not to act as a neutral organisation . . . rather the Security Council is to place all its resources at the disposal of my government". Lumumba protested against the agreement Hammarskjöld had made with Tshombe without consulting the Congolese government. The Congolese prime minister insisted that only African and Congolese troops should be sent to Katanga. In his first letter of reply, the secretary general refused to deal with this matter: "There is no reason for me to enter into a discussion here." *The Times* of 16 August commented that Hammarskjöld's second letter "clearly implied his doubt of Mr. Lumumba's right to speak . . . for his government". Lumumba ended the correspondence on 15 August as follows:

After the adoption of the last resolution, you delayed your journey to the Congo for twenty-four hours solely in order to engage in talks with M. Pierre Wigny, Belgian minister for foreign affairs, administrator of mining companies in the Congo and one of those who plotted the secession of Katanga. . . . Completely ignoring the legal government of the Republic, you sent a telegram from New York to M. Tshombe, leader of the Katanga rebellion and emissary of the Belgian government. . . . According to M. Tshombe . . ., you entirely acquiesced in the demands formulated by the Belgians using M. Tshombe as their mouthpiece. In view of all the foregoing, the government and people of the Congo have lost their confidence in the Secretary General of the United Nations. Accordingly, we request the Security Council today to send a group of neutral observers to the Congo immediately . . . The task of these observers will be to ensure the immediate and entire application of the Security Council resolutions.[20]

As soon as the break had become final, the secretary general sent President Kasa Vubu a letter with a thinly veiled political message:

Having great confidence in your wisdom, I am convinced that you will manage to lay the solid foundations that cooperation between the UN and the Republic demands. . . . I will be happy to continue [the cooperation] provided we find on the part of the Republic the trust over and above considerations of nationality and race that is necessary to reach our aim.

The "considerations of nationality and race" allude to Lumumba's demand that UNOC become more Afro-Asian. Hammarskjöld, for his part, drew his own conclusions. In an internal telegram of 16 August, US diplomats stated that the secretary general was going head on towards a confrontation with Lumumba. "H" had come to the conclusion that "the UN effort could not continue with Lumumba in office. One or the other would have to go." On 21 and 22 August, the Security Council again deliberated on the Congo crisis. Given that UN troops were stationed throughout Congolese territory, the secretary general had brushed Lumumba's criticism aside. He called the Congolese government and the illegal regimes of Elisabethville and Bakwanga to the negotiating table in New York. "The United Nations . . . is all over the area in charge of order and security, creating an umbrella under which the people of the Congo should be able to find its way to peace and to create the forms of government and administration under which they wish to live."[21]

However, the focus of attention shifted back to the Congo where Lumumba's government, abandoned by the UN, decided that it would itself deal with the secessions of Katanga and South Kasai, if possible with, but if not without, help from other parts of Africa. Léopoldville asked the Soviet Union for planes, lorries, arms and equipment. All Sabena aircraft were requisitioned. Shortly afterwards, on 22 or 23 August, about 1,000 soldiers left for Kasai. The Congolese government represented a sovereign nation, which had the legitimacy required to act against the secessionists, who threatened not only the existence of the government but also the elected institutions and structure of the state: "Resorting to federalism is the only means of getting rid of Lumumba's MNC, the only party to have support throughout the country, whereas the other parties, locally or tribally based, have no power at national level", observed *Le Figaro*.[22]

The ANC seized Bakwanga, the capital of Albert Kalonji, during the night of 26 to 27 August, without meeting fierce resistance. In the next two days it temporarily put an end to the secession of Kasai. Lumumba arrived in Stanleyville, the nationalist heartland, on 28 August, to prepare for the second phase, towards Katanga. During a public rally, he asked the population for volunteers:

> It is not from pleasure or indolence that I would lead you once again into the scale of battle we waged in 1959. But I warn you that, if a new ordeal by fire is to be our destiny, I will accept it with joy and will do what I consider to be my duty. And our country will have the added satisfaction of realising that it does not take lives, but gives them; that it does not make the Belgian people suffer, but is the one that suffers."[23]

However, an air bridge between Léopoldville and Stanleyville failed. The Soviet Ilyushin planes were grounded at Luluabourg when, on about 5 September, the United Nations refused to supply fuel. A second group of soldiers left Stanleyville at the beginning of September. They quickly reached the frontier with Katanga and set out for Kongolo, in the north of the province, where the population was openly anti-Tshombe. The offensive got bogged down around 8 September amid great confusion. On 1 September, Colonel Mobutu, the army chief-of-staff, unilaterally decided to end the war in Kasai, without consulting the Congolese government. This decision coincided with confidential information about preparations for a *coup d'état* against Lumumba. When on 5 September, Lumumba was stripped of his functions, the new military and political leaders in Léopoldville, with the help of the UN, did everything they could to withdraw the ANC.

After the breakdown in relations between "H" and Lumumba, the United States came on the scene. On 26 August, Allen Dulles, the head of the CIA, sent a telegram to Lawrence Devlin, the CIA station chief in Léopoldville:

> In high quarters here it is the clear-cut conclusion that if [Lumumba] continues to hold high office, the inevitable result will at best be chaos and at worst pave the way to Communist takeover of the Congo with disastrous consequences for the prestige of the UN and for the interests of the free world

generally. Consequently we concluded that his removal must be an urgent and prime objective and that under existing conditions this should be a high priority of our covert action.

Richard Bissell, the CIA's Deputy Director for Plans and its head of clandestine operations, said later: "The Agency had put a top priority, probably, on a range of different methods of getting rid of Lumumba in the sense of either destroying him physically, incapacitating him, or eliminating his political influence." At about this time, a CIA scientist named Sidney Gottlieb was ordered to collect biological material with a view to assassinating an unidentified African leader. US Ambassador Timberlake now sprang into action. In mid-August, he let it be known in a telegram that "Kasa Vubu will continue to be a political zero as long as Lumumba is active." He sang the praises of Joseph Ileo, the president of the Senate, and of Bomboko, the foreign minister, but recognised that compared to Lumumba they perhaps lacked aplomb in political matters. Timberlake tried to alert President Kasa Vubu, but in vain. Madeleine Kalb says: "Whenever Timberlake . . . went to see Kasa Vubu . . . to try and persuade him Lumumba was an extremely dangerous man, Kasa Vubu . . . would say nothing. . . . Timberlake noted in a gloomy cable to Washington: 'I confess I have not yet learned the secret of spurring Kasa Vubu to action.'"[24]

UN leaders persisted with their project to eliminate Lumumba politically. According to a telegram of 26 August from the US permanent mission to the UN, Hammarskjöld was convinced that "Lumumba must be broken."[25]

The *Christian Science Monitor* of 1 September reported UN diplomats in New York as saying that "few tears would be shed" if Lumumba were to disappear from the political scene. By means of coded telegrams, Bunche kept New York informed as to the details of possible actions against Lumumba. On 21 August, he wrote: "Bomboko . . . informed me that Kasa Vubu is observing now, permitting Abako to express his views, biding his time. . . . He hopes Security Council will strongly approve UN action and your position. He would, of course, wish the UN to be tough with the government, even to the point of using force against it."[26]

On 26 August, Hammarskjöld's assistant, the American Andrew Cordier, left for Léopoldville where he was to replace Bunche as head of the UN in the Congo. Cordier was part of the Congo Club, a group of senior UN officials intent on making sure that the international organisation safeguarded Western interests in the Congo. In August 1960, Cordier privately confessed that "Nkrumah is the Mussolini of Africa while Lumumba is its little Hitler", adding that: "The only real solution to the problem is a change of leadership." Cordier's stay was scheduled to be brief, and this predisposed him to take what he later called "necessary but unpopular measures".[27] With the military offensive against Kalonji and Tshombe, Lumumba had shown that he would not tolerate the *de facto* division of his country, and this is precisely what condemned him in New

York once and for all. The United Nations did not want the secession of Katanga to be called into question. When, at the end of August, dozens of civilians were killed in fighting between Kalonji's partisans and the Congolese army, "H" declared: "The UN force must receive mission to intervene, in order to prevent, by force if necessary, the massacre of African and European civilians." The principle of non-interference in internal affairs did not apply, according to "H", in what he called "a case of incipient genocide". Indar Jit Rikhye, a UN general, later wrote that "in anticipation of an invasion of Katanga by the ANC, our troops in the province, who were posted at all important population centers, were redeployed to block entry into Katanga from Kivu or Kasai". If an "invasion" were to take place, the UN would send the Blue Berets in to prevent the central government from re-establishing its authority in the copper province.[28]

Meanwhile, Brussels was busy too. The Belgian ambassador in Léopoldville embarked on a search for candidates capable of succeeding Lumumba. On 23 July, he sent his boss the message: "Opposition to the prime minister within the cabinet is growing. It is in our interest to follow the advice of that moderate faction that increasingly hopes to control and even constrain the prime minister's actions." These hopes soon had to be scaled down. On 16 August, Marcel Dupret, the Belgian consul in Brazzaville, sent word that Kasa Vubu was prepared to overthrow Lumumba, but he added: "The question is whether he will have the courage or the necessary foresight to intervene at the appropriate moment." So the Belgian prime minister decided to encourage Kasa Vubu. In his memoirs, Gaston Eyskens wrote: "On 18 August, I gave Jef Van Bilsen, legal adviser to Kasa Vubu, a confidential task. I led him to understand that Kasa Vubu had to kick Lumumba out." Shortly afterwards, Foreign Minister Wigny's assistants made contact with Georges Denis, another of Kasa Vubu's advisers. The subject of their conversation was "the overthrow of the government according to our wishes".[29]

At around this time, Louis Marlière, a Belgian colonel and key man in the war against the Congolese nationalists, retired to Brazzaville, on the right bank of the Stanley-Pool river. Most of the time he wore civilian clothes, which made him less conspicuous in these conspiratorial times. According to Vandewalle:

He found the former colonial intelligence officer André Lahaye still there as the envoy of M. [Ludo] Caeymaex [head of Belgian intelligence services]. Consul Marcel Dupret was in the conspiracy too. There was a radio link with Léo. Informers came and went between the two river banks. Radio Makala, which broadcast propaganda, enjoyed benevolent neutrality and effective assistance.

Subversion began to take more concrete shape. Leaflets were scattered in the "cités" of Léopoldville warning: "Congolese, Lumumba will sell your women to Russia", or "For Lumumba thousands of diamonds, for our women millions of tears." Vandewalle comments on this prose: "Obviously European instigated". A telegram sent by secret agent Lahaye to Wigny and the Belgian intelligence services gives an idea of the feverish activity going on at the end of August, aimed at overthrowing Lumumba's government:

> Opposition to Lumumba has grown stronger and more coherent over the past few hours. On the one hand, the defection of Baluba soldiers has been confirmed. . . . Bangala and Bakongo soldiers are also being worked on. Mbungu Joseph, editor of *Présence africaine* and a serious contact, has just informed me that 600 soldiers in Camp Léopold are ready to take action and to overthrow Lumumba. . . . Batshikama, a member of Abako, is still in Brazza writing anti-Lumumba leaflets and preparing a clandestine radio station's first broadcast. . . . President Youlou [of the Congo Brazzaville] supports these activities wholeheartedly. Last night, he stated "I am saving the West". . . . Added to this, a demonstration of the unemployed is planned for tomorrow. Since crossing the Pool is now allowed again, there is a veritable climate of conspiracy here in Brazzaville at the moment.[30]

At the beginning of September, Count d'Aspremont Lynden, one of the strongmen behind Tshombe, was appointed minister for African affairs in Eyskens's government reshuffle. It was a clear signal: Brussels remained on a war footing with Léopoldville.

Meanwhile, Youlou's support was appreciated. Consul Dupret told Foreign Minister Wigny in a telegram: "The moment has come to give Youlou and other members of his circle some important honorary decorations. The pretext: aid given to refugees. The effect: a considerable reinforcement of our collaboration in Congolese matters."

Apart from Tshombe, the ecclesiastical hierarchy was the most important Congolese source of support for the coalition of Western powers. Bishop Malula rejected the Congolese government's programme recommending the strict division of Church and State and total freedom of worship. (The country to date had been governed by a tightly knit alliance of missionaries, trusts and colonial administration. Catholicism was the state religion.) Applying such bourgeois-democratic principles would provoke considerable upheaval, he suggested. "Secularisation is an attack on the religious life of the Bantu people for whom private, family and public life is totally impregnated with religious meaning. I make a solemn appeal . . . to reject atheist materialism as the worst form of slavery."[31]

Kasa Vubu finally took sides in the conflict. On 5 September, a few hours before making his radio speech, the president got his adviser, Jef Van Bilsen, to ask the United Nations for the immediate closure of the radio station and all airports. Referring to his visit to Andrew Cordier, the American who succeeded Bunche at UNOC, Van Bilsen writes that Cordier had already been informed: "The UN representatives insisted they could not interfere in internal affairs and that, if the president could keep the initiative, the presence of the UN and the [Blue Berets] could work to his advantage." According to an internal US report, Van Bilsen ended this message by indicating that Cordier was going to do the necessary: "Officially, I [Cordier] must be able to say that you gave me these letters [from Kasa Vubu asking for UN assistance] one half hour from this time", that is, after Kasa Vubu's radio message. That same evening, Kasa Vubu read on the radio his message announcing that he was relieving Lumumba and six of his ministers of their offices. Shortly afterwards, also on the radio, Lumumba denounced Kasa Vubu's action and dismissed him. Lumumba called on the United Nations "not to forsake its mission, not to get involved in the dissension that has brought the government and M. Kasa Vubu face to face. We are going to settle this matter ourselves through democratic procedure within our parliament."[32]

In his memoirs, UN General Carl von Horn described the atmosphere in the UN headquarters after Kasa Vubu's radio broadcast as one "of relief, almost of satisfaction". Hammarskjöld wired Cordier immediately, telling him that "the right to liberal interpretation of" the United Nations mandate "is automatically widened in state of emergency." The secretary general ended his telegram with these words: "May I add an irresponsible observation: that responsible persons on the spot may permit themselves, within framework of principles which are imperative, what I could not justify doing myself – taking the risk of being disowned when it no longer matters."

The veiled language does not conceal the message: if need be, Cordier's powers ("responsible persons on the spot") could go beyond the brief of the UN. He had the right to take politically desirable but legally questionable measures which may later be denied when they have already taken effect, in other words when Lumumba has been eliminated. In another telegram sent the same evening, the secretary general told Cordier:

> The chief of state clearly has authority under Article 22 to dismiss the prime minister and to appoint new prime minister . . . prime minister's apparent attempt to dismiss chief of state . . . and set up "popular government" is clearly extraconstitutional and puts prime minister "hors la loi". General legal conclusion that in present circumstances UN is compelled to deal with chief of state as only clear legal authority. "[33]

Cordier did exactly what was expected of him. Kasa Vubu received the protection he asked for and the UN closed the radio station and the airports "in the interests of the maintenance of law and order". In a telegram to Hammarskjöld, Cordier explained: "This seems to go as far as we can to affect situation favourably and stay within the terms of our mandate." Closing the radio station and the airports undeniably hurt Lumumba. An anti-nationalist station broadcast out of the Congo-Brazzaville, while Lumumba had no similar medium for mobilizing his supporters in Léopoldville and the surrounding area. And closing the airports to non-UN aircraft not only thwarted the nationalist troops' offensive against the secessionists in South Kasai and Katanga, but also kept them hundreds of kilometres away from the political hub of the capital.

The Blue Berets placed a security cordon around the president's residence. On 6 September, Minister Bomboko, who countersigned Kasa Vubu's decree dismissing Lumumba from his duties, was pursued by nationalists and took refuge in the United States Embassy in Léopoldville. The US asked the UN to escort him to Kasa Vubu's residence. US Ambassador Timberlake wired the state department: "I intend allow Bomboko remain temporarily Chancery and protect him if I can." The secretary general then gave Cordier instructions which are worth remembering: "Bomboko should in circumstances be given safe conduct by UN as would any civilian threatened with violence irrespective of his official status and of where he wants to go."[34] Six weeks later, however, when Lumumba was in his residence surrounded by Mobutu's soldiers, the UN refused to take him to Stanleyville for the funeral of his still-born daughter Léonie. And at the beginning of December, the UN even denied Lumumba protection when he was on the run from Mobutu.

On 7 September, the United Nations clearly showed its bias when a Sabena aircraft carrying 9 tonnes of weapons was allowed to land at Elisabethville without any difficulty. The telegrams exchanged on this subject between the UN stations at Léopoldville, Elisabethville and New York are revealing. On 7 September, Cordier and von Horn (UN Léopoldville) refused to comply with the request of Ian Berendsen (UN Elisabethville) to open the airports for Tshombe. "H" approves: "Confirm instruction. Blow-up on Tshombe side would just show that he does not understand his best interest." Nevertheless, UN Elisabethville insisted. Elisabethville was in great danger now that the ANC was advancing and threatening to join up with Baluba guerrillas in north Katanga. A new telegram from "H" to his colleagues gave the green light for a breach of UN directives, if it would serve Tshombe's strategic interests: "When you are forced to give a reply to authorities, you should if order still generally valid, as I fear it will be, tell them (a) that order stands; (b) that we cannot enforce it in E'ville with military means; (c) that they must shoulder full international responsibility for disregarding our order."

On 9 September, aircraft took off from Elisabethville to stop the nationalist troops' offensive against north Katanga. According to Jules Gérard-Libois, without this support the *Gendarmerie* might have been defeated by the ANC near Kongolo.[35]

During this period, the Western press stressed the part played by the UN in the development of the situation. *The Times* reported on 7 September: "There then the United Nations stands, ostensibly in the middle as always but leaning perceptibly in one direction." *La Libre Belgique* of 15 September stated: "If Kasa

Vubu and Ileo finally got the victory they deserved, they would owe it to the UN. Without the UN, Lumumba could turn the situation round with a few hundred followers." The overthrow of Lumumba's government was the result of a whole chain of unconstitutional actions. The United Nations played a decisive part. By its *de facto* recognition of the secession of Katanga and its protection of the province, the UN contributed to the secession of South Kasai and the dismantling of the Congolese state. And finally, the UN finished off the job in Léopoldville by supporting Kasa Vubu's coup against the Lumumba government. Kasa Vubu's action was clearly not constitutional. Congolese law gave parliament, not the president, the right to relieve a minister or the government of its functions, and stated that, while awaiting the formation of another government, it is the retiring team that deals with ongoing business. However, the famous Article 22, a literal copy of Article 65 of the Belgian constitution, though totally obsolete ("the King names and dismisses his ministers"), was invoked by Kasa Vubu and his followers. This legal argument could be resolved only by a law or a revision of the constitution, passed by a parliament with confidence in Lumumba.

There is no doubt that the Belgian legislator who wrote the Congolese Basic Law used the Belgian situation as a model: a parliamentary regime with a titular head of state. That is the conclusion reached by CRISP researchers, and that is the conclusion, prior to independence, hence *in tempore non suspecto*, of François Perin, a constitutional expert, of the Belgian minister Raymond Scheyven and of many others. Evan Luard, for instance, wrote in his reference book on the history of the United Nations: "Of Kasa Vubu's move . . . it can reasonably be said that the way he used his power without referring to parliament amounted to an abuse of the constitution".[36] The United Nations, Belgium and the United States removed politics from parliament and put it in the street, where the balance of power is played out in a brutal fashion, in numbers of soldiers, battalions and weapons. It was there that UN generals, Belgian officers and Joseph-Désiré Mobutu awaited Lumumba.

IN THE STEPS OF THE CIA: OPERATION BARRACUDA

No sooner had Kasa Vubu's coup taken place than Lumumba was ready to regain the initiative. On 7 September, he made a masterly speech to the Congolese House of Representatives condemning Kasa Vubu's coup and the balkanisation of his country. His opponents in parliament were present in force and made their voices clearly heard, but the House rejected the dismissal of the president and the prime minister by sixty votes to nineteen. The following day, the Senate rejected Kasa Vubu's decision by forty-one votes to only two. US Ambassador Timberlake, the most active anti-nationalist on the Congolese scene, commented on Lumumba's speech:

At his very best, Lumumba devastated the points raised by the opposition . . .
He made Kasa Vubu look ridiculous. He attacked the UN saying the country
was not really free if arms, airports and radio facilities were controlled by the
UN. How could the UN justify this interference if it refused to liberate
Katanga? . . . He had turned to the Russians for planes only when Belgium
supplied planes to Tshombe and after both the UN and the US had abandoned
him by failing to furnish transportation.

Rajeshwar Dayal, Cordier's successor as UN Congo representative, gave this
assessment of the Senate vote: "Kasa Vubu is thus greatly weakened politically.
. . . the day's developments have greatly strengthened Lumumba's position."[37]
Ileo, Kasa Vubu's candidate for prime minister, did not even attempt to present
a government to parliament.

In a confidential memo, the CIA expressed the view that Lumumba's removal
was not irreversible: "Lumumba in opposition is almost as dangerous as in
office." The Belgian Consulate in Brazzaville also feared the worst. The day
after the coup, Consul Dupret wrote to Foreign Minister Wigny that Brazzaville
had been caught unprepared: "The plan to eliminate Lumumba was set in
motion forty-eight hours too soon." Another telegram stated: "Kasa Vubu's
action was started earlier than planned. . . . In fact, widespread demonstrations
including union, youth and parliamentary action were envisaged." In two other
telegrams, Dupret mentioned that a message from Kasa Vubu was to be taken by
helicopter or boat from Léopoldville to be broadcast from Brazzaville.[38]

On 9 September, Timberlake went to see Dayal, who commented on the
visit:

Timberlake said that Kasa Vubu had missed his opportunity and was now
politically ineffective. The immediate danger was that Lumumba would be
free to set up a dictatorial police state. The best that could be hoped for in the
circumstances would be to strive to return to the position before Kasa Vubu's
abortive proclamation last Monday (5 September), although this would not
be easy.

Brussels opted for further steps. On 10 September, Foreign Minister Wigny
wrote to his assistants in Brazzaville: "The constituted authorities have the duty
to render Lumumba harmless." Although he does not specify how the operation
was to be carried out, the message is clear. According to Colonel Vandewalle,
it was "invaluable encouragement for those discreetly but effectively supporting
the opponents of the leader of the Congolese government".[39]

Wigny's message bore immediate fruit: three days later, a secret telegram from
Colonel Louis Marlière fell on d'Aspremont Lynden's desk. Of the measures to
be taken against Lumumba, he wrote: "Examining a plan of action to be taken in
Léo in accordance with Ileo government – success very possible if perpetrators

as firm in action as in words. Impossible if Ghana takes Lumumba's side." Did he intend to have Lumumba arrested by units of the Congolese army and then killed, at least if the Ghanaian Blue Berets let them? But Marlière had an alternative in mind: "Operation Barracuda will be given to *Major* Dedeken [in] E'ville to study and will be executed without the participation of the Congolese government." The barracuda is a voracious and dangerous (sub)tropical fish. Vandewalle mentions Noël Dedeken in his *Mille et quatre jours*: on orders from "a Belgian general", Major Loos, assistant to d'Aspremont Lynden, sent Dedeken to Katanga during the summer of 1960. The former head of a Force Publique commando company, Dedeken was to kidnap Lumumba, and about thirty Baluba tribesmen were trained for that purpose. Soon afterwards Dedeken settled in South Kasai, from where he was able to reach Leopoldville more easily.

Major Dedeken would not be operating alone. The messages that Marlière and Loos exchanged mentioned "two children": an intelligence expert and an officer of a commando unit. Major Loos said that two intelligence experts would be arriving: J. Van Gorp, an official Belgian intelligence agent, and E. Pilaet, who was freelance. The matter had been dealt with at the highest level, because it was the minister for African affairs who gave the operation the green light. Loos wrote to Marlière: "On order from minister coordination guaranteed by Marlière who must inform Minaf [African Affairs]; he will, except emergency, judge opportuneness." The message was clear: the minister was to evaluate the opportuneness of eliminating Lumumba, except in an emergency, in which case Marlière should go ahead anyway and the minister would cover up the assassination. Brazzaville was equally implicated in the action, because Marlière promised Loos he would discuss the matter with Consul General Dupret. These telegrams show beyond doubt that a few weeks after Washington's decision to make Lumumba's "removal" an absolute priority, Brussels intended to take things into its own hands.[40]

A young assistant of Foreign Minister Wigny's, Viscount Etienne Davignon, who was in Brazzaville at that time, sent a telegram to his boss saying that the problem had still not been solved: "complete disorganisation in Léo. . . . General symptoms: lack of determination in taking action, which explains why Lumumba has not yet been rendered harmless. So the overwhelming problem seems to be to remove Lumumba and unite Congolese leaders against him." Operation Barracuda had got off to a difficult start. The situation was changing by the hour. Sometimes Lumumba could count on the support of certain Congolese army units and was protected by them; at other times different units pursued him and wanted to arrest him. The conspirators did not have adequate information and Pilaet, the intelligence expert code-named "Achille", did not come up to general expectations. Worse still, according to Marlière, "Achille is a dangerous gossip". Marlière also complained to Major Loos about "too many licensed plotters on the spot already" and about the lack of discretion in Brussels where certain people had been talking too much. In addition, Colonel Marlière had much more urgent matters to deal with at the end of September. Loos had given him the task of trying to get Congolese soldiers to support Mobutu, who could be overthrown at any time. The minister's right-hand man therefore made 20 million Belgian francs available to Marlière to pay the soldiers.[41]

Still, the "plotters" in Brazzaville and Léopoldville were doing their best. At the beginning of October, when Lumumba was still free and trying to win the population of the capital over to his side, they quadrupled their subversive efforts. A coded telegram sent by Consul Dupret mentioned talks with Gaston Diomi, an Abako leader, who wanted no less than that Lumumba be "removed once and for all". According to his own account, Dupret answered him: "No serious result is ever achieved without taking risks. On the other hand, if he has the courage to take the recommended initiative, the population will follow, the police will rally and money will flow." Colonel Marlière received yet more encouragement for Belgian action. He wrote to the African Affairs Minister d'Aspremont Lynden:

> Emissaries from Brussels or E'ville lead me to believe that Minaf considers action opportune. . . . I am giving orders to prepare to act. If Minaf agrees I will start action forthwith. If there is agreement I request authorisation trip to Brussels to finalise plans or send Minaf representative here.

A few days later, on 5 October, Major Loos, the minister's assistant, replied "agree prepare action". During this time, one of Loos's collaborators was commuting between Brussels and central Africa for discussions with Marlière and his colleagues. Collaborators of Foreign Minister Wigny, such as the diplomats Rothschild and Westhof, were involved in discussions on the subject (see ch. 3). If necessary, the minister for African affairs himself would explain the agenda. On 6 October, the day after Loos authorised Marlière to begin Operation Barracuda, d'Aspremont Lynden wired Brazzavillle and Elisabethville to report a rumour that a national cabinet including, among others, nationalist ministers was about to be formed. His words do not forecast a return to the pre-5 September situation, but predict the massacre of 17 January 1961: "Particularly dangerous because in my view it tends to put Lumumba indirectly in the clear . . . The main aim to pursue, in the interests of the Congo, Katanga and Belgium, is clearly Lumumba's *élimination définitive*." At the same time, in the presence of journalists, Prince (and future King) Albert, Baudouin's brother, summed up the prevailing public opinion in Belgium in these terms: "The Congo crisis is the responsibility of a single man, Patrice Lumumba."[42]

While Colonel Marlière worried about a risky commando action, the weight of Western intervention was concentrated on more structural actions. The iron logic inherent in the neo-colonial assault on the Congolese government would lead directly to military dictatorship. In effect, eliminating Lumumba meant doing away with parliament, where he had majority support. On 13 September, a joint session of the Congolese chambers gave Lumumba's government full powers.

With parliament about to regain the initiative, the elimination of Lumumba was the top priority on the political agenda. The colonels' time had come and a military coup on 14 September heralded its beginning. The day before the coup, *The Times* of London reported from Léopoldville:

> At the moment it is believed that the bulk of the army here is with Colonel Mobutu, the Chief of Staff, who has obviously done a deal with President Kasa Vubu and agreed to accept UN help with the army. . . . In Leopoldville, more pay parades financed by the UN were held at Camp Leopold this morning, and it seems clear that most of the army in this district has been neutralized, while a part of it seems ready to give open support to President Kasa Vubu."

In an article written before the putsch, *Time* magazine of 19 September produced evidence of cooperation between UN troops and units of the Congolese army:

> Hammarskjöld had decided to act in Léopoldville. . . . Behind the premier's back, Congolese army leaders and UN officers had worked out arrangements of their own: weapons were to be kept locked in central arsenals, and a cease-fire was arranged in the Katanga campaign. . . . The Premier, already deprived of his airports and his radio stations, was now in danger of becoming a premier without an army. . . . For the United Nations, all this was a venture into uncharted political water, far beyond anything that its original architects had envisioned. . . . [The United Nations] were trying to undo the actions of the premier who had invited the UN into the country in the first place.

2

UNITED AGAINST "SATAN"

MOBUTU'S APPEARANCE ON THE POLITICAL SCENE

On the evening of 14 September, Colonel Mobutu announced on the radio that he was "neutralising" politicians until 31 December 1960. In the Congolese government a College of Commissioners was established, comprising a group of young intellectuals including figures like Marcel Lihau, Albert Ndele, Mario Cardoso and Etienne Tshisekedi, and headed by the former minister Justin Bomboko. As on 5 September, the United Nations and the United States played an important role in the success of the operation of 14 September. Both actions of 5 and 14 September were originated by the same social forces and had the same objective: the removal of the legally elected government and parliament by the mediation of neo-colonial politicians and sectors of the officer corps. On the days before and after 14 September, the UN won support among the ANC by giving it money and food supplies. On 6 September Dag Hammarskjöld sent a telegram announcing a transfer of $1 million. The money came from the United States, and was transferred "to help meet pay and food costs of ANC. We are authorizing this action as measure in aid of law and order."

This UN support for Mobutu was substantially complemented by other financiers. Dayal, the UN representative in the Congo, subsequently pointed out:

UN liaison officers . . . reported that from time to time Western military attachés would visit Mobutu with bulging brief-cases containing thick brown paper packets which they obligingly deposited on his table. We could not tell what they contained, but could not help making guesses.

In any case, money for Mobutu was forthcoming from Brussels as well. At the end of September the assistant to the minister for African affairs sent a message saying he had released 20 million Belgian francs for pay, in order to rally support for Mobutu.[1]

The United Nations and Mobutu came to Tshombe's aid as well. He was grappling with a growing Baluba nationalist uprising in the north of the copper state, and the UN Congo representatives, Dayal and von Horn, were afraid that the ANC, which was carrying out an offensive, would make a pact with the insurgents. They proposed paying ANC soldiers' wages on condition that they retreated: "Mobutu is being approached . . . to abide by cease-fire. . . . We had promised to provide the ANC in the Kindu area with food. They are being reminded that this air shipment will be withheld if their part of the bargain is not kept."[2]

On 18 September, Mobutu agreed to the manoeuvre, and the ANC offensive got bogged down. On 17 October, the United Nations put the finishing touch on the operation by an agreement with Elisabethville by which "neutral zones" would be established in north Katanga within which only the Blue Berets could operate. Yet a proposal to this effect from Berendsen, the UN representative in Elisabethville, had been rejected by Tshombe earlier in September on the not unreasonable grounds that it would revive the question of the sovereignty of Katanga over part of his territory.

But practical considerations rapidly overtook objections of principle: the growing strength of the Baluba rebellion forced Tshombe to accept UN help. On 15 October, UN observers informed Dayal that in Manono (north Katanga) "UN troops had almost completely taken over the responsibility for law and order since Katangan administration ceased to exist". In a dispatch from Elisabethville to Brussels, the diplomat Jan Vanden Bloock recognised that Katanga itself had proposed setting up these zones, given "the weakness of their forces of order and so that strength can be concentrated elsewhere".[3] The United Nations agreed to protect the mines, factories and railway lines in these zones against Baluba attack. In exchange, the Katangan soldiers were called on to suspend their offensive operations there. The Blue Berets, whose original function was to act as a buffer between Elisabethville and Léopoldville, were now facing the internal Katangan opposition to Tshombe. At the end of November, following a clash with Balubakat fighters at Luena, Moroccan forces of the UN handed over Baluba prisoners to Katangan soldiers who promptly massacred them. The Katangan *Gendarmerie* defended the residential areas in Luena, while the Moroccans held the mines and the station. The agreement with the UN gave the Katangan secessionists breathing space, enabling them to create the repressive apparatus used to crush the nationalist insurrection during the spring of 1961.

The population of Léopoldville took a wait-and-see attitude to the September coups. The Congolese were badly informed, indeed, not informed at all. Following the closure of the radio stations, the only sources of information were the daily newspaper *Le Courrier d'Afrique*, which was hostile to the government, and broadcasts from the anti-nationalist radio stations in Brazzaville. Without properly organised political parties, trade unions or other mass associations, people in the poorer districts could only get a very vague idea of how the overall situation was developing. Events seemed to be the work of inaccessible actors dabbling in diplomatic intrigues and secret consultations in Washington, New York and Brussels, over which the Congolese people had no control. The prevailing mood for the average citizen was one of anxiety and doubt. The lightning developments which followed independence amounted to a chain of demoralising failures and reversals which disorientated many Congolese: the soldiers' revolt, seen in the light of the European exodus and administrative breakdown; the occupation of the country by the Belgians, symbolised by the attack on Matadi and the secession of Katanga; the welcome arrival of the UN forces, quickly followed by disappointment and hostility towards the Blue Berets ("a new occupation force"); the undermining opposition from Brazzaville and the overt hostility of the ecclesiastical hierarchy to the government; and finally, continual economic decline.

Furthermore, in the days following Kasa Vubu's coup, Patrice Lumumba – convinced of his political and constitutional rights, and of his mastery in the parliamentary arena – did not call upon the army and the people to rise up against the instigators of the coup. It would, however, be wrong to conclude that the population had become apathetic. Vandewalle describes the situation at the end of September 1960 in his *Mille et quatre jours*:

> The anti-Belgian hostility of the Congolese masses had grown apace since the intervention of metropolitan troops. Observers from Léo, Stan and Bukavu were fully aware of the enmity between the former colonisers and the former colonised. It was futile to think the new regime would modify this attitude in the short term.

Bomboko, who had secretly thrown his whole weight behind Brussels, was also aware of the situation. According to a confidential telegram:

> Bomboko complained bitterly about articles in which he is described as pro-Belgian. Bomboko maintains such articles do him harm with Congolese public opinion which is still influenced by Lumumba propaganda. He asks Belgian newspapers to stop publishing this kind of article; he feels obliged to attack the Belgian government in order to maintain his credibility. He assures his correspondent he wishes to return to a real entente between Belgium and the Congo and confirms that he is more Western than Congolese."[4]

It was certainly the attitude of the population which forced Kasa Vubu and Mobutu to use foreign aid discreetly and sparingly. Since it was their only source of support, however, this contributed to the new duo's fundamental weakness. The people did not prevent Lumumba's overthrow, but at the same time they were not prepared to let the new regime become established.

Even in the capital, Lumumba's active opponents were extremely few in number. On 15 September, Kasa Vubu managed to gather no more than 300 anti-nationalist demonstrators. When Lumumba decided to go out and meet the population of Léopoldville, appropriate measures had to be taken. Colonel Marlière, an active member of Mobutu's entourage, wrote to his bosses in Brussels that the freedom of action accorded Lumumba, Maurice Mpolo, Gizenga and Mulele constituted a permanent threat. A "top secret" reply from the African Affairs Minister d'Aspremont Lynden informed him that 500 million Belgian francs had been set aside by the Central Bank for the regime, in order to pay soldiers among other things. Marlière was also authorised to use other funds to pay wages, on condition, according to the minister, that Lumumba's "effective neutralisation" would be the result. On 9 October when Lumumba went out and about in the capital for the last time, he held several meetings attended by enthusiastic crowds. The following day, Colonel Mobutu ordered his troops to surround Lumumba's house, the former residence of the governor general in the administrative centre of the city, beside the river Congo. Lumumba was now "protected" by a double cordon of soldiers, the inside circle made up of Blue Berets, the outside circle by ANC soldiers. This formation anticipated the wishes of the Western coalition, which wanted to cut Lumumba off from his power base, and it also satisfied the UN leaders. In fact, the double cordon suited all those who believed that a stable neo-colonial regime was only possible if a weakened Lumumba was reduced to a position of little influence.

Thus Lumumba was under house arrest and this ruled out the possibility of his returning to Stanleyville. In a letter of 17 September, he told Nkrumah that he intended to transfer his seat of government to Stanleyville, and it is not impossible that the UN leaders knew of this intention. In any case a UN agent in the capital of the Eastern Province wrote in a letter: "I hope everyone in Léo realizes that Lumumba's arrival here or even a simple speech by him could alter the situation in half an hour."[5]

Lumumba was now a political exile in his own country. US Ambassador Timberlake noted in a reassuring telegram that "Lumumba's physical isolation would mean his political death". Dayal told Hammarskjöld that: "Lumumba . . . is in fact a virtual prisoner in his house without free access to anyone and he is without a telephone." Shortly afterwards, the UN leaders told the former prime minister that he was only under their protection while in his own residence. In short, Lumumba could only count on protection as long as he was inactive politically. The Belgian press challenged Lumumba's "protection", but Eyskens's government reacted with more reticence, appreciating the role the UN leadership played in the events of September, and wanting to avoid the African countries suspending their contributions to the UN. Brussels received the following telegram from Brazzaville: "ANC soldiers are sleeping round Lumumba's residence. The UN only guarantee his safety if he stays inside his residence."[6]

The former prime minister was a *de facto* prisoner. Thus ended Operation Barracuda, the risky, improvised, emergency solution hatched by Marlière, Loos and d'Aspremont Lynden. Belgium, meanwhile, was working non-stop on using Katanga as a bridgehead, the safest way to fight Congolese nationalism, which was still very much a live force.

THE COPPER STATE, "AN OASIS OF PEACE"

The secession of Katanga was the West's prime weapon in its fight against Lumumba's government. Brussels had amputated Katanga from the body of the Congo in the hope that Léopoldville would not survive the operation. Later, when the Congo had been purged of its nationalists, an inverse movement could graft Léopoldville on to Katanga. The copper province's centre of economic gravity was in the south, which is made up of a series of plateaux rising more than 1,000 metres above sea level. Their enormously rich subsoil was called a "geological sensation" by the Belgian scientist Jules Cornet at the end of the nineteenth century. The most important mines, most of Katangan industry and the largest towns, Elisabethville, Jadotville and Kolwezi, are located there. To ensure the export of Katanga's riches, a railway line running parallel to its southern border linked its main towns with (then) Rhodesia and Angola.

The province was the domain of the Union Minière du Haut-Katanga (United Mines of Upper Katanga, UMHK), founded in 1906 by the Katanga Special Committee (in which Léopold II held huge interests), Tanganyika Concessions and the Société Générale de Belgique. The Société held the exploitation rights over all the copper deposits in an area of 15,000 km^2 – nearly half the size of Belgium. The UMHK later became the jewel in the crown of Belgium's Société Générale, which controlled about 70 per cent of the economy of the Belgian Congo. Katanga was pretty much run by the Union Minière; the company controlled the exploitation of cobalt, copper, tin, uranium and zinc in mines which were among the richest in the world. The Union Minière had a concession of 34,000 km^2, and employed 21,000 African workers and 2,200 European administrators. In the 1950s, its net profits came to between 2.5 and 4.5 million Belgian francs per year. The colony's tax on the Union Minière made up 66 per cent of its revenues. The production of copper ores rose constantly, oscillating in the second half of the 1950s at around 250,000 tonnes. This figure placed the Congo fourth in the table of the world's copper-producing countries. In 1956, cobalt extraction in Katanga represented 75 per cent of entire world production.

Shortly after independence, when Belgium sent troops to its former colony, the main objective was to protect its colonial treasurehouse. The three small, pale green crosses which adorned the flag of the state of Katanga were a triple reminder of its copper wealth, of what was really at stake in the Congo crisis. Vandewalle admits that "[t]he unofficial aim of Belgian policy in July 1960" was to "keep operating [. . .] the productive machinery that all the mining and industrial installations in Katanga represent." In any case, the secession was a blessing for the Union Minière in the short term. The UMHK did not lose a single day's work in 1960. Copper production even rose from 280,000 tonnes in 1959 to 300,000 tonnes in 1960. Katanga had only just seceded when the Union Minière paid 1.25 billion Belgian francs into Tshombe's bank account, an advance on the 1960 taxes which it should in fact have paid Lumumba's government. Vandewalle comments: "Without this injection of funds, the secession could not have survived. . . . It was . . . a manoeuvre that Katanga's enemies could classify as neo-colonialist. They made no bones about it."[7]

Tshombe and his political party, Conakat, were in the hands of associations of Europeans such as UCOL. When it was founded in 1956, its initials – significantly – stood for Union for Colonisation, the implication being that continual immigration of settlers from Europe would keep Katanga in white hands for centuries. But when, in October 1958, it became clear that anti-colonialist ideas were gaining ground in the Congo, the association changed its name to Union pour la collaboration des classes moyennes au Katanga (Union for the Collaboration of the Middle Classes in Katanga). This name meant it could keep the acronym UCOL, battle cry of the more combative settlers. UCOL and the Katangan Union, an organisation of European settlers determined to fight "the abandonment" of the Congo, took over Conakat and made it an instrument of neo-colonialism. The party's African poster depicted Moïse Tshombe, a Lunda from an important family of merchants and plantation owners, and Godefroid Munongo, grandson of M'Siri, a former king of the Bayeke.

Conakat's position can be defined by reference to its 1959 manifesto in which it distanced itself from other Congolese parties which were demanding the formation of a Congolese government by the beginning of 1961 at the latest. A declaration in the introduction to the manifesto, written by Monsignor Jean-Félix de Hemptinne, Bishop of Katanga (who had since died), is shocking by any standards: "A sector of humanity has inherited no civilisation, no energy, no ideas, no interests to defend. . . . The black race has nothing behind it. It is a people without writing, without history, without philosophy, without any consistency." Tshombe (or rather, his Belgian mentors who wrote the text) clearly stated in the conclusion to the manifesto that one of its fundamental political aims was to "maintain the trust of the good people who came to help us out of our state of stagnation. With the Belgians, we need not bother about international opinion [which favours independence for colonies]."

The absence of any real support for secession on the part of the Katangan population was one of the reasons why Marc Mikolacjczak, editor of the Katanga daily *L'Essor du Congo,* was opposed, discreetly but firmly, to such a step. On 19 July, he wrote to former Governor André Schöller:

> In the minds of the Congolese (whatever certain European idealists may think) the independence of Katanga is not their doing but the Europeans'. . . . The presence of Belgian troops allows the country to carry on as normal, but it appears this will be [necessary] for a long time. It is highly probable that terrorism will take root in the interior of the country in the not too distant future. . . . The regime we adopt must necessarily be a dictatorship.

An internal UN memo dated October 1961 states: "The idea that the Katanga resistance [to the Congolese government] is a native and African affair is a myth put out for foreign consumption and is scoffed at in private by Europeans here." And Major Guy Weber himself, the embodiment of the Belgian military presence in the secession, a Katangan *par excellence*, would later recognise: "There is no doubt the secession of Katanga would not have happened without the intervention of metropolitan troops. The conditions that sparked off this desire for independence would not have come together."[8]

Secessionist propaganda did not disguise the incontestable fact of the occupation by Belgian troops. Brassinne also recognised it: "The Katangan state depended on the framework provided by Belgium." From day three of Katangan independence, Tshombe had to combat persistent rumours. He stated on the radio: "Certain ill-meaning individuals are spreading the rumour that we want to cede power to the Europeans." Vandewalle explains why:

> The Whites were too much in the spotlight. Lieutenant-General Cumont [commander-in-chief of the Belgian army] had come to inspect the troops. A big talker, he had held a press conference, placed Belgian troops at Tshombe's disposal, promised to appoint black officers and introduced J. M. Crèvecoeur as the new commander of the Katangan army. . . . [Major] Weber had publicly congratulated the Katangan government and Minister Munongo for having prevented Lumumba from coming.[9]

Somewhat formal congratulations since in fact Weber himself had prevented Lumumba from coming.

It was not Tshombe, but men like d'Aspremont Lynden, Rothschild and René Clémens who were pulling the strings in this comic-opera state. The president of Katanga was, in Vandewalle's words, "guided by his triumvirate of political tutors". Though impregnated with racism, the gently ironic terms the colonel uses recognise the real relationships of power. The "political mentors" at Tshombe's side who discussed the Blue Berets' arrival in Katanga with UN leaders at the beginning of August 1960 "had admonished him" beforehand.

Vandewalle goes on to say that the Katangan justice minister, Valentin Ilunga, acted as spokesman for his assistant J. Hellemans, and not the other way round. Furthermore, "[we] had to put a lot of pressure on Tshombe to stop him doing the many stupid things which irresponsible people advised him to". Influential Belgians in the copper province joined forces to form Mistebel (Mission technique belge), the Belgian techical mission. Vandewalle describes them as "string pullers" or even "Katanga's tutors". When these bigwigs sat round a table "all the grey matter ruling Katanga was gathered together".[10] Eyskens's government claimed "these string pullers" had been put at the disposal of the local authorities in accordance with a clause in the Congo's constitution: a trick which naively covered up the fact that it was actually Tshombe and his putschist friends who were making a mockery of the constitution and openly demanding it be discarded. Weber and his colleagues' mission orders show that Brussels, not Elisabethville, was in the driving seat. Weber's orders, signed by the minister for African affairs, stipulated that he was "to carry out a one-year mission in Katanga, which can be terminated at any moment by the minister for African affairs".[11]

The constitution of the secessionist state was "Made in Belgium", like the very concept itself and all the other pillars of the government. This Katangan constitution was written by Professor Clémens and his assistant A. Massart, on the basis of a confidential paper by Professor Mast of Ghent University. Supporters of the secession claimed the constitution brought together Bantu wisdom and Western efficiency. In fact, it set up a presidential regime with a Grand Conseil of notables as a conservative force backing it up. Article 32 was explicit: a simple majority on the Grand Conseil could decide to retain colonial legislation on the mines. In accordance with the constitution, a joint meeting of the National Assembly and the Grand Conseil at the beginning of August appointed Moïse Tshombe head of state. Vandewalle's opinion on the subject is: "That did not change the *de facto* situation but it did provide a veneer of legality which, in a world to a certain extent ruled by law, was a good cover to have."

Everyone understood the situation, even in New York. During a visit to Elisabethville in August the UN secretary general himself noticed the repressive and artificial nature of the armed forces of secession, the Katangan *Gendarmerie*. He wrote in an official telegram:

> The most depressing impression was that the so-called National Army (of 500) which may be "loyal", lacks the most elementary judgement. Obviously, it is influenced by Belgian colonialist tactics in their handling of the Congolese. To stop utter nuisance developing around house put at our disposal, . . . somewhat unexpectedly declared it "international territory" . . .; we really cannot permit UN to become compromised by bad manners of Force Publique taught them by Belgians and now executed under Belgian officers.

Journalists quickly discerned the real foundation of the regime behind the politico-diplomatic façade: the iron hand of its praetorian guard, the Belgian occupation force. From the Katangan capital, Manu Ruys reported for the Flemish daily *De Standaard*:

> In reality, Katanga is a police state too, and this illustrates the fragility of Tshombe's government. . . . Belgian soldiers move round Elisabethville as if in occupied territory. . . . Order and discipline reign in the copper capital, but the order and discipline of a military occupation."[12]

At the end of October, when both King Baudouin and Tshombe were writing letters enthusiastically describing Katanga as an "oasis of peace", the regime decreed a state of emergency, although in practice this had been in force since July. All public gatherings, demonstrations, meetings, propaganda activities and the sale of maps were forbidden. A restricted ministerial committee was also created to deal with current emergencies. It comprised five ministers (plus their *éminences grises*): Tshombe, Jean-Baptiste Kibwe, Munongo, Evariste Kimba and Paul Muhona. This centralisation and militarisation of power illustrate the tension in a regime which was finding it increasingly difficult to maintain its self-proclaimed "oasis of peace". During the last months of 1960, the internal pressure of the Baluba uprising increased day by day. The regime was up to its neck in mud, and the secessionist state's Belgian mentors had to handle matters as far as possible with the Katangan president, and with him alone. They decided on a division of labour according to which the Bureau Conseil, a phantom Belgian cabinet created in the meantime, took the decisions, but referred them to Tshombe for signature and for an air of Katangan legality. [13]

In this newly hatched African state the old colonialist reflexes had free rein. In the words of *De Standaard*'s correspondent quoted above:

> What makes a particularly unpleasant impression in Elisabethville is the mentality of a lot of the Whites who have clearly learned nothing from recent events. At the airport we witnessed aggressive barracking by Whites of Blacks who had just arrived from Belgium or Léopoldville, attacking the nationalist policies [of the Congolese capital]. "Katanga is our country," shouted a white woman to a Black, "our husbands must be allowed to finish their careers here." The Black nodded, not very reassured.

It should be no surprise therefore that journalists wrote articles denigrating black leaders who play the secession game under the leadership of their former masters. Writing in *De Standaard* E. Troch claimed that Tshombe and his colleagues "bear the burden of odious colonialist protection". The world over, the state of Katanga was seen as the vassal of Brussels, an area of Africa occupied by colonialists, where they were trying to eradicate the growing tide of nationalism.

Even Tshombe himself in a letter to Prime Minister Eyskens mentioned the high price of subjection: "The continual concern which [Katanga] has, with sincerity and courage, shown for Belgian interests since independence [. . .] has brought it a lot of opprobrium both within the Congo and abroad."[14]

THE OFFENDED KING BAUDOUIN

Baudouin, the young, shy, rather sad-looking king, left Léopoldville for Brussels immediately after the independence celebrations. How different from his visit to the Belgian Congo in 1955! The king was then head of state of the Congo, and it gave him a triumphant welcome on his first official visit. He went home with the nickname "Bwana Kitoko", the handsome young man. Five years later, his visit turned into a real disaster; the catastrophe was attributed entirely to Lumumba and his independence speech.

In retrospect, the incident has many more nuances. True, Lumumba's speech was very unusual for that kind of ceremony. But then Baudouin's speech was also rather humiliating for his hosts, and a committed nationalist like Lumumba surely had no choice but to address those who had elected him, to use the occasion to reassure them, to reinforce the Africans' sense of dignity, and to set out what would happen in the future. And should he not do it in plain language? Should not a nationalist leader call a spade a spade?

Baudouin, however, had no interest in such considerations. Reporters simply said that he turned livid and consulted with Prime Minister Eyskens. For Baudouin it was "a slap in the face. Prime Minister Eyskens had trouble persuading him not to return to Brussels immediately." Not surprisingly, Lumumba had from that day burned his boats with Baudouin, "who had inherited the stubbornness and implacability of the Saxe-Coburg line".[15]

This incident should not be reduced to a conflict of personality between two people of very different psychological make-up. Such an analysis was intended for public opinion in general and taking it seriously would mean underestimating the Belgian ruling class. Brussels did not create a crisis as serious as the Congo crisis to avenge a *faux pas*. What was at stake in Lumumba's and Baudouin's speeches was more important than a question of diplomatic *politesse* or a different interpretation of the colonial past. Any illusion about a privileged relationship between Brussels and its former colony appeared to have been buried once and for all. And Lumumba's plan to re-examine all the laws of the colonial period in the light of the Congolese people's current needs did not bode well for Belgium's neo-colonial aspirations. The incident also showed that Lumumba was no "drawing-room politician". In the eyes of Belgian strategists, Lumumba was "capricious" and "whimsical"; that is, they could not manipulate him or use him to defend Western interests.

It was the Congolese government's Africanisation measures, announced a few days after the incident on 30 June, that set off warning lights for Brussels. Lumumba was taking the first step towards weakening the neo-colonial hold on his country, and Brussels reacted immediately. The monarchy's place in the ruling class and its historic role in Belgian–Congolese relations explain why Baudouin played such an important role in the crisis and why the 30 June incident has been given such an important symbolic function in the literature a posteriori. The political class lined up to a man behind King Baudouin and urged him to influence public opinion in favour of Katangan secession. The Belgian government had always wanted national opinion on Congolese affairs to be unanimous, under the patronage of the palace. Hence the Social Democrats, in opposition since 1958, associated themselves with the Catholic and Liberal majority.

The unity of the nation received the support and enthusiastic encouragement of the king. Baudouin was thus following in the steps of his predecessors who, ever since the independent state of the Congo was founded by Léopold II, had a tradition of intervening personally in Belgian colonial policy. The palace was at the centre of an economic and financial network in which links between the dynasty and the Belgian elite were woven together around the defence of the colonial purse. This should come as no surprise, since the history of Belgium, the dynasty, the Société Générale de Belgique and the Belgian Congo are tightly intertwined.

When the Congo crisis broke out, the network operated like this: Gobert d'Aspremont Lynden was Lord Chamberlain at the court. He was also a commissioner of the Société Générale de Belgique, and administrator of the Compagnie Maritime Belge and the Compagnie du Katanga. Together with the honorary Lord Chamberlain Prince Amaury de Mérode, he represented the royal house on the college of twelve commissioners which was the ruling body of the Société Générale. Gobert's nephew, Harold d'Aspremont Lynden, ran the Belgian technical mission in Katanga (Mistebel) and then became minister for African affairs. Count Robert Capelle, former secretary to Léopold III, and Jean-Pierre Paulus, King Baudouin's former assistant private secretary, had administrative functions in the Union Minière and several other colonial societies. Deputy Prime Minister Lilar was a former president of Titan anversois et des Ateliers de Léopoldville. The president of the Belgian chamber, Baron Kronacker, and Ministers Scheyven, Wigny and Albert De Vleeschauwer were administrators of a whole series of colonial enterprises.[16]

This list is only the most visible tip of the iceberg. The incontrovertible political conclusion is that the political class, including the court, had a considerable direct material interest in the outcome of the Congo crisis.

The palace itself had a lot to lose. But there were also other forces impelling the court to pose as the providential saviour in the Congo crisis, including certain conservative Catholic groups, the colonial trusts and the officer corps of the Force Publique, with their offshoots in certain military circles. At the height of the crisis, when the entire political class was on alert, traditional politics were radicalised very quickly. Newspapers like *La Libre Belgique* and *Le Soir* called for "an iron fist". The public was exhorted to rise above national humiliation, the shame of being Belgian, and close ranks round the dynasty. Influential sectors began to envisage replacing Eyskens's government with an emergency cabinet.

The palace was unequivocal about what the unity of the nation should mean. In his speech of 21 July, King Baudouin condemned Lumumba's government in no uncertain terms and, demonstrating his esteem for Tshombe, expressed his wish to see the Congo rebuilt around Katanga. The attack on Lumumba was far removed from the silky language of diplomatic niceties, and was most unusual for a reigning sovereign:

> Belgium had hoped that the peoples of the Congo would be capable of governing themselves and they would have been if those whom we chose to guide their destinies would have loyally accepted the help we generously offered them. Unfortunately this was not to be. A movement of terrible cruelty occurred among the Congo's Force Publique and the authorities responsible, far from combating it, have tried to turn the Congolese people against the Belgians.

These words are in striking contrast to the equally bald declaration of love for Tshombe: "Entire ethnic groups, led by men of honesty and courage, have pledged their friendship and begged us to help them build their independence amid the chaos of what was once the Belgian Congo. It is our duty to respond to all those who loyally ask for our help."

The following day, Moïse Tshombe held a press conference during which he could find no words strong enough to express his appreciation of the royal initiative: "I thank King Baudouin for having spoken those words. Without false modesty we accept His Majesty's tribute to our honesty and our integrity. It expresses before the entire world what I have always stated to be the truth."[17]

Baudouin missed no opportunity to treat the Katanga regime as if it were a legitimate state. On 3 August 1960, he received three Katangan ministers who stayed at the Château de Val Duchesse where official foreign delegations are usually lodged. At the end of October 1960, amid constantly increasing Western pressure on the Léopoldville and Elisabethville regimes to form an anti-nationalist alliance, the king sent Tshombe the following letter:

> Mister President,
>
> I was very moved by your letter of 6 October in which you convey to me the affection you continue to feel for Belgium and its dynasty.
>
> Since my great-uncle King Léopold II brought civilisation to the lands of the former Belgian Congo, the destiny of its peoples has been, as you know,

one of the major concerns of the sovereigns who have succeeded to the Belgian throne. Faithful to this tradition, I have myself followed with great attention, and over recent months with intense anxiety, the development of the events that have shaken the Congo. Therefore, the drama that has plunged a large part of this territory into mourning is for me a constant source of sadness; an association of eighty years like the one that has united our two peoples creates affective bonds too close to be broken by the policy of just one man.

This explains the emotion aroused in me by the affirmations of constant friendship from the president of Katanga, whose actions and role in the development of these events have been followed very attentively and with great sympathy, first in Belgium but also, more recently, in most Western capitals. As you write in your letter, Katanga constitutes an oasis of peace, a bridgehead from which it will be possible to stop the expansion of communism in Africa. It is this principle that inspired your declaration of 6 September on the Confederation of United States of the Congo. It is the same principle that moves you to discuss a federalist system with other provinces of the Congo.

Belgium cannot intervene further in the internal affairs of a country which has been independent since 30 June, but it cannot help having special feelings with respect to its fate. It is this which allows me to express in this letter how much I appreciate the efforts you are so tirelessly making to bring about the policy of entente that you have defined on several occasions.

It is my hope that world opinion will soon appreciate your efforts as fully as they deserve and that it pays Katanga and its leader the special tribute due to them.

Please accept, Mister President, the expression of my deep esteem,

Baudouin

The letter's political message lends specific meaning to the policies on the Congo that Belgium was championing at the time. Clearly, Baudouin accorded Katanga the main role in the anti-nationalist alliance Belgium and the West were seeking ("an oasis of peace, a bridgehead from which it will be possible to stop the expansion of communism in Africa") as an axis and the driving power behind a weak central government ("the Confederation of United States of the Congo"). The court would rather entrust the Congo's political future to the secessionists than to a hastily created alliance between Elisabethville and the weak regime in Léopoldville. The palace was pleading for a fundamental restructuring of the Congo, not for Katanga's rapid reintegration into the unitary state to the detriment of the neo-colonialist advantages gained so dearly by secession. Colonel Vandewalle recognises that this letter and other messages from the palace demonstrated "it was moving in the direction of total independence [for Katanga]. Belgian encouragement was not lacking."[18]

At the beginning of December 1960, the president of Katanga addressed the Belgian press on the tarmac of Brussels airport. There had been little fuss when he left Katanga, where – significantly – cheering came almost exclusively from Europeans. But once in Belgium, reflecting the aura of the royal palace, his star shone brightly. *De Standaard* transcribed the president's remarks in its 6 December issue: "I have come back to Belgium today primarily to honour its king and show my gratitude to him and through him to the dynasty which has shown continual foresight and concern for the peoples of the Congo."

An article by Manu Ruys questioned whether this visit was politically opportune, at a time when Léopoldville was preparing an initiative to unify the bastions of anti-nationalism. Tshombe's visit, not to mention a possible audience with the king, would be interpreted by his regime to mean approval of his policies; this might harden Elisabethville's attitude towards Léopoldville. The article was headlined significantly: "A political visit. Does the government agree?" Ruys added that according to opposition circles the king's entourage had been scheming "to try and force some kind of official recognition of Katanga by making Tshombe come to Belgium ostensibly to give the royal couple a present [for the marriage of Baudouin and Fabiola on 15 December]".

That same day, President Tshombe was granted an audience with King Baudouin at Laeken Palace. After this visit, Tshombe receivesd a prestigious decoration from the Belgian minister for African affairs. "It pleased the king to award President Tshombe the Grand Sash of the Order of the Crown", proclaimed the African Affairs Minister d'Aspremont Lynden during a dinner at Le Cygne in the Grand Place in Brussels. He continued : "This honour shows Belgium's gratitude for President Tshombe's courage." Of the many jokes going around, one of the most popular was that the Belgian national motto had been changed to "L'Union Minière fait la force" (meaning "The Mining Union is strength", a play on the words of Belgium's actual national motto, "Unity is strength").[19]

Tshombe immediately used the king's attentiveness to put pressure on the Eyskens government. In an interview in *De Standaard*, the holder of the Grand Sash of the Order of the Crown declared himself disappointed by the Belgian government's level of support to Katanga. The newspaper commented:

> The visit to Belgium and the great distinction given him at the palace have strengthened the Katangan president's position. He is not afraid to voice his criticism of the Belgian government, and he plays to the crown as well as to the Belgian people. . . . As for the situation in the Congo, Tshombe does not say he is in favour of a confederation with the other parts of the republic. On the contrary, he emphasises the sovereignty of his state and foresees at most an economic and financial association with other regions. This policy is not

compatible with the federal project Léopoldville is working towards. Tshombe gives the impression that it is for Kasa Vubu to take the first step and that Katanga will study Léopoldville's proposals with indulgence. That attitude will certainly not facilitate reconciliation with Léopoldville.

Wigny, the Foreign Minister, told the directors of the Union Minière that Tshombe had been received by the king "only because he wanted to thank him personally for the courageous and understanding attitude he has taken regarding Belgian nationals in Katanga".[20]

Even after the assassination of Lumumba, the palace continued discreetly to protect the Katangan secession. The eulogy Baudouin sent Tshombe on 13 March 1961 is reproduced on p. 159 below. When the king wrote this letter, news of Lumumba's assassination in Katanga had been officially known for only a month. But, for the Belgian monarch, the crime was no reason to distance himself from a regime that, in the eyes of the world, had blood on its hands. A note from Major Guy Weber, one of Tshombe's strongmen, clearly shows that even at that stage, the court was still following matters in Katanga very closely. On 19 May 1961, the Belgian government decided to recall Weber to Belgium. In a significant internal memo, Weber reported that Jean Oldenhove, the emissary from the Foreign Ministry who came to notify him of the decision, said: "I must warn you that the palace knows and shares the government's views." Aware that Weber and the Belgo-Katangan lobby would be loath to accept the recall, the authorities had obtained the king's agreement beforehand to pre-empt any resistance.

In mid-1961, by which time Congolese nationalism no longer appeared to represent any danger, the United Nations, Washington and Brussels joined forces to put together a government under Cyrille Adoula. The West was desperately trying to gather the diverse Congolese regimes into this government of national unity. However, the Katangan secessionists clung stubbornly to their isolationism. The Belgian sovereign reassured them: "I heartily thank you and the members of your government. It is very satisfying for me to know that calm and tranquillity reign in Katanga, thanks to your wisdom. I send you the most heartfelt wishes for the prosperity and happiness of your peoples."[21]

At the end of October 1961, Colonel Vandewalle became Belgian chargé d'affaires in Katanga. He received a letter from Marcel Dubuisson, rector of Liège University, who played an influential behind-the-scenes role in Katangan politics through what was called the "action committee". In August 1960, Dubuisson had been one of Baudouin's favourite candidates for the emergency cabinet proposed to replace the Eyskens government. The action committee included Harold d'Aspremont Lynden as well as Dubuisson and others. The members of the committee wanted to influence government policy in favour of Belgo-Katangan interests. Dubuisson's letter reveals that Baudouin continued to sympathise secretly with the "Katangan option", while Brussels, Washington and New York had for some time resolutely opted for a unified Congo:

Dear Colonel,

. . . The main reason why I'm writing you this letter is to tell you that I had a very long conversation with King Baudouin a couple of days ago, principally about Katanga. It is quite a delicate matter informing you of the content of this exchange of views, but I feel I have to give you a message. The king is following our action in E'ville with particular interest and it appears, from information he already had and some I was able to give him, that he has special admiration for you, something I am sure you will appreciate.

Due to this mark of esteem, and other things I cannot say in this message, I am asking you to continue your mission with the same courage and enthusiasm you have been good enough to demonstrate up till now. In short, we hope you will be in the copper capital for a long time to come.[22]

King Baudouin does not reappear in this account of the assassination of Lumumba. Too many protected witnesses still refuse to talk, too many archive doors are still closed. However, the palace undoubtedly played a behind-the-scenes role throughout this period. In 1960–61 Baudouin was no longer the twenty-year-old prince of 1951, who listened to Count Jacques Pirenne, former secretary to King Léopold III, explaining a contract negotiated between Brussels and Paris to supply Léopoldville with electricity from Brazzaville. Pirenne warned him that the contract threatened Belgian sovereignty over the Congo. Although the prince reacted to these words with strong emotion, according to Pirenne, he said there was nothing he could do about the situation. Pirenne replied that he could put pressure on the minister concerned by pointing out that it went against his wishes. He explained to the inexperienced young man that the power of the king went beyond his strict prerogatives. The king did not forget the lesson, according to a book by Professor Stengers.[23]

He certainly remembered it in 1960. Baudouin soon found the channels through which he could translate his power into action. His Court Chamberlain, Gobert d'Aspremont Lynden, was the nephew of the minister for African affairs and worked in the palace itself; its shadow fell on the neighbouring building, the Ministry for African Affairs, where Harold d'Aspremont Lynden and his assistants were preparing the next act of the drama.

THE BELGIAN GOVERNMENT

Gaston Eyskens's coalition government was not unprepared for the Congo crisis. It had come to power in November 1958 when peace still reigned in the colony. Soon after the unrest in Léopoldville in 1959, Brussels was faced with the rapid spread of nationalist ideas and the incipient dismantling of the colonial edifice. This government conceded independence at the beginning of 1960.

A permanent committee was created to deal with the crisis. After a government reshuffle on 2 September 1960, a Congo Committee was formed comprising three of the governing Christian Social Party's (PSC) ministers: Prime Minister Eyskens (aged fifty-five), Foreign Affairs Minister Pierre Wigny (also fifty-five), and African Affairs Minister d'Aspremont Lynden (aged forty-six). Eyskens and Wigny played a key role in the undeclared war on the Congolese government in 1960. Eyskens even introduced the conspiracy theory into official terminology, referring to the Congolese government's role in the mutiny and the Africanisation of the Congolese army. On 14 July he told the Belgian House that "the spectacular collapse of the Force Publique . . . is not the work of fate. It has been prepared, the indications are now all too obvious."

Wigny, his foreign minister, agreed, telling the Senate: "We are the victims of a diabolical plot . . . which was most certainly premeditated. . . . Imagine my surprise when I learn that a cargo ship – apparently of Polish origin – loaded with arms and ammunition was at the mouth of the river Congo a few days ago." Colonel Vandewalle's comment was damning: "the mention of this phantom cargo leaves us quite dumbfounded. . . . With a naval base in Banane, and the air force in Kitona, it would not have been difficult to verify a piece of information of that kind. But fibs and a diabolical plot were apparently preferable to the truth." In the same speech, Wigny added that he had always respected "the principle of non-interference". However, by then Belgian troops had already captured the Congolese army's camps in Katanga, put Tshombe on the presidential throne and banned the Congo's legal authorities from entering the copper province.[24]

From September 1960, when the battle against Lumumba entered its decisive phase, the undisputed linchpin of Belgium's Congo policy was the African Affairs Minister Harold d'Aspremont Lynden, the scion of an old and powerful aristocratic family which had held important positions in the state apparatus since Belgium was created in 1830. His father Charles d'Aspremont Lynden was a Senator, a former minister and the former chairman of the employers wing of the Catholic Party which later became the PSC. Harold's nephew Gobert was Lord Chamberlain at court, administrator of colonial companies and director of Belgium's Société Générale. Harold himself was administrator of the Banque de Bruxelles and mayor of Natoye where he lived with his wife, Baroness Doris van der Straten, and his father, in the Château de Mouffrin, the family seat.

Behind Harold d'Aspremont Lynden's political rise stood none other than King Baudouin and Prime Minister Eyskens, to whom he had been assistant private secretary since June 1958. When the Congo crisis broke out, Eyskens sent his assistant to Katanga to organise the secession. During the intervening months, d'Aspremont Lynden proved himself the right man to lead the battle against Lumumba's government. His memos to the Belgian government, with their perspicacious analyses and strong-arm remedies, reflected the view of the palace and the Société Générale. In a note at the end of February 1960, he wrote with brutal clarity that "a moderate Congolese government, that is to say, one basically willing to collaborate with Belgium, must be created before 30 June 1960". Figures like Lumumba must be kept out of government, or at least should not hold important positions: "So we need to 'win' the elections, by legitimate indirect means, with support from the private as well as the public sector." He then pleaded for King Baudouin to be proposed as the Congo's transitional head of state or as leader of a Belgo-Congolese community. A few weeks earlier, Count Jacques Pirenne, who was very influential at the court, had made the same request in a letter to Eyskens' government. At the beginning of March 1960 , d'Aspremont Lynden had noted down the conclusion of a discussion he had with Professor Arthur Doucy of the Université Libre de Bruxelles: "Political action. The man to eliminate is Lumumba."

On 10 July, as Belgian military intervention was under way, he came straight out and asked for a military operation that would result in the formation of a new Congolese government. Moreover, in his view the war situation demanded a tri-partite government in Brussels, which would include extra-parliamentarians, a request taken up later by King Baudouin.[25] On 17 July, the count arrived in Katanga to run Mistebel, nerve centre of the break-away province, with help from Robert Rothschild, a diplomat of socialist tendencies.

Harold d'Aspremont Lynden's appointment as minister for African affairs on 2 September 1960 was the most important feature of Eyskens's cabinet reshuffle. In August 1960, Belgium's ruling class asked for a firm hand to deal with both the Congo crisis and the strict austerity measures to be imposed. King Baudouin suggested the politically weakened government be replaced by an emergency cabinet made up, among others, of public figures like Paul Van Zeeland and Ganshof van der Meersch, advocates of a tougher policy in the Congo. Gaston Eyskens refused to resign, but agreed to a reshuffle which met the demands of the king and Belgian employers.

According to Major Weber, Count d'Aspremont Lynden was "the most dedicated of Katangans, the man behind the machine, the Belgian proconsul in central Africa". The weekly Pourquoi Pas? called him "practically more Katangan than Tshombe". La Libre Belgique commented that "Katanga is putting its hopes in the minister of African affairs. . . .We assume the new head of Mistebel in Elisabethville laid down his conditions before accepting the African affairs portfolio."[26] The count's promotion did not go unnoticed in Elisabethville and Léopoldville. His appointment spoke volumes. Brussels remained on a war footing as far as the Congo's government was concerned. The minister and his military adviser Major Jules Loos would play a crucial role in the impending drama. This duo had authority not only over Belgian officials in Katanga, but also over the Belgian army officers put at their disposal by a colleague at the Ministry of Defence to create the Katangan *Gendarmerie*.

Major Loos's sphere of influence also included the anti-nationalist pockets in Brazzaville and Léopoldville. The minister's right-hand man was involved in the preparation of Operation Barracuda. He sent funds to the Congo to buy the support of soldiers for Mobutu's coup of 14 September. In November 1960, he sent an intelligence officer, Armand Verdickt, to Brazzaville. Before returning to Katanga some time later, he and Colonel Marlière perfected a coding system for Belgian messages in which Lumumba was called "Satan", and Tshombe "the Jew".[27]

Powerful Belgian institutions gave Major Loos the freedom and the means to put Belgium's policies into operation on the ground. Vandewalle indicates that Loos had access to "a special account funded by the profits from copper mining". Would it be fanciful to claim that this account had been provided by the Société Générale? Probably not, for according to a telex sent in August d'Aspremont Lynden had given the anti-nationalists "one million lent [to me] by the Union Minière" to oppose the Congolese government. [28]

Loos used the funds in a variety of ways. In October 1960, he handed the press so-called intercepted messages in which Lumumba allegedly ordered nationalists "to lead the Republic's inhabitants as if they were sheep to . . . the first phase of dictatorship". These falsified messages end with the words: "Long live the Soviet Union. Long Live Khrushchev." The Belgian press lapped up this prose. At the beginning of 1961, Loos recruited Polish mercenaries for the Katangan army, soldiers who had stayed in Great Britain when they were demobbed after the Second World War. Loos handed out the funds so generously that Dupret, now the Belgium ambassador in Brazzaville, wrote to him: "I also request stop distributing money to Congolese through Belgian advisers. This behaviour queers the pitch and prevents us knowing the true attitude of the Congolese vis-à-vis us and the current problems."[29] Loos's most masterly achievement was to bring Colonel Vandewalle onto the Katangan stage. On his recommendation, Minister d'Aspremont Lynden appointed the colonel the *de facto* commander-in-chief of the Katangan *Gendarmerie*. Vandewalle would not disappoint his comrade-in-arms in the war against "Satan".

THE DEATH CELL

D'ASPREMONT LYNDEN AND LOOS IN AFRICA

Getting rid of Lumumba remained a top priority even after Mobutu's *coup d'état* of 14 September 1960. Georges Denis, Kasa Vubu's Belgian adviser, wrote to Minister Wigny on 16 September:

> Act of Authority of September 5 must prosper . . . first and only problem was and is to eliminate one man: Lumumba. Use the army to this effect. . . . Ordered Mobutu to stop both chambers meeting this morning at 9 hours; this was done, a new fact of considerable importance . . . our present policy is to support Mobutu without intervening too openly and without damaging his so-called neutrality which allows him to rally the entire army. . . . circumstances have forced me to play an important role . . . I am conscious of being part of a major struggle for the West's ideal of freedom. . . . I am in good shape, despite crushing responsibility and sometimes psychologically trying moments.

At some 6,000 kilometres from there, people were thinking along the same lines. A telegram of 6 October to Mistebel and the consulate general in Brazzaville from Minister of African Affairs d'Aspremont Lynden is worth quoting in full:

> Minaf to Mistebel
> For Rothschild
>
> Primo wait for you on Monday in USA [Usumbura in Burundi].
>   Clémens has to come back to Belgium, so couldn't he attend the meeting if it is not too much trouble for him?

Secundo from circles close to Thomas Kanza and Lumbala we have information that a third central government is apparently being formed in Léo. A lot of the MNC's members who have spectacularly deserted Lumumba could be part of it. It is also said that Godfroid [sic] Munongo will be deputy prime minister. All this seems to me

a) improbable

b) particularly dangerous because in my view it tends to put Lumumba indirectly in the clear.

It might be opportune to inform Godfroid Munongo of these rumours and possibly warn him of such an attempt. The main aim to pursue in the interests of the Congo, Katanga and Belgium is clearly Lumumba's *élimination définitive*.

Aspremont

Tell Dupret
Copy for Foreign Affairs

Foreign Minister Wigny said likewise on 10 September: "the constituted authorities have the duty to render Lumumba harmless."[1] Like his colleague, d'Aspremont Lynden left his assistants free to think up a practical solution to this problem themselves.

While the Belgians were preparing Operation Barracuda in Brazzaville, and the Congolese were being encouraged to take action themselves, the CIA worked with greater speed. Devlin, the CIA station head in Léopoldville, was afraid the Congolese leader could make a political comeback at any time: "Only solution is to remove him from scene soonest." At a later date the CIA scientist Gottlieb said he had been sent to the Congo with a box of poison to "mount an operation . . . to either seriously incapacitate or eliminate Lumumba". On 21 September, during a meeting of the National Security Council with President Eisenhower, CIA Chief Allen Dulles stressed that "Lumumba . . . remained a grave danger as long as he was not disposed of." Three days later in a personally signed telegram to the US Embassy in Léopoldville, Dulles confirmed that he would take responsibility for the whole operation: "We wish give every possible support in eliminating Lumumba from any possibility resuming governmental position or if he fails in Léopoldville setting himself up in Stanleyville or elsewhere." CIA agent Gottlieb made a brief visit to the Congo at the beginning of October. He left the poison in Léopoldville. At the beginning of November, the CIA told Devlin that a foreigner with a criminal past, recruited in Europe, would shortly be arriving in the Congo. This hired assassin's code name was QJ/WIN and he was "capable 'of doing anything'." QJ/WIN arrived in the Congo on 21

November. Not long afterwards, Lumumba managed to escape from his residence but then fell into Mobutu's hands. In consequence the CIA cancelled its operation and recalled QJ/WIN. At a later date Devlin said he threw the poison into the Congo river.[2]

All these machinations prove that it is wrong to see, as several authors do, the massacre of 17 January 1961 as an *accident*, to be ascribed to an emotional outburst by a few black leaders – an unfortunate mistake caused by a panic reaction in Léopoldville and unfathomable feelings of hate in Elisabethville. In fact, Lumumba's assassination was the culmination of six months of intervention by the West in the Congo.

Brussels, Washington and New York all took fright at Lumumba, or, to be more precise, at the anti-colonial movement he personified and led. This movement pushed the masses to the fore for the first time, with hundreds of thousands of people attacking the colonial edifice. This particular assault was only one expression of the worldwide anti-colonial movement, which encompassed more than half the globe's population and shook whole continents. This powerful movement, which forced Brussels into temporary capitulation in 1960, saw Lumumba as its leader and its symbol. His charisma, his solidarity with the Congolese masses, his radical commitment and strong principles, created an explosive cocktail for Western strategists. Brussels feared that Lumumba and the nationalist movement would bar the way to neo-colonial rule. This was the logic that brought the Western powers to an ultimate confrontation with the nationalist leader. These were the underlying reasons, the hidden agenda, for what Jean Kestergat, star reporter of *La Libre Belgique,* recognised in an internal memo at a much later date: "From September 1960 onwards, Lumumba can have had no illusions as to his future."

Kestergat sought the explanation in the Congolese leader's personality. The journalist *demonized* and *psychoanalysed* Lumumba. He makes him "a devil of a man", someone who "must know he has lost, but still wants to strike, like a lion at bay". General Janssens, former commander-in-chief of the Force Publique who opposed Lumumba from the start, has written about him in the same way: "Lumumba was the devil who spread terror in Maniema and the Eastern Province in April and May 1960. . . . More fiend than man, without scruples, without any real knowledge, he was however a brilliant thinker, a leader of men, of tireless perseverance."[3]

Once Lumumba had been portrayed as a dangerous madman, they had of course already half explained and justified that he must at all costs be stopped – and – why not? – killed. This campaign was organised by powerful people. King Baudouin had publicly condemned Lumumba in his 21 July speech. Several days later, after the Belgian National Day, in an editorial in *La Libre Belgique*, Professor De Corte regretted the opportunity missed by Belgian soldiers: "one virile gesture" would have rid the planet of Lumumba. In this bellicose atmosphere, when the king publicly took sides and a professor could publish with impunity what is tantamount to a call for Lumumba's death, the way was clear for people who, in the shadows, were ready to put words into action.

Back in Belgium for August and September, the former head of the Congolese intelligence services, now (temporarily) unemployed, was a keen and well-informed observer of what Brussels was plotting for its ex-colony. Vandewalle writes: "Lumumba's Belgophobia (no one advised moderation) got so bad that he became the enemy to be laid low, no matter what the cost." His conclusion would be correct if "Lumumba's Belgophobia" were replaced by "Brussels' Lumumbaphobia". At the beginning of October, Baudouin's brother, Prince – later King – Albert, put the prevailing Belgian views in a nutshell. He laid responsibility for the crisis squarely at the door of the Congolese prime minister by saying: "The Congo crisis is due to just one man, Patrice Lumumba." A few days later, the minister for African affairs called for the nationalist leader's *élimination définitive*. Colonel Vandewalle devotes a chapter of *Mille et quatre jours* to the period after the beginning of October, using a subheading which spelt out this aim. This time it is not Lumumba must be "laid low no matter what the cost", but "Lumumba must be eliminated".[4] During this time, the nationalist leader's return to the political scene was never off the agenda. Lumumba went to Léopoldville regularly to speak to enthusiastic crowds, and the president of the Congolese chamber intended to convene parliament.

Brussels spared no effort to ward off the danger. On 6 October, Major Loos left Brussels for a brief mission to Pointe-Noire in Congo-Brazzaville. He had discreet contact with Colonel Marlière, who was busy preparing for Operation Barracuda. It is easy to guess what was on the agenda: the day Loos left for Africa, d'Aspremont Lynden's telegram to Mistebel called for Lumumba's *élimination définitive*. Loos was not the only one carrying the message. While he looked after Léopoldville, the minister himself took care of Elisabethville. d'Aspremont Lynden telegraphed his arrival at Usumbura on 10 October. He wanted to meet Rothschild there and also Clémens of the Katangan Bureau Conseil. Vandewalle's comment on receipt of the 6 October dispatch about the elimination speaks for itself: "That's clear, then!" And in the margin of the copy of the telegram, someone made a note: "Bartelous will talk to Tshombe about it."[5]

Nor was Foreign Minister Wigny sitting idle. His dispatch of 8 October dealt entirely with the battle to prevent Lumumba returning to power. It was crucial that parliament should not reopen. Wigny insisted that Kasa Vubu and Tshombe must meet and send a communiqué to the world opening up the possibility of reuniting the Congo. However, it was not appropriate to fix a precise date for this meeting, because Léopoldville must first "confirm its authority by action". Vandewalle deftly points out that Wigny did not specify what actions he had in mind. The dispatch ended with the words "This is confidential and cannot be transmitted in writing." The colonel's conclusion is unequivocal: "Lumumba had to be eliminated!"

Foreign Minister Wigny, however, had no problem letting people know what he thought. In the same telegram he said that Westhof, an official who would be leaving shortly for Africa, was fully aware of his opinions.[6] On 13 October, a meeting was held in the Belgian consulate in Brazzaville. Consul Dupret received Westhof, an adviser of Wigny, and Jean Cordy, a member of Governor General Pétillon's cabinet and that of his successor Hendrik Cornelis, who after independence had become adviser to Justin Bomboko, president of the College of Commissioners set up by Mobutu. The discussion centred on Lumumba's removal. In a telegram from Dupret and Westhof, the talks were described as "interesting". Cordy wanted to keep the cordon round Lumumba's residence, and "meanwhile get a helping hand from a small independent squad of the Force Publique [ANC]". In *Mille et quatre jours,* Vandewalle describes Loos's plan to entrust the Belgian officer Dedeken with a commando action against Lumumba. In Vandewalle's archives there is a handwritten note which talks of delivering commando material "perfectly suited to long-distance guerrilla action". This material was to be smuggled to Katanga via Usumbura to await Dedeken. However, like other projects, this one came to nothing. That same 13 October, a telex from Brussels arrived. Its contents are unknown but, replying on the 14th, Westhof wrote: "Cordy felt the project was for the time being – I repeat – for the time being impracticable." In *Mille et quatre jours* Vandewalle comments: "Jiggery-pokery, like decolonisation, was not simple."[7]

The last months of 1960 saw more evidence of Belgian support for the regime in place in the Congolese capital. Belgian officers arrived to reinforce the ANC in Léopoldville. Three Belgians tutored the regime: Georges Denis was President Kasa Vubu's adviser; André Lahaye was in charge of the intelligence services and internal affairs; and Louis Marlière, who shared a flat in Brazzaville with Lahaye, took care of Mobutu and the ANC. Both Marlière and Lahaye had special links with the men who, structurally, had become their bosses. In the days of the Belgian Congo, Sergeant-secretary Mobutu had been one of Marlière's subordinates in the Force Publique. Victor Nendaka had been an informant for Lahaye, a former commissioner of the colonial intelligence services. And the colonial past had another beneficial legacy: Lahaye still had his antenna in Elisabethville in the shape of Jules Allard, a former colleague in the Congolese intelligence services.

As the war against Lumumba and the nationalist movement approached its final stage, the focus of Belgian action moved from Wigny to d'Aspremont Lynden, and especially his cabinet, to Major Loos and his assistants on the ground: Marlière and Lahaye in Léopoldville, Vandewalle and Clémens in Elisabethville. In a confidential interview with Brassinne, Marlière admitted that the transfer of Lumumba to a "safe" place was first envisaged not in January 1961, but much earlier. Since Lumumba's dismissal on 14 September, the situation had been "very precarious. . . . He still has a lot of followers, even among the young 'commissioners'". The conclusion was obvious. "We do not wish him ill, but we must 'neutralise' him properly. . . . We must act quickly. . . . Nobody knows what to do with him, but we must absolutely prevent him from getting back to Stan!" In a telegram in mid-October, Marlière wrote to Loos:

> Lumumba's arrest is going badly. The Thysville troops are disappointed with the lack of action. [. . .] Our personal part in this matter is on course. Reinforcements are needed following new activity being tr [transferred] promised by E'ville and ex-Sûreté Van Steenbeek. Request you remember promises tr [transfer] made by Verdickt when Charles came [Magnette or Van Overstraeten, Loos's assistants].

Meanwhile, Brussels was kept informed of possible attempts on Lumumba's life. In a note at the end of November, *Major* Verdickt pointed out that Kasa Vubu "told Abbé Fulbert Youlou, president of the former French Congo, HE DID NOT want to liquidate M. Lumumba P., because the latter could help reconquer Katanga. M. Kasa Vubu's remarks were violently anti-Belgian". The capital letters are in the original document.[8]

LUMUMBA DELIVERED TO MOBUTU BY THE UN (2 DECEMBER 1960)

At the end of November Lumumba's political future was still a burning issue. For weeks the UN headquarters in New York had been shaken by a fierce diplomatic battle. Which delegation should represent the Congo at the UN? Kasa Vubu's or Lumumba's? On 24 November, after a stormy debate, the General Assembly recognised Kasa Vubu's delegation as the legal representative of the Congo by fifty-three votes to twenty-four with nineteen abstentions. An analysis by Catherine Hoskyns shows that most of the countries that changed from Lumumba's side to Kasa Vubu's during the deliberations "were those susceptible to pressure from the countries of the Western alliance". Dayal, the UN secretary general's special envoy in the Congo, later described this as "one of the most glaring examples of the massive and organized application of threats and pressures – along with inducements – to member states to change their votes".[9]

On Sunday 27 November, a triumphant Kasa Vubu, in the grand white and gold uniform of a lieutenant general, made his solemn entry into the Congolese capital. And that evening, a grand banquet gathered together national and foreign dignitaries to honour the brand new general who had just conquered New York. Lumumba watched the parade from his residence, isolated by the cordon

of Blue Berets and Mobutu's men. He decided that it was time to try and escape
and get back to Stanleyville where Gizenga, his former deputy prime minister,
was regrouping the nationalist forces. Now that the vote in the UN General
Assembly had definitively cut off all chance of his returning to power by legal
means, retaking Léopoldville from Stanleyville had become the only realistic
option. Seven other nationalists prepared to make the journey: former ministers
Gbenye, Joseph Mbuyi, Mpolo, Anicet Kashamura and Mulele, Deputy
President of the Senate Okito, and Governor of the Central Bank Barthélemy
Mujanay. Of these eight nationalists, only Gbenye, Kashamura and Mulele
reached their destination. Lumumba, Mpolo and Okito were arrested and taken
back to Léopoldville, while Mbuyi and Mujanay were killed in the Charlesville
region.[10]

That same evening of 27 November around 8 o'clock, it was pouring with
rain when a Chevrolet drove out through the cordon of soldiers encircling the
residence. It was taking the former prime minister's servants home, as usual. But
this time the car was also carrying Patrice Lumumba, who was pressed against
the front seats, under the feet of the passengers in the back. This precaution
turned out to be unnecessary: because of the tornado, the ANC guard was
even less careful than usual to check the car as it left. For safety reasons,
Lumumba left that car at the Astoria hotel, and got into a Guinean Embassy car,
driven by an official. A little further on, at Nsele, a column of three vehicles was
formed: a Fiat with Akunda, former head of Mpolo's cabinet, and Wingudi,
Lumumba's administrative secretary, inside; the former prime minister's nearly
new blue Peugeot, driven by Bernardin Mungu Diaka and carrying Lumumba,
his wife Pauline Opango and their little son Roland; and the Chevrolet.[11] At
some 2,000 kilometres from there, on the other side of the province of
Equateur, Stanleyville was impatiently awaiting its leader.

Dayal informed Hammarskjöld by telegram that he had had an interview with
Kasa Vubu, Bomboko and Ileo two days after the dismissed prime minister had
slipped away from his residence: "My interrogators were obsessed by
Lumumba's escape. . . . Bomboko was obviously most concerned and highly
excited at the possibility of Lumumba reaching Stanleyville."

Léopoldville had reason to be worried. Dayal's first reaction was to wire his
superior: "If Lumumba manages to get to Stanleyville the situation would change
in a flash."

US Ambassador Timberlake recognised later that Lumumba "more than
likely . . . would have been able to regain control of the Central Government
from that vantage point had he ever managed to reach it".

Meanwhile, Hammarskjöld told the US ambassador to the United Nations
that he would position UN troops between Stanleyville and Léopoldville if
Lumumba reached his objective. The secretary general thought Mobutu's army
"could not match" the forces of Stanleyville.[12]

In a press communiqué from Lumumba dispatched on the evening of his departure, he openly defended his political project. The dismissed prime minister denied the rumours broadcast on national radio which had him leaving the capital "like a coward". He defended the principles of national unity and territorial integrity, and held out his hand to all those wanting to join this fight. He hoped soon to be able to take part in round-table discussions with both Kasa Vubu and Tshombe. Lumumba presented himself as a national conciliator and unifier, accusing his political adversaries of dividing the nation. At the same time, he made not the slightest concession on constitutional and democratic principles. He would take part in the round table "as prime minister of the only legitimate government, together with M. Tshombe, president of the provincial government of Katanga".[13]

Dayal kept New York posted hourly: "[H]e has reached the area of Kikwit where he has strong adherents. Pongo, the hysterical security chief, has followed in pursuit in a Sabena helicopter." In 1966 Heinz and Donnay published a small, well-documented book which is still of interest today, *Lumumba Patrice. Les cinquante derniers jours de sa vie* (Lumumba: The Last Fifty Days of his Life). They say that Mobutu asked for technical assistance in the search for Lumumba "from a European airline. He was provided with a European aircraft and a pilot, a specialist in low altitude reconnaissance flights. . . . the Katanga and South Kasai security services were alerted." Brussels and its helpers did not stand inertly watching their number one enemy try to regain his freedom. Since 20 November, a Belgian intelligence services agent in Léopoldville had been warning that some nationalist detainees were making plans to escape. Dupret passed the information on to Wigny, adding that Mobutu's College of Commissioners had been informed. On 28 November, Dupret wired that the guard round Lumumba's residence had been reinforced. All to no avail, however, since on that very day Wigny learned, even before Kasa Vubu and Mobutu, that Lumumba had escaped.[14]

The convoy made very slow progress; torrential rains and road blocks slowed Lumumba down and besides, all along the way his supporters invited him to speak. Heinz and Donnay describe the group arriving on the evening of 29 November at Bulungu:

> The fugitives want to stock up on provisions but a local man recognises P. Lumumba. The news spreads like wildfire and at 10.30 Lumumba is practically forced to hold a public meeting in the centre of Bulungu in front of a very enthusiastic African crowd. He explains his problems in Léopoldville. He is not going to Stanleyville as a runaway but to liberate national territory and protect the people.

Dupret, who was keeping Brussels informed by telegram, mentioned this meeting and added: "The commissioners are starting to realise the gravity of the situation." In another dispatch the same day, Dupret was hard pressed to restrain his animosity: "The consequences of Lumumba's escape and the prospect of a central revolutionary government being installed in Stanleyville are at the moment unpredictable but undoubtedly very serious."[15]

On 1 December, Lumumba reached Port-Francqui, in the east of Kasai province, where the people were decidedly nationalist. The group was stopped on the outskirts of Mweka, some 150 kilometres further along the road to Luluabourg: "The district commissioner greets them with the elected representatives and local authorities. The crowd is waiting for the prime minister and wants to hear him." The same day, the consul in Brazzaville sent another telegram to Ministers Wigny and d'Aspremont Lynden, and to the head of the Belgian intelligence services. Jean-Baptiste Crokart, a Sûreté agent, had talked to a man with the code name "e070/a", who promised to do "the impossible" to stop Lumumba reaching Stanleyville and forming a "popular democratic regime". A certain "Raymond" and his company were mobilised to find Lumumba – this was probably Raymond Linard, pilot and co-owner of Air Brousse. Contact was also made with the military authorities in South Kasai to prepare "an ambush" there if Lumumba appeared in the region.[16] Did they intend to kill Lumumba? (See p. 24 for an account of *Major* Dedeken's missions first to Katanga and then to South Kasai to organise an operation against the former prime minister.)

Lumumba's journey towards Stanleyville was triumphant, and it is indeed this which led to his downfall. On 1 December around midnight, Lumumba was intercepted near Lodi by a unit of the ANC. The group had left the road from Port-Francqui to Luluabourg near Mweka. Rather than drive south towards the capital of Kasai, they took the northern road to the left, which would take them to Dekese, Lomela, Ikela and finally Stanleyville. At Mweka, with still about 1,200 kilometres between them and the bastion of nationalism, the population lit bonfires to celebrate the announcement that the former prime minister would be arriving soon. On the evening of 1 December, the group reached Lodi, on the left bank of the Sankuru. This river, about 600 metres wide, was the last real obstacle for the travellers on the road to Stanleyville, 1,000 kilometres distant. On the other bank, they could expect a welcome from a strongly nationalist population and a relatively good road to the capital of the Eastern Province. Lumumba, Mulele, Valentin Lubuma and Mathias Kamishanga crossed the Sankuru in a dugout while the others, among them Lumumba's wife and little Roland, waited on the bank for the boat to return. Lumumba was on the way back to fetch his family when he was captured. Mobutu's soldiers caught up with the group on the river bank. Some say Lumumba didn't know they were there; others that he did know, and went back across the river precisely to argue for the release of the rest of the group – which in fact he seemed to be doing successfully at first. Pierre Mulele, who did not go back, was able to escape and reach Stanleyville.

On 2 December, the convoy with the prisoners was back in Mweka. According to Heinz and Donnay, this is what happened then:

> Taking advantage of a lapse in the vigilance of the ANC guards, Lumumba's driver [. . .] dashes off to a camp of Ghanaian soldiers of the UN Congo force. In the version given by this driver [. . .] a Ghanaian lieutenant . . . explained to Lumumba that it was not his mission to offer him protection. Congolese soldiers then arrive, find Lumumba leaning on the back of the Peugeot, beat him with rifle butts and take him away. Rebelling against their officer, the Ghanaian soldiers free the other fugitives who were taken prisoner and threatened in the centre of Mweka, but they intervene too late to save the Congolese premier.

An internal UN document and a coded telegram from Dayal confirm the driver's version. The UN was directly responsible for the former Congolese prime minister's arrest. On 30 November, the Ghanaian command at Luluabourg gave orders to its regiment in Tshikapa, where Gilbert Pongo was looking for Lumumba; the battalion must remain neutral in the hunt for Lumumba and, what is more: "In the event arrival Lumumba take him into protective custody if in danger of arrest or causing trouble."

General von Horn, commander-in-chief of UN forces, later issued this counter-order from Léopoldville: "No, repeat no, action is to be taken by you in respect of Lumumba. We were responsible for his personal safety only in his house at Léopoldville. It has always been understood and made known that he would venture out of his house at his own risk and responsibility."

The same day, the UN leadership was twice reassured by the Ghanaian command: "Position Lumumba discussed with ANC Commander Kasai. . . . Agreed UN would not interfere legal arrest Lumumba by ANC." Dayal confirmed von Horn's counter-order in a telegram to Hammarskjöld on 1 December: "[The Ghanaians] yesterday casually mentioned their intention to provide protective custody to Lumumba in case it was requested. We have taken firm position that he was under UNOC guard at his residence only."

The events in Mweka were subsequently the object of a report by the Ghanaian command:

> At 0730 hours on the morning of 2nd December, the Ghana platoon commander was near the entrance to his platoon location when he saw three cars being driven down the road at high speed. They stopped some distance down the road and there was a scuffle. Lumumba was dragged by ANC from his car, hit with rifle butts, slapped and kicked. The Ghana platoon commander ordered his men into position around the car and stopped the maltreatment. Lumumba was then hustled into a car by the ANC and driven away quickly in the direction of Luluabourg.

This report which, in its very – and very significant – title, talks about "the arrest of Lumumba" sums up:

> Their original reaction [of the Ghanaians] when it was learned that he [Lumumba] had left UN protection in Léopoldville was that he would be taken into protective custody if in danger of arrest or harm. They . . . received very clear instructions that on no account was any action to be taken in respect of Lumumba. These instructions were rigidly adhered to.[17]

These documents contradict Hammarskjöld's assertions that it was not within the UN's mandate to protect Lumumba, and would contradict the principle of the (active) non-use of force, because protecting Lumumba would imply a military initiative. On that morning of 2 December, Lumumba was again free, and the Blue Berets were present when he was rearrested. They stopped the brutality, but refused him their protection and allowed him to be arrested, on the orders of their superiors. Moreover, these documents clearly show that the explanations given by Hammarskjöld to the Security Council after Lumumba's death contain a lie:

> Mr Lumumba escaped from his residence in a way unknown to the United Nations and travelled East, without any possibility for the Organization to give him protection. He was arrested out in the country without any possibility for the UN to stop this action, as it was not in control of the situation."[18]

After his arrest Lumumba was handed over to Gilbert Pongo (assistant to Victor Nendaka, the chief of Mobutu's intelligence services) in Port-Francqui on 2 December. There was some talk of whether or not to transfer him to Léopoldville. Heinz and Donnay write: "At that moment, a European present, who had played a large part in locating him, strongly advised G. Pongo to go ahead with P. Lumumba's immediate transfer to Katanga, where he would be judged for common crimes or offences." This was not the first time that this kind of transfer was considered as a means of ridding Léopoldville's weak regime of troublesome nationalists. On 23 September 1960 the Belgian consul in Brazzaville had sent a telegram to Katanga via Brussels (!) with a request from Kasa Vubu to deliver the nationalists Gizenga and Mpolo "to be tried there". This plan would have been carried out, had it not been for pressure from the local UN leadership on an indecisive and weak Mobutu, who eventually ordered their release.[19] Nevertheless, Pongo kept to the orders he received, and Lumumba was transferred to Léopoldville in an Air Congo DC-3. The idea of the transfer to Katanga was abandoned and that seemed to be the end of it.

Lumumba's capture came as a huge relief to Léopoldville. General von Horn subsequently described the atmosphere in the UN quarter: "Most of us felt quite rightly that there was now a genuine chance of the Congo returning to some degree of tranquility. To put it frankly, had Lumumba got to Stanleyville, the whole Congo might have gone up in flames." Hammarskjöld was of the opinion that, without Lumumba, Gizenga would not be able to "crystallize" the situation in Stanleyville. Colonel Mobutu stated somewhat prematurely: "That's the end of Lumumba, and Stanleyville, that hotbed of agitation, is in theory neutralised."[20]

CAMP HARDY AT THYSVILLE

On 2 December, shortly after 5 p.m., an Air Congo DC-3 landed at Ndjili, Léopoldville's airport. On board were Gilbert Pongo, Lumumba and a military escort. Dozens of people were waiting on the tarmac: journalists and photographers, ANC soldiers and dignitaries of the regime. The minutes of the College of Commissioners' session for that day read: "A large number of members suggest Monsieur Pongo deserves to be promoted to a higher military rank . . . The session rose at 5 p.m. to allow certain commissioners to go to the airfield and watch the big rabbit [code name for Lumumba] disembark."

UN soldiers were standing slightly further away but did not intervene. Lumumba was the second person to come out of the aircraft, behind a triumphant Pongo. His arms were tied behind his back by a big rope. He was wearing a white shirt, sleeves rolled up. According to a 3 December telegram from Rothschild, Lumumba "gave the impression of complete weariness and dejection" on arrival. But Heinz and Donnay say he was "very dignified but passive, apparently weary". Lumumba and the few other prisoners were pushed roughly onto the back of a lorry where, huddled together, they awaited the next stage of the journey. For the benefit of the photographers and cameramen, a soldier grabbed Lumumba by the hair to raise his head, and twisted his arm. According to UN observers, he had lost his glasses, his shirt was stained and there was blood on his cheek.[21]

The prisoners were taken to the Binza paratroop camp, near Mobutu's residence which was built by the Belgian Congo Bank. A journalist who was present says Lumumba was again made to pose for the press. Mobutu watched calmly as his men manhandled the prisoner; he was thrown to the ground, surrounded by soldiers, and kicked and punched. Pongo shouted at them to hit harder. A soldier read a recent statement by Lumumba in which he declared he was the head of the country's legitimate government. The soldier then crumpled the piece of paper and stuffed it into Lumumba's mouth. After that Lumumba was thrown into a room where he was once again savagely beaten.[22] During the night, Nendaka took Lumumba into custody again. According to Alfred Cahen, a young Belgian diplomat who arrived in the Congo shortly after the events, his friend Nendaka subsequently told him that he locked Lumumba in the garage of the residence of Vandewalle, former head of colonial intelligence. Lumumba was again mistreated. Minister Wigny was given more details in a telegram from the Belgian Embassy in Brazzaville, dated 3 December: "Badly mistreated during the night of the 2nd to 3rd by commandos who notably burned his beard. Bomboko intervened to calm tempers down, but to no avail. According to an eyewitness, the party concerned is in a very bad way."

Nevertheless, Rothschild said in the telegram (cited above, see Note 21) sent the same day that steps were being taken to make sure Kasa Vubu was "firm" with the detainee.[23]

The foreign press photographed and filmed the punishment inflicted on Lumumba at Ndjili and the Binza camp. US Ambassador Timberlake sent Secretary of State Herter a telegram asking him to stop these images being disseminated since they would have an "atomic bomb" effect. However, thinking there would be little chance of self-censorship, Timberlake suggested to his boss that the affair could be minimised by drawing attention to Mobutu's supporters detained in Stanleyville and concluding "that violence breeds violence in return".[24] Sure enough, the images did have their effect. The international community's indignation brought shock waves which crashed onto the UN offices in New York, and even the openly neo-colonialist regimes in Africa felt obliged to distance themselves from UN policies. People did not understand how Hammarskjöld, who had a huge intervention force in the Congo, was able to protect the Belgians in Stanleyville and elsewhere, but was not capable of protecting Lumumba who enjoyed parliamentary immunity. Several African and Asian leaders threatened to withdraw their contingents from the UNOC.

Both Hammarskjöld and Dayal lodged protests about what had occurred. Dayal protested to Bomboko against this "arbitrary arrest" and demanded the prisoner be treated appropriately. Hammarskjöld reminded Kasa Vubu in a letter that Lumumba was a member of parliament, and that "the principle of parliamentary immunity exists throughout the world as a means of protecting . . . the structure of parliamentary democracy". This protest only made the UN position worse. If Lumumba's arrest was arbitrary and endangered parliamentary democracy, why did UN leaders not demand his release or release him themselves? According to Hammarskjöld's report to the Security Council, the UN intervened in the Congo because "the breakdown of the instruments of the Government for the maintenance of order . . . had created a situation which through its consequences represented a threat to peace and security". How could helping to maintain law and order be reconciled with standing by and allowing the country's very constitutional structures to be violated? As Vandewalle subsequently admitted, the UN officials' only purpose in lodging protests with Kasa Vubu and Bomboko was to "cover themselves" vis-à-vis Afro-Asian repugnance at the ill-treatment of Lumumba.[25] The UN's unfortunate behaviour at Ndjili and Binza can be seen in a sense as a precursor to that of 17 January 1961 at Elisabethville airfield, on Lumumba's last journey. The

December dress rehearsal taught Mobutu and Tshombe that as far as their treatment of the nationalist leader was concerned, they had not much to fear from the UN, apart from a few verbal protests.

On 3 December 1960, Patrice Lumumba was transferred by military convoy to Camp Hardy, in Thysville. According to journalists, he had difficulty getting into the lorry, and his face bore marks of beating. Camp Hardy housed the regime's elite troops, under the command of Colonel Louis Bobozo. At independence, Bobozo was a sergeant. The Africanisation of officer ranks and his family ties with Mobutu allowed him to rise rapidly through the ranks. He was even interim commander-in-chief of the ANC during Mobutu's absence in October 1960. Other important prisoners were detained at Camp Hardy, among them Georges Grenfell who had been a minister in Lumumba's government. Nothing is known of where they were kept, but Lumumba was put in a guardroom near the entrance to the camp. His cell was a brick construction with a corrugated iron roof next to the soldiers' quarters.[26]

Moroccan Blue Berets, responsible for training the ANC, were stationed near Camp Hardy. This UN contingent was quick to address complaints about Lumumba's fate to the UN's top brass. Dayal summarised the criticisms: "He is said to be suffering from serious injuries received before his arrival. His head has been shaven and his hands remain tied. He is being kept in a cell under conditions reported to be inhuman in respect of health and hygiene." Lumumba's detention worried not only the Blue Berets but also Congolese soldiers in Camp Hardy. In a coded telegram to Hammarskjöld on 5 December, Dayal reported that: "The Moroccan detachment at Thysville reports that there is considerable discussion amongst the ANC rank and file over Lumumba's treatment. The argument has not yet concluded." On 22 December, Dayal informed his superior that the garrison was deeply divided about the matter: "Lumumba's incarceration in Thysville is causing embarrassment to his jailers [Kasa Vubu and Mobutu] because of the feelings pro and contra it has aroused among the troops."[27]

On 4 January 1961, thirteen days before his death, Lumumba managed to smuggle two letters out of his prison. The first was a message to the UN leaders, in which he described the conditions of the political prisoners in Camp Hardy:

I am here with seven other members of parliament – among whom is the president of the Senate, M. Okito – a government employee and a driver. There are ten of us in all. We have been confined in damp cells since 2 December 1960 and have not been allowed out once. The meals brought to us (twice a day) are very bad; I often eat nothing for three or four days except a banana. I reported this to the Red Cross doctor sent to see me; the colonel in charge of Thysville was present at the time. I have asked for fruit to be bought with my own money because the food I am given here is so bad. Although the doctor gave his permission, the military authorities here have refused to allow it, saying they have orders to that effect from the head of state, Colonel Mobutu. The doctor here at Thysville has prescribed a short walk every evening so I can get out of my cell for a while, but the colonel and the district commissioner refuse. The clothes I have now been wearing for thirty-five days have never been washed. I am forbidden to wear shoes.

In a word, we are living in absolutely intolerable conditions, in contravention of regulations.

What is more, I have received no news of my wife and I don't even know where she is. I should be receiving visits from her, as laid down in Congolese penal law.

In the second letter, to his nephew Albert Onawelo, Lumumba gave more details about his detention, and also talked of the support he received from some of the soldiers:

I am here with seven deputies, among them Joseph Okito. We have been locked in dark cells continuously since 2 December 1960. The food we're given (chikwangue and rice) is disgusting and dirty and I don't eat for three or four days at a time. In addition, my stomach hurts (constipation). . . . It is really hard and worse than under the colonialists. If a soldier gives us so much as a banana, he's arrested and put in a cell. Despite everything several soldiers come secretly to try and help me.

Lumumba also revealed in this letter that his third wife, Pauline Kie, the mother of his little François, "is doing all she can to come here often and leaves messages for me with soldiers who are on our side". Lumumba worried about his family and his friends, as if he was preparing for the worst: "I've sent a letter telling Socobanque to give 30,000 francs to [Cléophas] Kamitatu" (a nationalist leader and president of Léopoldville Province). His fourth wife, Pauline Opango, was instructed to share the money between his elder brother Charles (6,000 francs), Pauline Kie (3,000 francs), his assistant Michel Tshungu (2,000 francs), and his nephew Albert Onawelo (2,000 francs). Pauline Opango was to keep 17,000 francs for herself "to look after the child and feed him sparingly. I don't want him to go hungry or eat food that's not good for him." We do not know if the bank released the money because d'Aspremont Lynden asked his colleagues to start proceedings to block Lumumba's accounts.[28]

At the beginning of January 1961, Hammarskjöld visited Léopoldville where he was welcomed by demonstrations in support of Lumumba. When the nationalist leader Kamitatu tried to give him Lumumba's letter describing the conditions in which the nationalists were being held at Camp Hardy, Hammarskjöld turned red and asked him to give the letter to his private secretary. The embarrassment of the UN secretary general, who was jointly responsible for the pitiful situation of the man who had asked for UN help for his country, is understandable. The sentence where Lumumba described the arbitrary nature of his detention must have especially embarrassed the UN head. Was it not to help restore law and order that the UN had rushed to the aid of the Congolese authorities? Yet several months later, the UN forces stood passively by as a man with parliamentary immunity was arrested and tortured, what's more by the rabble army of Mobutu, a man whom Dayal himself called the main author of the troubles which plunged Léopoldville into "a state of terror". Lumumba wrote:

> The penal code in effect in the Congo expressly stipulates the prisoner must be taken before the examining magistrate investigating the charges on the day following his arrest at the very latest. After being detained for five days, the prisoner must appear before the judge again for him to determine whether or not he should continue to be held in preventive custody. Whatever the circumstances, the prisoner is entitled to a lawyer.
>
> The law regarding preliminary hearings states that the person under arrest be "automatically" released if after five days the magistrate decides he should no longer be held in preventive custody. . . . Since our arrest . . . we have not been taken before an examining magistrate, nor have we been visited by one. No warrant for our arrest has been served. We have simply been kept in an army camp for thirty-four days, in punishment cells intended for soldiers.

Kamitatu enclosed this message in a letter of his own:

> M. Lumumba has been suffering inhumane treatment for 35 days. During that time he has been allowed only 3 baths; he is served food fit for dogs (excuse the expression). He has worn the same clothes for 35 days. He lives in a damp cell. He has not been taken before a magistrate, and he has even been forbidden visits from his wife.[29]

The UN leaders did not react to these letters.

Incidents and even revolts were a constant danger in Thysville and the camps controlled by Mobutu. Lieutenant Schoonbroodt, assistant to Colonel Bobozo, said the origin of the troubles in the Thysville camp "was political. A section of the troops in the camps were Lumumbists". On 27 December, Colonel Bobozo had to put his life on the line to keep Lumumba under lock and key: that night he stood in front of the cell door to stop a few dozen soldiers setting the former prime minister free. According to Schoonbroodt, Colonel Bobozo told the soldiers: "You have no choice, if you want to free the prisoner you'll have to kill me." The soldiers finally withdrew one by one.[30] But how long would that last?

About fifty nationalist soldiers were arrested at Thysville at the end of 1960. And later, on 5 February, another group of forty men were transferred to other units. Lumumba, who was "in good form" at Thysville according to André Lahaye (a Belgian commissioner of the Sécurité Congolaise), appeared to be strengthening his hold over the soldiers. A rumour that the prisoner had shared Christmas dinner with some of the officers in the garrison was spread. Luis López Alvarez, a former assistant to Lumumba, wrote that at the beginning of January the leaders in Brazzaville were very worried:

> [they] started wishing the Thysville prisoner a Happy New Year and offered their hospitality to Lumumba's companion, whom they presented to world opinion as his wife. . . . They ask me, "If Lumumba comes back, would you act as mediator to find a *modus vivendi* between us and him?"[31]

On 4 January 1961, panic-stricken, Belgium took a further step in its war against the former prime minister. Brussels sent the Léopoldville regime a telegram drawing their "special attention to the disastrous consequences if Lumumba were freed". The following day, the Belgian government was reassured by a dispatch from Brazzaville telling them that the College of Commissioners would not free the nationalist leader.

Shortly after, the authorities in Léopoldville started intensifying their moves to get rid of Lumumba. On 8 January, Albert Delvaux and Cyrille Adoula, who collaborated with the Léopoldville regime, were in Katanga to discuss, among other things, transferring Lumumba. The following day, the College of Commissioners decided, in consultation with Kasa Vubu and Mobutu, to transfer him first to the fort at Shinkakasa, near Boma, in Lower Congo. This fort had long been abandoned but was then renovated for use as a military prison. Commissioner for Defence Ferdinand Kazadi maintains that this transfer seemed at that time to be the only way of avoiding "a revolt in Thysville and surrounding areas". Vandewalle summarises the arguments: "Surveillance would be easier there and the danger of influencing the population almost nil."[32] The next day, Commissioner for Internal Affairs Damien Kandolo left for Boma to arrange the transfer. Local Abako leaders strongly opposed the plan, and the district commissioner considered that Lumumba's presence in the region could be a potentially subversive element.[33]

According to Heinz and Donnay, "an authorised Belgian observer" was following these events for Brussels. This was probably André Lahaye, who had gone back to the Congo on 5 September – the very day Lumumba was dismissed – to become adviser to Damien Kandolo. It would be interesting to know the details of the correspondence between Lahaye and Brussels, where people must surely have been waiting impatiently beside phones and telexes, anxious for information about the latest developments. However, neither Heinz and Donnay in their *Lumumba Patrice* (1966), nor Brassinne (1990), nor Brassinne and Kestergat in *Qui a tué Patrice Lumumba?* (1991) say anything about it. In the interviews Brassinne did for his doctoral thesis, he did not even ask the question.

In the pile of telegrams from Brazzaville to Brussels which I was able to consult, there is one dispatch of 9 January from Ambassador Dupret to Wigny, stating that the decision to transfer Lumumba to Boma was taken on the advice of the intelligence services. Dupret explains, however, that certain neo-colonial Congolese politicians like Jean Bolikango, short-sighted and power-crazy, were seeking an agreement with the nationalists by which, in exchange for freeing Lumumba who would be given the post of foreign minister, Bolikango would become prime minister.[34]

THE BELGIANS WAIT IN KATANGA

Secession had been a stab in the back for the new Congolese democracy, a bridgehead established in Katanga to overthrow the legal government. The last uniformed Belgian unit had left Katanga at the end of August 1960. In its place came a disguised occupation force, the Katangan *Gendarmerie*, which had a core of about 200 Belgian officers, later swelled by mercenaries. Vandewalle writes: "It is this nucleus of regular Belgian officers . . . which maintains the structure." A Katangan, Joseph Yav, was appointed defence minister, but this did not fundamentally change the *Gendarmerie*'s command, which remained entirely in Belgian hands. At the end of September, the Belgian diplomat Rothschild pointed out in a telegram to Brussels that removing the Belgian cadre from the *Gendarmerie* could bring about "the collapse" of the Katangan forces.[35]

The *Gendarmerie*'s favourite tactics were blind and merciless repression. On 16 September, Katangan soldiers summarily executed sixty-eight Lumumbist Balubas in Luena. A Belgian *Gendarmerie* captain declared to a stunned UN officer: "Killing these people is the only way of controlling them." But many of the officers had guilty consciences. Vandewalle writes: "Bloodthirsty actions, carried out more and more frequently, were not on their agenda". According to the journalist Pierre Davister, a fervent pro-secessionist with some experience on the ground: "In December 1960, an estimated 7,000 [nationalist] rebels were killed in reprisals in north Katanga. We know what these kind of figures mean in Africa. We can generally multiply them by two, three, ten, and still not be sure whether they are far below the truth."[36]

The Belgian government claimed it was observing the rule of non-interference in the internal affairs of its former colony. In theory, the Belgians in Katanga's army or administration were considered Congolese officials of Belgian nationality: that is, the Eyskens government had no authority over them. In practice, however, things were quite different. The Belgians took orders from the minister of African affairs and were paid by Brussels. Major Weber wrote in a confidential memo in mid-1961, after Brussels ordered him back to Katanga: "1.

I am an officer. If the government gives me an order, I obviously have to obey. 2. I have always said that here I consider I am defending 'a Belgian presence' in Africa."[37]

At the beginning of October 1960, Mistebel, the nerve centre of Belgian intervention in Katanga, was abolished and replaced by the Bureau Conseil, headed by Professor René Clémens of Liège University. According to Vandewalle, it functioned like a "shadow government, solving logistic problems". Its permanent members were Clémens, Jean-Marie Crèvecoeur, the *Gendarmerie* commander-in-chief, Lieutenant-Colonel André Grandjean and Major Guy Weber. Weber, a former colonial army officer and a relative of Pierre Bauchau, the secession's banker, was appointed Tshombe's military adviser by Belgian army Commander-in-Chief General Cumont. From January 1961, Colonel Vandewalle, the man Brassinne calls the *Gendarmerie*'s "hidden boss", was also on the Bureau Conseil. There were proportionately a large number of military men on it – a result of the increasing militarisation of the regime in response to the threat from Baluba rebels and their allies. Not a single African was allowed into the daily meetings. The Bureau Conseil reported directly to African Affairs Minister d'Aspremont Lynden, who regularly recalled Clémens or Weber to Brussels for consultation. It was these men, and only these men, who took the strategic decisions in the Katanga that would be playing host to Lumumba in January 1961.[38]

TSHOMBE SAVED AGAIN BY THE UN

When in October 1960, the internal revolt against Tshombe's regime gathered strength and external military pressure continued, he had to do his best with the means at his disposal. His regime did not collapse there and then because Lumumba's offensive was suppressed by Mobutu, and the UN set up neutral zones. If Tshombe's fragile state was to last till the New Year, he would owe it to the Belgians and the support of the UN leaders. On 17 October, Tshombe and the UN issued a joint communiqué to the press: they had agreed to set up two "neutral zones" inside which the UN would take over responsibility from the Katangan *Gendarmerie* for maintaining order. The first zone was made up of Nyunzu, Kabalo, Manono, Mulongo and Bukama in north Katanga; the second of Mukulakulu, Luena and Bukama in the centre. Shortly before the agreement was made public, weapons were used, demonstrating that this breach of Katanga's sovereignty was the lesser evil for the regime. On 15 October, Second Lieutenant Raymond Capiot was wounded during a skirmish with Baluba warriors at Luena, and on the same day a unit of the *Gendarmerie* was ambushed at Mukulakulu. Lieutenant Walter Smets died on the spot, Police Chief Goffinet was wounded and Commander Paul Janssens, one of the "heroes" of July, was seriously wounded. (In this war, only European victims were counted.)

In the meetings in which UN representatives and leaders of the Katanga regime decided the neutral zones, what was really at stake was containing the nationalist rebellion. During one of these meetings, Rikhye, Hammarskjöld's military adviser, stated:

[T]here was political opposition but also plain banditry. The aim of the UN was to restore order using resources put at the Katanga government's disposal. . . . Rikhye did not want "to neutralise the *Gendarmerie*". He preferred a cease-fire. He did not want either the local authorities or the Gendarmes to be withdrawn from the zones where the UN force was operating, but he did want the cessation of hostilities to be respected.

Vandewalle rightly regards this agreement as an assault on the very principles of the copper state. But Tshombe had no choice: the *Gendarmerie* was not in a position to control the rebellion, and without reinforcements, it could only hang onto the coat-tails of the UN forces. A *Gendarmerie* intelligence officer said: "This agreement . . . certainly prevented the rebel-controlled zone extending to Lubudi and Kolwezi [in the south)] where vital road and rail traffic between Elisabethville and the Angolan coast wold have been in danger of disruption."[39]

The UN helped Katanga in yet another way. What it refused Lumumba's legally elected government, it granted the putschist Tshombe: authorisation to receive unilateral aid from abroad. In September a UN General Assembly resolution had called on all member states to cease all military aid to any Congolese authority whatsoever, except that channelled through the UN. A note from Secretary General Hammarskjöld to the Belgian ambassador to the UN, dated 8 October, referred to this resolution and stipulated that Belgian aid to Katanga and South Kasai "is not in conformity with the requirements of the General Assembly".[40] If the contents of this note were implemented, the situation would not look good for Kalonji and Tshombe. Both Brussels and Washington, however, were of the opinion that the document was only intended "for the record", as Vandewalle put it. The UN was going to take no action against Belgian control over the Congolese and Katangan states, apart from a few symbolic protest notes.

On 1 January 1961, in a short speech, Tshombe acclaimed the army as the main architect of independence. In another message, Colonel Yav, Katangan defence secretary, paid tribute to the six officers and junior officers who had fallen in defence of the copper state. All Belgians, they all received posthumous promotion. Paul Janssens, who had recovered from his wounds, was made a *major*.[41] On New Year's Day, the officer corps of the Katangan forces comprised 194 Europeans and seventy-eight Katangans. In the ranks were 1,702 Katangans and forty-four foreigners. In addition, 2,049 recruits were still being trained. The *Gendarmerie* also had about 1,425 reservists, and forty-nine men of the volunteer corps – a European paramilitary militia from colonial times. In total, 5,541 men could be counted on to defend the secession.[42] The officer corps was thus about a third Katangan, but this figure is deceptive for anyone examining the true power relationships between Belgians and Katangans: all the core commands were still in Belgian hands, whatever UN resolutions might stipulate.

In mid-December, the diplomat Vanden Bloock wrote a memo on the situation in Katanga. Classified "top secret", the document contained no good news for Brussels. The UN had suffered defeats at the hands of the rebels in Manono, Nyemba and Luena. The only encouraging point was a real improvement in relations between the regime and the Blue Berets. The UN force respected an effective distribution of functions: "The UN . . . has agreed to leave to the Katangan *Gendarmerie* in Luena responsibility for guarding the work being done on the airfield and for some coal-mining activities there." In addition, Bloock was very pleased with the UN decision that about fifty of the Baluba rebels were common criminals; it had therefore handed them over to the Katangan authorities to be tried. At about the same time, the UN leaders in Elisabethville confirmed once again to Tshombe that the Blue Berets would respect the 17 October agreement. This letter was addressed not to the "President of the provincial government of Katanga, Republic of the Congo", as was customary for documents to be made public, but to the "President". The UN leadership had less friendly terminology for the nationalists. It promised Tshombe to "strive" to pacify the neutral zones and prevent "armed bands" from leaving these areas.[43]

Hammarskjöld was afraid the African and Asian Blue Berets would sympathise with Lumumba. He tried to ensure a strong Western component in the UN Congo forces and he saw that it was well represented in Katanga. Deployed in Katanga were Irish, Swedes, Moroccans, Ethiopians and Malays. The officer corps of the UN forces was not unfavourably disposed to secession. The actions and declarations of officers such as von Horn, Rikhye, Byrne and others speak for themselves. On 1 January 1961, Irish officers went to Tshombe's residence to wish the Katangan president a happy New Year. *Gendarmerie* officers and UN contingents were on good terms. At the beginning of 1961 a tradition was established: in Vandewalle's words, "There were contacts between officers of the *Gendarmerie* and the UN. Some afternoons Crèvecoeur got them together round the bridge tables at HQ. Irish coffee had become a popular drink with the Belgians."[44] But how long could Dag Hammarskjöld continue to protect Moïse Tshombe? To stop the nationalist offensive at the end of 1960 and beginning of 1961, he would need more extreme measures: sowing genocidal terror in the rebel regions and murdering nationalist leaders.

4

THE GREEN LIGHT FROM BRUSSELS

COLONEL VANDEWALLE'S NEW MISSION

In the autumn of 1960, the Katangan army succumbed to a crisis of leadership. Jules Loos, military adviser to the Ministry of African Affairs, was dissatisfied with Lieutenant-Colonel Jean-Marie Crèvecoeur, the commanding officer of the *Gendarmerie*. He considered nominating a "secret" military chief to spare local sensitivities and his candidate was Colonel Frédéric Vandewalle, former head of the colonial intelligence services. The African Affairs Minister was reticent but, at the end of 1960 when events in Katanga took a dramatic turn for the worse, Major Loos got his way. Count d'Aspremont Lynden gave the go-ahead on 4 January 1961: "Lieutenant-Colonel Vandewalle, a reserve colonel in the Force Publique, has full authority over all military personnel of technical assistance in Katanga." Vandewalle described his mission as follows:

> The point was to help the embryo *Gendarmerie* get over its teething troubles and, in particular, to co-ordinate the activities of the three officers in charge . . . A *chef d'orchestre* was needed . . . The minister's patience ran out and he sent Colonel Vandewalle back to Africa with . . . orders to put an end to the debacle.[1]

With his appointment, the Belgian stage was finally set for the final act of Lumumba's martyrdom. On 4 January, the day Vandewalle left for Africa, Brussels sent an urgent telegram to Léopoldville asking for a firm solution to the Lumumba problem.

The crisis in the Katangan army had a lot to do with the difficulties the secessionist province as a whole was going through. Tshombe's regime had only survived because of foreign aid. At the beginning of 1961, the situation looked very much like that later described by Rothschild in his 11 October 1960 telegram to Wigny and d'Aspremont Lynden:

[Belgian] supervision of the Katangan *Gendarmerie* . . . is an essential and a decisive element in maintaining order in Katanga. It is necessary to fully understand that, if they [the Belgians] withdraw, the *Gendarmerie* will collapse within 24 hours, followed not long afterwards by the Tshombe government.

In mid-January, Colonel Vandewalle wrote: "[Tshombe's] 'regime' is increasingly viewed as a hundred-odd Katangans who have sold out to the Whites. This idea has now spread [to the Lunda people, Tshombe's power base]. Everyone else has thought it for a long time."

With the Baluba rebellion advancing, the Belgian weekly *La Relève* predicted a gloomy scenario in which Tshombe's state would consist "solely of copper mines defended by Belgian officers".[2] By the end of 1960, nationalist forces had gained a serious amount of ground. At Christmas, Gizenga's troops took Bukavu, the capital of Kivu Province. At New Year a counter-attack by Mobutu's troops ended in disaster for Léopoldville; the majority of the soldiers, including Major Pongo, were taken prisoner. On 7 January, a nationalist force of 600 men arrived in Manono, north Katanga, where they tried to join forces with the Baluba guerrillas who already controlled north and central Katanga – about a third of the total area. The rebels were about to take Albertville in the north, the province's second largest town, Kolwezi, a mining town in the south, and the railway linking Elisabethville with the port of Lobito in Angola. UN officers were finding it increasingly difficult to suppress the Blue Berets' nationalist sympathies, especially in Kongol in the north, where troops from Mali were stationed, and in Kolwezi, Jadotville, Lubudi and Luena, where the Moroccans were stationed. Tshombe's regime protested to the United Nations, blaming it for the nationalist successes in the north, and stating confidently that it would feel free to act in the neutral zones if the UN proved ineffective. The *Gendarmerie* commando was perplexed by this statement, according to Vandewalle, since the troops were in no position to carry out the ultimatum. On 11 January, flying over the Bukama region on a reconnaissance flight, *Major* René Vandamme was killed by a rebel missile. He was the eleventh Belgian soldier to die in Katanga since July 1960, and fifteen other names would be added to the Belgian list before the end of the year.[3]

PATRICE LUMUMBA MUST DIE

While Lumumba was detained at the army camp in Thysville, a plethora of discussions as to the fate of the eminent prisoner took place. On 3 December, only a few hours after the prisoner's arrival at Ndjili airport, Rothschild sent a telegram from the Belgian Embassy in Brazzaville to Foreign Minister Wigny, with copies to African Affairs Minister d'Aspremont Lynden and the head of the Belgian intelligence services Caeymaex. Rothschild had received his information from Crokart, the former colonial intelligence collaborator now very active again in central Africa: "It appears the authorities in Léopoldville are going to contact the Katanga authorities with a view to getting them to agree to transfer Lumumba to a prison in Katanga." Rothschild added: "No information yet as to what Kasa Vubu thinks, but action is taken through the progressive wing of the Abako and his entourage to press him to be firm."

On 13 December, President Tshombe left the Katangan capital to attend a conference of Francophone African countries in Brazzaville. In his pocket he carried a memo from the Bureau Conseil. Accompanying him were Kimba, Weber and Jacques Bartelous. The Léopoldville delegation comprised Kasa Vubu, Kalonji, Bomboko, Kamitatu, Bolikango, Mobutu and Ileo. There was a moment during the meeting when Brazzaville President Fulbert Youlou proposed including Lumumba in rebuilding the new Congo. Major Weber was keeping a watchful eye, however, and told Youlou categorically that that scenario was "unthinkable".[4]

This was not the first time anti-nationalist leaders had met to discuss Lumumba's political fate. A previous meeting had taken place at the end of November 1960, during the Congo-Brazzaville's independence celebrations, when news of Lumumba's escape from Léopoldville first broke. President Fulbert Youlou received Kasa Vubu, Ileo, Adoula, Bomboko, Tshombe, Kimba and Kalonji at the Beach Hotel for an improvised round table. They discussed transferring the Lumumbist prisoners, hopefully soon to include Lumumba himself, to Katanga.

The Léopoldville regime's state of health did not improve and the Eyskens government and its antennae in Léopoldville and Brazzaville continued to fret about how to put Lumumba *hors de combat*. On 24 December 1960, Dupret (Brazzaville) sent a coded telegram to the *Gendarmerie*'s headquarters in Léopoldville, containing Bomboko's request for Lumumba's transfer to Katanga, to which Tshombe had already agreed in principle. In the second part of the telegram, Dupret wrote: "An affirmative reply is desirable, despite the failure of previous attempts. It is feared the troops at Thysville are being influenced." Dupret's telegram was sent to the Belgian Foreign Ministry and the Ministry for African Affairs and to the Belgian intelligence chief, Caeymaex. Brussels immediately sent it on to the Belgian consulate in Elisabethville.

A few days later, Vanden Bloock in Elisabethville sent a top secret telegram to Brussels, saying Elisabethville did not consider a transfer to Katanga opportune: it would provoke "a general outcry" in Africa and Asia in which Belgium, "suspected of colluding with Katanga", would be pilloried. Besides, the Katangan regime feared that accepting Lumumba would imply recognition of formal ties between Léopoldville and Elisabethville. Vanden Bloock ended his message as follows: "So Bakwanga seems to me a good compromise." This telegram was sent to the Wigny–Rothschild duo, to d'Aspremont Lynden and to Dupret.[5] No immediate reaction to this proposal is known. For Lumumba, however, being delivered into the hands of Kalonji in Bakwanga would mean a certain and horrifying death. A few days later, Brussels took the initiative once again and put Lumumba's transfer to either Elisabethville or Bakwanga on the political agenda.

The editors of Gaston Eyskens's memoirs, elsewhere very detailed in their account, gloss over this crucial episode in the Congo crisis. Eyskens says that his government "stuck to its previous stance of non-interference in internal Congolese affairs during this particularly confused period at the end of 1960". Brussels was aware of "the possibility of Lumumba's return to power. The government was certainly not happy about this prospect . . . The government would obviously have preferred a reconciliation between moderate elements." That is all. But contrary to what Eyskens wanted his readers to believe, Brussels did not stand passively by and his government would definitely try to influence the course of events.

Just in the first few days of 1961, at least two initiatives from the Eyskens government were set down in writing. In early January, the Belgian Embassy in Brazzaville produced a report on the situation in Léopoldville which was far from encouraging: another new soldiers' mutiny was on the cards and all the military leaders were shirking their responsibility. Furthermore, the American press was spreading rumours that Lumumba celebrated Christmas with officers at the camp. Alarmed, Brussels did not wait to investigate the situation more fully. On 4 January 1961, Brussels sent a telegram to Brazzaville in which Léopoldville's "special attention" was drawn "to the disastrous consequences of releasing Lumumba. The danger of such a step must be made absolutely clear to the general commissioners." The draft of this message is in the archives of the Belgian Foreign Ministry. Its author was Minister d'Aspremont Lynden, and its addressee was André Lahaye. In their 1966 book, Heinz and Donnay write that at the time "an authorised Belgian observer" was corresponding with Brussels about Lumumba's removal from Thysville. This "Belgian observer" was undoubtedly André Lahaye. Heinz and Donnay are the pseudonyms of Jules Gérard-Libois and Jacques Brassinne himself. In his dissertation, Brassinne is silent on the subject of this correspondence and its possible link with the telegram.[6]

Brassinne's silence is totally understandable. In his doctorate he tries to present Lumumba's transfer as the panic reaction of certain Congolese leaders. What happened between 4 and 12 January does not really interest him. For Brassinne, the story begins on the night of 12 to 13 January, when a soldiers' revolt broke out at Thysville and for a time it looked as if Lumumba was about to be freed; at this point Léopoldville hastily decided to transport him to Katanga. Yet, in actual fact, the decision to effectively neutralise Lumumba, perhaps actually to kill him, was taken months earlier. Léopoldville, Bakwanga, Elisabethville and Brazzaville had been discussing the Congo's future since

September 1960, and Lumumba's fate was the burning issue at the centre of the talks. Like it or not, Lumumba came up over and over again. For instance, the participants wanted to organise a round table on the country's institutions with a view to reaching a compromise on a provisional central government. But could this be done without Lumumba? Would he be brought to trial or kept in prison awaiting a political compromise between the "moderates"? A permanent solution to the Lumumba problem was the *sine qua non* of progress in every other field.

The Belgian government's view was clear. From October 1960 onwards, the demand for the former prime minister's "*élimination définitive*" was voiced by Minister d'Aspremont Lynden, and this position never changed. The 4 January telegram demonstrates that, for Brussels, this meant more than mere detention at Thysville. Lumumba had to be removed from there at all costs, whatever the price of the operation in terms of international diplomacy.

It is impossible to analyse the debate over Belgian political decision making in all its detail without first examining the entire correspondence between Brussels and its African outposts. Only then does the role of the Belgians in the discussions of 2 and 8 January become clear. During these discussions, Léopoldville's emissaries to Elisabethville pleaded for Lumumba's removal from Thysville (in the Léopoldville area) since the authorities were not in a position to guarantee the detention of the nationalist leaders. Only then do we learn if a meeting on 10 January in Paris, between Bomboko and Ambassador Rothschild, speeded up the developments. At this time, Rothschild was continually travelling between Brazzaville, Elisabethville and Brussels, and was also co-ordinating Belgian intervention in the Congo from Brussels on behalf of Foreign Minister Wigny. In Paris, Bomboko and "R" discussed all aspects of co-operation between Léopoldville and Brussels. Wigny referred to these discussions in a coded dispatch containing instructions for Elisabethville and Brazzaville. The text clearly shows Belgian involvement in building a stable neo-colonial order in the Congo. Wigny noted with some satisfaction that "preparations are being made for a vigorous reorganisation of the ANC. Internal subversion is the greatest danger. The garrisons at Thysville, Luluabourg and Coquilhatville are wavering." It is not known whether anything was planned for Lumumba, but a telegram of 19 January from Dupret to Brussels says Rothschild promised Mobutu equipment for an airborne battalion, monthly aid of 120 million Belgian francs and Belgian officers.

Wigny's communication stressed that Tshombe must stop "vying for prestige" with Kasa Vubu: co-operation between the "moderates" in order to fight the nationalist peril was crucial. Wigny mentioned that telephone contact between Léopoldville and Elisabethville had been restored, and that telephoning was "a better procedure than sending telegrams via Dupret. . . ."[7] Wigny's criticism of Tshombe and Kasa Vubu for their power struggle had some practical importance: at the end of 1960 the Katangan regime had refused Lumumba's transfer to Elisabethville because, among other reasons, it would have implied *de facto* recognition of formal links between it and Léopoldville.

The power brokers in Brussels did not even need direct information to understand the critical position of the Léopoldville regime. They only needed to read the press. On 9 January, *De Standaard* reported that the conference held in Casablanca for African countries sympathetic to Congolese nationalism "insisted on the return to Lumumbist legality. Whether Lumumba as a prisoner is still a legal political entity or not, it is hard to deny he is still a symbol of the decolonised Congo, while most of his opponents pass for the servants or the instruments of their former masters."

In its 12 January edition, the Brussels daily reproduced an article from the Belgian news agency Belga. Under the headline "Léopoldville Alarmed", it read:

> The political climate in the Congolese capital yesterday indicated a certain anxiety and nervousness. A variety of rumours . . . were spread by followers of Lumumba stressing "the offensive by friendly troops in the north of Katanga" and suggesting that we could soon expect a political about-turn in the province of Léopoldville.

Partition of the country in two – the larger part under the Lumumbist regime – "seems inevitable if measures are not taken immediately on the economic and military front. It remains to be seen if the authorities in Léopoldville, given the current level of disorganisation, will be capable of taking the necessary steps."

One of the obstacles to any successful initiative was the diffuse nature of the weak centres of power in Léopoldville, a source of despair for Brussels. Power there was in the hands of what Colonel Marlière – now Mobutu's adviser – called "a nebula": an informal network of people and groups, affiliated in one way or another to certain units of the army and to Western diplomatic missions. There were very few formal meetings. "Meetings are sometimes held at the Zoo restaurant, sometimes in people's houses." At the end of 1960 a centre of gravity formed within this network which was subsequently called the Binza Group. Ranking the people with the greatest political clout, Marlière put Mobutu in pole position: as head of the army, he was the linchpin, but "not yet the uncontested leader. He knows, but he does not 'get his feet wet'." Then came Nendaka, Bomboko, Kasa Vubu and Adoula. Jules Gérard-Libois, a Congo expert, presented a similar picture: he cast Kasa Vubu as the main man, given his legal status as elected president and his role as the regime's figurehead and port of entry to the United Nations. Also on the list were Mobutu and commissioners Bomboko, Ndele and Nendaka. According to Gérard-Libois, Nendaka and Ndele were the real leaders in Léopoldville at the end of 1960 and beginning of 1961.[8]

Marlière claimed that Mobutu "acted like Pontius Pilate . . ., he always maintained everything happened unbeknownst to him while he was perfectly aware of what was being plotted". Such a diluted power structure, one devoid of any real command centre, was not very robust and left a free hand to all sorts of advisers manoeuvring to secure an influential space for themselves. A striking example was 18 January, when an important delegation from Léopoldville arrived in Elisabethville to talk about military co-operation. One of its members was Colonel Marlière, appointed by Mobutu "to represent him, with all his powers". It is no surprise, then, that Vandewalle describes Marlière as Mobutu's "prompter."[9]

One additional shock – the threat of Lumumba's political return in mid-January – was needed to make the Congolese dignitaries and their *éminences grises* act in concert. Stanleyville sensed what was going to happen and feared the worst. On 10 January, Gbenye, interior minister in Gizenga's government, declared from within his nationalist bastion: "The health of Gibert Pongo [captured by Stanleyville] depends on our prime minister Lumumba being freed immediately."

Pongo was worried too and sent message after message to Léopoldville. Tormented by the fear of death, he begged for the nationalist leaders Lumumba, Jean-Pierre Finant and Jacques Fataki to be freed in exchange for his own release. Dupret passed the message on to Wigny but added reassuringly: "In any case, Léopoldville will take no notice of his demand."[10] Soon after, Pongo, Lumumba, Fataki and Finant were all dead. Almost a hundred years earlier, Léopold II had had a marble medallion carved with the saying: "Belgium needs a colony". This dream had come true. But to preserve the benefits of colonialism for the future, they needed to establish in Léopoldville a Congolese regime with which they could do business. Patrice Lumumba was standing in the way. Now Marlière and his colleagues convinced themselves that there was only one solution. *Belgium needed an assassination.*

MUTINY IN THYSVILLE, PANIC IN LEOPOLDVILLE AND BRUSSELS (12–14 JANUARY 1961)

Camp Hardy is situated in Thysville, about 150 kilometres from Léopoldville. During the night of 12–13 January, Second Lieutenant Schoonbroodt, the camp commander's chief-of-staff, was woken by noises and voices: mutiny was breaking out at Hardy. Soldiers were also stirring at Sonankulu, the city's other army camp.[11] Small groups of soldiers passed in front of Schoonbroodt's quarters. Their objective was the houses of the African officers, situated higher up in the hills. Schoonbroodt immediately telephoned Lieutenant-Colonel Bobozo, the camp commandant. He was out, but his wife was at home. Frightened, she talked of soldiers coming and going, and her fear of being attacked. Officers had been taken prisoner, several officers' wives had been raped. That night Bobozo telephoned Léopoldville. The situation had become untenable. The soldiers were demanding a pay rise, a new government and freedom for Lumumba. The officers vacillated. Instead of taking action, Colonel Bobozo pretended nothing was happening. The main problem was that Lumumba's imprisonment (Bobozo's *raison d'être*) was becoming more difficult to guarantee by the day. The general climate of insecurity, the nationalist sympathies of a section of the soldiers and the threat to release Lumumba (made in part as a bargaining tool for a pay rise) all meant that the nationalist leader could on no account remain in Thysville. It was imperative that he left – and anyway Mobutu had promised to transfer him to a safer place in the New Year.

When Léopoldville learnt of the mutiny the following day, the Europeans panicked. Rumours circulated about Lumumba's release: that he was going to march on Léopoldville at the head of the Thysville troops and install a revolutionary government. As in July 1960, many Europeans made for the Beach to try and cross the river to Brazzaville.

The situation was serious enough for government ministers to go to Camp Hardy and take stock of events. That same day, 13 January, Kasa Vubu, Mobutu, Nendaka, Bomboko and Ileo landed on the camp's runway in a Dragon rapide, a small aircraft belonging to Air Brousse. According to Madeleine Kalb, Kasa Vubu, Mobutu, Bomboko and Nendaka visited Lumumba in his cell and offered him a ministerial post in a government headed by Ileo. Lumumba refused, saying he would only agree to be freed as head of the legal government. Again according to Kalb, Lumumba's attitude was both courageous and foolhardy, and ultimately caused his downfall.

In fact Kalb is probably wrong, since the entire regime shared the Belgian government's view that setting the former prime minister free would have disastrous consequences. Léopoldville knew what Lumumba's attitude was: he was the country's legally elected prime minister and must remain so unless parliament decided otherwise. Over the previous months, Lumumba had remained politically consistent. Given that the nationalist movement was gaining strength by the day, it was highly unlikely that he ever considered capitulating to his enemies. Neither Lumumba nor Kasa Vubu and company were inclined to accept a compromise. If Lumumba was offered a ministerial post, it was no doubt to trap him into leaving prison, whereupon he would immediately be killed, presumably while "attempting to escape". Lumumba was on his guard, for at no moment did he leave his cell.[12]

Jacques Cordy, a journalist then in Léopoldville for the Belgian daily *Le Soir*, described the atmosphere as tense and the wait for the return of the president and the other leaders as "particularly difficult". When Bomboko came back that evening with news that the matter would be settled, the atmosphere in the capital remained agitated. The city panicked at the prospect of the former prime minister's possible political return. The troops at Camp Hardy formed an armoured brigade, renowned as the "regime's elite unit". Moreover,

Bobozo brought Mobutu more bad news, impressing on him (they were both Ngbandi and related by marriage) that Lumumba must be moved as it would be impossible to keep him in prison should a further mutiny break out. On 15 January, UN chief Dayal stated in a telegram to Secretary General Hammarskjöld: "It is generally thought here that Lumumba's release is only a question of days."[13]

Chaos reigned. On 7 January, Mobutu and Defence Commissioner Kazadi went to Camp Nkokolo (in Léopoldville) to negotiate with dissatisfied soldiers – with no lasting success, however, since a new uprising broke out on 14 January. Lumumba's influence was growing there too, as Dayal remarked on 18 January, the day after Lumumba's transfer to Katanga: "The reasons for delivering Lumumba etc. to the tender mercies of Tshombe is to make a sacrificial offering to him and also because of the developing pro-Lumumba sentiment in the Thysville garrison and indeed in Camp Nkokolo as well." Much later on, Dayal assessed the situation as follows: "Lumumba behind prison bars had been no less potent a force than Lumumba free. There was no prison in Kasa Vubu's Congo secure enough to contain him."

By mid-January, troops loyal to Lumumba controlled roughly half the country. The failure of Mobutu's new-year offensive clearly showed what little chance of success his troops had against a motivated army. Colonel Marlière confirmed such a view at Elisabethville when he spoke of the ANC's "grave crisis" and admitted that Léopoldville was capable of gathering together "only a few platoons, at most a few companies, for operations".

Meanwhile, Kasa Vubu was in a shaky political position. During November and December 1960, the news sent from Brazzaville to Foreign Minister Wigny became increasingly ominous. At the beginning of November, Ambassador Dupret informed his boss that his French counterpart in Léopoldville:

> is very concerned about Lumumba's renewed prestige and influence, particularly in the interior and with young people in Léopoldville. He feels the only way to counter Lumumba's return is a Congo–Katanga entente. . . . Without this entente, he is of the opinion that the current regime will collapse within a month.

Half-way through November, he pointed out: "The College of Commissioners realises the situation has deteriorated in the provinces but does not have the guts to take practical measures." On 5 and 9 January, Dupret warned that certain neo-colonial politicians like Bolikango were demanding the release of Lumumba as "blackmail" in their negotiations with their rivals for power. In another telegram dated 9 January, Dupret mentioned that the president of the Congo Brazzaville had done an "about-turn in favour of Lumumba":

Youlou's anti-Lumumbism probably only set its sights on the overthrow of the man and the movement which in his eyes embodied the unity and integrity, and consequently the power, of the neighbouring Congo. Now that he has succeeded in bringing down Lumumba, of course he wants to restore him, so that his enemies do not become too strong. So Youlou is doing a Congolese balancing act, playing off Lumumba against Kasa Vubu and Mobutu, and Elisabethville against Léopoldville, and watching to see no one tendency wins out permanently over the other. It is a dangerous policy, because Youlou does not have the means with which to maintain the balance he seeks, and his policy risks being swept away by the tide of Lumumbism. It goes without saying that I am endeavouring by all means possible to warn the abbé against a disaster of his own making.[14]

During January, Mobutu's College of Commissioners disintegrated. The Léopoldville regime had been more or less paralysed since mid-December because of imminent financial catastrophe. The president of the Chamber of Representatives, Joseph Kasongo, who in mid-December had agreed to be part of a government under Ileo, now demanded Lumumba's release. At the beginning of January, in a scathing letter to Hammarskjöld, he rejected any solution obtained by means of a round table: "As if the Congolese people, by freely electing its parliament, had not by the same token chosen its leaders. . . . The Congolese crisis is essentially a crisis of legality. . . . The solution is to restore parliament's constitutional powers."

This letter, together with Gizenga's recent successes, led the US ambassador to some sombre conclusions which he put in a telegram: "The prospects for installing a moderate government, which about a month ago were reasonable, have considerably dimmed."[15]

In mid-January Dupret sounded the alarm. He sent messages to all those with authority over Belgian actions in the Congo: to Foreign Minister Wigny, his boss, but also to African Affairs Minister d'Aspremont Lynden and Belgian intelligence chief Caeymaex. He writes on 11 January:

Léopoldville: a serious malaise exists, mainly among the Europeans who say this is the calm before the storm, and among the soldiers of Camp Nkokolo where a mutiny is always on the cards. This malaise can be explained by the Bukavu disaster, the presence of Lumumbist troops at Manono, the lack of resolve at the centre and the difficulties with the round table.

Two days later, he wrote:

There is blatant inertia in Equateur [province] where no apparent precautions are being taken to repel an almost certain attack by Lumumbist troops, which would be welcomed by the local populations in the Djolu and Boende regions. The same source says it is feared Lumumbist troops will take Bumba and Lisala and reach Coquilhatville directly via Yahuma, Djolu and Boende, thereby tightening Stanleyville's hold on Equateur before attacking Kwilu. Gizenga's goals apparently are to show his government controls most of the Congo, convene parliament at Stan, and gain international recognition. By so doing, he hopes to create divisions among the commissioners and the politicians, prevent the round table, spread confusion in Léopoldville and ultimately obtain Lumumba's release.

On 16 January, Dupret reiterated Marlière's opinion of Mobutu's troops: "In the ANC, the officer cadre does not think, does not organise, and does not command, the soldiers do not obey and do nothing. The equipment is in a bad state. This army is completely useless. It even constitutes a danger for the country."[16]

The Congolese press openly called for action. On 10 January, the daily paper *Le Courrier d'Afrique* lectured the regime: "We have to admit that the share of the cake still belonging to the capital is really negligible. . . . We must face facts. . . . There is no question that what we need . . . is effective leadership." On 14 January, the weekly *Présence Congolaise*, which had good relations with the Léopoldville regime, printed under the headline "Sounding the Alarm": "How to save the country? . . . Something . . . has to be done and done quickly." The paper called for Lumumba to be transferred to Elisabethville, "for his personal safety and for public order in Léo province". The conservative Belgian press was also outspoken. *La Libre Belgique* of 14 January mentioned the mutiny at Thysville, commenting in its leader: "In the present situation the Congo is heading for an even greater catastrophe than that of July 1960."

In Washington, Lumumba's possible political return caused panic – in the CIA, in Eisenhower's outgoing government and in Kennedy's new administration. The attitude of the White House and its Congolese friends is aptly conveyed in Madeleine Kalb's account of President Kennedy's first cabinet meetings at the end of January (by which time Lumumba was already in Tshombe's hands):

> They did not believe Kasa Vubu would ever agree to reconvene parliament. . . . all the embassy and CIA reports indicated that even if they started out with a solid anti-Lumumba majority, Lumumba could easily swing it around in his favor, if he were released from prison and permitted to take part in its deliberations. Lumumba still dominated the Congolese political scene, even from his jail cell in Katanga (where he was presumed to be).

A few hours before the revolt at Thysville, CIA station chief Lawrence Devlin reported to Washington: "[The CIA] station and embassy believe present government may fall within few days. Result would almost certainly be chaos and return [Lumumba] to power." Lumumba's release would inevitably mean his political victory: "The combination of [Lumumba's] powers as demagogue, his able use of goon squads and propaganda and spirit of defeat within coalition [Kasa Vuba and Mobutu] which would increase rapidly under such conditions would almost certainly insure [Lumumba] victory in parliament." Devlin concludes with a great deal of perspicacity: "Refusal take drastic steps at this time will lead to defeat of [US] policy in Congo."

Devlin's forceful language hides his desperation: it was, quite simply, the only weapon at his command. Washington, however, was clear about its adversary. As early as 22 July 1960, CIA chief Allen Dulles had declared during a meeting of the US National Security Council, presided over by President Eisenhower himself, that Lumumba was "a Castro or worse . . .". Fidel Castro! At that time, no one could evoke as much horror in the White House as the man who brought the Soviets into the US backyard.

On 18 August 1960, during another National Security Council meeting, Eisenhower had made it clear, without explicitly saying so, that he favoured Lumumba's elimination. An assassination operation was planned with the support of CIA chief Dulles. But as soon as Lumumba had fallen into Mobutu's hands at the beginning of December, the risky operation against the former prime minister was called off. As Kalb put it: "There was no longer any point in surrounding his residence [the army camp at Thysville] with hired assassins armed with poisoned toothpaste; he could simply be left to the tender mercies of his enemies."[17]

Examination of the Foreign Ministry archives shows that Brussels drew the same conclusion. By the end of October, the risky operation known as Barracuda had been dropped. The nationalist revival at the end of the year, the decline of the Léopoldville regime and the growing unrest in the Léopoldville and Thysville army camps took the West by surprise. The regime seemed less and less capable of keeping its prisoner locked up. A goodly number of CIA agents must have bitterly regretted the error of judgement of thinking Lumumba was finished. Whatever. claims are made to the contrary, the US and the CIA played no role in either the preparations to transfer Lumumba, the transfer itself, or the events in Katanga of 17 January and the following days.[18]

Eyskens's government was well aware that any salvage operation would have to come from Brussels. As already shown (p. 62), Brussels, in no less of a panic than Washington, wired Léopoldville on 4 January emphasising that Lumumba must not be allowed to escape. A few days later, the minister for African affairs wrote to Lahaye and Marlière that Lumumba's release or exchange must be avoided "at all cost, I repeat, at all cost". Ambassador Dupret noted in his 14 January telegram to Brussels:

Around 16 hours on the 13th departure of the head of state for Camp Hardy where apparently no incident involving soldiers took place. . . . Lumumba stayed calm, understandable since he is kept in what is in fact a real cell. . . .

Pay seems to be at the bottom of all difficulties. Calm reigns at Léo.

So the mutiny was over. But Wigny and d'Aspremont Lynden did not relax. Now that Lumumba's release seemed imminent, the entire Belgian apparatus, from the rue de la Loi in Brussels to Brazzaville, Léopoldville, Elisabethville and Bakwanga, swung into action.

Who can claim responsibility for the idea of removing Lumumba from Thysville? According to Brassinne, on the morning of 14 January, at the very moment that a revolt was breaking out at Camp Nkokolo, various people arrived at the Congolese president's residence: apart from Kasa Vubu himself, these included Mobutu, Bomboko, Ileo, Kazadi, José Nussbaumer, Kandolo, Nendaka and a European – probably Georges Denis, Kasa Vubu's Belgian adviser. Again according to Brassinne, "a collective decision was taken at this 'important gathering': Lumumba would be sent to Bakwanga". Brassinne, who is at great pains to lay the entire responsibility for transferring Lumumba firmly at the door of the Congolese, clearly exaggerates the importance of this meeting. Jean Cordy, Bomboko's adviser, agreed unreservedly in Brassinne's hearing that he knew about the transfer decision in advance, but is equally certain that he had no knowledge of a meeting at Kasa Vubu's on 14 or 15 January.[19]

Vandewalle indirectly confirms Cordy's testimony. The decision to remove Lumumba from Thysville had been taken long before. There was broad consensus on the subject in Léopoldville. According to Vandewalle, the dubious honour of originating the transfer decision falls to

the active nucleus of the college of commissioners: Bomboko, Kazadi, Kandolo with his adviser A. Lahaye. . . . General Mobutu's idea, certainly shared by L. Marlière, was to protect the ANC from Lumumbist contagion. Kasa Vubu . . . was certainly au fait with the transfer plan. His adviser G. Denis and Bomboko's adviser J. Cordy also knew.

Colonel Vandewalle goes further: he implicates the Eyskens government:

The Belgian *éminences grises* all knew that Minaf in Brussels thought the interests of the Congo, Katanga and Belgium were best served by keeping Lumumba out of power. P. Wigny also let it be known . . . that Minaffreta [Foreign Affairs] shared this aim. . . . The advisers, each in his own particular sphere of influence, helped conceive the transfer plan in keeping with this policy. . . . The head of the national intelligence services, V. Nendaka, was the main agent in carrying out the matter.

Colonel Marlière, Mobutu's adviser, is also quite clear on the subject. He maintained at a later date: "There was 'consensus', and no 'adviser', Belgian or

American, considered dissuading the [Congolese] leaders." Like Cordy, Marlière told Brassinne that he was not aware of what the latter called "an important gathering". Marlière did not really need this hypothetical meeting anyway because *in the course of the morning* of 14 January he contacted Elisabethville, from Brazzaville, about handing Lumumba over to Tshombe. They had been working hard on the removal of the prisoner from Thysville ever since the 4 January telegram from Brussels; the mutiny simply made Marlière decide to expedite the operation. Years later, Marlière made no attempt to conceal from Brassinne the fact that Lahaye and he "were intimately involved in the preparation of this operation". Mobutu's adviser, who was the Brussels number one in Léopoldville at the time, thought that "Lumumba had to be eliminated", that it was "a public health measure".

Once Lumumba was on the plane to Bakwanga or Elisabethville, for Marlière the matter was closed. He was not concerned with humanitarian issues. Of the cruel treatment Lumumba received during his transfer to Elisabethville, Marlière simply said: "As for what happened in the plane, I only know what I was told. We were very pleased to know the 'package' had arrived. And we have always been grateful to those who were kind enough to deal with it." Marlière had not the slightest doubt that Lumumba's transfer meant certain death. He acknowledged this by reducing the Westerners' role in the transfer to that of technical support: "The decisions were taken by the Zairians and by them alone . . . and they [Westerners] could sense, fear or hope for what would happen after the plane took off, but it was nothing to do with them."

Objections to eliminating Lumumba were not so much concerned with the humanitarian aspect, but were more of a diplomatic and political nature. The consequences of transferring Lumumba to Tshombe's or Kalonji's regimes were unpredictable. Throughout the Third World there was enormous sympathy for the Léopoldville regime's most important prisoner. Lumumba's liquidation under the noses of the Blue Berets could have caused several African and Asian contingents to withdraw from the UN, and to direct support for Lumumbist forces from countries like Ghana and Guinea. The UN operation could have disintegrated and led to heavy military engagements well beyond Congolese borders. These considerations had been restraining Brussels, Léopoldville and Elisabethville since the beginning of December from effectively liquidating Lumumba or transferring him, which came to the same thing. This was despite the fact that they had unanimously agreed in principle to try and keep the former prime minister out of the political arena at all costs. It was only when Lumumba's political return seemed inevitable that all hesitation disappeared in both Brussels and Léopoldville. At the height of the crisis, they made necessity a virtue. "There is now only one solution," as Kestergat wrote later.[20]

On the morning of 14 January, Colonel Marlière crossed the Congo river and went to the Belgian Embassy in Brazzaville. He knew the road well. Although he worked in Léopoldville, that January he spent most nights in Brazzaville where he had access to a radio transmitter. After talks with Ambassador Dupret, it was decided that Marlière would stay by the radio at Brazzaville. André Lahaye returned to Léopoldville where, according to Brassinne, he would be "better able to follow the situation and influence it". That same morning, Colonel Marlière sent this radio message to *Major* Verdickt, the Katangan *Gendarmerie*'s intelligence officer in Elisabethville: "Request Jew's agreement to receive Satan." (As mentioned earlier, "Jew" was the code name for Tshombe, "Satan" for Lumumba.) Verdickt discussed it with Tshombe and Weber, his military adviser, during their daily meeting and replied to Marlière that they were studying the question.[21] Still on the same day, Lahaye returned to Brazzaville and at about 15.30 hours, he told Dupret to send another message to Verdickt:

> The College of General Commissioners insists on receiving agreement to transfer Lumumba to Katanga. His presence at Hardy may provoke new reverses. Despite inevitable drawbacks, it would be advisable to arrange a transfer to a secure region. Commissioner Kandolo insists on behalf of his colleagues.

Dupret telegraphed a copy of the message to Brussels, adding: "It will no doubt seem appropriate to you to support the operation in view and to be firm with the Katangan authorities." The fact that the ambassador was convinced that Brussels would welcome the message clearly demonstrates the climate of opinion at the time.[22] Confirmation of the part the Eyskens government played in the decision to transfer Lumumba comes not only from the telegram of 4 January, but from three other documents as well. The first is a telegram from d'Aspremont Lynden to Tshombe dated 16 January insisting that Tshombe must receive Lumumba as soon as possible. He also sent Brazzaville the message that: "An urgent approach is being made by Minaf to the president of Katanga." As for Foreign Minister Pierre Wigny, his efforts in arranging Lumumba's transfer to Tshombe or Kalonji are clearly stated in his telegram of 18 January to Elisabethville:

> The message signed by Kandolo [of 14 January] was sent directly to the Katangan authorities to ask them to reconsider their refusal to transfer Lumumba to Katanga. In view of Katanga's reluctance, agreement has been reached for transfer to Bakwanga on that day. The operation is being carried out without the knowledge of the UN. Wigny.[23]

As is made clear below, Brassinne and Kestergat maintain that by 14 January Tshombe had decided to accept Lumumba. Therefore, they say, the telegrams from Wigny and d'Aspremont Lynden did not really influence the success of the transfer. Even if Tshombe had already agreed on the 14th, their claim is not valid

from the political point of view. It has already adequately been demonstrated that
Brussels, Léopoldville and Elisabethville consulted each other on several occasions on the subject of Lumumba's possible transfer during the months preceding
the Thysville mutiny. Neither Kasa Vubu, Mobutu or Tshombe, nor Wigny or
d'Aspremont Lynden were caught unprepared. Each was well aware of what the
other was thinking. They all agreed that, whatever the cost, Lumumba must be
kept away from the centre of power. But as long as it was not absolutely necessary to liquidate him immediately or to transfer him from Thysville or
Léopoldville, political considerations for not eliminating him physically carried
more weight. The Katanga lobby was particularly adamant on this score. The
Elisabethville regime's Belgian "advisers" realised the copper state would pay the
highest price for this transfer.

The 16 January telegram had a direct bearing on the outcome of the drama
on 17 January. But there is something else: Brassinne and Kastergat write in *Qui
a tué Patrice Lumumba?* that d'Aspremont Lynden's message was "too short" to
clarify the motives which led him to make this intervention. They add:

> We can rest assured that in his [d'Aspremont Lynden's] opinion, whatever
> happens, they cannot run the risk of removing Lumumba physically. He cer-
> tainly thinks that if they really must get him away from Léopoldville, it would
> be better to transfer him to Katanga where the presence of Belgian advisers
> would guarantee the prisoner's safety, rather than to South Kasai where
> Kalonji is not a man to listen to moderate advice.[24]

That assertion is totally unsubstantiated. The basis for Brassinne and Kestergat's
attribution of humanitarian motives to d'Aspremont Lynden – that is, the claim
that in Katanga "Belgian advisers" would look after Lumumba – contradicts
both their true intentions and their actual actions (as will be seen subsequently),
as well as Brassinne and Kestergat's central premise that the Belgians in Katanga
were not able to influence the dramatic course of events. Was d'Aspremont
Lynden such a bad judge of the power relationships in Katanga and the intentions
and opinions of his subordinates? Of course not.

In his "Enquête sur la mort de Patrice Lumumba", Brassinne recognises that
in Brussels "certain figures were still in favour of tough action" against
Lumumba. In an attempt to clarify the term "tough action", he quotes an article by Professor Marcel De Corte. Published six months earlier in *La Belgique
Libre*, it is a barely veiled appeal for the physical liquidation, purely and simply
the murder, of the Congolese prime minister. But after that, Brassinne clouds
the issue. He does not name names. Although he recognises that the 16 January
telegram reflected the "state of mind" of hard-line partisans, he writes that
Ministers d'Aspremont Lynden and Wigny aimed to eliminate Lumumba politically, without seeking his "physical liquidation". D'Aspremont Lynden had the
opportunity to clarify his thinking "during various one-to-one conversations

with the author": "It was necessary to take Lumumba to Katanga to save the rest of the Congo", but, Brassinne reassures us, "that did not mean he had to physically disappear". He says the same thing about Wigny. Brassinne does not quote the ministers' words verbatim. He summarises and paraphrases their ideas himself. The reader cannot check the accuracy of the summary, nor whether he picked out the facts that would support his thesis.[25]

The responsibility of Brussels is, however, overwhelming. The message from the minister of African affairs demanding Lumumba's "*élimination définitive*" is as clear as day. This same minister gave Operation Barracuda the green light, as has already been noted. If it is supposed that the minister only envisaged eliminating him politically, the question then arises: how could Lumumba be eliminated from the political scene once and for all without being eliminated physically? And did not Foreign Minister Wigny insist he be transferred to Bakwanga, where Albert Kalonji was burning with desire to kill him? But let us take Brassinne at his word for a moment and suppose that d'Aspremont Lynden thought Lumumba did not necessarily have to be physically eliminated. Could his transfer to Katanga mean anything other than his death? Or similarly, can a regime be regarded as innocent when it has deliberately sent its enemy into the lions' den and, after the fact, maintained that it did not intend to physically eliminate him, and that it was not an accessory to murder?

Minister d'Aspremont Lynden knew perfectly well that Katanga was waiting impatiently to murder Lumumba. He was the man running Katanga when the first directive concerning the Congolese prime minister's assassination was sent out. He was the head of Mistebel when, in mid-August, Munongo and his Belgian advisers sent a directive to the *Gendarmerie*'s commanders in north Katanga. Elisabethville was afraid of Lumumba's imminent arrival in a region which was about to fall to the nationalist rebels. This is what it says: "If Lumumba entered Katanga, he would disappear."[26] And on 12 September, *La Cité* reported a statement by Munongo about Lumumba's fate if he were found on Katangan soil: "If he comes here, we will do what the Belgians couldn't do, we will kill him." The Belgian government was perfectly aware of all this. Bartelous, Tshombe's principal private secretary, admitted to Brassinne that, during the period before the transfer, Elisabethville's European elite knew all too well that Lumumba's transfer to Katanga meant his death. And later, once Lumumba's death was official, Victor Larock, an opposition leader, reminded the Belgian government that a document from the Katangan regime about the treatment Lumumba would receive if he set foot in Katanga was discussed at the beginning of January 1961 in the Foreign Affairs Committee, with both Wigny and d'Aspremont Lynden present: "It was a revealing document. Why did the two ministers present at the committee not take it more into account?"

Even after the assassination, when the harm had been done and the regime and its collaborators were mounting a cover-up operation, the secessionist leaders continued to speak openly. Hence, on 28 January 1961, Munongo told a delegation from South Kasai that Lumumba would not be transferred to the République de la Forminière: "It is an honour for us to kill this man on Katangan soil, we will not give anyone else this honour."[27]

BAKWANGA OR ELISABETHVILLE?
(14–17 JANUARY 1961)

It is clear from the telegrams of 16 and 18 January from Ministers d'Aspremont Lynden and Wigny that the Eyskens government chose to transfer Lumumba and not to liquidate him immediately in Thysville. Thus far, we can only guess at the motives which led the Belgian ministers to prefer transferring him. They probably wanted to spare the fragile regime in Léopoldville. They needed Kasa Vubu in the long term, as the legal figurehead behind which the Congo would be reconstructed. It seemed preferable, therefore, to delegate the "dirty work" to Elisabethville or Bakwanga. Moreover, the transfer suited the Belgian authorities and their intelligence services down to the ground. Unlike the United States, they had neither the apparatus nor the tradition to mount an effective assassination operation quickly thousands of miles from home. Besides, Brussels was convinced that a solution to the Lumumba problem was an integral part of any political solution, one aspect of which was collaboration between Léopoldville and Elisabethville. Lumumba's transfer was the concrete expression of that incipient collaboration and cleared the way for a permanent solution. Had not Vanden Bloock suggested at the end of December that Katanga was afraid that accepting Lumumba would imply the recognition of formal ties between Léopoldville and Elisabethville? And this was precisely one of the Belgian government's aims. They wanted Katanga to participate in the reconstruction of the Congo.[28]

It was not Kasa Vubu, therefore, but Kalonji or Tshombe who had to get rid of Lumumba. And settling accounts meant that blood would flow, as everyone knew from the outset. In Bakwanga, Albert Kalonji was champing at the bit, waiting to receive the former prime minister and leaving absolutely no doubt as to the fate awaiting him. He had sworn to use Lumumba's skull as a vase. On 10 October, the day Mobutu and the United Nations placed Lumumba under house arrest, Kalonji declared Lumumba was "bloodthirsty" and "a murderer who must be tried and executed". One of Kalonji's Belgian officers described what would happen if the *mulopwe* got his hands on Lumumba: "There would be no chance of keeping the secret for a single minute after Lumumba landed at Bakwanga. The president [Kalonji] could picture thousands of Baluba men and women fighting over a scrap of flesh, a lock of hair or a piece of clothing!"[29]

Since the nationalist offensive against South Kasai at the end of August 1960, the Kalonjists saw Lumumba as evil personified. Several dozen innocent civilians were killed during battles between Congolese government troops and Baluba militias. Lumumba's enemies lumped together that tragedy and the accusation "H" levelled at the ANC – according to him, they were embarking on genocide – with the thousands who had died in battles between Balubas and Luluas over the past few months, and the growing number of victims of the famine raging in Kalonji's separatist state. The anti-nationalists accused Lumumba of a whole amalgam of ills and considered him the perpetrator of genocide against tens of thousands of Balubas. It was obvious Lumumba would not be spared in Bakwanga. Brassinne wrote in his "Enquête":

> We can reasonably ask ourselves what the chances of the prisoners' surviving would be, were they handed over to the South Kasai authorities. Considering what happened three weeks later [the murder of Finant and the other nationalist leaders at Bakwanga in February 1961], they would appear to be nil.

For its part, Elisabethville's plans for the former prime minister were hardly different. Brassinne admits Lumumba was going to certain death in Katanga: "We knew for a fact what was going to happen. And it did!" The choice between Bakwanga and Elisabethville is limited, therefore, to knowing who will actually carry out the deed. That Lumumba will be killed is an already established fact.[30]

From 14 January, Léopoldville was working on the premise that Lumumba would be transferred to Bakwanga. On that day, Léopoldville CIA chief Devlin learned that South Kasai was to be Lumumba's (probably final) destination. Colonel Jean Gillet, nicknamed "Long Kangaroo", the officer commanding Kalonji's troops, had said earlier in the day that Lumumba could be transferred to Bakwanga without any preconditions. Gillet had been listening to radio communications between Marlière and Verdickt, in which they talked of transferring "Satan". He had joined in the conversation and reminded them that he was still prepared to receive the "parcel". Marlière did not hide his satisfaction: "So we have the green light for departure whatever the landing strip. For me, the matter is closed."[31]

But was Tshombe prepared to "receive" the prisoners? Brassinne and Kestergat maintain that, on 14 January or the following day at the very latest, the Katangan president agreed the venue for the nationalist leader at a meeting of the Katangan government. Brassinne and Kestergat do not know exactly when this important decision was taken. But they are sure of two things: that agreement was reached before Brussels pleaded with Tshombe to allow Lumumba's transfer to Katanga and that the president's Belgian entourage was not aware of it. Brassinne and Kestergat maintain that Tshombe kept quiet about this decision, even after Bartelous, his private secretary, informed him on 16 January of Minister d'Aspremont Lynden's telegram bearing the urgent request to receive Lumumba in Katanga.[32] Readers of *Qui a tué Patrice Lumumba?* are supposed to believe that the Katangans consented to the transfer completely independently of their Belgian advisers. Brassinne and Kestergat suggest that "on 17 January the

Belgian political advisers [in Katanga] still do not know anything". They write that "the Katangans, who are determined President Tshombe's Belgian advisers should not know of their decision to accept Lumumba", succeeded in their plan. "The testimonies [these advisers gave to Brassinne] all concur." Brassinne and Kestergat use Tshombe's agreement to minimise the importance of d'Aspremont Lynden's plea for a transfer. Since President Tshombe had already agreed, the practical value of the ministerial missive is reduced to zero. The sub-heading in Brassinne's doctorate concerning the contentious decision reads as follows: "15 January, the Katangans accept." The 16 January telegram from the minister for African affairs is not even mentioned in the section on the transfer decision, but comes in a separate section entitled "The Position of Brussels".[33]

Brassinne and Kestergat's assertions are unfounded. It is true that Lumumba's transfer made certain sectors in Elisabethville very happy. Many of them were after his hide. A draft telegram about Lumumba's possible transfer exists, dating from the beginning of January 1961 and compiled by Louis Duray, one of the regime's legal advisers. The document should have been given to Tshombe to sign. It obviously did not reach its destination, but it is quite typical of certain people's mentality at the time: "The government commissioner on the permanent military tribunal of the Katangan armed forces has today accused the deputy Lumumba Patrice of a breach of internal and external security of the state, of encouraging civilians to riot and soldiers to disobey." He demanded that the prisoner be handed over, claiming that parliamentary immunity did not apply, given the gravity of the crimes committed.[34]

Certain people actually hoped to gain from agreeing to the transfer by asking Léopoldville for the political elimination of Jason Sendwe. Sendwe, who at the time was roaming free in the streets of the Congolese capital, was the leader of the Balubakat, which was threatening the Tshombe regime in north Katanga. In a draft text of 14 or 15 January 1961, an exchange was again proposed. This quid pro quo was sent "according to some" by Verdickt (in Elisabethville) to Brazzaville. In the text Tshombe tells Léopoldville that Lumumba could be sent to Katanga "if the leader of the Balubakat, Jason Sendwe, is also in the plane".[35] These proposals, however, were left pending, among other reasons because Léopoldville believed (rightly) that Sendwe had a somewhat moderating influence on the nationalist forces and that he could play a useful role in reintegrating Katanga into a future unified Congolese state.

Within the Katangan government and its Belgian entourage, there was neither a white majority, nor a black, in favour of receiving Lumumba. Brassinne and Kestergat maintain that no Belgian was present at the Katangan ministers' evening meeting on 14 January when partisans of Lumumba's unconditional delivery apparently held sway. But we know from Vandewalle and Weber that at least three or four Belgians always attended these meetings: civilians like Bartelous, Clémens, F. Renard, François Thomas and Victor Tignée, and military men like Vandewalle, Weber and the *Gendarmerie*'s chief of staff, Paul

Perrad.[36] Brassinne's "Enquête" states that the following Belgians were among those present at the select committee of Katangan ministers held during the second week in January which dealt with the question of Lumumba's transfer: Major Weber, Professor Clémens and Perrad. Other Belgian advisers, like Bartelous, Thomas and Tignée, joined in the debate. A few pages further on, Brassinne talks about the "relatively heavy weight of European elements" during the 14 January cabinet meeting. During that meeting, Marlière's radio message demanding "Satan" be accepted was widely discussed. The answer was no, which in effect reflected the point of view of the Bureau Conseil: Lumumba represented "a poisoned chalice" for the copper state.[37]

Colonel Vandewalle writes that the ministerial select committee of 14 January went back to its former bargaining position (Lumumba = OK if Sendwe = imprisoned). This negotiating proposition was sent to Brazzaville the next day. But during the daily meeting of the Bureau Conseil on 14 or 15 January, according to Vandewalle, it was decided "unanimously . . . that there could be no question of accepting Lumumba in Katanga. It was decided that those meeting Tshombe would take him in hand." This they did, and Tshombe was indeed brought round to his Belgian advisers' point of view yet again. The argument suggesting that Tshombe and his ministers accepted the transfer behind the Belgian advisers' backs has no basis at all. Vandewalle is absolutely clear about this: "That does not correspond to reality."[38]

Brassinne writes that on 15 January Tshombe dictated a letter to his secretary which she had to type confidentially, making two copies, one for Kasa Vubu, the other for Bomboko. In it Tshombe just said he accepted Lumumba's transfer; he expressed no demands about Sendwe: "With reference to the message we have just received from you, we agree to the immediate transfer of the communist Lumumba to Elisabethville. This operation must be done discreetly: can you advise of his arrival as soon as possible?" What happened to these letters? Brassinne admits in the "conclusions" to his dissertation: "It has never been proved that when those responsible in Léopoldville took their decision, they were aware of the Katangans' agreement." Furthermore, he notes in the dissertation's "testimonies" section that the letter could not possibly have reached Léopoldville by the time the decision to transfer Lumumba to Elisabethville was taken. In the body of the text, Brassinne writes that during the course of 15 January Verdickt would have taken the necessary steps to send these coded letters by radio-message to Marlière in Brazzaville. But according to Brassinne and Kestergat's book, the radio-message was only found much later on – "possibly during the day of 16 January" – on the foreign affairs telex in Léopoldville.

It is out of the question that Tshombe's important letters, typed by his secretary, were not known to the Belgians. Servais, Tshombe's Belgian secretary, was an informer for the *Gendarmerie*'s intelligence services. The first thing she would have done would be to alert her Belgian bosses. But above all, it is unthinkable that *Major* Verdickt, who was at the *Gendarmerie* headquarters and would have transmitted the content of these letters to Brazzaville, would not first have told his Belgian colleagues about them. On 14 January, Verdickt had had further talks with Tshombe and Weber, his military adviser, on the subject after having communicated by radio with Marlière. The attitude of the *éminences grises* in the Bureau Conseil and in the select council of ministers was undoubtedly hostile to the transfer. Nevertheless, Brassinne and Kestergat insist that Verdickt sent a positive response and kept absolutely silent on the matter to his colleagues. Brassinne and Kestergat explain this silence by saying that the intelligence officer was not "a very expansive character".[39]

But Brassinne should be heard out. If it is true that Tshombe did not want the Belgians in Katanga to know of his affirmative decision, the following very simple question arises: why did he transmit his decision by the (Belgian) radio network of the Katangan *Gendarmerie* or intelligence services, and not by plane with a courier or simply by telephone? The telephone lines between Léopoldville and Elisabethville had been repaired. As discussed below, on 16 January Kasa Vubu and Tshombe discussed this matter on the telephone. That same day, Delvaux, a messenger from Léopoldville, back from Elisabethville, told the press that Kasa Vubu and Tshombe had a very long telephone conversation.[40]

Vandewalle admits that on 15 January, a letter was written in Tshombe's name for the attention of Kasa Vubu, in which Elisabethville unconditionally agreed to Lumumba's transfer. But he says he does not know whether or not it was actually sent. But it is unthinkable that it could have been sent without Colonel Vandewalle being informed by one of the senders: by Verdickt, who was in charge of radio correspondence between the *Gendarmerie* (G2) and Brazzaville, or by Renard, who dealt with the correspondence between the Katangan intelligence services and Lahaye (Léopoldville). It seems that this draft letter stayed in the drawer. In his dissertation, Brassinne writes that Verdickt stated in an "additional testimony" that this letter was sent to Marlière by radio. But this is not the explanation found in the annexes to the thesis. What *is* there is Verdickt's testimony in which he stated that no radio message was sent from G2 of the *Gendarmerie* (Elisabethville) to Marlière (Brazzaville). Marlière's testimony does not mention Tshombe's affirmative reply either, although he, Marlière, was the recipient of these letters.

According to Jean Cordy, an affirmative reply reached Bomboko in Léopoldville, before Lumumba's transfer. It could not have come over the radio from either Verdickt or Renard, or Vandewalle would have known. It is not impossible that during the day of 16 January, or the night of 16–17 January, confirmation did actually arrive, either by telephone to the president of the college or through the office of Kasa Vubu who telephoned Elisabethville that same day.[41] That would explain why, as will be made clear below, Léopoldville was still working on the premise of transferring Lumumba to Bakwanga. And the reason why the message giving Tshombe's agreement did not reach Léopoldville until "16 January during the day" becomes equally clear, as Brassinne and Kestergat write. Brassinne (Kestergat is now dead) will not like hearing this, but Minister d'Aspremont Lynden's telegram had the effect he intended and forced the Belgian lobby in Katanga to accept the transfer. That finally explains why during the afternoon of 16 January, André Lahaye in Leopoldville was still trying to persuade Elisabethville to agree to the transfer – a fiat already given some hours earlier. Lahaye says that he was with Nendaka until 17 hours on 16 January. When they parted, transferring Lumumba to Bakwanga was still the preferred option. It was not until after 17 hours, during the evening or night of 16–17 January, that Nendaka learned Tshombe had agreed and that Lumumba's destination had changed to Elisabethville.[42]

Brassinne reveals a significant fact about Tshombe's place in the Katangan chain of decision making dealing with the transfer. Minister d'Aspremont Lynden's 16 January message, in which Brussels urged the regime to agree to the transfer, was not even given to Tshombe: "Only the contents of the telex were relayed to Tshombe, he was not given a copy!"[43] In the light of this unequal relationship between the Katangan "dignitaries" and the Belgian "advisers" and known historical facts, we can confidently assume that Tshombe did not give the transfer the green light behind the Belgians' back, or against their will.

D'ASPREMONT LYNDEN ORDERS LUMUMBA'S TRANSFER TO KATANGA (16 JANUARY 1961)

At precisely what time on 16 January 1961 did the crucial telegram from the minister for African affairs arrive at the Belgian consulate in Elisabethville? The time is not without importance. If, for instance, it arrived in the evening, its impact would obviously be less than if it arrived earlier in the day. Vandewalle writes in his *Mille et quatre jours* that the telegram had been studied by the Bureau Conseil. Meetings of the Bureau Conseil are known to have adhered to a strict pattern, with the daily meeting held in the morning. So the telegram arrived on the morning of the 16th, before the meeting, or at the latest during the meeting. The Foreign Ministry archives say that the draft was written on 15 January. The text leaves nothing to the imagination: the minister was anxious to close the matter as quickly as possible. Lumumba's transfer must take place "with the least possible delay". In a message to Brazzaville, the minister classified the telegram "urgent action". It is clear that the text, drawn up on 15 January, was sent first thing the next morning. Brassinne and Kestergat confirm this: they write that Tshombe's private secretary had already conveyed the contents of the message to the president by the morning of 16 January.

The minister's telegram arrived in time to inform all the people involved (Henri Créner, the Bureau Conseil, Bartelous) and to influence the course of events. Vandewalle writes that on 16 January, the Bureau Conseil's advice on the transfer "was unanimous. It was negative." But the Bureau Conseil decided not to take its own advice and did not prevent Lumumba's transfer. The minister's telegram leaves no room for interpretation. It was short, clear and extremely authoritarian. The text was not sent "in Jules code", by the parallel line between the minister's office and the Bureau Conseil, but officially addressed to Consul General Créner and preceded by a directive. This is the whole text:

Consubel E'ville. For Créner.
06416/Cab.
For the attention of President Tshombe.
Quote Minaf [Ministry of African Affairs] Aspremont personally urges President Tshombe to allow Lumumba to be transferred to Katanga with the least possible delay. *Unquote*
Please keep me informed.
Minaf.

This message was to be given to Tshombe. In other words the traditional procedure, whereby the minister's telegrams were discussed at the Bureau Conseil and, if necessary, "translated" into decisions for Tshombe and his government, had been bypassed. The Bureau Conseil had been forced to give tacit approval. Bartelous, Tshombe's private secretary, only had one item on his agenda that morning: to give Tshombe the message. Tshombe, amused, might have reacted with the following remark: "Your minister wants me to receive Lumumba and you propose the opposite?"[44] Bartelous probably replied that a transfer could have heavy repercussions for the secession, but that Lumumba's release, from the Katangan point of view too, must be avoided at all costs. This was why the minister of African affairs had opted for the transfer to Katanga.

On 16 January, everyone knew that the Bureau Conseil and the Katangan government had agreed to Lumumba's transfer after learning of the contents of d'Aspremont Lynden's telegram – although the date of his arrival was still uncertain. When, on 17 January, the pilot of the plane circling Elisabethville told the control tower that he had "three important parcels for Munongo", the airport staff understood the message perfectly – as Brassinne himself writes. On 18 January, Consul General Créner sent a telegram to Brussels: "The Katangan government agreed on principle but was surprised by the speed of the arrival."[45] The argument that the Katangans acted on their own initiative on 15 January and decided to agree to Lumumba's transfer without the knowledge of the Belgians falls on stony ground. In fact, this thesis repeats in not a very subtle way what one of Tshombe's assistants much later told a United Nations inquiry set up to wash its hands and those of its Belgian colleagues of the affair. It does not correspond to reality, as Vandewalle rightly concludes.[46]

On 16 January, the two hundredth day of Congolese independence, Kasa

Vubu telephoned Tshombe about the transfer of their common enemy. Jacqueline Dumba, the president's cousin, who was in his office at the time, has confirmed this. Tshombe said to Kasa Vubu: "I know about it. . . . For the practical details, I am passing you over to the minister of the interior [Munongo]." That same day, E. Longerstaey, head of the new Belgian diplomatic mission in Léopoldville, had a meeting with the Congolese president. The subject of the transfer was touched on.[47] Meanwhile, Nendaka, the intelligence chief, was already dealing with the practicalities of the plan. At 10 a.m. on 16 January, a meeting was held in the office of Jean Annez de Taboada, chairman of Sabena-Afrique, at Ndjili, Léopoldville's airport. Sabena's representatives at the meeting were: Annez de Taboada himself, Jean Jonniaux, head of operations and his assistant Michel Doutreloux, Captains Piet Van der Meersch and Bob Watson. Representing the Congolese authorities were: Kandolo, Kazadi and Lahaye, joined later by Nendaka who explained that "Lumumba's powers of persuasion would in the end probably overcome the doubts of the soldiers guarding him at Thysville . . . there is no doubt that he would have been released before long." The conclusion was obvious: Lumumba must go, and two planes were requisitioned for this purpose.

During the conversation, Lumumba's possible destinations were reviewed: Bakwanga and Elisabethville. It has been seen that Bakwanga wanted nothing better than to receive the prisoner. But risks were involved since Bakwanga's airport was controlled by Ghanaian Blue Berets who had a lot of sympathy for the Congolese nationalists. Would the Ghanaians try to protect Lumumba? This "security problem" would not arise at Luano, Elisabethville's airport. Under the August agreement between the United Nations and Tshombe, Belgians and Katangans were in charge of the control tower and the military section of the airport, with the Blue Berets patrolling the airport's civilian area. Hence, there would be no problem landing Lumumba in the military section of Luano.

However, the people at the meeting had not yet heard that Elisabethville had already given permission for the transfer, and so they were still working on the hypothesis of a transfer to Bakwanga. They decided to use three planes. A small transport aircraft (a Dragon rapide) would take Lumumba to the airport at Matadi, where he would be put in a DC-4 plane captained by Piet Van der Meersch. (Lahaye and Marlière explained later that he was chosen because he was soon going back to Belgium for good.) A DC-3, captained by the Australian Bob Watson, would be sent in advance to Bakwanga. If there were no Blue Berets at the airport, he would radio permission for the DC-4 to land with Lumumba on board; otherwise the DC-4 would have to go on to Elisabethville. The DC-3 and the DC-4 belonged to Air Congo, a new domestic airline managed by Sabena. The Dragon rapide belonged to the private company Air Brousse, run by pilots De Coene, Tabutaux and Linard, with a fleet of seven light aircraft running flights into the interior of the country. Captain Van der Meersch later gave his end of mission report in the office of Annez de Taboada and subsequently also in Brussels, in the office of Gaston Dieu, the chairman of Sabena. Dieu no doubt listened with sardonic pleasure to the exploits of Van der Meersch: in July 1960, he had taken "a malicious delight" (according to Belgian Ambassador Van den Bosch) in exposing Lumumba to the insults and blows of the Belgian repatriates at Ndjili.[48]

The meeting at Ndjili lasted barely half an hour. Later that day, at about 5 p.m., André Lahaye, Kandolo's adviser, crossed the river Congo to send another message to Elisabethville from Brazzaville in which he urged Tshombe to approve the operation. He then asked Ambassador Dupret to urge Brussels to encourage Tshombe to support the action.[49] But meanwhile Tshombe and his assistants had already discussed Minister d'Aspremont Lynden's telegram, and the presidents of the Congo and Katanga had agreed to Lumumba's uncondi-tional transfer to Katanga. During the evening or night, Nendaka, Lahaye and the others were informed of this agreement: they could therefore proceed with transporting the "package" in total safety. The hard core – Nendaka and doubt-less Lahaye and Marlière – who were in charge of the practicalities of the transfer, were confident of the outcome now that the risky journey to Bakwanga could be avoided.

Jonas Mukamba, one of Mobutu's commissioners and a close associate of Kalonji, was dispatched by DC-4 to Matadi and on to Elisabethville – instead of going by DC-3 to Bakwanga as previously planned – following instructions given him by Nendaka during the evening of 16 January. The same instructions applied to Ferdinand Kazadi, commissioner for defence, so on 17 January, at 4 a.m., they both boarded the DC-4. It took off shortly afterwards, not for Matadi where the fog was too thick but for Moanda, 240 kilometres further away on the Atlantic coast. Moanda was a small colonial seaside resort and a favourite week-end place for UN officials. At Moanda airport, as at Matadi, there were no Blue Berets. The Dragon rapide, which was to take Lumumba to Matadi, flew to Lukala on the morning of 17 January – not to Thysville so as not to "stir up the garrison", as Schoonbroodt subsequently stated. For his part, Victor Nendaka left Leopoldville by road on that night of the 16th, accompanied by a military escort. They drove to Thysville in two cars, and took Lumumba from his cell on what would be his last journey.[50]

LUMUMBA'S LAST DAY

FROM THYSVILLE TO LUKALA, THEN TO MOANDA

Nendaka's retinue was made up of three soldiers, chosen with care: Baluba from Kasai, whose hatred for the former prime minister ensured that orders would be strictly executed. Their leader was Lieutenant Zuzu, a "bloodthirsty brute" according to Brassinne. They meant to cover the 150 kilometres from the capital to Thysville before dawn. The camp commander Colonel Bobozo had insisted Nendaka come as soon as possible. Because of the very recent mutiny, he wanted Lumumba gone before the soldiers woke up — otherwise fresh scuffles or worse were feared. Nendaka arrived at the entrance to Camp Hardy at around 4.30 a.m.[1]

According to Brassinne, they already had two prisoners with them: Maurice Mpolo and Joseph Okito who would accompany Lumumba on this last journey to his death. Maurice Mpolo, aged thirty-two, had been the sports and youth minister in Lumumba's government, and also, for a brief period, the Congolese army's chief of staff. Joseph Okito, fifty, had been vice-president of the Senate before it closed down. They had both fallen into the hands of Mobutu's soldiers during Lumumba's attempt to escape to Stanleyville. Okito was arrested near Kikwit. Mpolo made the mistake of addressing a gathering of his supporters at Lake Léopold II before leaving for Stanleyville; he was arrested at Mushie. They were probably held in Luzumu, near Léopoldville, and Nendaka went to fetch them there before continuing to Thysville. However, at one stage Lumumba mentioned his fellow-prisoner Okito in a letter (pp. 59 and 60 above). If Brassinne is right about Nendaka having Okito with him, then Okito had probably already been transferred from Thysville prison. Mpolo and Okito had been leaders of the MNC, and were considered by the Léopoldville regime to be potential figureheads for a nationalist attempt to rally support.[2]

Nendaka and his retinue went straight to see Colonel Bobozo. Nendaka probably had a letter from Kasa Vubu ordering that Lumumba be handed over. Bobozo had asked him to bring such a document. Bobozo, Nendaka and the ANC soldiers then headed for Lumumba's cell. As soon as Lumumba saw Nendaka he must have realised the situation had taken a turn for the worse. His comrade of yesteryear had become his worst enemy. As Mobutu's security chief, Nendaka was responsible for torture and murder in the newly established camp for prisoners at Binza, on the hill outside Kinshasa where the commandos had their barracks. He was also the brain behind the terror in the capital's poorer residential areas. At the beginning of December, just before his transfer to Thysville, Lumumba had been severely beaten by Nendaka. Kazadi said later: "Patrice Lumumba knew straight away that things were bad." According to Second Lieutenant Schoonbroodt, "Lumumba didn't want to [go with him], he was apprehensive."

At about 5.30, shortly before dawn, Lumumba left the camp in a convoy. Bobozo had provided Nendaka with additional men and three cars, as he knew that the Congolese soldiers were in contact with the Moroccan Blue Berets stationed in Thysville. (The Moroccans made up the ANC's third commando battalion in Camp Sonankulu, which was in Thysville itself, unlike the large Camp Hardy, which was outside the city.) Since the recent mutiny at Hardy, surveillance of the Moroccan garrison had increased. Bobozo was not taking any risks and had forbidden the Moroccans entry to the camp for the last few days.

Schoonbroodt woke at 6 o'clock. During his early morning tour of the camp, he noticed that its main entrance was wide open. The door had been kept closed ever since Lumumba's arrival, so he immediately surmised that Lumumba, who he knew had to be got rid of, must have gone. A little later, Bobozo sent the following radio message to Léopoldville: "the parcel has been dispatched". Bobozo's role in Lumumba's elimination stops here. A dazzling career was awaiting him in Mobutu's army.

Much later, a journalist giving evidence to the UN inquiry into the assassination of Lumumba, Mpolo and Okito stated that a strategy had been employed to lure Lumumba out of Camp Hardy. He was told there had been a coup in Léopoldville, that Kasa Vubu, Mobutu and Bomboko were in jail, and that he was eagerly awaited in the capital to form a government as quickly as possible. However, our evidence shows that Nendaka himself went to fetch Lumumba.

Lumumba can have had no illusions as to the intentions of Mobutu's right-hand man when the convoy turned left towards Matadi and the ocean, instead of right towards the capital. The convoy probably travelled for at least an hour and a half to cover the 60 kilometres to Lukala on a partially paved road with dangerous inclines and bends winding through the hills. Around 7 o'clock, the convoy arrived at the plain of Kimbala Zolele, near Lukala. There an hour later, a Dragon rapide landed on the grass air strip. Lukala was home to the headquarters of the Congolese Cement Company (CICO). The pilot had not followed usual procedures: he had not informed CICO of his arrival, and had not flown over the village. Normally, the company sent someone to greet passengers on their arrival or to unload freight.[3]

CICO's European staff could not see what was happening. The cement works was 1.5 kilometres from the runway and the Europeans lived in a compound surrounded by a 3-metre-high fence. After work, they went back to the compound and stayed there until the next morning. But on this particular morning, hearing a plane, several Congolese employees headed for the air strip to see what was happening. When the Congolese arrived back at work, they related the *matatas* (events) to Maurice Renous, the finance manager. After the Dragon rapide landed, soldiers pulled Africans dressed in civilian clothes from one of the cars parked there, and pushed them onto the plane. The clerks recognised one of them: Patrice Lumumba, his face covered in blood. In the course of the same morning, André Mezo, one of the leaders of President Kasa Vubu's party Abako, visited Renous. Mezo must undoubtedly have expressed what the leaders in Léopoldville were feeling: "Light at the end of the tunnel at last . . . Lumumba is finished!"

François Beaumont, the French pilot of the Dragon rapide, took seven people on board: Nendaka, the three ANC soldiers, and the three prisoners who were shoved inside the plane. Beaumont ordered the soldiers to remove the bayonets from their guns as he feared they might damage the aircraft. They took off at about 8.15 and landed at approximately 9.30 in Moanda, some 240 kilometres from Lukala. The next day, Beaumont told his boss, Raymond Linard, also a pilot and joint owner of Air Brousse, what happened during the flight. As the plane was taking off, the soldiers began manhandling the prisoners. The pilot asked them to stop immediately, fearing an accident. (The Dragon rapide is a small light aircraft and easily destabilised. It weighs less than 2.5 tonnes and can only carry eight people.)[4]

A DC-4 with its crew and two passengers on board had been waiting in Moanda, on the Atlantic coast, since 7 a.m. Nendaka disembarked from the Dragon rapide, followed by his escort and the prisoners. As soon as they were on the ground, the prisoners were beaten up again. Meanwhile, Nendaka talked to the two passengers in the DC-4, Commissioners Kazadi and Cléophas Mukamba. He disclosed the three prisoners' final destination: Elisabethville, where they were to be taken immediately. The DC-4, its tanks refuelled, took off at about 10 o'clock. Above the ocean, the pilot turned to take a shorter route to the copper capital via the Angolan corridor in the south-east, reducing the distance to about 1,800 kilometres. On board the plane were Kazadi, Mukamba, Zuzu, some Baluba soldiers, the three prisoners and four crew members: the Belgian captain, Piet Van der Meersch, the Australian first officer Jack Dixon, the Belgian radio operator Jean-Louis Drugmand and the French engineer Robert Fau.

Half an hour later, a DC-3 took off from Ndjili airport for Bakwanga with no passengers, only the crew comprising the Australian captain Bob Watson, the

Belgian radio operator Guy Goblet and a Belgian engineer named Pachenko. Before taking off, Watson told his crew: "We're going to see if there are UN troops in Bakwanga. . . . We want to see if we can take Lumumba to Bakwanga without him being freed by UN troops." It was only after the DC-3's departure that the DC-4's captain informed Ndjili that his destination was Elisabethville. Ndjili then sent a message in morse code to the DC-3, which was by now past Kikwit, saying its mission had been cancelled and ordering the pilot to return to Léopoldville. Radio contact with the DC-4 was established on the return journey. The radio operator Jean-Louis Drugmand told his counterpart Guy Goblet on the DC-3: "We know you're going back to Léopoldville; we're going straight to Elisabethville." During the journey, DC-4 Captain Piet Van der Meersch did not try to contact either Elisabethville or Léopoldville. Morse code can be picked up everywhere in the Congo. After the DC-4's departure from Moanda, Victor Nendaka, finally rid of his awkward prisoner, returned to Léopoldville in the Dragon rapide.[5]

That same morning, while the DC-4 was en route to Katanga, Ambassador Dupret sent a telegram from Brazzaville to Foreign Minister Pierre Wigny, saying that Lumumba was being transferred to Bakwanga, in accordance with what was agreed at Ndjili:

> Lumumba's transfer to Bakwanga has been decided with Kalonji's consent. It will be carried out this morning as follows: leave Thysville for Moanda by Air Brousse; from Moanda to Bakwanga on board a DC-4. Moanda has been chosen because there are no Blue Berets there. Kazadi will accompany Lumumba to Bakwanga. We insist Lumumba be treated decently. Nevertheless, it is possible he may be prevented from leaving Camp Hardy. All operations are carried out without UN knowledge, and with all the usual precautions.[6]

Was this a deliberate error to mislead the United Nations and disrupt any possible intervention by the Blue Berets? Or did Dupret himself then know no better or had Crokart, Lahaye's contact, lied to him? Or did Crokart not know either?

On the evening of 17 January, a UN officer visited Emmanuel Kini, the Congolese president's private secretary. The plan to keep the UN in the dark concerning Lumumba's departure had apparently succeeded. The UN officer wanted to know more about Lumumba's fate, and particularly about the destination of the DC-4. UN radar had tried to track the plane's flight path but failed. Kini asked President Kasa Vubu but, true to his reputation, he remained silent as the grave.[7]

Patrice Lumumba arrives at the Palais de la Nation in Léopoldville
for the independence ceremony, 30 June 1960. (Popperfoto)

Lumumba and Gaston Eyskens, Belgian Prime Minister, sign the
Declaration of Congolese Independence, 30 June 1960. (Popperfoto)

Kwame Nkrumah (in white suit), first President of the Ghanaian Republic, bids farewell to the outgoing Governor General of Ghana Lord Listowel, 1 July 1960. (Popperfoto)

Lumumba being interviewed with Maurice Mpolo, the new commander-in-chief of the Congolese army, at Ndjili airport, 17 July 1960. (Topham Picturepoint)

Lumumba with UN Secretary General Dag Hammarskjöld, after their conference at UN headquarters in New York on the critical situation in the Congo, 24 July 1960. (Topham Picturepoint)

Joseph Mobutu in Léopoldville on 15 September 1960, having just announced that the Congolese army would be taking over the running of the country. (Topham Picturepoint)

British Prime Minister Harold Macmillan making a speech at the United Nations General Assembly, 30 September 1960. (Topham Picturepoint)

Allen Dulles, head of the Central Intelligence Agency. (Popperfoto)

Lumumba and his aides in a truck at Léopoldville airport, on the day after their arrest by Mobutu's army in Port Francqui, 2 December 1960. (Associated Press/Topham)

US President Dwight Eisenhower and President-elect John F. Kennedy, 6 December 1960. (Popperfoto)

Officials next to the Ford sedan car alleged to have been used by
Lumumba and his aides to escape prison, 12 January 1961. Left to
right Pius Sapwe (commissioner of the Katanga police), an unidentified police commissioner, Jules Allard (a Belgian agent of the
Katanga intelligence service), and the captain in charge of the
prison guards Julien Gat. (Popperfoto)

The Brouwez house where Lumumba, Okito and Mpolo were tortured on the evening of 17 January 1961, before being executed. The painted poster of Lumumba, just visible in the centre, is captioned "Le pays exige des martyrs. Je me présente". Today, the house no longer exists. (Photograph taken by Tom Küsters on 27 July 1977, © Tom Küsters, Holland)

Protesters in London's Piccadilly on their way to the Belgian
Embassy, 19 February 1961. (Associated Press/Topham)

FROM MOANDA TO ELISABETHVILLE IN THE DC-4

The DC-4 carrying Lumumba, Mpolo and Okito to Elisabethville was a large four-engined plane with seats for fifty passengers. Everything had been prepared for a long flight – there were forty-two meals on board.[8] All the crew members subsequently stated that the prisoners were badly abused throughout the flight, which lasted several hours. Lumumba, Mpolo and Okito were seated next to each other, wearing seat belts and tied with ropes. The prisoners' eyes, ears and mouths were covered with adhesive tape. One after the other, they were made to kneel in the aisle where the soldiers kicked them or beat them with their rifle butts. Even while Lumumba was sitting in his place, they did not leave him alone for a minute. One of the soldiers, leaning against the side of the plane, kicked him repeatedly in the stomach. The prisoners' only respite was when the soldiers, themselves tired, took a rest and passed round a bottle of whisky. The violence eventually started to bother the crew, and Van der Meersch tried to make the soldiers calm down, explaining that their abrupt movements threatened the safety of the plane. The captain asked Kazadi if he meant to kill the prisoners on board. Mobutu's defence commissioner replied that they would reach Katanga alive. A khaki beret on his head, the rather stout Kazadi went on calmly smoking his pipe, observing his soldiers' behaviour in silence.

They tore out Lumumba's goatee and several tufts of his hair which they then forced him to swallow, a spectacle which apparently made one of the soldiers ill. The radio operator Jean-Louis Drugmand was made actually sick by the display of cruelty which, according to Goblet, so traumatised him that the events haunted him all his life. The crew repeatedly tried to restrain the soldiers, but they finally locked themselves in the cockpit from which they emerged only after landing in Elisabethville. In an interview with the *Durban Sunday Tribune* shortly after the transfer, the Australian co-pilot Jack Dixon said he tried in vain to keep the soldiers away from Lumumba and apparently told the unconcerned commissioners: "Say, we have to hand Lumumba over alive." In 1966 Kazadi admitted to Jean Van Lierde that the prisoners were brutalised during the flight: "It's true, but you know the ANC soldiers, they are brutes and we couldn't stop them beating the prisoners! We had no authority over them." Even during these moments, Lumumba kept his fighting spirit. At one point, while his torturers were having a break, he recognised Jonas Mukamba's voice. The former prime minister started talking to him. Mukamba later claimed that Lumumba nearly succeeded in persuading him not to hand him over to Tshombe.

Jack Dixon filmed some of the torture the soldiers inflicted during the flight and also captured the moment the prisoners got off the plane at Luano later that day. According to Captain Bob Watson, the film Dixon had developed in South Africa was lost. In fact when Watson tried to recover the film, he was simply told that it was totally "black". Someone probably warned the authorities in Katanga and South Africa, as they had obviously become very wary after the interview Dixon gave to the *Durban Sunday Tribune* about the eventful flight. Is the film still securely in the safes of the South African security services? In any case, the prisoners were in a very bad state on their arrival. Christian Souris, from *Pourquoi Pas?,* wrote: "It is a fact that the poor wretches are in a pitiful state. Tufts of Lumumba's beard and moustache have been torn out. His face is all swollen, and bears the marks of cuts from his glasses which his torturers smashed on his face."

It is nevertheless untrue that Zuzu and his men tortured Lumumba, Mpolo and Okito almost to death as the plane was landing. This argument was made by people like Tshombe who wanted to dodge responsibility for the events that occurred in Katanga. Captain Van der Meersch stated later that the prisoners were seriously abused during the flight, but that they were certainly not dying on their arrival. This was confirmed by Bob Watson, the DC-3's captain, who had good relations with the crew of the DC-4.[9]

At about 4 p.m. local time, the plane was approaching Katanga's capital. At the control tower in Luano, Elisabethville's airport, a man called Lambol was on duty. When Van der Meersch asked for permission to land, Lambol immediately informed the airport chief Guy Dedeken, whose office was one floor below. In turn, Dedeken sought advice from Gerard Lindekens, who was in charge of airport communications. A plane from Léopoldville, unannounced, in Katanga? Lambol requested further information from the pilot who gave him the plane's identification number, the flight's purpose and destination, and his name, and then declared: "We have some precious parcels on board!" Lindekens and Dedeken immediately realised what was going on: "OK, now we have to inform the intelligence services, we have to inform the minister of the interior, we have to inform the president."

President Tshombe's residence was located in the former offices of the Katanga Special Committee (CSK). François Thomas, Katanga's provincial secretary during the colonial era, answered the telephone. He then informed Tshombe's private secretary Bartelous, who was talking to Weber at the time. Dedeken also informed the *Gendarmerie*'s chief-of-staff Perrad who passed the information on to Munongo.[10]

In order to take the necessary safety measures in the zone reserved for Katanga's military aviation (Avikat), Major Perrad ordered Dedeken to keep the DC-4 in the air for a little while longer. The airport chief immediately blocked off the runway with barrels and fire engines. After consulting Munongo, Perrad called Camp Massart. He then ordered Captain Julien Gat to go to Luano with a squad of military police. The intelligence officer at the *Gendarmerie*, Joe Verdickt, was assigned to following the events at the airport *de visu*. Immediately aware of what the "parcels" were, he jumped into his jeep and rushed off, alone, to Luano. Even before Gat could assemble his men, he was summoned to the Interior Ministry. When he arrived at about 4.30 p.m., he found Munongo and several other of the regime's bigwigs gathered there: Victor Tignée, the minister's private secretary; Pius Sapwe, Elisabethville police commissioner; Raphaël Mumba, inspector general of Katangan police; Frans Verscheure, Mumba's adviser; and Jérome Disase, Munungo's brother-in-law and head of the Interior Ministry's security services.

Victor Tignée put Gat in the picture and gave him orders to take charge of the prisoners. As an interim measure, it had been decided to take the prisoners to the Brouwez residence, an empty house not far from the airport and about 8 kilometres from the centre of Elisabethville. Police commissioner Verscheure, who according to Gat was co-ordinating the whole operation, went immediately to see Brouwez, a white settler, to requisition his house. He then went to the house, and waited.[11] Police commissioner Georges Segers was to bring a detachment to Luano to reinforce Gat's soldiers. For his part, Gat hurried to Camp Massart to assemble his troops. The *Gendarmerie*'s military police battalion was made up of two companies of military police and the presidential guard. Officially Major Norbert Muke was in command of the battalion, and was also commander of Camp Massart. But, according to Brassinne, Captain Gat was the real boss. Muke did all the "palavers" with the soldiers and Gat took charge of all the other tasks. (This was actually the system within the *Gendarmerie*; in the subaltern ranks, Africans were officially in charge, but, according to Lieutenant Grandelet, the Belgian officers "effectively control everything that is not routine".) In practice, then the first battalion of military police was commanded by Lieutenant Michels and Lieutenant Grandelet; the second by Captain Gat, Lieutenant Blistein and Second Lieutenant Léva.[12]

Julien Gat and his battalion constituted one of the pillars of the regime. In July 1960, when soldiers from the Katangan army camps demanded the army be Africanised, and then opposed Belgian intervention and the secession, Gat's units stayed loyal to Tshombe. Ever since then, Captain Gat and his battalion were constantly called on to carry out special missions. Maintaining order in the Elisabethville shanty towns, repressing nationalist resistance, commando actions against supposed opponents, and putting down an incipient mutiny in the capital's police barracks – these were always the work of Captain Gat and his men. Gat was one of those involved in the operation to "neutralise" the Lebanese businessman Habib, who was suspected of backing the Balubakat. It was no accident that there was a direct telephone line between Gat and the Interior Ministry: urgent missions went straight to Gat, bypassing the *Gendarmerie*'s commander. "I had the confidence of the authorities", the officer boasted subsequently.

At Camp Massart, Gat requisitioned all available senior and junior European officers, as well as the two squads which were always on duty for urgent missions. Three jeeps, two lorries and an armoured vehicle transported the fifty men. Captain Gat later confirmed that he took some officers as reinforcements, because he feared that confrontation with Lumumba would revive nationalist sentiments in his troops: "I had a large proportion of Balubas from north Katanga in my unit at the time." The significant number of troops represented another safety measure: he did not know how many UN soldiers were at the airport, or whether they would intervene. Moreover, he was afraid that if Katangans with nationalistic leanings got wind of Lumumba's arrival, they "will come en masse to the plains as happened before when the visit of Sendwe [the Balubakat leader] was announced".[13]

The airport was crowded that day, as a Sabena aircraft from Brussels was about to land. The bustle on the military tarmac 250 metres away was followed with great interest from the terrace. At around 4.45 p.m., the full security arsenal had been deployed: Gat's MPs, Segers's police and Lieutenant Grandelet and Sergeant Son's Greyhound armoured vehicle. All obstacles had been cleared from the runway. Captain Van der Meersch was allowed to land. When the landing gear touched down at 4.50 p.m., the plane had just enough fuel for another ten minutes in the air. The prisoners' six hours of horror had ended. They had exactly seven more hours to live. On 19 January, the Tshombist newspaper *L'Essor du Katanga* reported the prisoners' journey and claimed they were safe and well in a Katangan prison: ". . . no brutality whatsoever has been inflicted on Lumumba and his co-detainees, although the former prime minister, who was convinced he would be killed, was talking to his guards in eloquent terms in an attempt to dissuade them."

From the Congolese capital, Commissioner Bomboko informed the UN that "rumours that they have been harmed have been denied" and the prisoners "are very well". The truth was very different, and much bloodier. At the root of what happened next was no blunder by a few drunken Katangans, but a methodical policy which had already been in place for months in Brussels, New York and Washington. Lumumba's transfer and liquidation were the culmination of a drama in which the war against the Congolese nationalists was the central theme of a stage-managed campaign. Colonel Vandewalle subsequently admitted: "the sequence of events on 17 January in Elisabethville would bring the matter of Lumumba's elimination to an end. First mooted in August 1960, it entered its final phase on 5 December."[14]

ARRIVAL IN KATANGA

This was the second time Lumumba had been taken to Katanga to be imprisoned. When he was sentenced following the unrest at the end of October 1959 in Stanleyville, the colonial authorities had him moved to Katanga's Jadotville prison. His transfer and imprisonment then represented the reaction of a moribund regime which not long afterwards had to free its prisoner and send him to Brussels, where he took part in the round-table negotiations at which the colonial power committed hara-kiri. His transfer in 1961 was no less symbolic – although this time it was a desperate action by Léopoldville's tottering regime which hoped thereby to ensure its survival. The connection between the two transfers may also be seen from another angle. Police Commissioner Georges Segers had arrested Lumumba in 1959, and after his trial Police Commissioner Frans Verscheure had taken him to Katanga. Segers and his police were involved in Lumumba's landing at Luano on 17 January 1961, and Verscheure went to the house where the prisoners would spend a few more horrific hours.[15]

At 5 p.m., the DC-4 was on the military tarmac near Avikat's hangar, its nose pointing towards the city, its tail facing the airport building 250 metres away. About 50 metres away, parallel to the DC-4, was the Greyhound armoured vehicle, its gun pointing at the plane. Nearer the aircraft was a jeep, with quite a long body, a CG6 type Minerva. The military policemen under Second Lieutenant Léva were deployed in a semi-circle, their backs to the plane, watching the airport building and closely following the movements of the Blue Berets who were observing the scene from a distance. About thirty policemen protected the entrance to the area. A crowd of people were on the tarmac awaiting the prisoners: about fifty military police with Gat and Michels; two squads of policemen headed by Segers; Police Inspector Mumba and Police Commissioner Sapwe; the Katangan ministers Munongo, Kibwe and Gabriel Kitenge; senior Belgian officers Weber, Vandewalle and Crèvecoeur; *Major* Smal and *Major* Verdickt; Captain Protin; and some civilians, Carlo Huyghé, Lindekens, Tignée and Betty Jacquemain. Gat ordered a group of soldiers to form a double line from the door of the plane to the jeep where the prisoners were to be taken.

According to his own account, Verdickt was standing at about 25–30 metres from the plane as the steps were rolled out and placed against the door. Kibwe, Kitenge, Sapwe and Mumba, as well as Gat, Protin and Michels, were among those waiting at the bottom of the steps. The first to appear at the door was an ANC soldier, who was over six feet tall. Gat recognised Zuzu, "a volitile character" who had been under his command before independence. But the first down the steps were the Léopoldville men, Commissioners Kazadi and Mukamba. Shortly afterwards the three prisoners were pushed onto the steps. They were tied together, but had sufficient freedom of movement to be able to walk down the steps by themselves. They were in an appalling state and, according to Major Perrad, "Lumumba is worse than the two others". Major Weber later described the prisoners as "a human mass. . . . their shirts torn, blood coming out of their mouths, their faces swollen, [they were] dazed, defeated, more dead than alive, that was the state in which 'the rare birds' were delivered to Katanga".[16]

Major Weber, Tshombe's military adviser, wanted to emphasise Léopoldville's responsibility in the dramatic course of events and make out that the prisoners were nearly dead when they arrived. Subsequently, Tshombe often repeated this argument. The secessionist leader, no stranger to deception, even embellished to prove his point. He claimed that Kazadi set an example on the tarmac, hitting the prisoners with his bare fists and showing all and sundry the hair pulled out of Lumumba's beard and moustache.[17] However, it was obvious that the prisoners had been brutally treated during the flight. Several witnesses saw blood on Lumumba's face and noticed that tufts of hair and part of his goatee had been pulled out. His khaki trousers were torn and his white shirt was in tatters and stained with blood.[18] As soon as they reached the ground, the prisoners were surrounded by soldiers and onlookers. *Major* Smal later testified that: "there was some bustling in the crowd, but no shouting". Everything happened very quickly. The three men were beaten with rifle butts. According to Brassinne, who takes up Gat's played-down explanations, "there was no beating, only some roughing up which at the time was nothing unusual coming from soldiers, be they Congolese or Katangan".[19]

According to Vandewalle, the three prisoners "disappeared from sight into a group of Europeans and Katangans who were gesticulating and yelling. There was shouting, arms waving, guns brandished."

As an intelligence officer Verdickt was quite used to observing events. He wrote a daily *Bulletin de renseignements* for the Bureau Conseil, Tshombe, Munongo, the *Gendarmerie*'s high command, the public prosecutor's office, the government intelligence services and the Union Minière's security services. Verdickt saw "a European NCO, dressed in the uniform of the Katangan *Gendarmerie*, hitting Lumumba who by now is hardly reacting to the blows". After the prisoners had left, the same NCO bragged about it to Verdickt and "anyone willing to listen". Verdickt added: "he punched Lumumba to avenge . . . the excesses in Thysville in July 1960 [the rape of white women]". He also said that someone shouted "Don't let them sully Katangan soil", and "Carry them, carry them!" This was Lieutenant Michels, according to Lieutenant Blistein. The prisoners were dragged, pulled and beaten all the way to the jeep. There, soldiers went on beating them with their rifle butts until, according to Lindekens, Captain Gat shouted: "That's enough now!" Only then were they thrown into the jeep "like sacks". Segers testified that a soldier took Lumumba by the neck and pushed him down onto the floor. Six military policemen sat at the sides with their feet on the prisoners. Lumumba had not uttered a word since he landed. According to Lieutenant Grandelet, he showed courage and dignity. The signal was given for the convoy to depart and it moved off, headed by a black car belonging to the intelligence services, and followed by Tignée and Huyghé's car, Gat's jeep, the jeep carrying the prisoners, Grandelet's armoured vehicle and, some distance behind, the car carrying Sapwe and Segers. In front of the airport building, a huge banner bore the words "Welcome to Free Katanga" in French, Swahili and English.[20]

The control tower was located a few dozen metres in front of the airport building and 225 metres from the military tarmac. At the foot of the tower was the UN guardroom, occupied since mid-August 1960 by a Swedish detachment. Six soldiers were there that day, under the command of NCO Lindgren who observed the scene – no doubt with binoculars – and wrote in his report:

[The soldiers] kicked them, beat them with their rifle butts and threw them onto the jeep. Four gendarmes then jumped into the jeep and sat down. At that point, one of the three prisoners screamed. The jeep then led the vehicle convoy and drove off along the runway towards the far end of the airfield where there was an opening in the fencing.

Only five to ten minutes had elapsed since the plane door was opened. But Lindgren's report – the only testimony from an outsider – corroborates the Belgo-Katangans' statements on a few important facts that can be established about Lumumba, Mpolo and Okito's rapid evacuation.

First: Katangan soldiers abused the prisoners under the eyes of their Belgian officers. At least one Belgian NCO took part in the beating. Second: the Belgian officers' complicity in what happened in Luano makes them, to some extent, accomplices to what happened to the prisoners next. The attitude of the officers during the public battering in Luano can only be interpreted as approval for worse brutality to come once the prisoners and their guards were away from public scrutiny. After the prisoners had been taken away, still standing on the tarmac Minister Kibwe said to Vandewalle: "It's a good thing you're here!" But no Belgian officer ordered a halt to the subsequent violence. And that they knew it would continue is proven by a conversation between Brassinne and Gat who, according to Brassinne, "is in charge of co-ordinating the operation". Only once did Brassinne ask a critical question, and the officer's answer is revealing: "Were they badly ill-treated at the airport?" "At the airport, no. There was no time."[21]

Soon afterwards, Pierre Davister, the journalist who covered Katanga's secession, filed his piece on Lumumba's arrival in Katanga in *Pourquoi Pas?* As usual, words came easily to him – and as usual, he was ready to protect the Katanga regime. In his view, responsibility for initiating the transfer lay with President Kasa Vubu and Mobutu, and no one else. Everyone present when the prisoners landed could see that they had been "visibly harmed" during the journey. If Davister is to be believed, even on Katangan soil the fate of the three nationalist leaders lay in Léopoldville's hands:

> Mobutu's soldiers put on a great show of raining blows on Lumumba with rifle butts. It was probably all about impressing people, and people, in this case the airport staff, were suitably impressed. The prisoners were literally thrown into the jeep and the same ANC soldiers stamped with both feet on Lumumba, who was lying in the vehicle, to demonstrate yet again that he was nothing more than a mere prisoner whom it is appropriate to handle harshly and to thrash frequently.

The journalist hoped that the transfer would bring political dividends for Katanga which, by accepting Lumumba, had demonstrated that it had taken over anti-Lumumbist operations.[22]

AT THE BROUWEZ HOUSE

During the rainy season, the sun rises at about 5.30 a.m. and sets at around 6.45 p.m. So it was still daylight when the convoy arrived at approximately 5.30 p.m. at the Brouwez house, 3.5 kilometres from the airport along the old road from Luano to Elisabethville, through overgrown savannah, past L'Etrier riding school and Le Pondoir farm where Lucien Brouwez, a poultry farmer, lived with his family. They were about to move to a new, as yet sparsely furnished house a few hundred metres away and it was here that the prisoners were to be lodged. The police had closed all access routes; nobody could see the convoy, except perhaps the people living in the few mud and straw cottages half-way between the airport and the house. The armed forces knew the area well: the president's mounted guard used the area for training and units of the guard often visited the Verlaines who ran L'Etrier.[23]

The Brouwez house was built in classical colonial style, a more or less square bungalow with a façade some 10 metres long, fronted by a veranda or *barza* with a corrugated iron roof. A french window opened from the *barza* into a living room from which one door led to the kitchen and another, on the left, opened into a corridor off which were four rooms: two bedrooms, a bathroom and, at the end, the toilet. On reaching the veranda, Captain Gat noticed that the french window was open. Verscheure was in the house already as he had not gone to Luano but had come straight there. Gat did not go into the house at once: "I did a recce first. A tour of the house, followed by the immediate surroundings, in order to establish a plan in case there was a massive demonstration. For as soon as the news was known in town, we had to be able to withstand a possible attempt to free the prisoners."

After his inspection, Gat came across Verscheure. They agreed on how to organise the guard because, as Gat put it: "I couldn't hold back my reserves who had other missions to carry out, like maintaining law and order in the native areas."[24] By this time, apart from the prisoners, there were six or seven Katangan military policemen and six Belgians (Gat, Verscheure, Grandelet, Son, Tignée and Huyghé) inside the house or around it. Shortly afterwards Sapwe, Mumba and Commissioner Segers arrived with two or three policemen, followed at about 6 p.m. by Lieutenant Michels and second Lieutenant Léva with a squad of military policemen. The task of guarding the house fell to the soldiers, while the police kept an eye on the nearby roads. Grandelet settled himself down on the *barza*. His armoured vehicle was parked in front of the house, its gun pointing towards the town.

Léva, who had organised the defence of the house, came into the living room where the prisoners were sitting on the cement floor, hands tied behind their backs. Léva saw that the rope tying Mpolo and Okito together "was cutting deeply into their flesh. I untied the two prisoners but one of them insulted me, saying 'filthy White!' so I punched him in the face." Police Inspector Raphaël

Mumba (who later became a lawyer at the Appeal Court in Brussels) stated that Lumumba was "pretty beaten up" and dressed in "a torn white vest", which implies that he had been manhandled again inside the house. Captain Gat said he could not confirm this since he went to inspect the surroundings as soon as he got to the improvised jail. Only after finishing this task did he go into the living room "where the prisoners were being guarded by my squad commanders and other men". Colonel Vandewalle, however, does not beat about the bush: he admits the prisoners were tortured again soon after arriving at the Brouwez house.[25]

Gat locked the three men in the bathroom, and put the key in his pocket. Later, he gave contradictory reasons for what he did, saying both that he wanted to stop the soldiers beating the prisoners, and that he wanted to prevent Lumumba from trying to persuade the soldiers to set him free. Given the large number of Belgian officers present, the second reason does not hold water. The first one is no better, and in the light of what happened has to be dismissed as a misplaced and *post factum* humanitarian concern. The explanation of Huyghé, deputy private secretary at the Defence Ministry, is more convincing. Any attempt to liberate the prisoners from outside had to be avoided at all costs: "[W]e feared the arrival of the Ghanaians and also of the crowd . . . the people might come."[26]

According to Brassinne, Julien Gat was in charge of "all operational measures". Captain Gat, Lieutenant Michels, Sergeant Son, Major Muke and Warrant Officer Sakela were involved in all the events of the evening; Grandelet and Léva went back to Camp Massart. Gat subsequently told Brassinne: "Nobody [had] access to the prisoners unless I [said] so, this [was] to avoid them being ill-treated by the soldiers or any visitors." What visitors? Between 5.30 and 7 p.m., Ministers Munongo, Kibwe and Kitenge, then Munongo alone; later, Grandelet and Son; and, at about 6.45, Tshombe. Gat and Huyghé were present during the Katangans' visits. At about 7 p.m., Verscheure, who had gone to Tshombe's residence, arrived with Tignée. Later in the evening, Commissioner Segers came, as well as Warrant Officer Rougefort whose men relieved Michels's detachment. Tshombe, Munongo and Kibwe paid another visit to the prisoners who were subjected to serious brutality during one or several of these visits.

The authors of *Qui a tué Patrice Lumumba?* talk in veiled terms of "pretty rough visits" to disguise the crimes committed under the responsibility of a Belgian officer, Captain Gat. A string of declarations from witnesses and observers all point in the same direction, however. Vandewalle writes: "Tshombe had visited Lumumba who had asked for his protection. Other ministers followed. Each appearance prompted new violence from the guards and perhaps from Their Excellencies."[27] In his dissertation, Brassinne concludes: "At least a dozen visitors saw the prisoners and it is obvious that they were ill-treated in their presence by the military policemen." According to Son, "the prisoners had completely had it." He saw their swollen faces, nasty bruises on their bodies, but no sign of open wounds. Lumumba no longer had shoes on. At about 7 o'clock, Verscheure, accompanied by Tignée, came to the house for the second time. He noticed that the prisoners were "tied up in a bundle, their faces swollen by the blows . . . they were no longer talking, they were inert."

Segers went to see Lumumba in the bathroom. The commissioner had played a part in repressing the anti-colonial demonstrations in Stanleyville in 1959 and in Lumumba's arrest at that time. Segers told Brassinne: "He knew me, I knew him, and of course, I didn't like him at all." He only stayed a few minutes with Lumumba, without even speaking to him. He was waiting for the former prime minister to take the initiative, but in vain: ". . . he didn't complain . . . he didn't say anything to me!" Lumumba said to a soldier: "I'm thirsty." The soldier went away and came back with a bucket half full of water which he threw in his face, saying, "Here, have a drink!" Segers added: "The soldiers were excited and I found that really unpleasant. . . . I stayed deliberately because my presence restrained their brutality a bit." He also stated that during a short period when he had gone outside to talk to Sapwe Lumumba "had been hit very hard": " I didn't see the blows being struck but Patrice Lumumba seemed to have been ill-treated." When Lieutenant Grandelet visited the prisoners in the bathroom, Lumumba was sitting on the floor with his hands tied behind his back. The attitude of the badly beaten prisoner impressed him: "I remember being struck by his dignity." Vandewalle learned later that at one point Lumumba banged his head badly on the bidet on receiving a particularly hard blow.[28] When Huyghé went to see the prisoners, Lumumba "was groaning weakly, bent double". When Kibwe told him he was about to die, Lumumba apparently said: "At this stage, it doesn't matter!" and "No problem!"[29]

Bartelous, Tshombe's private secretary, had not the slightest doubt that Tshombe and his ministers went to see the prisoners at least once, and that "they each hit Lumumba once or several times". For his part, Warrant Officer Rougefort stated that, during the visit Tshombe and his ministers made at about 9.30 p.m., the prisoners were taken to the living room where soldiers and ministers alike all "began hitting him". The soldiers went on beating them after most of the ministers had gone; only Tshombe, Munongo, Sapwe and Kimba stayed to confer with Captain Gat.[30]

Commissioner Verscheure is one of the few to have written a complete account of his own, rather than are prompted by Brassinne's ambiguous presence. Verscheure was not directly in charge of guarding the prisoners and so shows less of a tendency to embellish the facts. He knew what he was talking about: he went to the Brouwez house several times that evening. His account dated February 1961 states that "Lumumba [was] dazed from the beatings" when Tshombe, Munongo and Kibwe visited him. Sitting on the floor, he silently listened to Kibwe: "Lumumba, I told you at the round-table conference in Brussels that if you set foot in Katanga, you would piss blood and your head would roll at my feet. Tomorrow we will glorify our men who died fighting the Balubas you unleashed against us. You will be dead by then." Verscheure saw that "bits of wood had been stuck under [the prisoners'] toenails and fingernails."

It was not only the Katangan ministers who abused the prisoners, the guards did too. Colonel Vandewalle is quite clear on this matter, and his observation is important. Vandewalle admits that the torturers were either Belgians or men under the command of Belgian officers, but for the guards too Lumumba's physical well-being was clearly not a priority. Lieutenant Grandelet subsequently stated that at the Brouwez house Michels gave him an order. "If Swedish or Moroccan troops from the UN arrive, he is ordered to shoot them on sight . . . if a disaster happens, better to kill Lumumba than have him freed by the UN!" Elsewhere he says that Lieutenant Michels ordered him to "finish Lumumba off" if he attempted to escape.[31]

"NO BLOOD ON OUR HANDS"

The authors of *Qui a tué Patrice Lumumba?* summarise the events as follows: "One thing is certain: Katanga's government was not prepared, so it was bound to react hastily and to improvise without consulting its Belgian political advisers. It is regrettable, for things could have turned out differently. . . ." Here Brassinne and Kestergat follow the line of Colonel Vandewalle who, to play down his own role, wrote in 1975:

> During the evening, without any of their European advisers, Tshombe, Kimba, Kibwe, Samalenge, later joined by Munongo, conferred together. They decided to get rid of him. . . . What were their motives? Revenge, tribal hatred, the need to erase all trace of the violence inflicted? . . . They did not assess the political consequences of their collective behaviour.[32]

However, the events actually unfolded quite differently. Soon after 5 p.m., Vandewalle and Smal were at the *Gendarmerie*'s headquarters where they met the Belgian senior officers Weber, Perrad and, a little later, Verdickt.[33] Verdickt told them what Munongo had said to him at the airport about the prisoners' fate: "It will be over tonight!" Brassinne's thesis makes few references to discussions among the Belgian officials about Lumumba's last hours. This should come as no surprise. Brassinne, who himself was present at one of these meetings, hardly broached the subject with his witnesses. He admits, however, that when they met at the army headquarters, Vandewalle said he was convinced Lumumba's execution "was only a matter of hours away". Verdickt was equally "pessimistic". But, writes Brassinne, the other officers were hoping Tshombe would change his mind about the execution. Had he not agreed with his Belgian advisers who had unanimously considered the transfer of the political prisoners inopportune? At that point, according to Brassinne, they still did not know Tshombe had agreed in principle to the transfer behind their backs. Whatever the truth, no initiative was taken at army headquarters to save the lives of Lumumba, Mpolo and Okito.

After the meeting, Vandewalle, Weber and Smal went to see Professor Clémens who lived on the third floor of the Immokat building, in the centre of the city. Present at this emergency meeting were Professor Clémens himself, officers Vandewalle, Weber and Smal, and the two Belgian assistants to the Bureau Conseil, Grosjean and Brassinne. It was about 7 p.m., as Brassinne recalls, when Weber opened the meeting with these words: "We wanted him, we've got him . . . and now we are in the shit!" Brassinne describes the general mood as pessimistic: "Nobody had any illusions about what was in store for the prisoners." Brassinne, despite his presence there, says nothing about what was decided at the meeting; he only mentions that nothing was done to save the prisoners. Brassinne and Kestergat wriggle out of it in the following way: "What could be done but wait for the results of the discussions the Katangan government was about to have at the president's residence?" According to the two authors, the Belgian top brass, including the usually enterprising Colonel Vandewalle, simply went home, while their subordinates organised the assassination on orders from the Katangan government.

Again according to Brassinne and Kestergat, the Belgian top brass did not have sufficient authority to intervene successfully and speedily. Yet they could see for themselves that Captain Gat had taken charge of the prisoners and left the airport with them. Brassinne, it will be recalled, describes Vandewalle as the *Gendarmerie*'s "hidden boss". It is clear that had the colonel ordered Captain Gat and the other Belgian officers to save Lumumba's life, events would have taken a different course.

The real reason for Belgian passivity, resignation or tacit agreement with the evolution of the tragedy was not practical but political. Vandewalle and Weber knew that Lumumba's physical integrity was not a priority for Brussels. With Lumumba's transfer, it had achieved its main objective: preventing Lumumba's political come-back and saving the Léopoldville regime. This was the real reason behind African Affairs Minister d'Aspremont Lynden's 16 January telegram (p. 90). But this telegram put Elisabethville in a very difficult position. Politically, Lumumba's presence was a time bomb planted on the regime. To kill him, to hold him without trial, to "try" him – any of these solutions would be enormously damaging politically for the copper province. Whatever the decision, Katanga was bound to pay the price for Brussels' wishes. As Police Commissioner George Segers said to Sapwe at the Brouwez house, "they are walking on eggshells".[34]

Smal remembered taking a short walk with Vandewalle that evening. The former intelligence boss used his former assistant as a sounding board, thinking aloud about the least damaging solution for Katanga: "His idea was to put

Lumumba on trial for the crimes he had committed. . . . We would have followed traditional Congolese customs. The court would have been made up of the Congo's traditional chiefs . . . and the verdict would not have been in doubt. . . ." The "hidden boss" faced a huge dilemma. Any attempt to give the murder an appearance of legality would cause worldwide indignation and unleash incalculable consequences. In a telegram to Washington, the US consul in Elisabethville, William Canup, described the situation on the day after the transfer by saying there could be such international pressure on Tshombe that it would be "impossible" to keep Lumumba alive and that there was a "certain chance" of "suicide or other mishap".

After Lumumba's transfer, it became clear that keeping the former prime minister any longer would have been very detrimental to the Katangan regime. A bulletin dated 23 January mentioned that the UN was worried about a wave of nationalist sentiment. At Luena, Moroccan Blue Berets had been distributing arms to nationalist rebels. At Lubudi, the Blue Berets had called on Katangan soldiers to break with Tshombe, their officers openly declaring their support for "Lumumba and the Balubakat". And at Jadotville, shooting almost broke out between the *Gendarmerie* and Moroccan Blue Berets who had taken some nationalists under their protection.[35]

Police Commissioner Frans Verscheure crudely explains in his secret report that killing Lumumba was the only solution:

This execution had to take place, since none of the crimes committed by Lumumba could, without proof, and especially without any legal basis, serve as a pretext for a regular conviction. Lumumba had to disappear . . . Lumumba alive, even in jail, represented too serious a danger. He had the ears of the masses, except in Upper Katanga, and would have continued to have a real majority in the Parliament.

On the evening of 17 January, after some thought, Vandewalle and company decided not to reprieve Lumumba; thus they gave the green light for his death while hoping that the storm would quickly abate. In the medium term, the death of the nationalist leader could be advantageous. Weber admitted as much to Brassinne in 1987. According to him, the assassination was a matter the "Bantus have sorted out between themselves". But Weber "realised that, for the European advisers, Lumumba was at the centre of the post-independence chaos in the Congo and that his 'neutralisation' would be good for the future."[36]

D'Aspremont Lynden's telegram putting Lumumba's fate in Tshombe's hands limited the political freedom of movement of the Belgo-Katanga lobby. While their subordinates played a crucial role in transferring the prisoners to the Brouwez house, in the assassination, in fabricating their attempted escape, and ultimately in physically getting rid of the bodies, Vandewalle and Clémens, for their part, tried to limit the political fallout. Pierre Adam, a military chaplain, clearly expressed Belgian concerns when, on the evening of 17 January, he sent the following telephone message to Major Weber at the *Gendarmerie*: "Above all, no blood on our hands!"[37] The chaplain knew how Lumumba's detention would end. The soldier-priest simply looked the other way and waited until everything was over. Amen! The senior Belgian officers did not intervene to save the three prisoners.

Is it plausible that during the infamous evening of 17 January, neither Vandewalle, nor Weber, nor Perrad, nor Smal, nor Verdickt, nor Clémens, nor Brassinne, nor Grosjean had any contact with the outside world? This is what the authors of *Qui a tué Patrice Lumumba?* claim. Although there is no irrefutable proof, this is highly improbable. Did the G2 intelligence officer Verdickt really not contact anybody while he was at the *Gendarmerie* headquarters writing his *Bulletin quotidien de renseignements*, which was based on information given him by the police, the *Gendarmerie*, various informants and Renard, chief of Katangan intelligence, the SCCR? Did Perrad not consult anybody when, after having dinner at his home, he went back to the *Gendarmerie* headquarters for the three hours from 7 to 10 p.m.? He said he did not remember exactly whom he telephoned on that particular evening. But in a footnote recounting a conversation he had with Perrad, Brassinne reveals that on the evening of 17 January the Major "was informed of what was afoot".[38]

Is it conceivable that the senior Belgian representatives in the entourage of Tshombe and Munongo did not contact Vandewalle, Weber or their colleagues? Vandewalle and his men were not at the Katangan ministers' meeting which took place at Tshombe's residence, a few minutes away from the Immokat building (see p. 114–15 below). This was out of character. The regime usually looked to the Belgians to manage things. This was clear at Luano, soon after the prisoners left, when Kibwe said to Vandewalle: "It's a good thing you're here!" The *Gendarmerie*'s "hidden boss" had indeed taken the initiative on one matter. Captain Protin, commanding officer at the *Gendarmerie* in Mitwaba, in the centre of Katanga, informed him that the Ministry of the Interior was considering a temporary transfer of the prisoners there. The idea of receiving Lumumba did not exactly enthuse Protin, who was devoting all his efforts to controlling the 3,000 pro-Lumumbist workers in the mining company Sermikat. Vandewalle advised him to leave for Mitwaba immediately. Protin understood that this was the end of the matter for him. Later that same evening, Vandewalle and the other Belgians stayed away from Tshombe's residence. If what Brassinne says is true, they were all suddenly seized by an attack of lethargy. But were not Weber, Vandewalle and Clémens part of the president's circle of advisers?

As will be detailed later, the president conferred with Bartelous, his private secretary, before going back to join the other Katangan ministers. It is unlikely Bartelous's advice was entirely his own. Créner, the consul general, has admitted that he discussed the arrival of the "parcels" in Katanga with Bartelous on the evening of 17 January. The diplomat Vanden Bloock and Créner talked about it at least twice during the evening, although the consul general was "generally kept out of important conversations": "The 'good man' is not much liked in Katangan circles", according to Brassinne and Kestergat. Their conservative opinions and narrow minds clashed with what they called "his timid convictions" and "excessive caution".[39] Créner was a good diplomat in peace time, but utterly unsuited to the needs of the Congo at that time. The siege of Fortress Katanga relegated people like Créner to the sidelines and brought military men like Vandewalle and Weber to the fore. If the consul general was consulted on the final decisions to be taken in the war against the Congolese leaders, it is absolutely certain that the Belgo-Katangan regime's senior officers and advisers were consulted too.

In Brassinne's dissertation, only two pages are devoted to the meetings at the *Gendarmerie*'s headquarters and the Immokat building. Yet these are key moments in assessing the responsibility of the Eyskens government representatives in the crime committed that evening. The Belgians failed to take any action to prevent their unanimous prediction of a violent death for Lumumba, Mpolo and Okito. They refused to save the prisoners' lives and tried to avoid doing anything that might implicate Belgium in this death foretold. But while keeping their distance, they monitored the situation. In that sense, they would be guilty of "non-assistance" as defined today in the Belgian Penal Code, Art. 422b: "the person who fails to help or arrange help for someone exposed to serious danger, either when he has himself recognised that person's situation, or when the situation has been described by those who seek his intervention".

However, the senior officers' responsibility goes further than non-assistance to a person in danger. Brassinne writes, without drawing any conclusions, that: "Vandewalle knew that Huyghé from the Defence Department was in charge of the Katangan guards' supplies." Elsewhere, Perrad is said to have been kept in touch with the main developments.[40] While Lumumba and his companions were struggling to stay alive, Vandewalle, Perrad and company were giving their subordinates *carte blanche*. Not only did they look the other way, but by doing so, they allowed their subordinates on official duty to finish off the task. Bartelous has admitted he had been informed of the dramatic course of events before he arrived at his office on the morning of 18 January. After the assassination, Verscheure for his part telephoned the Interior Ministry immediately. He did not ask to speak to Munongo who was at the scene of the crime, but probably to Tignée, the minister's private secretary. A few hours later, on 18 January, Huyghé was summoned by Vandewalle. When he rangs the bell at 6 o'clock in the morning, Smal opened the door. Vandewalle took notes of the conversation. As for Gat, he went to report to Perrad.[41]

The secessionist state's Belgian leaders did not stop the developments of that night. The telegram from the minister of African affairs did not give the Bureau

Conseil much freedom to act otherwise but – and this is important – the Bureau was quite happy about that. Lumumba's liquidation was a necessity or rather a necessary evil. The Bureau Conseil shared Marlière's view that the assassination was "a public health measure". And of course Major Weber had admitted that the assassination would be a good thing for the future of Katanga. Again, complicity went further than a case of non-assistance to persons in danger. Brassinne's silence on these meetings indicates that nobody went out of their way to save Lumumba, Mpolo and Okito. It is too easy to focus solely on the actual executioners; on Gat, Michels, Verscheure and Son. The Bureau Conseil members were themselves accomplices in acts "intended to cause death", according to Article 393 of the Belgian Penal Code. If, as in this case, a homicide is committed "with premeditation", it is a murder according to Article 394. An indictment of complicity is, by extension, applicable to Jules Loos, to Ministers Pierre Wigny and Harold d'Aspremont Lynden and to Prime Minister Gaston Eyskens, those responsible for Belgian government policies at that time.

The United Nations presented no obstacle for either the Katangan regime or its core of Belgian advisers who could do away with their "parcels" without being disturbed. Lindgren, head of the Swedish Blue Berets at the airport, had informed his bosses. The head of the UN in Katanga, the New Zealander Ian Berendsen, said the Blue Berets informed him of the prisoners' arrival "barely one or two hours" after the DC-4 landed, that is between 6 and 7 p.m. Lindgren minuted the landing. This document was telegraphed to New York, and Lindgren and his men were questioned by Berendsen himself. Lindgren's report made it quite clear that the prisoners were in danger. "They were pushed 10 to 15 metres to a jeep. As they were pushed, they were hit with rifle butts in a way the Swedish soldiers described as violent and even brutal." Berendsen subsequently declared that he only read the report the next day, after his conversation with Tshombe on 18 January. However, it seems clear that he knew that same evening that the three prisoners had landed and that their situation was serious. Berendsen understood the Katangans well and knew – or should have known – that the prisoners were in mortal danger.

The head of the UN in Katanga made no attempt to put any pressure on Tshombe or the *Gendarmerie*'s commander. Berendsen, a Belgo-Katangan in a UN uniform, stuck to the UN agreement of August and October 1960 on the arrival of the Blue Berets in Katanga and the setting up of "neutral zones". Katanga was treated as an independent state, which meant it could count on the UN forces' help. Berendsen did not speak to Tshombe until 18 January when, according to a UN report, he met the president "to discuss something else . . . but took the opportunity to discuss the news, now public, of the transfer of M. Lumumba and his two fellow prisoners to Katanga".[42] The UN reaction was, therefore, no different from that of the Belgian officials in Katanga: they turned a blind eye while Lumumba, Mpolo and Okito were tortured and assassinated.

Given the policies followed for months by their bosses in Brussels and New York, Clémens, Vandewalle and Berendsen were unanimous in saying that they did not have the political freedom of movement to prevent the crime.

TSHOMBE CELEBRATES

Moïse Tshombe, the president of the copper state, was not at the airport when the DC-4 landed with its precious "parcels" on board. Major Perrad had tried to contact him at his residence, but without success, as the president was at the Palace Cinema watching *Liberté*, a film by the Swiss Moral Rearmament Association. His private secretary Jacques Bartelous finally reached him by telephone and informed him of Lumumba's arrival. Tshombe hurried to his office where he arrived at about 5 p.m. By 5.45, a few ministers were also there. Brassinne describes the activities there on that day as "a Katangan cabinet meeting" which lasted "several hours". The subject of conversation was "the thorny issue of what to do with the prisoners".[43]

What Brassinne calls a cabinet meeting was in fact the disorganised to-ings and fro-ings of the Katangan dignitaries trying to decide when and by whom Lumumba should be killed. Any alternative was unacceptable. Releasing Lumumba was ruled out. D'Aspremont Lynden had been firm: Lumumba must go to Katanga. But he could not be kept in prison indefinitely, as that would only increase international pressure on the regime. The United Nations would be compelled to take action. In the worst-case scenario, UN forces in the Congo would splinter and the United Nations would have to remove their protective hand from Elisabethville. Furthermore, imprisonment made little sense. Keeping Lumumba in jail as a bargaining chip to achieve a political solution to the Congo crisis would mean giving him a role in a new Congo. This is precisely why it was ruled out by the Katangans and their Belgian paymasters who had been doing their best to erase all traces of Congolese nationalism. Executing Lumumba after a show trial was not considered a valid alternative either. How would the international community react if a government "tribunal" condemned Lumumba to death, a suggestion made by Colonel Vandewalle at one point?

Soon after 5 p.m., Tshombe and Bartelous were talking the problem through in the president's office. Were any other Belgians present, or had any others been consulted, by telephone perhaps? Probably, because Bartelous told Brassinne that as their first response "the European advisers" suggested "sending Lumumba back to Léopoldville". François Thomas was not at the airport, so does that mean he was at Tshombe's residence? Bartelous was with Major Weber when the news of Lumumba's transfer reached him. The two men discussed the situation before Weber went to Luano to await Lumumba's arrival. Bartelous says that, during his conversation with Tshombe, the possibility of

keeping Lumumba in prison was ruled out because of the anticipated international reaction. Brassinne and Kestergat recount: "Tshombe hesitates. He
weighs the pros and cons. . . . The president confers with Bartelous for a long
time, then tells him his final decision. Tomorrow at dawn, a Katangan plane
will take the three prisoners to Bakwanga." This was evidently the most elegant
solution for Katanga: certain death for Lumumba, and no blood on the
Tshombists' hands.

After the meeting, the private secretary Bartelous went home while the
Katangan ministers arrived at the presidential residence. Brassinne and Kestergat
understand that this plan compromised Bartelous as well as the other Belgian
officials, but they attempt to mislead their readers:

> Isn't that [Bakwanga] where Léopoldville wanted to send him in full knowl-
> edge of the facts? Could he [Tshombe] be blamed for sending the prisoners
> where they were meant to go? . . . After all, won't Lumumba have a chance
> of surviving in Bakwanga, given that the UN will be informed of his arrival
> and could easily intercept him in Kalonji's territory where there is a Ghanaian
> garrison?[44]

The gathering at the presidential residence was not a regular meeting where
"rational" decisions were taken. D'Aspremont Lynden's telegram had set the
tone; eliminating Lumumba was the only way out. The telegram from Brussels
which ruled out returning the three prisoners to Léopoldville; the conversation
between Bartelous and Tshombe and the provisional solution of getting
Lumumba killed by Kalonji; the behaviour of the Belgian officers at Luano, the
attitude at the army headquarters and finally at the Brouwez house: everything
leads us to believe there was a Belgo-Katangan consensus on a rapid liquidation
of the Congolese leader. Verscheure's report mentions that Kibwe told
Lumumba at about 7 p.m. that he would soon be dead, i.e. even before the so-
called "cabinet meeting" where a "verdict" on the prisoners was supposedly
given. In *Qui a tué Patrice Lumumba?*, Brassinne and Kestergat's account of this celebrated cabinet meeting is entitled "Fever and whisky at Tshombe's". In any case,
the image of a drinking session gives a better idea of what really happened that
evening than the term "cabinet meeting".

At about 5.45 p.m., as the "cabinet meeting" began, the regime's most important figures – Ministers Munongo, Kibwe and also Kitenge – were on their way to
the Brouwez house, and Kazadi, Mukamba and Zuzu were at Tshombe's residence.
Later in the evening, the delegation from Léopoldville went to have dinner with
Cléophas Mukeba, one of the Katangan ministers.[45] A strange cabinet meeting:
several top ministers were absent; members of a regime Elisabethville did not trust
were present; alcohol was flowing freely; and ministers and the president came and
went . . . to have dinner or go and ill-treat the prisoners. At 6.30 p.m. Tshombe
himself, accompanied by Munongo and Kibwe, paid the prisoners a short visit.

The Katangan ministers did likewise at around 9.30 p.m. Meantime, at Tshombe's, people came and went, talking and . . . drinking.

Tshombe's Belgian secretary Servais was at the residence. She subsequently stated that Tshombe, Kibwe and Kimba drank a bottle of whisky each that evening. Breuer, the Belgian butler, said they drank all night long and that excitement and voices rose as the hours passed. He also noticed that Tshombe and his ministers came back late in the night, after the crime was committed. He told Weber they were "completely drunk". Bartelous, the private secretary, was also categorical: "the ministers are drinking, some of them are drunk".[46]

Brassinne says that the ministers met without a single European present. The origin of this rash assertion is the testimony of Verscheure[47] who was not involved in guarding the prisoners and spoke openly of Lumumba's treatment. But it was in his interest to present the deliberations at Tshombe's as a purely Katangan affair. He admitted he went to the president's residence at least three times: before and after Tshombe and Munongo's visit to Brouwez and later in the evening, after a telephone call from Tshombe. Later, his role in the prisoners' assassination would be central: this is exactly why Verscheure took pains to present himself as executing a proper verdict taken by the Katangan cabinet ministers; and why Verscheure put the entire significance of the discussions firmly at the Katangans' door; and why Verscheure and Gat – who played an equally crucial role in the execution – are the only ones to claim that on the evening of 17 January the Katangan ministers were not under the influence of alcohol. However, while awkwardly trying to exonerate himself, Verscheure reveals that the truth was quite different. He said that in the garden after dinner, between 8 and 9 p.m., he was present at a conversation between Kazadi, Tshombe and Munongo. Kazadi suggested "taking a hand or an ear from each prisoner to Léopoldville to prove they are dead". To this Verscheure said [T]hat would be stupid. If the Katangans did that, the whole world would be against them." According to Verscheure, Tshombe agreed.

Everybody gradually left the residence. Kazadi and Mukamba went to a restaurant. Lieutenant Zuzu was taken to the Grand Hôtel Léopold II in the centre of the city. When at about 9.15 p.m. Tshombe, Munongo, Kibwe, Kimba, Kitenge and Verscheure went back to the Brouwez house, the decision to assassinate the prisoners had already been taken. Not a single concrete element in all the testimonies gathered by Brassinne confirms the argument defended in "Enquête" and *Qui a tué Patrice Lumumba?* that Tshombe "had his back to the wall. In the next few hours, he will have to take crucial decisions and go to great pains to try and assuage those who hate Lumumba". There is no evidence that any alternatives were seriously considered and that Tshombe finally had to "capitulate" to the "hawks" Kibwe and Munongo, who wanted to shoot the prisoners straight away. Brassinne tries to explain this attempt to make Tshombe "the dove" by referring to the traditional difference between the Bayeke, "conquerors who lived from plunder and *razzias*" (Munongo was a Muyeke), and the "Florentine" Balunda (Tshombe is a Mulunda).[48] But the only people to claim Tshombe suggested keeping Lumumba in jail pending his 'trial' (except for Tshombe himself) were Paul Perrad, Tshombe's daughter Marie, Mario Spandre and Professor Clémens. The latter three referred back to statements made by Tshombe himself. Brassinne did not ask Perrad to identify his source. Perhaps this was Tshombe too. The rest of his account is curiously similar to Tshombe's version of Lumumba's end.

Tshombe's statements served only one purpose: to pin responsibility for the crime on others. Everything points to Munongo and Mumba's assertions being correct: everyone agreed to massacre the prisoners that same evening. It was not a concrete decision taken after a lot of discussion, but a solution that slowly emerged during the course of the evening and became the only way out to which nobody could see any obstacle. The decision was not taken during a formal cabinet meeting, as claimed by Tshombe (who likes to present himself as opposing the crime), and as described by Brassinne and Kestergat (who protect Brussels and the Belgo-Katangan lobby). Everybody, Blacks and Whites alike, unanimously accepted the principle that Lumumba must disappear. This included the *éminences grises* who stayed discreetly in the background to avoid "blood on their hands" but who meanwhile gave clear signals to the Katangan ministers and their Belgian subordinates in the army and the police. One thing was certain: Lumumba must not be allowed to escape. The option of a risky transfer to Bakwanga was quite rapidly dismissed, since the Ghanaian Blue Berets there made the option of an execution in Kalonji's territory hard to carry out. It was obvious that the affair had to be dealt with in Katanga.

Several of the people involved have suggested that the final decision to assassinate the prisoners that same evening was taken in a moment of euphoria: it was late in the evening, and the alcohol had already had its effect. Bartelous said that there were "many libations at Tshombe's residence to celebrate Lumumba's arrival". And moreover: "the ministers had not made the decision to kill Lumumba, but, being drunk, they made the mistake of going to visit him". There is no doubt that the solution of a quick liquidation became inevitable as the evening wore on, and no one can prove anyone was against it. Whatever the truth, at some stage the decision was taken and it was agreed that Verscheure would organise the execution. To give the crime some semblance of legality, Brassinne and Kestergat announce that "the Katangan government" "condemned Lumumba, Mpolo, and Okito to death".[49]

BACK AT THE BROUWEZ HOUSE

In *Qui a tué Patrice Lumumba?*, the ministers' last visit to Lumumba is described thus:

"Not long before 9.30 p.m., the oppressive calm reigning at the Brouwez house is disturbed by the arrival of big cars crammed with people."[50] The calm did not extend to the prisoners who, as stated above, were being seriously ill-treated; the arrival of Tshombe, Munongo, Kibwe, Kimba, Samalenge, Kitenge and Verscheure gave them no respite. Two soldiers brought the prisoners into the living room where the ministers were waiting, one more drunk than the other. The Belgians Gat, Son, Léva, Rougefort and Verscheure were also there at one point or another. According to Rougefort, the Katangans immediately began hitting the prisoners. Bartelous said that all the Katangan ministers beat Lumumba, adding that Samalenge "brags about it the following day". The president's private secretary noticed next day that Tshombe's suit was "stained with blood". The butler at the residence told Bartelous that when the president came back late in the night, he was "covered in blood".

Brassinne only gives a footnote to Captain Xavier Blistein's testimony. Yet his statements are interesting from several angles. On 17 January, he was on leave in Brussels and, therefore, not involved in the prisoners' imprisonment and death. This could be why he was less tempted to embellish the facts. As an officer in the military police's second company, he was certainly one of the Belgians best informed about the events at the Brouwez house. He knew all the officers involved in the drama, and took over command of the second company after Captain Gat's departure. Blistein's testimony does not try to conceal the Belgian officers' responsibility, and his comments on his colleagues' actions and personalities show a sense of proportion and objectivity. Hence, he labels Warrant Officer Rougefort, a Belgian mercenary who enlisted in the *Gendarmerie* in Katanga, as "simple-minded".

According to Blistein, Lumumba was almost beaten to death by Michels, Rougefort and the Katangan soldiers. Rougefort injured his hand beating the prisoners. Lumumba was "a human wreck". According to the officers present he was "little more than a corpse" and, says Blistein, probably "dying". Colonel Vandewalle cites "his diverse sources of information" to claim that, at about midnight and shortly before their execution, the prisoners were dying from the beating which the guards and probably the Katangan ministers themselves had given them.[51] But in fact, the prisoners were far from dying before their execution. Vandewalle and the others use the battering to excuse the worst, to justify the execution on humanitarian grounds. But in their zeal, they reveal the damning fact that the prisoners were the victims of violent brutality for which the Belgians were partly responsible.

At about 9.45 p.m., some of the ministers went back to the president's residence, leaving Tshombe, Munongo, Kimba, Kibwe, Kitenge, Sapwe, Gat, Rougefort and Verscheure at the Brouwez house. While Tshombe, Munongo and Gat conferred together, the prisoners were again beaten by the guards. According to Rougefort, Munongo said to Gat: "We know you will carry out all the missions we ask of you regarding the persons concerned." The witness added that Munongo said "Anakufa" ("he must die" in Swahili) to which Tshombe answered: "No, no, no." As is made clear later, the decision had already been taken by that time and preparations for the execution were already under way. Even Brassinne admits that this dialogue was undoubtedly invented, but it "conveys the state of mind at the time". What this anecdote clearly shows is the central argument defended by all the former collaborators of separatist Katanga: that the Katangans were calling all the shots, the "hawks" (Munongo) prevailed over the "doves" (Tshombe), and the Belgians were their instruments. In reality, Police Commissioner Frans Verscheure was directing operations during Lumumba, Mpolo and Okito's last hour. No sooner had Verscheure arrived at Brouwez than he informed Gat that the prisoners were to be taken away, and that, to use Brassinne's words, they had been "sentenced to death by the Katangan government". At Verscheure's request, Captain Gat arranged an escort of loyal soldiers.[52] By that time, the place of execution and the policemen chosen to perform the task had all been decided. The policemen were taken to the killing field to prepare the prisoners' grave. Gat and Verscheure later testified that it had already been dug when the convoy arrived.

The decision to carry out the crime was taken, therefore, before Tshombe and company's last visit to the Brouwez house, probably at Tshombe's residence, after 8 p.m. but no later that 9.15 p.m. Verscheure says that he went to see the prisoners at about 7 p.m., then had dinner at home where Tshombe telephoned to ask him to come straight to the residence. Verscheure arrived there between 8 and 8.30 p.m., a little before the police had been given the green light to make the necessary preparations for the execution.[53] These facts are interesting, and make it impossible to exonerate anyone by describing the assassination as a *faux pas* by a few drunken Katangans. At some point, the balance shifted in favour of immediate liquidation. When this decision was taken, there were at least two Europeans at Tshombe's residence: his secretary Servais and Frans Verscheure who was to play a key role in the drama's final act in the hours to follow. And in the background were the other Belgians – sober, impassive, discreet, but organising the liquidation very efficiently.

Who gave the final signal to carry out the task that same evening? It seems unlikely that Frans Verscheure and Godefroid Munongo would act without previously seeking the advice of Victor Tignée, the minister's private secretary. The relationship between Tignée and Verscheure, who was officially adviser to Chief Inspector of Police Mumba, is clear: according to Huyghé, Tignée was Verscheure's "immediate superior". This would imply that Munongo's private secretary was the real motor behind the operational decisions. Tignée was highly regarded. According to Vanden Bloock, Tignée and Clémens were "responsible for civilian action in Katanga", and Tignée was a private secretary who kept "his minister under control". In December 1960, Vandewalle had even thought of replacing the Bureau Conseil by "periodic meetings with Tignée and Clémens, chaired by Vanden Bloock".[54] During the evening of 17 January, Tignée was everywhere: in Munongo's office at around 4.30 p.m. when the message about Lumumba's arrival was received; at the airport when the prisoners landed; at Brouwez when the prisoners arrived; at Brouwez again at 7 p.m. Each time, Tignée was surrounded by the men actually carrying out the operation, Gat, Verscheure and also Huyghé. As will be seen, Tignée also played a crucial role after the assassination. In the absence of research material, we must limit ourselves to the following hypothesis, which should be treated cautiously: on the Belgian side, Tignée and Bartelous played the largest part in the decision to eliminate Lumumba, probably after asking Colonel Vandewalle's advice; the "hidden boss" of the Katangan armed forces was kept informed as events panned out – for instance, he knew that Huyghé was responsible for supplying the Katangan guards at the Brouwez house.[55]

In a conversation with Brassinne and Verdickt in 1988, Verscheure said that he learned that night, at the residence, that the prisoners were to be eliminated, although he did not know, and these are his own words, where it would happen. According to Verscheure, the place was chosen by the Katangan security services. However, the operational end of the drama was handled by the Katangan police, and they were under the orders of Verscheure, Mumba and Sapwe. The *Gendarmerie*, responsible for the prisoners' detention at the Brouwez house, provided twelve military personnel for the assassination: eight soldiers, three officers and one NCO. The military police escort chosen by Captain Gat consisted entirely of Balunda and Bayeke. The Lunda and the Bayeke are from the south of Katanga and supported the regime passively. The twelve military men were Warrant Officer Sakela, two sergeants, three corporals and two privates second class, plus Captain Gat, Lieutenant Michels, Major Muke and Sergeant Son.[56] The other units were ordered to stay at the Brouwez house under Léva's command.

LUMUMBA'S LAST HOUR

At about 10 p.m., the prisoners were pushed inside a car in a convoy made up of four black American cars and two jeeps.[57] In the first three cars, apart from the drivers, were President Tshombe, Ministers Kitenge, Munongo and Kibwe, Commissioner Sapwe, and probably Minister Kimba. Captain Gat was in the fourth car, driven by Commissioner Verscheure, with the handcuffed prisoners in the back. In the first jeep, which had a short-wave radio, were the driver plus Michels, Son and Muke. In the second were the driver, Sakela and five military policemen. The cars left the Brouwez house and turned right towards the nearby junction. After a few hundred metres, the convoy took a narrow track to the left which led to the road linking Luano to Elisabethville. Then it turned left again onto the tarmac road to Jadotville. The convoy cut across the savannah and the villages of Kibembe, Lukuni (a mining centre), Tumbwe and the station of

Tshilatembo. The American cars drove at full speed and the jeeps had difficulty keeping up with them. Six kilometres past Tshilatembo, they reached a cross-roads. The convoy followed a track to the right leading to Mwadingusha, known for the Cornet waterfalls and the Emile Francqui hydro-electric plant, an area of swampland home to huge colonies of birds. Three hundred metres further on the convoy arrived at a clearing in the wooded savannah. The time was 10.45 p.m.: it had taken less than forty-five minutes to cover 50 kilometres.

The spot was illuminated by the headlights of Verscheure's and Sapwe's police cars, which had arrived first. The preparations, made by torchlight, were complete and they were awaiting the rest of the convoy. As well as the eight soldiers, nine policemen (also Balunda or Bayeke) had been chosen for the execution. The grassy clearing was bordered on the right by a 5-metre-high anthill covered with small shrubs, and 8 metres further on to the left, 10 metres away from the road, was an imposing tree 10 metres high and 80 centimetres in diameter. The policemen had not had much trouble digging the grave because the soil there was sandy and loose. The passengers got out of their cars and joined the policemen – except for the prisoners, who stayed in Verscheure's car. Captain Gat exchanged a few words with the Katangan ministers standing in front of the grave. Kibwe, in his customary bowler hat, and Munongo were the only ones talking. According to Verscheure, they were in a good mood and cracked a few jokes. Kitenge, on the other hand, was nervous and chainsmoked.

Soon afterwards, the prisoners were taken out of the car. They were bare-foot, and dressed only in their trousers and vests. Verscheure removed the handcuffs. He was walking behind Lumumba who asked him: "You're going to kill us, aren't you?" to which Verscheure simply answered "Yes". These were the first words exchanged with the prisoners since they left Brouwez. According to Verscheure, Lumumba "took very well" the announcement of his imminent death. The prisoners stood on the path, surrounded by the policemen and soldiers. Verscheure said "they were still on their feet", implying that they bore the marks of the previous few hours' beatings. Verscheure told them they were going to be shot. According to Gat, they were "given time to prepare, to pray". Verscheure said that Lumumba rejected the offer.[58] Meanwhile, the first firing squad of two soldiers and two policemen got ready. The police had Vigneron sten guns, the soldiers FAL rifles. Someone apparently intoned a native oath. Verscheure took Joseph Okito to a tree. According to Verscheure, Okito said: "I want my wife and children in Léopoldville to be taken care of." Somebody answered: "We're in Katanga, not in Léo!" Okito leaned against the tree, his face turned towards the firing squad already in position 4 metres away. A short hail of bullets, and the former vice-president of the Senate was dead; his body was immediately thrown into the grave. After "the little one", it was the turn of "the big one", as Verscheure said later. The commissioner placed Maurice Mpolo against the tree; a round of bullets from another squad mowed him down. Finally a third firing squad faced Lumumba. Verscheure, who had taken him to the big tree, later said that Lumumba trembled when led to the edge of the grave, but "mute, completely dazed, his eyes misty, he put up no resistance". An enormous hail of bullets riddled the former prime minister's body. "After the execution, we picked up half a kilo of cartridges," the police commissioner said. When Brassinne visited the spot twenty-seven years later, the big tree was still riddled with bullets.

Lumumba knew all too well that he could be destined for a violent death. A few months earlier he had said: "If I die tomorrow, it will be because a White has armed a Black." On the day he died, Patrice Lumumba was not yet thirty-six years old, the same age as Robespierre, that other great defender of the modern nation state, when he died. Vandewalle writes, with more than a hint of racism, in *Mille et quatre jours*: "His career ended on the 201st day of Congolese sovereignty, in the horror of a bloody night, after a horrific journey, with a final vision of black faces, their eyes full of hatred, vengeance, cruelty, feelings he had incited."[59]

The whole operation took barely fifteen minutes, and passed without any unforeseen eventualities. Who was in charge of the execution? The known facts point to Commissioner Verscheure and Captain Gat. Verscheure later told Commissioner Soete that Captain Gat was in command, and that he himself had been appointed solely to "prepare the prisoners to die", and he also said he had advised them to pray. In his secret report, Verscheure writes that the signals to the firing squad were given by "a European officer" – therefore by Captain Gat.[60] The prisoners were resigned to what was going to happen, they were calm and "fatalistic" according to Verscheure. Okito and Lumumba "shuddered" as Verscheure took them to face the firing squad. But others were also shivering on that cold rainy-season night, and the Katangan ministers were wearing coats. Julien Gat, who admitted he was shivering too ("the evenings are very cold in January in Katanga"), later told Brassinne that the three men were very brave. According to Kazadi, Kasa Vubu told him later that Lumumba lived the few hours before his death "with supreme contempt and extraordinary courage". Other testimonies in *Qui a tué Patrice Lumumba?* fully concur.[61]

Brassinne's "Enquête" creates the impression of a more or less legitimate trial, with Blacks as judges and black executioners carrying out the sentence. The role of the Europeans is obliterated, as if they were simply court clerks or ushers. Those Belgians directly involved will of course uphold this argument. According to Verscheure, the "judges", i.e. the Katangan ministers, spoke to the "convicted men" before their assassination, an assertion denied by other witnesses. Verscheure, who took an active part in the organisation of the massacre, subsequently tried to veil the crime in a mantle of "legality". He was helped by Brassinne who in his dissertation uses the judicial term "appear" (before a court) to describe the hypothetical meeting between the judges and the condemned.

The terms "firing squad" and "execute" suggest that a sentence was carried out. Brassinne agrees with Son's and Grandelet's attempts to minimise the role of the Whites: "From the start, the Europeans were dragged into events they did not control, receiving instructions as the situation progressed." And "at no time did any officer or NCO intervene in the physical liquidation." In *Qui a tué Patrice Lumumba?* Bassinne and Kestergat tell the same story: "None of the Europeans take any direct part in the execution, not even for a *coup de grâce* which obviously is not necessary." Of Verscheure's role, they specify: "He only obeyed orders, he had no choice."[62] But is the officer who commands a firing squad exempted a priori from any responsibility? Anyone using this argument to excuse the involvement of officers in Nazi Germany's war crimes or, for instance, of Habyarimana's followers in Rwanda, would get little sympathy.

Brassinne and Kestergat write that the three Belgian soldiers who took part in the execution "are devastated and very worried about the consequences of the drama". Of Commissioner Verscheure, they say that "his conscience will torture him for a long time . . ." Brassinne claims the civilian officials in the Belgo-Katangan lobby felt the same. He writes that, on the day after the drama, when news of the killing had reached a few limited circles, Ugeux, Samalenge's private secretary, was "shattered", and Bartelous, Tshombe's private secretary, "distraught". Obviously, the Belgo-Katangan lobby was very worried about the future. But to say that Gat, Michels and Son were "shattered" is a spurious assertion. Nowhere will that claim be proven, either in testimonies or in interviews. The Belgian officers in the *Gendarmerie* were part of the hard core of the former Force Publique. They played a vanguard role in July 1960 in sabotaging the Africanisation of the army and in pressuring the Belgian government to come to their aid. These "Heroes of July" were fiercely anti-nationalist and sworn enemies of the Congolese government. They were bitterly resentful of Lumumba. We have seen how Captain Gat let his men beat the prisoners on their arrival at Luano and how none of his superiors intervened. The Belgian NCO who hit Lumumba was neither stopped nor punished.

Several years later, Captain Gat claimed he had bad memories of the events. But the reasons he gave have nothing to do with the crime itself. He said the police should have been in charge of the execution and that the army should not have been involved. At some point, as a crucial witness in such a compromising crisis for the Belgo-Katangan regime, he even feared for his life. He also complained of problems, including death threats, he had encountered for his part in the massacre. Brassinne's thesis claims Ugeux and Bartelous were "shattered" and "distraught" when they learnt about the assassination next day. The reason soon becomes apparent. After a discussion with Tshombe on the matter, both men realised that any hope of gaining diplomatic recognition of the copper state's independence had vanished for good.[63]

Commissioner Verscheure had taken Lumumba from Stanleyville to Jadotville prison only a few months before independence. The colonial authorities had sentenced Lumumba for subversive activities. As stated above, Verscheure was also at Tshombe's residence when the decision to kill the three prisoners was taken, and he played an active role in the assassination itself. Later Verscheure showed Verdickt a 7.62 calibre bullet from an FAL rifle which came from Lumumba's skull and "has been slightly dented by the impact". In the months following the assassination, Verscheure gave a bonus to the soldiers and policemen who took part in the execution.

Neither do Gat, Michels or Son look like men dragged into a nightmare against their will. Gat was a former "Hero of July" and his military policemen were among the pillars of the regime. The captain organised Lumumba's last abode on Katangan soil in the Brouwez house. His men abused the prisoners at the airport and he was in charge of the prisoners at the Brouwez house while they were being beaten up. Finally, he commanded the firing squad. According to Blistein, it was Lieutenant Michels, commander of the first company of military police, who shouted at the airport that the prisoners shouldn't sully Katanga's soil, and was one of the Belgians who beat up Lumumba at the Brouwez house.[64] Michels gave the order to Grandelet and the other guards at Brouwez to kill the three prisoners if they were freed by UN forces. And Son had been a legionnaire in Algeria and Indochina.

It is no accident that Belgian protagonists were in the foreground when the drama reached its conclusion. The list of anecdotes and remarks from Belgo-Katangans about their hatred for Lumumba is never-ending. Chaplain Adam, who had fought to defend Katanga's cause with the gun and the cross since July 1950, had only one concern: in no way must Lumumba's blood soil Belgians' hands. As described later, Soete, who was on holiday in Belgium in July 1960, wanted to go back to the Congo "among other things, to kill Lumumba". A military expert and a veteran of what became Belgian military co-operation with Mobutu, Jean-Claude Marlair writes that the Belgian soldiers' loathing for Lumumba was "unanimous" and "total", and that "Louis Marlière's men in Léopoldville, Noël Dedeken's in Bakwanga and Frédéric Vandewalle's in Elisabethville did not shed a single tear over the fate of the fallen prime minister!"[65]

The civilians were every bit as tough as the military. Even the top dignitaries passionately defended the Katangan cause, although a certain reserve might have been expected on their part. After the massacre, Verscheure went for advice to Joseph Cornélis, the archbishop of Elisabethville, who reacted like all the other Whites around him. This Benedictine monk, who "never hid his deep antipathy for Lumumba", "put his mind at ease". According to Vandewalle, Cornélis told Huyghé, another penitent, "it is a forgiven sin". Roger Jaspar, then head of Radio Katanga, who had earned the nickname "Fearless John" by his action in the summer of 1960, wrote later: "Lumumba is dead and the man committed all the atrocities it is possible to commit in one lifetime. He is dead, never mind how."[66]

This attitude was equally common in high circles. Did not the diplomat Vanden Bloock (at the end of 1960), and Foreign Minister Wigny (in January 1961) offer to hand Lumumba over to Kalonji so that he could die a martyr? The Belgians in Léopoldville chose to deport him to Bakwanga because, as Brassinne puts it euphemistically, "they were sure Kalonji's Baluba would take special care of the prisoners".[67] Brassinne interviewed nearly all the Belgians who were involved in the events one way or another. Not one of these Belgians, in positions where they could have influenced the course of events, expressed a single word of regret for the three nationalists, *not a single word!*

6

OPERATION "COVER-UP"

ANXIETY OR CELEBRATION?

At about 11 p.m., the key figures left the spot while the policemen quickly covered the grave with earth.[1] The Katangan ministers hurried back to Tshombe's residence, while Michels, Son and the Katangan soldiers headed back towards the Brouwez house. For his part, Gat returned directly to Camp Massart. It was about midnight when Gat paid a visit to the mess, together with Michels who was already back at the camp. They were joined by other Belgian officers and NCOs. The mood was pretty low. As Gat said, "In the military, we don't like this kind of thing!" The officers stayed less than half an hour, for they were expected at their posts the next morning at 8 o'clock. Gat concluded: "To suppose the day ended in a booze-up would be wrong!"

Commissioner Frans Verscheure, however, was finding the events were too much for him. After leaving the scene of the crime that night, he went straight to the Le Pondoir farm, where he found Carlo Huyghé, as well as the Brouwez family who lived there. Earlier that evening, Huyghé had delivered food to the prisoners' guards at the new Brouwez house nearby. Léva had apparently taken the sandwiches, saying: "Gat has gone with the soldiers and the prisoners." Soon after Huyghé's return at around midnight, a black car driven by Frans Verscheure arrived at Le Pondoir. According to Huyghé, Verscheure got out of the car "staggering as if he's drunk, the right side of his trousers covered in mud. . . . I'll never forget it. He looks so strange." Verscheure wanted to talk about the evening's events. Huyghé asked him if he felt all right and if he had fallen over. According to Huyghé, Verscheure rang the Interior Ministry. He left soon afterwards to go and see Chief Inspector Mumba who said later "He was shaking . . . he was afraid of what had happened . . ." Verscheure simply told him that Lumumba was the last to be executed and that he had been "brave".

Verscheure and Mumba went together to Tshombe's residence, where they

found the Katangan ministers. Breuer, the butler, later said that the Katangan
ministers had queued up to wash the blood off their hands, and then more bot-
tles of whisky had begun to appear.[2] While most of the Katangans were sleeping
the drink off, the top Belgians in Katanga conferred discreetly. Lumumba's
body was barely cold and they were already gearing up to conceal the story of his
death from the Congolese people who had been robbed of their leader.

Meanwhile in town, the fate of the three prisoners was on everyone's lips. The
civilians who saw Lumumba arrive in Luano immediately alerted the city's
European colony. The devil himself was in town! Two hours after Lumumba
landed, Carlo Huyghé met the Moreau family from the Union Minière on the
road to Elisabethville. They pounced on him, saying "You've heard the news,
Lumumba is here!" That same night, Secretary of State Lucas Samalenge went to
the Relais, one of the town's busiest bars, and told anyone willing to listen that
Lumumba was dead and that he had kicked his corpse. He went round repeat-
ing the same story until the police took him away. Others believed Lumumba's
tragic end was due to a stupid accident: that following a particularly hard blow,
he had banged his head on the bidet.[3] In any case, the elite and general population of Katanga's capital alike knew that Lumumba was dead. On the evening of
18 January, Whites at the Cercle d'Elisabethville uncorked champagne to celebrate the murder. In the course of the day, they were kept informed through
Samalenge himself who put various members of the Katangan information service in the picture about the events.[4]

Twenty-four hours after Lumumba's arrival in the copper state, rumours
were spreading like wildfire in Elisabethville; white colonials and the black elite
both rejoiced over the disappearance of their prime public enemy and worried
about the consequences of the crime. Meanwhile, a Convair landed at Luano,
with certain members of the Léopoldville regime on board: Minister Delvaux,
Major Puati from the ANC and Colonel Marlière, the ANC's "technical adviser".
They would conduct the military dialogue between Léopoldville and
Elisabethville while Vandewalle, Marlière and Vanden Bloock conferred behind
the scenes. Nendaka, Mobutu's security chief, arrived a few days later. Some of
the drama's main actors – Nendaka, Marlière, Vandewalle and Smal – took this
opportunity to meet at the Sabena restaurant. What was said remains unknown
but, according to Vandewalle, "the handshakes were very hearty".[5] They
undoubtedly mentioned the sad end of the former prime minister: was not his
elimination a prime example of political co-operation between the Léopoldville
and Elisabethville regimes and a foretaste of their future union? And was not the
murder of paramount importance for those contemplating the Congo's future?
And did it not bring the neo-colonial reconstruction of the country closer?

The assassination seemed to have opened the way for a rapid construction of
anti-nationalist bastions in the former colony. On 23 January, in a ceremony at

Camp Nkokolo in the Congolese capital, Kasa Vubu upgraded Mobutu to major general. This promotion, initiated by the president's entourage, was not due to the respect the former Force Publique sergeant commanded among his officers, or indeed to his military successes. It was political, and aimed to strengthen the army, the president's sole support, and Mobutu's position within the army. Elisabethville also wanted to strengthen its armed forces: the day Mobutu received his promotion, an emissary from Elisabethville finalised the purchase of twelve armoured vehicles in Brussels. They were to be transported from Britain to South Africa which had agreed to let Katanga have them. Colonel Vandewalle informed Loos, the military adviser, of the transaction and told him to help in any way he could. At almost the same time, a Persian Airlines plane landed at Elisabethville with fifty Belgian mercenaries on board. They were to join the Katangan *Gendarmerie* which was preparing a devastating attack on the Baluba rebels.[6]

MASQUERADE IN KATANGA

On the morning of 18 January, the day after Lumumba's arrival, there was a climate of intense excitement in Elisabethville. Passers-by discussed events and combed the newspapers for more information. A journalist at *La Libre Belgique* assessed public opinion as follows:

> Little groups of passers-by fight over the newspapers announcing Lumumba's arrival. The African and European population in the city rejoice at the news of Lumumba's transfer to Katanga's capital. In fact, there had been fears he might be released due to the deterioration of the situation in Lower Congo, and particularly the threat of mutiny by the Congolese troops guarding the prisoners in Thysville. . . . Some observers, however, do not share the satisfaction of the majority in Elisabethville.

These "observers" thought the small, not very stable, state would come under enormous pressure if it kept the former prime minister within its borders any longer. *De Standaard* commented: "The general opinion is that they [Tshombe, Kasa Vubu and Mobutu] are incurring serious problems with the transfer of Lumumba and his two colleagues."[7]

That day, one item dominated the agenda of the Bureau Conseil's daily meeting: "The prisoners are dead. What to do now?" According to Colonel Vandewalle, there was only one thing to do pending a final solution: confirm that the three nationalists were safe in jail and being well treated. Perrad, the *Gendarmerie*'s chief-of-staff, summoned Captain Gat to headquarters for a meeting with several senior officers. They agreed upon total discretion. Grandelet recalls that several officers did the rounds of the bars spreading the rumour that they had kept Lumumba until noon, then taken him to a secret hide-out. In its one o'clock news bulletin, Radio Katanga announced that the prisoners had arrived the previous evening and immediately been taken to a more secure place outside the city. In the course of the afternoon, a press release specified that the transfer of the "traitor Lumumba" had been organised "at President Kasa Vubu's request and with the agreement of the Katangan government". Another communiqué was issued by Tshombe's entourage that same day: "Following certain rumours spread in foreign press circles, the President of Katanga categorically states that, on his arrival at Elisabethville Patrice Lumumba did not suffer any ill-treatment from either Katangans or European members of the Katangan *Gendarmerie*."[8]

However, Elisabethville had to face the reality of the crime sooner than it expected. The morning after the assassination, Commissioner Frans Verscheure answered a telephone call in Munongo's office. Jadotville's commissioner was on the other end of the line and his message made Verscheure queasy: a missionary was saying that some Blacks had seen Blue Berets in the vicinity of Tshilatembo where the prisoners had been killed. This was a coal mining area and some miners had also heard shooting. At daybreak in the clearing they had come across a pile of freshly dug earth with an arm sticking out of it.[9] While the police sealed off the area, Munongo, Verscheure, Sapwe, Tignée, Mumba and Soete held an emergency meeting in the Interior Ministry. Gerard Soete was a man of experience, who had been in the Congo since 1946. He was on holiday in Belgium at the time of the Congo crisis. He quickly returned, however, and was promoted from chief inspector to chief commissioner in charge of the training and reorganisation of the Katangan police in the Balubakat rebel areas.

Soete was furious and shouted: "You're in the shit now." He talked of "war crimes" and reminded them that "the Nuremberg tribunal, if it still existed, could condemn them for what they had done." He blamed Verscheure and Munongo for losing their heads: "They hadn't a clue what to do!" In front of Brassinne, Soete openly referred to "Verscheure's inability to deal with events that need a cool head". A decision was taken: Soete and Verscheure would dig up the corpses and "make them disappear once and for all! There must be no trace left." Soete, a man of action, took matters in hand. With his brother Michel, an engineer in the public works department, he would personally take charge of the task.[10]

While they were wondering how to get rid of the bodies, another crucial question emerged. Sooner or later, Katanga would have to announce the death of the three nationalist leaders: how to minimise the political fallout? According to Verscheure, Victor Tignée was the brain behind the answer.[11] Tignée, Verscheure and Alexandre Belina, a legal adviser to the Katangan president, studied the matter. On 26 January, Belina came up with a proposal which was implemented in full, except for a few details. Nobody could be allowed to see the bodies or take them away. It would certainly not be possible to claim that the corpses had been mutilated by crocodiles for, as Belina subsequently said, "generally speaking, crocs don't leave bullet holes in bodies. . . ." The scenario was as follows: the prisoners had managed to escape in one of the guards' cars which got stuck in a ditch; they had to continue on foot; some villagers recognised them and murdered them on the spot.

Perrad immediately ordered Captain Gat to stay on the alert with the soldiers and policemen who took part in the execution. They had to figure in a scene that the scriptwriter himself described as "totally indefensible".

On 27 January, Julien Gat and his men left in two black public works department cars, three jeeps and a lorry. Three of the policemen, dressed in civilian clothes, sat in the back seats of one of the cars impersonating the three prisoners. Their destination was Kasaji, on the Dilolo–Kolwezi–Jadotville road, in the south-west of Katanga, some 620 kilometres from Elisabethville. The cars stopped at Jadotville and Kolwezi for all to see that the prisoners were still alive. The convoy finally headed for Mugulunga, a village near Kasaji.

On the evening of 10 February, Radio Katanga announced that Lumumba, Mpolo and Okito were on the run. They had dug a hole in the wall of their prison and commandeered a car, which had been found. The regime promised a reward to anyone helping to recapture the escaped prisoners: 300,000 Belgian francs for Lumumba, and 50,000 for each of his two companions. The United Nations also put out a statement in which Berendsen said "it is important that these people are treated humanely if they are recaptured". In Katanga, news of the escape was spoken of "with anxiety by Lumumba's followers, with ironic indifference by Conakat". A certain Jean Yumba, an ardent nationalist, asked the United Nations to help the escapees. The regime dashed the nationalist's hopes by putting him in jail.[12]

The scenario was viewed with scepticism from the beginning. The day after the announcement about the escape, during a press conference Munungo referred to articles he had read about a "put-up job". Munongo dismissed this allegation, pointing to the number of Katangan soldiers who had been mobilised to find the escaped prisoners to the detriment of the war against nationalist rebels in the north. Soon afterwards, the minister circulated photos of the improvised jail with the opening in the outside wall, and of the car stuck in the ditch. Julien Gat, Jules Allard from the intelligence services and Pius Sapwe were standing beside it. Gat left Katanga a few days later but the photos linked him to the assassination for ever. He said later that for a while his entourage feared he would be killed to erase all traces of the drama and transfer blame for the mistakes onto him. He received death threats for years and in 1965 *Jeune Afrique* published a photograph of him standing in front of his house: he had refused to talk to their reporter. At his own request, he was transferred to a Belgian military base in West Germany. Weber writes: "Harassed, the poor man asked to change his name. The Belgian authorities helped him to do so."[13]

"NO BLOOD ON OUR HANDS" (ENCORE)

As has been shown above, the reaction of the UN leadership in Katanga shortly after Lumumba's transfer was unlikely to help reveal the truth and make the regime do anything that might save the three prisoners' lives, had this still been possible. The UN head Berendsen was informed of Lumumba's arrival barely one or two hours after the DC-4's landing. Yet, he did not think it necessary to contact Tshombe on the matter immediately, and decided to wait until the next day to see him, as previously planned. During this meeting, he made it clear that the regime "would undoubtedly expose itself to a lot a problems" if it accepted the prisoners. Berendsen suggested returning the prisoners to their sender, and ensuring they were treated humanely in the meantime. He asked the regime to accept a delegation from the International Red Cross which might want to examine the prisoners. Berendsen mentioned rumours of the prisoners' death. Tshombe firmly denied them. The president reminded him that the three men were in "a pitiful state" due to the battering they got on the plane, and that Lumumba, "whose face was swollen, had asked for his protection, in a manner that inspired pity".

So Berendsen did not demand that Lumumba be handed over to the UN, although maintaining law and order was the specific purpose of the UN presence in the Congo. Had not Lumumba, as the Congo's legally elected prime minister with parliamentary immunity, the same right to protection as Minister Bomboko, for instance, who on Hammarskjöld's request was escorted by Blue Berets to Kasa Vubu's residence in September 1960? But the New Zealander simply suggested handing Lumumba over to none other than Mobutu's illegal regime, presumably to spare himself "a lot of trouble". He put no public pressure on the Katangan regime. The press communiqué on the evening of 18 January was short, vague and purely descriptive. It mentioned only that the day before, three people escorted by armed soldiers disembarked from a DC-4 and were "probably" political prisoners. Lumumba, Mpolo and Okito were not mentioned by name, not a word was said about their physical condition and no demands were made concerning their treatment. The same day, a UN spokesman in Elisabethville disseminated bland information that the Blue Berets at the airport "had not noticed Lumumba had been beaten. Moreover, he points out that the former prime minister was transported from the plane to his prison so fast there could not have been time to ill-treat him."[14]

In New York, reactions were also placatory. Heinrich Wieschhoff, Hammarskjöld's assistant, declared from the dizzy heights of the UN skyscraper that Lumumba's life was not in danger, because the Congolese "have no record of killing their political leaders", although they tended to "indicate their displeasure by beating them". But Hammarskjöld expressed another point of view in a personal telegram to Dayal: "What this may lead to is only too obvious." As the news of the ill-treatment at the airport and the rumours of the murder spread, the UN felt it had to do something. On 19 January, Hammarskjöld made his first official communication. The secretary general wrote in a letter to the Congolese president: "The transfer of Mr. Lumumba to Katanga necessarily involves a further interference of Mr. Lumumba's right to be tried without undue delay". He stressed that Lumumba must be removed from Katanga and, "unless released, he [must] be given the opportunity to answer the charges against him in a fair and public hearing by an impartial tribunal at which he will have all guarantees necessary for his defence."

This request to the Congolese president to have Lumumba taken back to Léopoldville was written solely for the sake of form: in a letter to Tshombe, who had enough power to take the initiative, Hammarskjöld mentioned neither the three prisoners' possible release nor their transfer to Léopoldville. The secretary general asked only that they be treated humanely and in accordance with the law. Then, if the regime really had been presented with a *fait accompli*, the Katangan president was asked to take measures "so that Mr. Lumumba and his companions may be given the benefit of due process of law" by the Katangan regime. In the letters to Tshombe and Kasa Vubu, there was no question of a formal protest against the transfer, as was the case in the message sent the same day to the nationalist authorities in the Eastern Province protesting against restrictions on the freedom of movement of foreigners.[15]

Nevertheless, the breach of "Mr. Lumumba's right to be tried without undue delay" was a serious offence. On 5 December 1960 – when Lumumba had just fallen into the Léopoldville regime's hands – Hammarskjöld emphasised in a letter to Kasa Vubu that respect for "human rights and constitutional freedoms for all" are the very essence of the United Nations Charter. This is why, the secretary general went on, the Congolese Basic Law and the Universal Declaration of Human Rights should be respected. Consequently, Patrice Lumumba, who enjoyed parliamentary immunity, should be able to assert certain rights regarding his arrest, for instance the right to a fair and public trial before an impartial court of law.[16]

The UN leaders knew they had enough legal grounds to take action. In a letter of 13 February 1961 to Iyassu, chief-of-staff of UN troops in the Congo, Hammarskjöld wrote that "according to the United Nations' Charter, Lumumba's fate . . . can not be considered an internal affair. . . . The repercussions of the treatment suffered by Lumumba are extremely serious in international terms." In the same letter, he stressed the fact that the *Gendarmerie*'s offensive against the rebels in north Katanga would justify military action by the Blue Berets: "No interpretation of the UN forces' mandate permits us to remain passive in the face of military measures against civilians, in circumstances that have the characteristics of genocide." The Katangan offensive had provoked a lot of feeling after disturbing images had been shown on Belgian television (RTB). The *Gendarmerie* had taken a village near Luana, and though meeting no resistance, the gendarmes and mercenaries had burnt it. Pictures showed a woman with a child in her arms. A mercenary, who found them in a hut, had shot her, tearing off part of her lower jaw.[17]

Lumumba's opponents like to flaunt the (unjust) UN accusation of "an incipient genocide" by the former prime minister during clashes in Bakwanga between the Congolese army and Baluba militias at the end of August 1960, during which unarmed civilians were killed. The secretary general used these accusations at the beginning of September 1960 to break, *manu militari* if necessary, Lumumba's offensive against the separatists. In February 1961, he was about to do the same thing, in the sense that he did not consider Lumumba's imprisonment and Tshombe's military offensive as belonging to the domain of internal affairs but as a threat to international peace and security, which would give the UN the right to intervene actively. In August–September 1960, the UN took action after the death of a few dozen civilians but in January, February and March 1961, when the former prime minister had been assassinated and *thousands* of civilians were massacred during the Katangan offensive against the rebels, the UN remained silent.[18] The UN made absolutely no effort to try and find Tshombe's prisoners and offer them its protection, although it could easily have located Lumumba. From the airport, the convoy went almost directly to the Brouwez house which was easily recognisable with its military police guard and had been cordoned off by the Katangan police.

It is easy to understand UN passivity in January 1961. On the one hand, in August 1960 the UN wanted to overthrow Lumumba. On the other, at the beginning of 1961, in the eyes of the UN the Katanga regime was playing an indispensable role in the reconstruction of a neo-colonial Congo. Hammarskjöld's letter to Iyassu was only a threat, part of the strategy of negotiations. It was not meant to be carried out. The very different treatments the UN reserved for Lumumba in 1960 and Tshombe in 1961 demonstrate clearly that the actions of the UN and other international institutions are not inspired by abstract rights and principles. The great powers employ these criteria (or, if it suits them better, ignore them) only to justify the actions or inaction of the organisations they control. No doubt Hammarskjöld intended, if it became useful later on, to publish this letter to prove that he made efforts, *in tempore non suspecto,* to save Lumumba. This was not the first time. On 6 September 1960, after Lumumba's overthrow, the secretary general telegraphed his assistant Cordier, setting out his instructions for when Lumumba's letters had to be answered: "The technique for reply . . . is memo without address handed to [Lumumba's government's ambassador to the UN Thomas] Kanza. . . . I think more of our record than of courtesy to a certain individual. It would be good to be able later on, if necessary, to publish replies as having been sent before an attack in parliament [on the UN's attitude to Lumumba]".[19]

In the days following Lumumba's transfer to Katanga, the UN Reconciliation Commission tried several times to visit the prisoners. The Commission's task, according to a UN General Assembly resolution, was to ensure respect for the

Congo's parliamentary institutions. Kasa Vubu and Tshombe sent the Commission's delegation from from pillar to post: a painful business for those concerned and a slap in the face for the UN. First, Kasa Vubu assured the members of the Commission of his good will and promised they would be able to see the three prisoners in Katanga. With this aim in view, he gave them a letter for Tshombe. On 22 January, Jaja Wachuku, a member of the Commission, arrived in Elisabethville where Tshombe initially said he did not want to see him. Shortly afterwards Tshombe did agree to meet him but only because he had recognised Wachuku as the Nigerian finance minister. Tshombe refused to accept Kasa Vubu's letter. He attributed all responsibility for Lumumba's imprisonment to Kasa Vubu and said the Commission should ask the president to send a letter to Lumumba's guards.

On 26 January, the members of the Commission again met Kasa Vubu, who promised to talk to Nendaka, the head of Mobutu's intelligence services. On 31 January, Nendaka reiterated that only Tshombe had the authority to deal with the matter. He said he had approached Elisabethville but had received no satisfaction. On 4 February, the members of the Commission again visited the Congolese president who asked them if the UN had really given them a mandate to meet the political prisoners and, if so, what names were on the list. This game of hide-and-seek lasted until 14 February when the Commission asked the president why Lumumba had been transferred to Katanga. As a result, Kasa Vubu abruptly ended the meeting. The Red Cross also tried to visit the prisoners, with as little success as the Reconciliation Commission.[20]

Needless to say, asking the Commission if it had the appropriate mandate was another in the long line of pretexts for putting off clarification indefinitely. But Kasa Vubu's action remains pertinent. The least that can be said is that the UN had not really thrown all its weight behind the demand to see the prisoners. The secretary general left it to the Reconciliation Commission and the International Red Cross to do this. The secretary general made no mention of the matter in his report to the Security Council on 1 February, although a request by eight member states for an explanation as to Lumumba's treatment was on the agenda. The fact that Tshombe was toying with the UN Reconciliation Commission would imply that, like his rival accomplice in Léopoldville, he knew very well that he would get away with his tricks. It should come as no surprise that after Lumumba's death was announced, Tshombe told a press conference he would refuse to meet any commission of inquiry and shouted: "I couldn't care less about the UN"[21]

MASQUERADE IN BRUSSELS AND NEW YORK

Brussels had been informed on 18 January of the three nationalists' arrival in Katanga. Smal sent the telegram: "To Major Loos. Report arrival in E'ville on

17/1/61 at 17 hours of Lumumba, Mpolo and Okito." Soon afterwards, the diplomats Vanden Bloock and Créner sent the following message to the Foreign Ministry:

> Lumumba, Mpolo and Okito were brought on a special flight yesterday afternoon to Elisabethville, where they are being detained temporarily pending their transfer to another place of detention. The Katangan government had agreed in principle but was surprised by the speed of their arrival. Bloock/Créner.

This telegram marks the first lie of the post-Lumumba era[22], given that they had held discussions on Lumumba's death in the course of the morning. Bartelous and Ugeux, Tshombe's and Samalenge's private secretaries, had discussed the matter at great length with Tshombe, after which Bartelous went to Immokat to talk to Vanden Bloock "so he can inform the department of Foreign Affairs". Vanden Bloock later admitted that Elisabethville wanted above all to play for time and keep the Belgian government out of it.[23] Brussels agreed to the line taken by its subordinates in Katanga: the three prisoners were being detained by the Katangan government; the Belgian government and its representatives on the spot had nothing, but absolutely nothing, to do with it.

Telegrams were sent solely to confuse the issue until the death of the three men was officially announced. For example, on 20 January, Afrian Affairs Minister d'Aspremont Lynden gave the following order: "It seems to me a political necessity, firstly to ensure a tight guard, repeat tight, on Lumumba, secondly, to avoid ill-treatment and suppression." The hypocrisy in Vanden Bloock's reply is obvious: "Can assure you that no Belgian has been involved in guarding Lumumba and company so far, and never will be since Katangan authorities consider Lumumba's treatment their own exclusive prerogative." A few days later, it was the same story. The minister for African affairs showed his humanity when he wired: ". . . insist in strong tone on humane treatment for Lumumba whose life cannot under any circumstances be put in danger. . . . No Belgian can be involved in this matter." The following incident recorded by Vandewalle shows that Belgium was taking every precaution, even in its coded messages. When, in a 23 January telegram, a Belgian adviser to Mobutu's intelligence services praised the healthy effect on the political climate of Lumumba's removal from the Congolese capital, and noted that other transfers of political prisoners from Thysville and Luzumu were being considered, certain people in Brussels were not pleased.[24]

The eyes of the whole world were on Elisabethville and Brussels. Had the unimaginable happened? Lumumba himself had invited the UN forces to come and help in the Congo. Were the Blue Berets unmoved by the assassination of a legally elected prime minister? Proof of Brussels' involvement in this crime would provoke violent demonstrations throughout the world and badly damage not only Belgium's position in the world and the UN operation in the Congo, but also the credibility of the United Nations as an institution. Elisabethville and Léopoldville, Brazzaville as well as Brussels, were all acting with caution. In the exchange of messages between Brussels and its African diplomatic missions, any reference to Belgian involvement in the drama was avoided at all costs. Hence, Vanden Bloock, the vice-consul in Elisabethville, refrained from informing Brussels of the prisoners' arrival on 17 January. He also failed to let them know of the prisoners' death after Bartelous told him about it. "I wished", he said later, "[that] the government would not be blamed, nor the Katangan *Gendarmerie* nor the police with whom the Belgians were working as advisers".[25]

However, it is inconceivable that Ministers Wigny and d'Aspremont Lynden's staff in Katanga failed to inform Brussels of the assassination. Lumumba's elimination was of crucial political importance. Did not Bartelous inform Vanden Bloock of the events immediately so that he could warn Brussels? Vandewalle rightly points out that there was not a single telegram from Elisabethville to Brussels mentioning the rumours circulating about the prisoners' death. The reason for this reticence must surely be that Brussels had been informed by other means. Vandewalle writes that the Katangan *Gendarmerie*'s internal bulletin of 19 January recounting statement by the the headman of Tshilatembo village about the suspicious nocturnal diggings was sent to both the Foreign and the African Affairs departments in Brussels: "It was probably thought that reading that was enough."[26]

Brussels knew much more than the documents would have us believe, and was kept informed by telephone, a more ephemeral means of communication. According to Brassinne and Kestergat, Vanden Bloock told Brussels what had really happened in a telephone call on the night of 21 January to A. Lebrun, the Foreign Minister's assistant. No doubt Vandewalle is right when he says Brussels already knew. At about 5 p.m. on 18 January, Rothschild, another of Wigny's assistants, had picked up the phone in his Brussels office to ask Elisabethville to clarify telegram No. 52 from the consulate about the transfer. Following this conversation, Créner sent telegram No. 56 that same day, agreeing to the general line of admitting no Belgian involvement in the events and making a plea for the prisoners to be treated well. The revealing passages of telegram No. 56, classified "top secret", are as follows:

> Following telephone conversation with Rothschild on 18 January at about 17 hours, confirm that: . . . Lumumba had been manhandled before his arrival and it is not true to say that he was violently hit at E'ville by white officers as well as Katangan gendarmes. . . . Minister Munongo and his private secretary Tignée have stated they will have him examined by a doctor to record the condition in which he was brought to Katanga.[27]

On 20 January, Vanden Bloock and Créner told Foreign Minister Wigny that no Belgian was involved in guarding the prisoners and that the place of their detention was a secret well kept by the Katangans. Years later, Vandewalle speculated as to whether the diplomats were really unaware of what was happening or whether it was Foreign Ministry tradition to introduce bland elements into their sensitive files. "We could assume the second hypothesis", he concluded. But, in the same telegram, Belgian diplomats stated emphatically that the Katangan authorities considered Lumumba's treatment as "their prerogative" and "despite being urged to be moderate, Katangan ministers unfortunately seem indifferent to the repercussions any ill-treatment may have". The text was meant for use later on, once the crime was out in the open, so as to prove the good will of Brussels and its representatives in Katanga.[28]

It was difficult for Brussels to sell its story abroad as its lies had already been too transparent. The torture at the Brouwez house and the assassination had been hidden from the outside world but the prisoners' arrival at Luano in front of several dozen onlookers and Blue Berets, the indiscretions of people like Samalenge and the Katanga regime's reactions and patently untrue statements had finally convinced the international press that it could presume the worst had happened and attribute to Brussels and its representatives in Katanga part of the responsibility for the affair. In a telegram of 18 January, Washington drew its consul's attention to press communiqués saying that Lumumba had been "severely beaten" in the presence of a white officer. If this turned out to be true, Consul Canup was requested to let Tshombe know that the US government deplored such treatment and must insist he receive "humane treatment". In his answer on 20 January, Canup said he had discussed the matter with Munongo, and he informed his chiefs in veiled diplomatic terms that Lumumba was probably dead: "Believe impossible totally disregard persistent rumors Patrice Lumumba died shortly after arrival as result mistreatment here. Minister Interior Munongo denied rumors to me but continuing mystery of Lumumba's whereabouts obliges me to keep open mind."[29]

Even the mouthpiece of Brussels and the Belgo-Katangan lobby, La Libre Belgique, could not claim ignorance. In its issue of 19 January, it quoted the Associated Press:

"It was sickening", one of the Swedish soldiers declared . . . "they were beaten, punched, hit in the face with rifle butts, kicked." . . . An aerodrome employee recounts: "I had to turn my back. It was more than I could bear." Under the blows, M. Lumumba and the two other prisoners groaned but didn't protest or ask for mercy.

In an article in De Standaard, E. Troch quoted a Swedish witness's report: "It was sickening . . . the Gendarmerie (Congolese and Whites) surrounded the prisoners and abused them. Lumumba and the two others fell on the ground. They were hit in the face with rifle butts and kicked." And Troch added in conclusion: "In addition, the pretence that the Belgian gendarmes were recruited by an independent Katangan government won't stop Congolese nationalists and other Africans hailing Lumumba as the martyr of the struggle against Belgian colonialism." These news reports and comment in the press prompted Foreign Minister Wigny's spokesman to declare:

> Lumumba's transfer has led certain organs of the international press to claim or insinuate that the Belgian authorities were involved in one way or the other . . . [the transfer] has in all probability been organised solely by the Congolese authorities who took the decision themselves and carried it out without intervention of any kind by Belgium. At no time were the Belgian authorities consulted; they learned the news in the press.[30]

On Monday 23 January, Prime Minister Eyskens and his ministers d'Aspremont Lynden and Wigny discussed the situation in central Africa. We will probably never know what they said, for in the Foreign Ministry archives' index there is no trace of the Eyskens government's select committee called Comité du Congo (Congo Committee) which was in charge of interventions in the Congo. We have only this official declaration: "Government circles insist that the Belgian government is in no way involved in Lumumba's transfer to Katanga. Moreover, we hope that he will be treated humanely." The foreign minister, finding himself in the international press's line of fire, continued in this combative vein. The next day, he declared in the Senate:

> I must solemnly declare that we have in no way been involved in the transfer, directly or indirectly. . . . My concern has been twofold. I telephoned Elisabethville immediately to verify that no Belgian – I do not only mean officials – participated in the operation. Our consul general there gave me the strictest assurances on that score, adding that Lumumba's guard was the exclusive responsibility of the Katangan authorities and that they, moreover, insisted it was their prerogative. My second concern was to ask . . . the Katangan authorities . . . to treat the prisoner humanely since he is a man and, because he is a prisoner and cannot defend himself, is entitled to respect and decent treatment.

Had not Wigny done all he could to deliver Lumumba *unconditionally* to his worst foes in South Kasai or Katanga, as his telegram of 18 January demonstrates? But he belied his own hypocrisy in this speech. Let us believe Wigny for a moment and suppose Brussels truly believed Lumumba was actually locked up in a Katangan prison. In that case, should not the minister take concrete measures to protect Lumumba's physical integrity? But Wigny did not demand the prisoner be handed over to the Red Cross or the United Nations, nor did he demand his release or repatriation to the Congolese capital. On the contrary, the nationalist leader's transfer and the refusal to take into consideration his parliamentary immunity did not seem to embarrass the minister: "I don't have to judge if the African authorities behaved well or badly . . . you naturally would not expect me to intervene in a more indiscreet manner in the decision of the current government."

Hounded by the press, accused by their political opponents, worried about the implications of the affair, the minister and his colleagues certainly did not have an easy task. Under the circumstances, they must have been pleased by the Belgian ambassador to the Vatican's report on the Pope's position:

The Holy See did all it could to help us. . . . The active benevolence John XXIII showed us . . . exceeded everything we could have hoped for. . . . Washington was derided here when it received and supported Lumumba, and it was thought that US machinations in the Congo might consolidate the regime of another Fidel Castro. . . . As for Katanga, we were constantly advised to be careful while wishing success to Tshombe in whom they were pleased to recognise the statesmanlike qualities totally lacking in the politicians in Léopoldville.

Belgian dignitaries, who do not have to take diplomatic or tactical considerations into account, felt freer than Foreign Minister Wigny. In the Senate, former Prime Minister Pholien could barely contain his glee. He saw in Lumumba's transfer the beginnings of a solid union between the Léopoldville and Elisabethville regimes: "We must . . . get Kasa Vubu to hold out his hand to Tshombe. Sending Lumumba to Katanga proves that the two men have not totally lost confidence in each other." Pholien's bold speech is revealing. The Belgian ruling class was free to settle the Congo crisis once and for all. The big political families shared the vision of the Congo's reconstruction around Katanga, and the working class did not oppose it. The strike of winter 1960–61 against the government's austerity measures did not change attitudes despite the fact that the workers' movement, which was fighting Eyskens's "loi unique" (unique law), and Lumumba's government both had the same adversary. It is no accident that a few weeks later former Prime Minister Pholien compared Patrice Lumumba to André Renard, a leader of the strike against the "loi unique', whom he hated. But instead of linking their struggle to the resistance of the Congolese nationalists and their African allies, the strike leaders focused purely on socio-economic demands.[31]

The attitude of the Belgian Socialists was typical of the unanimity of political opinion in Brussels. Even at the end of January 1961, when Belgian involvement in the dramatic events became clear, Rolin, the Socialist Party (PSB) leader, told the Senate he opposed withdrawing Belgian troops from Katanga. He said the military in Katanga must help "maintain order" and "protect the Whites" in a region where "we have important interests and many settlers", but not "get involved in reprisals or the civil war". In mid-February

1961 (by which time Lumumba's death had been announced and the press was full of news about Belgian involvement in the drama), Larock, another PSB leader, told the Chamber: "We in no way dispute that the presence of soldiers in Elisabethville is protecting Belgian and European women and children. For this defensive mission which they have accepted voluntarily, they deserve our gratitude."[32]

While the issue was being skilfully obfuscated, Brussels proved its awareness of many other aspects of the drama and the shock that the real facts might provoke. On 25 January, following the death of Sergeant Urbain, the thirteenth Belgian serviceman to die in the line of duty, Foreign Minister Wigny sent a note to New York, Brazzaville, Elisabethville and Shangungu advising women and children in the Eastern Province and Kivu to leave the region; if the men felt threatened, they should group together. On 8 February, a few days before the announcement of Lumumba's "escape", Wigny sent a telegram recommending "most insistently" that every Belgian in the Eastern Province and Kivu leave. Vandewalle subsequently asked: "Was this change of attitude the consequence of news . . . of events linked to the Lumumba affair?" The colonel admits in his own distinctive style that Elisabethville did actually send reports on the assassination to Brussels: "When the UN Commission of Inquiry was eventually established it asked for a copy of these reports, but the Belgian government claimed it had no knowledge of them. It ordered a search for them. But they never turned up. Maybe people looked in the wrong places?"

The United Nations was also braced for the shock. Dayal, Hammarskjöld's right-hand man, informed diplomats in the Congo that "the United Nations is offering protection to everybody on Katangan soil", meaning of course, that every *foreigner* could take advantage of the organisation's benevolence.[33]

Meanwhile, the Eyskens government and its tentacles on the spot, officially totally uninvolved in the events of 17 January, kept up their interest in Katangan affairs. At the end of January or beginning of February, Brussels and Elisabethville collaborated to ward off the danger of a French raid on the Katangan army. Belgian officials in Katanga kept d'Aspremont Lynden's military adviser Jules Loos informed hourly of the actions of French Colonel Trinquier, who was trying to make himself head of the *Gendarmerie*.[34] It is clear that this semi-permanent connection between Brussels and Elisabethville had been used to get rid of another equally serious problem: the elimination of Brussels' number one enemy. In any case, the Belgian government received a detailed report of the assassination on 1 February at the very latest. Vanden Bloock and Clémens had flown back to Brussels the previous day.

Meanwhile, Belgian radio and television news avoided the subject and the newspapers continued to incriminate the Congolese nationalists. The result of this campaign was a *Congolisation* and *banalisation* of the events. As always, *La Libre Belgique* set the tone:

According to a Swedish NCO on duty at the airfield, the former prime minister, on his arrival, was badly treated by Katangan policemen. It offends us that a prisoner could be beaten and manhandled. . . . It is certainly very regrettable that the Congolese don't always keep the "perfect gentleman's handbook" in their pockets. . . . We will never advocate police brutality, not anywhere. But the blows Lumumba received on the plane to Elisabethville may have an explanation. During the three months we just spent in the Congo, we gathered quite a few testimonies as to the former prime minister's real character. In Brazzaville . . . a French doctor [said that Lumumba] is paranoid. . . . In August, having become prime minister, Lumumba was forbidden to land in Elisabethville . . . [he had] a hysterical fit . . . if the soldiers in charge of escorting him knew, for instance, of the massacre of children in Bakwanga, it is comprehensible, if not excusable, that they showed little patience with their prisoner's tantrums.[35]

TO THE DEPTHS OF HELL

Shortly before nightfall on 18 January, a few hours after the meeting in Munongo's office, a convoy left for the scene of the execution. It was almost dark when Police Commissioners Soete, Verscheure and Sapwe and the nine policemen who took part in the assassination arrived. Exhuming the corpses from the sandy soil did not take much effort.[36] The bodies were rolled up in mortuary cloths and put into the back of a lorry. While Sapwe and the policemen returned to Elisabethville, Soete, Verscheure and three Congolese made their way in the lorry to Kasenga, 220 kilometres north east of Elisabethville towards the border with Rhodesia, in a region inhabited by the Bayeke whose *mwami* (chief) was Antoine Munongo, half-brother of Tshombe's minister. Not far from Kasenga, the lorry stopped and the bodies were interred in a hastily dug grave behind an ant-hill, a few paces from the road. On the way back, the mortuary cloths which had been removed from the bodies were burnt. The sun was already rising when, at about 5.30 a.m. on 19 January, the lorry got back to Elisabethville. Here ended Frans Verscheure's part in the drama. But he kept a souvenir of his last mission: a few days after the exhumation, he showed *Major* Verdickt a 7.62 calibre bullet which had been fired from an FN rifle and came, he said, from Lumumba's skull. Commissioner Soete also showed Brassinne several bullets recovered from the bodies while they were being unloaded because of the way they had been shaken about during the long journey.

Lumumba, Mpolo and Okito were not to stay in their new grave in Kasenga for long. A definitive solution was planned over the next two days. Early in the afternoon of 21 January, two Europeans in uniform and a few black assistants left for Kasenga in a lorry belonging to the public works department and containing road signs, geometrical instruments, two demijohns filled with sulphuric acid, an empty 200-litre petrol barrel and a hacksaw. According to Brassinne, all the equipment was provided by the public works department. According to Verscheure and Belina, the sulphuric acid came from the Union Minière. On their arrival, they unloaded the road signs and a theodolite to make passers-by think they were doing a land survey. But they could not find the grave, and had to stop searching at nightfall. Not until the evening of the next day did they find the grave and start their lugubrious task. The corpses were dug up, cut into pieces with knives and the hacksaw, then thrown into the barrel of sulphuric acid. The operation took hours and only ended the next morning, on 23 January. At first the two Belgians wore masks over their mouths but took them off when they became uncomfortable. Their only protection against the stench was whisky, so according to Brassinne, they got drunk. One of the black assistants spilt acid on his foot and burned it badly. They discovered that they did not have enough acid and only burned part of the bodies. According to Verscheure, the skulls were ground up, and the bones and teeth (that neither acid nor fire can destroy) were scattered on the way back. The same occured with the ashes. Nothing was left of the three nationalist leaders; nowhere could their remains, even the most minute trace of them, be found.

During his conversations with Brassinne, Police Commissioner Gerard Soete refused to formally identify himself and his brother as the two Europeans who disposed of the bodies. But he said "nevertheless, the possibilities he had to observe were such that no important detail of the operation could have escaped him. Thus his testimony had historical value". He also said that he described the frame of mind of the two Whites during the jobs in his book *De arena: Het verhaal van de moord op Lumumba* (The Arena: The Story of Lumumba's Assassination). On the basis of Verscheure's, Belina's and Mumba's testimonies, Brassinne and Kestergat conclude that the two men were indeed the Soete brothers. And very recently, Soete has confessed that the two Europeans were indeed himself and his brother.[37]

In *De Arena*, Soete describes in detail how a certain Schäfer and his companion Denys disposed of the bodies. What Soete calls "a diabolical job" represents in fact the culmination of seven months of intervention in the Congo by the West. The story is told in the chapter "To the Depths of Hell":

Twenty metres from the road, at the place of execution in the middle of wooded savannah, the stiff hand of the Prophet [Lumumba] rises towards the sky: a last attempt to accuse, to call upon his destructive troops. They still can't kill decently. They do not think of the corpse that remains after the destruction of the human being.

As soon as they put the bodies near the empty barrels and assemble their equipment, they realise that they are not prepared for that kind of job. They go back to the car and drink whisky. . . .

Unused to this task, they start by hacking the bodies to pieces like maniacs. This gets them nowhere, except into stink and filth, and they decide to tie towels round their mouths. Schäfer grabs the hacksaw and the Prophet's leg and starts sawing just above the knee, as if it were the branch of a tree. He delicately places the piece of the leg at the bottom of the barrel and continues separating the limbs from the torso one by one. . . .

When he is left with only the torso and the head, he suddenly realises the horror of what he is doing. Denys keeps as still as a stone statue, holding a torch to light the scene. It is Schäfer who awakens his hatred. Passion mixes with his drunkenness. His fingers grab the metallic fuzzy hair firmly, this is the decisive gesture. . . .

He puts the saw aside. It is no match for this monstrous head. He takes the axe, puts his foot on the jaw and splits the neck; he is out of breath; he swears profusely, cursing everybody like the brothers of his race. . . .

"I'm doing this instead of you, you white cowards." It is a grating oath spit out between clenched teeth through the cotton wool of the sanitary towel. . . .

Suddenly, gripped by an immense repugnance, he curses all the nationalist prophets with goatees and big glasses, all his own country's fops with silk hats and false promises. With the ferocity of hatred, he delivers the axe blow that separates the last vertebrae from the neck, takes the stinking head in his hands and spits on it. Then, his head resting on his crossed arms, he sits in the liquid soiling the grass, and begins to sob. Beside him, the limb-less torso. At his feet is the head, an impossible object. . . .

Here is the only material proof of the Prophet's death. If a cult of martyrdom ever appeared, he could provide it with relics. He takes some pincers out of the tool bag, and extricates with difficulty two gold teeth from the Prophet's upper jaw. Dentists can identify unrecognisable corpses by the prosthesis.

He takes the right arm out of the barrel and cuts two fingers from the stiff hand: the index finger has a bullet hole where the hand tried to protect the body, the index finger which had issued so many threats, which had shown the excited masses the way to destruction, to death and to his own end; and the little finger with the long nail which he used to clean his nose and ears while in prison.

He envelops the relics in a clean cloth, bends over to where a bullet has fallen out of the corpse onto the ground, adds it to the evidence and puts it all in his pocket. He picks up the torso, puts it in the barrel on top of the limbs and lays the head over it. He opens one of the demijohns and pours the contents on the dismembered body. A column of gas, white and whistling, rises to the sky. The acid turns the Prophet into a mass of mucous.

Alexandre Belina, Tshombe's lawyer, later told Brassinne that the Soete brothers went on leave for two weeks in South Africa to recover from the ordeal.[38]

Brassinne devotes several pages of his dissertation to clearing Gerard Soete's name. He claims that at each phase of the operation, "he was facing a situation which had already been prepared, and which he could not dodge. It was as if somebody else (Verscheure) who had been given this particular task had sneaked off at the very last moment each time, leaving him with the responsibility."[39]

But is it really true that "Soete was trapped", as Brassinne concludes uncritically? Soete had taken charge during the meeting; he even told Brassinne that in 1960, while on holiday in Belgium, he had wanted to come back to the Congo "especially to kill Lumumba". Soete also told him that the events took place "to save Katanga's government and men like Moïse Tshombe and Munongo whom everybody liked a lot". He did "his diabolical job" with mixed feelings, hatred (for Lumumba), repulsion, respect , but also contempt for the authorities. But in the end, Soete considers that he and his colleagues behaved correctly. The jacket of his book has a quote from *Rebels, Mercenaries and Dividends: The Katanga Story* by Hempstone Smith. What happened had to happen:

> Lumumba's death was, on the face of it, a crime. This should not be allowed to conceal the fact, however, that Lumumba was an erratic, incompetent, corrupt racist whose demagogic actions brought death and suffering to literally thousands of Congolese. He used his intelligence and diligence in the cause of evil, and in the end he was his own victim. If it was necessary for one man to die for the good of the Congo, the most logical candidate for this honor was Lumumba.

On his conversation with Soete, Brassinne writes:

> According to him, the act out was carried out for "laudable" motives. . . . He asked the author [Brassinne] the following question: "Is the man who did what was done a criminal?" Since the witness had not participated in the prisoners' execution, the answer was meant to be reassuring.

Gerard Soete went on to have a very good career under Mobutu.

THE WORLD IS INFORMED

The announcement, on 10 February, that Lumumba, Mpolo and Okito had escaped was interpreted as a portent of yet more news, that of the deaths of the three "fugitives". On Friday 13 February, soon after midday, during a press conference, Interior Minister Munongo said that the three escapees had fallen into the hands of bush villagers who had immediately killed them. He showed the three death certificates, all signed by Dr Guy Pieters, the head of a clinic catering for Belgian technical assistants in Katanga. Brassinne writes: "he signed

Lumumba, Mpolo and Okito's death certificates without seeing the bodies. . . . Pieters had asked Belina to swear to him that the prisoners were well and truly dead." For a while, the regime thought of taking the fingerprints of the dead men and smearing them on the "escape" car, but it was too late, as the saponification of the corpses made this impossible.

Munongo told journalists that the bodies

were immediately buried in a place which we shall not reveal, if only to prevent any pilgrimages being made to it. Nor shall we disclose the name of the village whose inhabitants put an end to the sorry exploits of Lumumba and his accomplices, for we do not want these Katangans, the name of whose tribe will not even be revealed, to be the object of possible reprisals by Lumumba supporters. Nor do we wish to be exposed to pressure to make us bring to trial for murder these Katangans who have perhaps acted somewhat precipitately . . . but whom we cannot honestly blame for having rid Katanga, the Congo, Africa and the world of a problem . . . which threatened to be a source of trouble to mankind.

Munongo concluded:

I should be lying if I said that Lumumba's death grieves me. You know how I feel about him: he is an ordinary criminal who is responsible for thousands of deaths in Katanga and tens of thousands of deaths in Kasai. . . . Mr. Hammarskjöld himself had said that the action against the Baluba of Kasai was nothing less than genocide. It is because of that that I am sure what the outcome of Lumumba's trial would have been: he would been sentenced to death.

And finally: "I am going to speak frankly and bluntly, as I usually do. We shall be accused of having murdered them. My reply is: prove it."[40]

Two questions arise from a careful study of Alexandre Belina's scenario of the pseudo escape. First, why did the Katangan regime, having announced the "escape", then proceed to say Lumumba was dead? Why didn't it arrange things so that the search for the "fugitives" ended in failure? By sowing doubt about Lumumba's death, the doubt about Elisabethville's role would have been easier to swallow. However, the regime was determined to eradicate any uncertainty about Lumumba's death. Verscheure wrote later on that they wanted to destroy the myth of a living Lumumba who could be resuscitated whenever useful.[41] Second, why didn't they attribute Lumumba's death to the beating he received in the plane? Tshombe regularly reiterated this thesis to exculpate himself. However, the prisoners' physical condition in Luano, though appalling, precluded this scenario. It would also raise other serious problems, for example what arguments could they then put forward for not handing over the three bodies?

A third reason for not attributing the deaths to the beatings, and one that carries somewhat more weight, is that it points the finger at Léopoldville. And, if the telegrams of 16 and 18 January are to be believed, this would go totally against d'Aspremont Lynden and Wigny's political objective. Léopoldville, the neo-colonial order's most recent protégé, was in mortal danger. This regime had to be protected first from Lumumba and then from the harmful consequences of the nationalist leader's assassination. The reputation of the elected head of state could not be sullied by the former prime minister's death being attributed to him. Kasa Vubu was the only actor on the neo-colonial Congolese stage able to invoke enough legitimacy to let him keep playing a central political role. Consequently, there was only one solution: Elisabethville, not Léopoldville, had to suffer the negative consequences. African Affairs Minister d'Aspremont Lynden and his colleagues were excellent strategists. "Pro-Katanga" from the early days, the minister always kept clearly in mind that secession was not an aim in itself, but an instrument for achieving a strategic aim, that is the construction of a neo-colonial Congo on what was left of Congolese nationalism. The *éminences grises* overseeing the escape scenario, the interests and instructions of Brussels, were never very far away.

Even *La Libre Belgique* finally admitted that few people believed the Katangan regime's explanation. In a leading article, the newspaper predicted that Belgium would be accused of having played a role in the three nationalist leaders' disappearance. The leader writer rejected the allegation, putting the blame squarely on the Congolese in a column tainted with racism: Munongo announced Lumumba's death "with a horrible African tranquillity". The explanation of events was obvious for the mouthpiece of the Belgian colonial world: "What has occurred demonstrates, alas!, that in Africa and certain other countries at the same stage of evolution, access to the democratic process remains a murderous affair." *De Standaard* told the same story: "Patrice Lumumba has died the way he always wanted: violently." If the journalist is to be believed, death for this "slender villager from the warrior tribe of the Batetela in the jungle of Kasai" was the logical end for a man who in his cell in Thysville refused to accept the inevitable: "[H]is eyes used to shine with a raging inner fire. Crouching in an armchair, his hands shaking with passion and fever . . . he felt power slipping between his fingers". *L'Écho de la Bourse*, the Belgian financial paper, best described the mood among the Belgian elite when it compared Lumumba's elimination to a necessary surgical operation: "the very existence of Lumumba was an abscess which had already infected the Congo and was threatening to infect it even further". It continued in a bout of frankness: "It is very hard for us to be sad . . . without being hypocritical!"

On 20 February 1961, Jacques Brassinne gave a speech at the Paul Hymans Centre in which he said: "Lumumba represented a permanent threat to Katanga, because only he could incite the Congolese masses and organise the invasion of Katanga." Tshombe did not have much choice, he had to kill or be killed: "In the Bantu mentality, it is natural for the stronger to get rid of the loser. One thing is certain, if Lumumba could have got hold of Messieurs Tshombe and Munongo, there would be no doubt as to their fate."

The influential weekly *Pourquoi Pas?* was already looking towards the future: the killing of Lumumba had created a myth, "which now crystallises the muddled aspirations of Congolese nationalism". But Lumumba's death also had

> enormous advantages: this stumbling block on the road to a possible agreement between more conciliatory leaders had to be swept aside. . . . With Lumumba gone it was possible to envisage a rapprochement between the majority of Congolese politicians and start again on the right footing.[42]

On Tuesday 14 February, African Affairs Minister d'Aspremont Lynden made a statement in the Chamber on behalf of the Belgian government: "M. Wigny and I asked our consular representative in Elisabethville several times to draw the Katangan authorities' attention to the moral and material consequences for Katanga as well as for Belgium of ill-treatment and acts of violence towards M. Lumumba." The minister, who had not shown much concern about Lumumba's treatment in his 16 January telegram, when there was still time, continued his speech by reading a telegram written solely for public consumption:

> I want to read you a telegram signed by me personally, and not the first: "I must insist in the strongest possible terms that humane treatment be reserved for Lumumba whose life cannot be put in danger under any circumstances. It is desirable that everything be done to have him examined by a UN doctor."

The minister could not bring himself to explicitly condemn Lumumba's assassination. But the man who was, more than any other, responsible for the military secession and the consolidation of Tshombe's state argued that Lumumba's death was the consequence of "morally unjustifiable acts . . . violence can never solve a political problem, violence does not make an argument valid, violence cannot realistically create a healthy political climate."

During the House's session on 14 February, some members uttered a few obvious facts. At one point, Pierson interrupted Wigny: "I note that the plane's pilot was Belgian, that the commander of the sixteen men guarding him was (what a coincidence!) Belgian and I remind you that the head of the juridical system in Katanga is Belgian!" On the same day, *La Meuse* took up the story of Captain Gat "of Antwerp" on Lumumba's escape. *Le Peuple* talked of horrific discoveries, and speculated as to which mining company had Lumumba's body preserved in cold storage.

In a reply, Wigny denied the glaringly obvious:

> The Belgian government has had no hand in Lumumba's arrest, detention, transfer, treatment and final fate. Like you, I read about M. Lumumba's

transfer in the press and my first concern, as well as M. d'Aspremont Lynden's, was to ask our consul there to immediately start the necessary procedures for ensuring this political prisoner be treated with the humanity to which every prisoner is entitled.

Meanwhile, behind the scenes, everything was being done to try and limit the damage. That same day, Major Jules Loos sent a message to *Major* Smal asking him to verify the rumour that Captain Gat had given an interview to an American newspaper about Lumumba's imprisonment. "Is it true?" wondered d'Aspremont Lynden's adviser. "And if it is, who gave him authorisation?" Wigny, for his part, sent a message forbidding Belgians to speak to the press about the Lumumba affair: "We were not involved, and didn't want to be involved in this affair, in any way whatsoever." Créner sent his boss a reassuring reply. Gat did not give an interview, he simply acted as a translator for a German journalist.[43]

The first potted biographies of the Congo's former prime minister started to appear in the papers. In its portrait of Lumumba, the editorial staff of *La Libre Belgique* repeated all the propaganda it had used over the previous months. The nationalist leader was represented as a man of unstable character, driven at best by infantile impulses, at worst by a psychosis which, according to the racist opinions of the day, only lives in black souls as described in Joseph Conrad's *Heart of Darkness*. Under the headline "Cruel and bloody . . . ", the article read:

He was a man of prodigious vitality. He was said to be paranoid, and probably was. He had the physical signs of it, slim hands with long fingers, an eager and animated expression, a feline mask, extreme agitation. His ambition was boundless, his hatred merciless. He would have sacrificed the whole world for his thirst for power. . . . Charming, an immensely talented orator, he could stir crowds, even European crowds. He was by far the most talented of the Congo's politicians. . . . He was a cruel man, incapable of governing, even of governing himself. He was not interested in governing. . . . He lived only for political struggles, showing exceptional stamina and physical courage, never hesitating to enter his adversaries' bastions, loving the challenge of it, and sowing fire and blood in his wake. . . . On 30 June, he read his speech insulting the King whom only the day before he had greeted full of smiles. . . . After the mutiny, he had words of consolation for the rebels' victims. . . . A few days later, he was spitting out the venom he had so far held in check. . . . He had a plan: to seize and hold power. All the rest was improvisation. And this in the end was his undoing. For him, politics was merely a terribly exciting game which he played with successive displays of audacity. The game turned out badly for him, and for the Congo, victim of his insanity. It will continue to pay the price with its blood, for killing will continue in his name. We must not forget this.

This infantilisation and psychiatric profile of Patrice Lumumba have been reiterated so many times already since the beginning of the Congo crisis! Here is one of hundreds of examples. In *La Libre Belgique* of 7 December 1960, the former Belgian Ambassador to the Congo described a discussion he had with Lumumba: "He got up; his eyes were flashing as if they were on fire; his height, his goatee beard, his long arms thrashing the air, personified some kind of new Lucifer in the silence of that African night."[44] Time after time, relentlessly, the fraternity of journalists symbolically dispatched Lumumba to the other world. This frenzy did not abate until the agitation surrounding his assassination had calmed down.

The announcement of the crime resulted in explosions of popular anger round the world. Demonstrations were organised in Belgrade, Cairo, London, Vienna, Warsaw, Moscow and New Delhi. In the Indian capital, protesters marched into the Belgian Embassy where they tore a photograph of King Baudouin from the wall. They carried banners with slogans such as "United Nations Out" and "Africa for the Africans". In Belgrade, hundreds of demonstrators forced their way through police barricades to the Belgian Embassy. The inside of the building was damaged and the protesters burned the Belgian flag. The French Embassy in the Yugoslav capital was also attacked. In Warsaw, demonstrators forced their way into the Belgian Embassy where a secretary and a diplomat were manhandled. Under the headline "Belgian Embassy Burned in Cairo", *De Standaard* described the assault on the building by thousands of protesters who put Lumumba's portrait in the place of Baudouin's before setting fire to the edifice. The Belgian ambassador, his wife and his staff had hastily hidden on the second floor from where they escaped in the nick of time through neighbouring gardens to reach the Canadian Embassy. There were student protests in Tel Aviv and Oslo. In Moscow, more than 5,000 demonstrators, among them a lot of Africans and Asians, tried unsuccessfully to attack the Belgian Embassy. The United States and the United Nations were also targeted. The UN Information Centre in Cairo, opposite the US Embassy, was destroyed. In Accra, demonstrators pulled the American Embassy plaque from the wall and trampled on the UN flag.

Several heads of state and governments aligned themselves with this massive wave of indignation. According to Moscow, the assassination was "an international crime, incompatible with the United Nations Charter". A spokesman for the French foreign minister called the murder "a violation of basic human rights". The Cuban government announced three days of official mourning for which the flags on every official building flew at half-mast. Mali also announced a period of official mourning. The editor of the Egyptian daily *Al Ahram*, President Nasser's mouthpiece, demanded the resignation of UN Secretary General Hammarskjöld, who "has lost the confidence of all African countries". A telegram from the Moroccan king Mohammed V to "H" declared: "This crime against African nationalism is a terrible blow to the prestige of the United

Nations and to the confidence recently demonstrated in it by independent states."

Ghanaians heard this broadcast speech by President Nkrumah:

Somewhere in Katanga in the Congo . . . three of our brother freedom fighters have been done to death. . . . About their end many things are uncertain, but one fact is crystal clear. They have been killed because the United Nations, whom Patrice Lumumba himself as Prime Minister had invited to the Congo to preserve law and order, not only failed to maintain that law and order, but also denied to the lawful Government of the Congo all other means of self-protection. History records many occasions when rulers of states have been assassinated. The murder of Patrice Lumumba and of his two colleagues, however, is unique in that it is the first time in history that the legal ruler of a country has been done to death with the open connivance of a world organisation in whom that ruler put his trust. . . . instead of preserving law and order, the United Nations declared itself neutral between law and disorder and refused to lend any assistance whatsoever to the legal Government in suppressing the mutineers who had set themselves up in power in Katanga and South Kasai. When, in order to move its troops against the rebels, the Government of the Congo obtained some civilian aircraft and civilian motor vehicles from the Soviet Union, the colonialist Powers at the United Nations raised a howl of rage while, at the same time, maintaining a discreet silence over the build-up of Belgian arms and actual Belgian military forces in the service of the rebels. . . . When Lumumba [after Kasa Vubu's coup] wished to broadcast to the people, explaining what happened, the United Nations in the so-called interest of law and order prevented him by force from speaking. They did not, however, use the same force to prevent the mutineers of the Congolese Army from seizing power in Léopoldville and installing a completely illegal Government. . . . the United Nations sat by while the so-called Katanga Government, which is entirely Belgian-controlled, imported aircraft and arms from Belgium and other countries, such as South Africa, which have a vested interest in the suppression of African freedom. The United Nations connived at the setting up, in fact, of an independent Katanga State, though this is contrary to the Security Council's own resolutions. Finally, the United Nations, which could exert its authority to prevent Patrice Lumumba from broadcasting, was, so it pleaded, quite unable to prevent his arrest by mutineers or his transfer, through the use of airfields under United Nations control, into the hands of the Belgian-dominated government of Katanga.

The *Observer*'s correspondent described the mood in New York as follows: "In small private wakes for Patrice Lumumba, the Afro-Asian delegates at the United Nations swallow their drinks as if there were a bitter taste in their mouths. Even the wiser among them let this bitterness slur their speech as they pronounce the name of Hammarskjöld."

On 15 February a pro-Lumumba demonstration disrupted a session of the Security Council.[45]

In the Congolese capital a funeral procession passed through the streets. About a hundred people walked in silence, their heads bowed. They carried a white flag to show their intentions were peaceful. They started their march near Lumumba's house in the African district and headed towards Le Royal, the hotel where the leaders had their offices. At the head of the procession walked Pauline Opango, aged twenty-eight, the wife of the former Congolese prime minister, carrying her son Roland, aged two, in her arms. Two other of the murdered leader's children, François, aged nine, and eight-year-old Patrice, were in Cairo and did not know of their father's death; nor of course could Guy, the son of his mistress Alphonsine Masuba, born posthumously. In keeping with local tradition, the women walked barefoot, their breasts bare. *Time* magazine struck one last blow. The magazine, which had organised a smear campaign against Lumumba and said his wife wore luxurious clothes, shoes and jewels, published a photo of the bare-breasted Madame Lumumba with the following caption: "Gone were the Paris frocks". A delegation comprising Madame Lumumba, Patrice's cousin Albert Onawelo and Joseph Lutula, the agriculture minister in Lumumba's government, was received by UN head Dayal. Pauline Opango asked that the body of her husband be handed over to her.

Tshombe turned down Dayal's request, saying "Bantu traditions" would not allow the bodies to be exhumed, even by members of the family. However, custom also dictates that the relatives of the dead have the right to visit the grave; in this case they would not be able to exercise this right, since the name of the village where the three men were buried was withheld. In another letter, Tshombe refused to allow a United Nations investigation into the events, calling the request an interference in Katanga's internal affairs.[46] Dayal's request soon lost its impetus when Pauline Opango and other Lumumbists were forced to flee to a camp for political refugees hastily built by the United Nations in Léopoldville.

Brussels and New York did their best to defend themselves against worldwide condemnation. In Brussels, the Foreign Ministry spokesman reiterated Minister Wigny's previous statement maintaining total innocence: "In accordance with its policy of non-interference in the internal affairs of the Congolese state, Belgium has absolutely nothing to do with the arrest, imprisonment, transfer and death of the former Prime Minister." On 15 February, the minister himself appeared on television:

> On this difficult night for Belgium, I would like to make a short statement. Patrice Lumumba is dead. If he was the victim of a political assassination, we condemn it in no uncertain terms. . . . Yet, because Patrice Lumumba is

dead, a victim of the Congo's internal divisions, the Belgian government and people have their flag and ambassadors insulted and threatened and their embassies ransacked and even burned. . . . you, my compatriots, [are] as indignant as I am at the defamation campaign which affects everything we have done and are doing, and which questions our intentions. . . . From the beginning of the Congolese drama to this day, Belgium has never pursued any aim which is not noble, generous and unselfish. . . . Our conscience is clear.

However, the minister's life was likely to be complicated by fresh news. The edition of *De Standaard* that printed Wigny's speech above also mentioned that a Belgian doctor was implicated in the affair. It named Doctor Guy Pieters, who said he had examined the bodies and certified the causes of death. Professional discretion would not allow him to say more.[47]

At the Security Council, Secretary General Hammarskjöld called the murder "a revolting crime against principles for which this organisation stands". Without batting an eyelid, the harassed UN leader said he would look into whether the international organisation could be partly responsible for Lumumba's fate. He lied about the UN's part in Lumumba's arrest by Mobutu's troops at the beginning of December, saying that the organisation did not know where Lumumba was, and consequently, could not offer him protection. And he stressed that Lumumba's transfer to Katanga "was entirely outside the control of the United Nations' organs". Then he noted: "Immediately, in demarches to Mr. Kasa Vubu and Mr. Tshombe, I exercised all the influence possible for the return of Mr. Lumumba to Léopoldville and for application of normal legal rules in protection of his interests." We have already seen what is implied by "immediately" or "all the influence possible" and what the United Nations means by Lumumba's interests. Hammarskjöld said that the UN took immediate measures after the announcement on 10 February that Lumumba, Mpolo and Okito had escaped: "the instruction was that if Mr. Lumumba were to seek protection from any United Nations unit, he would immediately be granted asylum." Would it be exaggerating to claim that this was another lie? I have not found a single document in the United Nations archives to support this statement.[48]

A general strike organised in Luluabourg to protest the assassination was a total success. But in Stanleyville, where the armed nationalists had begun the apparently unstoppable reconquest of the country, the announcement of the death of Lumumba, Mpolo and Okito produced no immediate visible reactions. On the contrary, a deathly, supernatural calm fell over the city, as if Lumumba's death could not be true, as if Lumumba's personality had already taken on the mythical proportions it would assume in the decades to come. Nationalist leaders like Jean Manzikala and Lundula called for calm. On 16 February, Monsignor Kinsch celebrated a Mass in memory of Lumumba. At the end of the service, at the explicit request of their leaders, the 25,000 members of the congregation went home peacefully. In the rest of nationalist Congo, outbursts remained limited. Stanleyville shot a few officers who remained loyal to Mobutu and who had staged an anti-nationalist coup during the autumn of 1960. On 14 February, two Belgians were killed on the streets of Kindu. The doctor who recovered the bodies said later that the people were in the grip of rumours circulating in town, that the Belgians had sent Lumumba's body to be eaten in Brussels. In Maniéma, some European nuns were manhandled. But on 15 February, all detained foreigners were released on orders from the Stanleyville authorities.[49]

A RIVER OF BLOOD

THE MARTYRDOM OF JEAN-PIERRE FINANT AT BAKWANGA (9 FEBRUARY 1961)

On 9 February 1961, President Kasa Vubu signed a decree announcing the official demise of the College of Commissioners. The college was replaced by a provisional government headed by Joseph Ileo. Real power, however, remained in the hands of Kasa Vubu, Mobutu, Nendaka and Bomboko. In a highly significant move, the very day Ileo's government took office, six nationalist leaders were put in a DC-3 and transferred from Léopoldville to Bakwanga, capital of the secessionist state of South Kasai. One of them was Jean-Pierre Finant, president of the Eastern Province. According to the pilot Captain Michaux, the prisoners were beaten during the whole journey. The injuries they received were "indescribable". Major Jacques Fataki was so severely beaten that his jaw was "completely dislocated. . . ." He was blind by the time he was taken out of the plane. The day after their transfer all six nationalists were dead. They had suffered the fate Wigny and his compatriots had originally planned for Lumumba, the details of which Commissioner Mukamba had predicted: "Patrice Lumumba would be transferred to Bakwanga where he would be immediately killed in the main square, then cut into little pieces so that each *muluba* could eat a bit." The massacre removed the remaining leaders of the Congolese nationalist movement in its anti-colonial stage.[1]

In the meantime, Elisabethville's long-planned offensive against the nationalist uprising in north and central Katanga began. A few hours after Munongo's announcement that Lumumba, Mpolo and Okito had "escaped", Operation Banquise was launched. A thousand Katangan soldiers, led by a Belgian, Major J. Matthys, advanced from Lubudi to Bukama, taking three days to cover 100 kilometres. In a secret telegram to Brussels, Elisabethville said that Moroccan troops of the UN force had handed over to the *Gendarmerie* fleeing Baluba who had asked them for protection.

The operation was one stage in a war that would eventually kill several thousand people and bleed Katangan nationalism to death. Bringing mercenaries into Tshombe's army had made the increasingly well-equipped *Gendarmerie* into a merciless war machine. At the end of March, the *Gendarmerie*'s capture of Manono represented a strategic turning point. The UN head Dayal said in a report: "the offensive launched by Mr Tshombe on 11 February is aimed . . . at the subjugation of the entire region populated by the Baluba tribe, by the use of overwhelming force, including the burning of villages and the elimination of all opposition, resistance and the terrorization of the population." Benoît Verhaegen, an expert on the subject, wrote: "From February 1961, fierce military repression devastated the whole of north Katanga. It decimated the population, destroyed the social and political structures in rural areas, exacerbated tribal conflicts and demoralised the whole population."[2]

It would take time and the experience of struggle to give Congolese nationalism a new face and a new direction.

COVER-UP IN NEW YORK AND BRUSSELS

Following the announcement of the assassination, there was pressure from many quarters to launch an independent inquiry into the deaths of Lumumba, Mpolo and Okito and to punish the guilty parties. Worldwide indignation led several countries to recognise Gizenga's nationalist government in Stanleyville as the Congo's sole legitimate government. On 20 February 1961, it was recognised by the United Arab Republic (the union of Egypt and Syria), the Soviet Union, the German Democratic Republic, Yugoslavia, Guinea, Morocco, Ghana, the provisional government of the Algerian nationalists GPRA, Mongolia, Albania, Cuba, Poland, Bulgaria, Iraq, Hungary and the People's Republic of China. The International Commission of Jurists in Geneva put out a communiqué demanding "an in-depth inquiry by a highly competent and impartial international committee". On behalf of the Belgian League of Human Rights, Léon Goffin and George Aronstein expressed their amazement at the fact that the Katangan government regarded the execution as a legal act of justice. The League demanded the crime be investigated and the guilty punished.[3]

Global indignation and a thirst for justice also dominated the debates in the UN Security Council. In its 21 February resolution, the Security Council declared "having learnt with deep regret the announcement of the killing of the Congolese leaders, Mr. Patrice Lumumba, Mr. Maurice Mpolo and Mr. Joseph Okito", the Council is "deeply concerned at the grave repercussions of these crimes and the danger of widespread civil war and bloodshed in the Congo and the threat to international peace and security". The Security Council finally took the decisions Lumumba had hoped for in vain seven months earlier. For the first time, Hammarskjöld's legal objections to "interference in internal affairs" and "the use of violence except in self defence" – objections used by the United Nations to justify standing passively by while Lumumba's government was destroyed – were formally dismissed. The resolution gave the UN the power to use "force", if necessary, to "prevent the occurrence of civil war in the Congo". Moreover, the Security Council recognised "the imperative necessity of the restoration of parliamentary institutions in the Congo in accordance with the fundamental law of the country [the Congolese constitution], so that the will of the people should be reflected through the freely elected Parliament". The Security Council also decided "that an immediate and impartial investigation be held in order to ascertain the circumstances of the death of Mr. Lumumba and his colleagues and that the perpetrators of these crimes be punished". The Council "calls upon all States to extend their full co-operation and assistance and take such measures as may be necessary on their part, for the implementation of this resolution". During the debates, the secretary general asked for an "international investigation" which he considers essential to determine who was responsible, and what the "appropriate counteraction" should be.[4]

On 15 April 1961, the UN General Assembly decided to entrust the investigation to a commission made up of a Burmese judge, a Mexican ambassador, a Togolese lawyer and a civil servant from Ethiopia. This Commission of Inquiry met sixty-six times between May and October 1961. Sixteen sessions were devoted to questioning witnesses in New York, Geneva and Brussels. In their report of 11 November 1961, the members of the Commission stated that their primary aim was to establish the facts, that their task was different from a purely judicial mission and that, consequently, they had not followed strict procedures either with regard to gathering evidence or to the functioning of the Commission itself, and finally, that the issue of punishing the guilty parties was not within their brief.[5]

The Belgian government's lack of good will towards the Commission knew no bounds. It did not even reply to the Commission's or Secretary General Hammarskjöld's request to make available any information they had about the events in question. Of the fifteen Belgians on the list the Commission gave the Belgian government, urgently requesting all necessary measures to allow the Commission to interview them, only three were questioned. Some, including Jules Cousin, director of the Union Minière, refused to appear. Others, according to the Commission's report, "did not even reply to the Commission's requests". Following persistent rumours at the beginning of February 1961 of a Katangan intelligence services report on Lumumba's death apparently sent to Brussels, the Commission asked the Belgian government for a copy. Brussels denied any knowledge of it and said it would investigate the matter itself. It did not even give the Commission "a definitive reply", according to Commission members.

Yet the Belgian government knew full well the juridical scope of the 21 February resolution. Hammarskjöld wrote to Brussels:

The resolution . . . must be regarded as a mandatory decision that all Members of the United Nations are legally bound to accept and carry out in accordance with Article 25 of the Charter. The juridical consequence is that all the Member States concerned are under a legal obligation to adapt their national legislation to extent necessary to give effect to the decision of the Council.

Respect for the United Nations Charter was certainly not going to offset Brussels' more practical concerns. The opinion so clearly and brutally expressed after the assassination by well-known journalists like Pierre Davister or Philippe Toussaint still prevailed in the corridors of power. *Pourquoi Pas?* observed that it would be "insane" to publish the identity of Lumumba's assassins. Why expose them to possible retaliation? According to them, these men "in fact did what everyone expected and even hoped for. For there are individuals we cannot mourn, we do not mourn. On the contrary. Hitler's demise was a relief for humanity. Lumumba's disappearance will also provoke this same feeling in all honest men who love freedom, dignity, progress."[6]

Neither the Léopoldville nor the Elisabethville regime was ready to cooperate with the Commission. The UN leadership even helped sabotage the investigation itself. In mid-June 1961, shortly before the Commission left for Europe and the Congo, its members had a meeting with Hammarskjöld who told them the opinion of his representative in the Congo: the decision to start the investigation in the Congo, he said, "might on the one hand appear unilateral and on the other prejudice the serious negotiations then taking place regarding the formation of a new Congolese government." At this time, the United Nations and the West were working together on a unified Congolese government around Kasa Vubu and Tshombe, with the participation of Stanleyville's nationalists. The UN did not want to upset the West's pawns, or the foundations for establishing a new regime, by imposing an investigation into the assassination on them. A few days after the conversation with the secretary general, three high-ranking UN representatives in the Congo wrote to the Commission:

The arrival of the Commission [in the Congo] will give rise to feelings of hatred, of revenge, which can be easily exploited . . . in Africa. For the United Nations as well as for the world at large, the solution of this political problem is of paramount importance.

A pretty clear message! Vandewalle, who did not really support UN intervention in the Congo, observed later: "Neither UNOC, nor the central government, nor the Katangan government, wanted the [Commission's] investigation to be a success."[7]

On 2 August 1961, a new national government took over in Léopoldville. Adoula's administration was a coalition between Léopoldville and Stanleyville, as Elisabethville (for the time being) remained isolated. The new regime was the first step towards a stable neo-colonial government. The reopening of parliament and the inclusion of nationalists in the cabinet were nothing more than cosmetic measures. Lumumba's previous parliamentary majority was no longer a danger. The overthrow of Lumumba's government, the assassination of the former prime minister and the crushing of the nationalist rebellion in north Katanga in the spring of 1961 had finally destroyed the momentum of the anti-colonial movement. The masses were trying to get their political breath back. The nationalist leaders who had sided with Lumumba during the anti-colonial revolution now turned to their new masters. They bowed their heads opportunistically before the neo-colonial offensive, or were completely demoralised. Their support for the new regime did not change its neo-colonial nature in any way.

Behind the democratic façade, with Kasa Vubu as president and Adoula as prime minister, Mobutu still held the military reins. The UN Commission quickly realised this. It had asked Adoula to set a date for its visit to the Congo. On 19 September 1961, Adoula's foreign minister replied that the new government reserved the right to investigate the matter which was "primarily an affair which concerns the Congolese people" and to punish the guilty. Consequently, the Commission's visit was "inopportune and pointless". The author of the letter was none other than Justin Bomboko, former president of Mobutu's College of Commissioners and loyal collaborator of Brussels, Washington and New York in their fight against Lumumba's government. For his part, Tshombe cared even less about sweetening the pill: he did not even bother to reply to the Commission's request to testify.[8]

The Commission's final conclusions state that Lumumba, Mpolo and Okito were murdered "in a villa not far from Elisabethville, and in all probability in the presence of high officials of the Government of Katanga Province". The murder was probably the work of "two Belgian mercenaries". The Commission stressed: "President Kasa Vubu and his aides, on the one hand, and the Provincial Government headed by Mr. Tshombe on the other, should not escape responsibility for the death of Mr. Lumumba, Mr. Okito and Mr. Mpolo."

In its final conclusion the Commission expressed the hope that its report might "serve as a basis for a further investigation, in the Congo, and also in judicial proceedings". But the United Nations would not investigate further nor prosecute the guilty since it was now supporting the new Kasa Vubu–Adoula–Mobutu regime in Léopoldville.

Moscow brought no hope either.[9] At no time during the Congolese crisis did the Kremlin ever intend to give the Congolese nationalists unconditional help.

Since Stalin *de facto* replaced internationalism with peaceful coexistence with the West, Moscow no longer questioned capitalist supremacy in (semi-) colonial countries. Moscow used the crisis for propaganda purposes. Khrushchev only condemned Belgian intervention and Katanga's secession to strengthen his diplomatic position in the Afro-Asian world. Moscow did not really oppose UN intervention: it adopted the views of Afro-Asian countries which pinned all their hopes on the UN's ability to solve the Congo crisis.

In fact four out of the five resolutions on the Congo crisis in the Security Council in 1960 and 1961 were supported by both Washington and Moscow. The Soviet representative abstained in the vote on the resolution of 21 February 1961. Lumumba's death would not change Moscow's opportunistic stance in any way. The Kremlin blamed Hammarskjöld for the part played by the UN in the events, but supported its plan for national reconciliation. Soon afterwards, when the Kremlin realised that its verbal attacks on Hammarskjöld seemed to alienate rather than attract its possible Afro-Asian allies, its criticism abruptly stopped. The direct support that the Soviet Union gave nationalist Stanleyville remained negligible, and when, in August 1961, the Adoula government came into being, Khrushchev congratulated him for strengthening the Congo's independence and unity. Therefore, Moscow was certainly not in favour of continuing the investigation into Lumumba's assassination.[10]

Consequently, the UN General Assembly did not act on its Commission's report. On 24 November 1961, with Soviet support, the Security Council approved its fifth resolution on the Congo, which made no further mention of Lumumba or of finding and punishing his murderers. And yet, Lumumba's spirit lives on in the resolution. The Security Council, which had promised "its full and firm support" for Adoula's government, now used the same language that Lumumba had used when the crisis began, a language rejected by the United Nations and the West while a nationalist government was in power in the Congo. Now that Lumumba was dead, they adopted his ideas; now that there was a real prospect of a neo-colonial parliamentary majority, the reconstruction of a unified Congo was acceptable: "All secessionist activities against the Republic of the Congo are contrary to the fundamental law [the Congolese constitution] and Security Council decisions."[11] Soon afterwards, the United Nations sent troops to force Katanga to return to the unified Congolese state.

THE PRICE OF BLOOD

The eight soldiers and nine policemen who carried out the execution and helped stage the prisoners' so-called escape got a bonus in the months following the assassination. One of the receipts reads as follows: "I, the undersigned private X, of the 1st company military police Camp Massart, have received this 16 June 1961 from Commissioner Verscheure the sum of 10,000 francs." The text was written by Frans Verscheure himself on the back of a piece of writing paper headed Comité Spécial du Katanga (Katanga Special Committee). Verdickt later stated that he had paid each soldier and each policeman separately, probably in Verscheure's presence. If certain witnesses in Brassinne's "Enquête" are to be believed, a few Belgo-Katangans also got money. Léopoldville's accomplices were not forgotten either. On the day Lumumba was transferred, Lahaye told Brussels that Kandolo's and Nendaka's children were on their way to Belgium. Tshombe's children had already gone a few months earlier. The message said: "Both Kandolo and Nendaka are in an energetic mood, and knowing their children are safe will encourage them to carry on." The Belgians in Léopoldville were not short of financial rewards for their efforts either. On 18 January 1961, Major Loos was informed about the financial resources available to Colonel Marlière in a letter explaining that he had at his disposal 10 million Belgian francs, US$20,000, £7,000 sterling and 26 million CFA francs (the currency used in France's African colonies). Marlière concluded that further payments were not really necessary.[12]

Subalterns and superior officers alike were rewarded with congratulations, official thanks and promotions. The reason was clear: political assassinations were not the exclusive prerogative of the CIA or the KGB, and the Belgian ruling class was at the heart of this political murder. Remarkably, the assassination did not jeopardise the palace's discreet support for the Katangan regime in the slightest. The court did not distance itself from a regime the whole world saw as having blood on its hands. On 13 March 1961, a month after the official news of Lumumba's assassination, King Baudouin writes to Tshombe:

Dear President,

I would like to tell you how moved I was [by Tshombe's letter to Baudouin of 21 February]. . . .
    The whole of Belgium and I myself are particularly aware of the loyalty you have always shown my country and me. Rest assured that I very much appreciate the wisdom with which you have governed Katanga in extremely difficult and delicate circumstances. . . .

Please accept, my dear President, the expression of my highest esteem.

Baudouin[13]

Tshombe was not the only one to benefit from royal magnanimity. Baudouin also looked after the Belgians who, in one way or another, contributed to the outcome of the Congo crisis and to destroying the Congolese national movement by massacring their leaders. He did so by bestowing titles on them – one of the few instruments left to the Belgian monarchy to publicly express appreciation for individuals or the ideas and actions they symbolise. For Baudouin, this was not a banal task linked to Independence Day rituals. Quite the opposite; anecdotes tell that he attached great importance to ennoblement and to the external signs of social promotion. Gaston Eyskens himself wrote that Baudouin once reprimanded him for not wearing his Sash of the Order of Léopold at some ceremony.

The Belgian monarch opened wide the doors of the nobility to the Belgo-Katangan protagonists in the Congo crisis. Their role in the 17 January assassination was no obstacle to his rewarding several of them with a gesture of eternal gratitude. Count Harold d'Aspremont Lynden was already a regular visitor to the court before the Congo crisis. Soon after Gaston Eyskens resigned as Senator, Baudouin told him that he would make him a viscount *motu proprio*, following a constitutional privilege the monarch rarely uses. Moreover, Eyskens also became minister of state. Other protagonists also joined the court's pantheon: Pierre Wigny was made a baron and Jacques Brassinne a knight; Guy Weber later became Léopold III's aide-de-camp. After Léopold III's death, in September 1983, Weber stayed at Argenteuil as secretary to Léopold III's widow Lilian, Princess of Retie, a position he still holds today.[14]

COLONEL VANDEWALLE AND LEOPOLD II

The African Affairs Minister d'Aspremont Lynden was very pleased with Colonel Vandewalle's performance during the first months of his Katangan career. In a letter dated 24 February 1961, the minister asked him to use "his moral authority, which I know is considerable, to persuade officers to stay there" in order "to maintain the cohesion of the Katangan *Gendarmerie* and the Belgian presence in Africa". He was grateful beyond words: "I congratulate you and I cannot thank you enough for the remarkable job you were able to do so successfully in so short a time in Katanga." The count did not go into detail, but the colonel had indeed succeeded in sorting out quite a few problems during this period. Against a background of worrying developments like the nationalists' military advance and the collapse of the Léopoldville regime, he had been sent to Elisabethville to solve the crisis in the Katangan army command. Within a few weeks, he had succeeded in taking control of the *Gendarmerie* and strengthening it. When the 17 January murder decapitated the nationalist movement, the colonel prepared the *Gendarmerie* to deal a final blow to the Balubakat rebellion which threatened Tshombe's regime.

At the end of February 1961, Léopoldville, Elisabethville and Bakwanga nearly reached a compromise. The *crème de la crème* of the three regimes met in the conference room of the Special Katanga Committee in Elisabethville. Sitting round the table were Tshombe, Munongo, Kimba, Muhona, Bartelous, Tignée, Belina and Weber for Katanga; Ileo, Adoula, Lihau, Charles Kisolokele and Puati for Léopoldville; Kalonji, André Kabeya, Raphaël Bintu and Gillet for South Kasai. On Weber's suggestion, Colonel Vandewalle was the main speaker, an honour which did not make him particularly happy since, as he said himself, he "does not like being in the spotlight". True to character, the *proconsul* gave himself a modest introduction: "I am not part of the Katanga *Gendarmerie*'s cadre. I am simply an observer. My role is to help Katanga with military technique and see to it that the Belgian officers at Katanga's disposal act at all times in the interests of Katanga and its government." (The colonel should have added "as long as Katanga's interests serve those of Brussels", to be perfectly accurate.)

Vandewalle suggested that his listeners pool their military resources: "I know I touch on a sensitive political issue and I apologise. It is not a soldier's place to do so. But in the present circumstances . . . it is absolutely impossible to dissociate the military problem from the political". They ended by drawing up a military protocol and agreeing to continue their collaboration at a summit in Tananarive[15] (now Antananarivo). In fact, it took several years for a stable neo-colonial regime to be established in the Congo.

On 25 April 1961, the Lefèvre–Spaak government took over from that of Eyskens–Lilar. Paul-Henri Spaak succeeded Pierre Wigny at the Foreign Ministry. The Ministry of African Affairs became part of the Foreign Ministry and Count Harold d'Aspremont Lynden left the cabinet.

Certain sources say that this change of government can explain the anti-Katanga stance adopted by Brussels from 1961, and that it mirrors the changes in Washington brought by President John F. Kennedy's more favourable attitude to Africa than his predecessor Eisenhower's. This analysis, which attributes social change to strong personalities, is not borne out by facts, however. That the new cabinet's anti-Katanga position was due to a changed situation is proved by the fact that central figures in the previous administration supported the policy reversal. In September 1961, none other than the former African Affairs Minister d'Aspremont Lynden wrote Tshombe a letter. The count did not beat about the bush: the secessionist state might be in a strong position, he said, but serious danger threatened. In Léopoldville, "extremism" was about to take over Adoula's administration which included Gizenga supporters. A "communist" regime or one "sympathetic to communism" in Léopoldville would sweep Katanga away. This is why the "Katanga issue has to be solved". D'Aspremont Lynden believed Tshombe should come to an agreement with the moderates in Léopoldville and should extend the hand of friendship in a letter offering talks between the two governments. The former minister asked Tshombe to mention "President Kasa Vubu's authority", without insisting too much on Katanga's "independence". "It is the only way to strengthen the position of Léo's moderates, which is now crucial. In the long term, Katanga's fundamental solidity will inevitably strengthen its position." Lesser gods also threw themselves into the arena. At the end of August 1961, after the *Gendarmerie*'s merciless offensive, the territory still controlled by Katangan nationalist rebels was reduced to a third of what it had been at the height of their power. But this did not solve all the problems. In early November 1961, an internal memo from Vandewalle and

Brassinne pointed out that an alliance between Léopoldville and the UN forces, were that organisation to agree, could easily terminate the secession. This is why they suggested Elisabethville face reality and consider taking Katanga back into the Congo fold.[16]

In implementing the Security Council's 21 February resolution, by not-such-gentle persuasion, the UN helped to put the Adoula government in the driving seat. From then on, it resolutely opted for reunification. Katangan secession, previously a powerful weapon with which to destroy Lumumba, had become superfluous. Tshombe was called to order and encouraged to play a more useful role in Léopoldville, to counterbalance nationalists like Gbenye, and to use Katanga's economic potential for the Congo as a whole. US Deputy Secretary of State George Ball resorted to anti-communist rhetoric to condemn the secession: "The issue in Katanga is not self determination. It is the threat of armed secession by a tribal area that happens to contain a disproportionate part of the wealth of the entire country. . . . The armed secession of Katanga plays into the hands of the communists."

The then Minister of Foreign Affairs Paul-Henri Spaak wrote in his memoirs: "Adoula and Kasa Vubu were wise. . . . They had to oppose Katanga's secession. Deprived of its richest province, their country's future was in jeopardy. They could not allow this."[17] But the secessionist spirit did not abate. Military clashes between the Blue Berets and the Katangan *Gendarmerie* in August and September 1961, then later at the end of 1962 and beginning of 1963 finally ended on 17 January 1963 with an agreement between Tshombe and the UN. The secession was over, but Tshombe and his supporters kept the mandates they held before their unconstitutional coup.

From the beginning of his mission in the newly independent Congo until the end of the secession, Vandewalle had spent 1,004 days on African soil. He had arrived as a soldier, but ended this chapter of his African career as a diplomat. On 17 October 1961, Colonel Vandewalle took over from Créner at the Belgian consulate in Elisabethville. The consulate's "manager" acted as a *de facto* curator and, in close collaboration with the Foreign Minister Spaak, oversaw the end of the secession. Then, on 9 March 1963, Vandewalle arrived back at Zaventem airport. Two days later he was granted an audience at the royal palace, then, a few days after that, he was the guest of honour at a dinner at the finance minister's residence, at which Foreign Minister Spaak toasted the work of the former head of the colonial intelligence services in Katanga. When the secession ended, Spaak had told Vandewalle in a telegram that he wanted "to express my deep appreciation for your conduct and my gratitude for your loyal and intelligent assistance". Vandewalle was made Commander of the Order of Léopold. Meanwhile, Tshombe lamented Vandewalle's departure. According to a witness, Katanga's former president told the new Belgian consul in Elisabethville: "my heart is broken and bleeds since Vandewalle left".[18]

True nationalists very quickly realised that Adoula's government did not embody the future of Congolese nationalism. The prime minister was part of the political decor, but the administration could only indulge in the luxury of a parliamentary façade, thanks to Mobutu's troops. Many nationalists took to the bush. In January 1964, Pierre Mulele launched a rebellion against Léopoldville in his native Kwilu region, east of the capital. Meanwhile, a second front was being prepared abroad. The most important nationalists fled to Brazzaville where they founded the Conseil National de Libération (CNL, National Liberation Council). In March 1964, Gaston Soumialot arrived in Bujumbura, the capital of Burundi, where he regrouped the nationalists who had been driven out of the Congo. His supporters occupied Uvira, near the border with Burundi, shortly afterwards, on 15 May. The east of the country also presented a very serious threat to the regime.

Mobutu and the Binza Group decided to appeal to Tshombe for help. His Western contacts, Katangan soldiers and mercenaries were apparently essential to combat the rebellions effectively. Spaak met Tshombe at his European residence and asked him to go back to the Congo. He accepted on one condition: he wanted the Belgian entourage which guided him through the secession with him again. The first person Tshombe had in mind was Professor Clémens, now holding the sociology chair at Liège University, but Spaak thought he was too tainted by his activities in Katanga to be acceptable to Léopoldville. So Tshombe asked for Frédéric Vandewalle and *Major* Joe Verdickt to join the mission.

On 8 August 1964, Vandewalle arrived in Léopoldville with instructions from the Foreign Ministry in his pocket. Mobutu, the new prime minister, Tshombe and Vandewalle hired a large number of mercenaries to fight the rebellion. A United Nations official wrote in a confidential telegram: "Belgian businessmen . . . are determined reassert complete control over Congolese government and economy to point that there will be in fact classic neo-colonialist system in existence."[19] This old dream of the West could only be realised, however, by open military intervention. It was only after 24 November 1964, when Belgo-American operations began in Stanleyville (the rebel capital where all Westerners had been taken hostage) and shortly after the operations in Paulis where Belgian paras had also dropped, that mercenaries under the command of 300 to 400 Belgian officers destroyed the revolutionary momentum of the nationalist rebellion. The rebels' strength could be gauged by the fact that 40 per cent of Congolese territory was still in their hands at the beginning of 1965. But then the rebels systematically lost ground till by the end of the year only a few pockets of resistance remained around Bunia (in the north-east), Fizi (in the east) and Idiofa (in Kwilu). Mobutu did not manage to get his hands on Pierre Mulele until 1968, when he gave him his word of honour as an officer that he would grant an amnesty to the remaining rebels. Mulele was hacked to death by Mobutu's torturers.

The Belgian officers and political advisers fighting the rebels were for the most part the same men who fought Lumumba in 1960 from within secessionist Katanga. Vandewalle himself led the armoured brigade which, in October 1964, set out from Kamina to reconquer Stanleyville, an operation known as Ommegang. Vandewalle recognises this continuity: without the Belgian training of the Katangan *Gendarmerie*, "there would have been no Ommegang". His brigade had Belgian and American equipment, supported by air power. Operation Ommegang caused a river of Congolese blood to be shed. It is impossible to calculate the loss of Congolese life, but mercenaries admit that they killed about 3,000 Congolese in Kindu alone, and according to the Belgian officer Jean-Claude Marlair, the rebellion and the subsequent repression cost the lives of "about 300 Whites and more than 200,000 Congolese". All the evidence implies that a much larger number of lives were sacrificed.[20]

Lumumba's assassination halted the revolutionary momentum which began in 1959 with the Léopoldville revolt. But the 1964 rebellions proved that the Congolese masses continued to dominate the political scene, and that Mobutu's rise in 1960, Adoula's government in 1961, and Katanga's return to the Congo in 1963 had not totally reversed the situation in favour of neo-colonialism. Although neo-colonialism had political control through Adoula, it did not qualitatively change the balance of power within society. Rebellions had to be crushed to fundamentally alter this balance, to the detriment of the Congolese people. It was as if the days of Léopold II had returned. Thanks to its military supremacy, the Belgian conqueror could again openly lay down the law.

On 12 October 1965, President Kasa Vubu relieved his prime minister Tshombe of his duties. On 24 November 1965, Mobutu in turn kicked out Kasa Vubu, suspended political life for five years, and proclaimed the Second Republic. A few months later, the general concentrated all power into his own hands, becoming president of the republic, head of state, commander-in-chief of the army and, later, president-founder of the one-party system. In 1965, foreign intervention finally accomplished what it had started in July 1960: the nationalist political and military leadership had been destroyed; the military capability of the various rebel groups had been smashed; the population was fragmented and demoralised; a stable pro-Western regime was running the country. The peace of neo-colonialism reigned.

8

DANSE MACABRE IN GBADOLITE

GUY WEBER'S CONFESSION

If the United Nations had taken its own resolution of February 1961 seriously, it would have opened a judicial investigation and had the murder suspects tried by a war tribunal. But humanitarian and ethical principles are only taken out of the legal cupboard when they serve *political objectives*, and in this case there were serious political obstacles to such a trial. The United Nations and the Western powers under its umbrella were all implicated in the overthrow, imprisonment and assassination of the former Congolese prime minister. And the neo-colonial power, constructed over the period from 1961 to 1965 on the defeat of the nationalist movement, counted among its ranks too many officials with Lumumba's blood on their hands. No form of justice could be expected from the UN. There was no follow-up to the Special Commission's report, submitted to the General Assembly on 11 November 1961. Thus, General Mobutu had his hands free for a devilishly cunning ploy. In 1966 he rehabilitated Lumumba, declaring the murdered former prime minister a "national hero". The anti-imperialist rhetoric of the Kasa Vubu–Adoula duo during the First Republic, then of General Mobutu during the Second Republic, served to justify their policies of favouring a local bourgeoisie closely linked to a state bureaucracy and international capital. The regime donned a nationalist mantle in the hope of strengthening its position in Africa and inside the country, where nationalist sentiments lived on among broad sectors of the population.

Proclaiming Patrice Lumumba a national hero and the presidential decree making the Brouwez house a place of pilgrimage (1966); the nationalisation of the Union Minière (1967); the politics of "*authenticité*" and Zaïrisation; and, towards the end of the 1980s, a demagogic campaign against the IMF to reduce the foreign debt repayment: these are some examples of the incidental favours the dictator granted the impoverished masses who were pushed into the background but did not disappear from the stage altogether and continued in various ways to cherish their nationalist ideals.[1]

An ill-digested past can easily lend itself to a settling of political scores. The murder in Katanga is a case in point. In the decades since then, Mobutu regularly hinted at "*contentieux*" ("contentious issues") to pressurise Brussels into giving him financial aid. The dictator then alluded to the material and moral debts still not settled by the former coloniser: what he and a large part of the Congolese population had in mind were of course the crimes of the colonial period and the elimination of the nationalist leaders after independence. Even during the 1990s, when his regime was on the wane, Mobutu missed no opportunity to attack his enemies. Although he himself had been complicit in Lumumba's assassination, he tried to discredit Etienne Tshisekedi, the UDPS opposition leader, by publishing a letter showing his anti-Lumumbism at the time of the Congo crisis, when he was a deputy commissioner in Mobutu's College of Commissioners. In the letter, dated 23 December 1960 and addressed to Kalonji, Tshisekedi expresses his satisfaction at Lumumba's incarceration and announces the extradition of the nationalists Pierre Elengesa, Finant, Emmanuel Nzuzi, Christophe Muzungu and Mbuyi to Kalonji for what he calls "exemplary punishment". To my knowledge, Tshisekedi has never denied writing the letter. In any case, at the end of September 1960, he was among the first to demand strong measures against the former Congolese prime minister who had by then been overthrown but was not yet under arrest. And at the end of December 1960, Tshisekedi took part in the negotiations between Léopoldville, Elisabethville and Bakwanga on Lumumba's fate.[2]

After Mobutu's fall in July 1997, the government of the new President Laurent Kabila announced, through his Justice Minister Célestin Luangy, that there would be a trial to punish those responsible for Lumumba's assassination. To this day, no trial has taken place. But Lumumba's death is ever-present in Congolese political life. In March 1998, the Congolese commission preparing a new constitution announced that Tshisekedi would be stripped of his political rights for the part he played in the former prime minister's death.[3]

Apart from a possible initiative by Kinshasa, it is unlikely that the public defence of Brassinne's dissertation, and the affirmation of Belgian innocence it contains, will be countered in a courtroom. Nevertheless, this present book now exists and its conclusions are that Vandewalle and Brassinne's speeches for the defence must be set aside as not very reliable.

In 1975, fourteen years after Lumumba's assassination, twelve years after the end of the secession and ten years after the bloody repression of nationalist rebellions in the east of the Congo and Mobutu's ultimate victory, Colonel Vandewalle, who had retired meanwhile, confided his reflections on the events to his book *Mille et quatre jours*. The author, who much of the time seems a cold and distant archivist, is here the advocate of the Belgo-Katangan lobby:

The Katangan authorities . . . apparently lost control of the affair. The impulsiveness of ministers and their secret advisers, not very aware of the possible political implications of the transfer, and incapable of measuring the consequences of the rabble army's brutality, led to a triple crime that influenced subsequent events decisively. Rid of something which they considered . . . a stumbling block to the defence of national interests, the Belgians responsible for Congolese affairs opted more and more for the unitarians in Léo. . . . Katanga was thus to lose the only outside support it could really count on.

All responsibility is thus attributed to "ministers", "secret advisers" (whoever they may be) and the "rabble army". The official advisers (among whom Vandewalle was number one) are totally exonerated, for "they had no responsibility for the assassination and the attempted cover-up. The machinery of technical assistance had dragged the Belgians involved, soldiers or policemen, into the drama."

To this day this plea for the defence establishes the political context for official historiography. The same argument reappears in Brassinne's "Enquête". In his conclusions, Brassinne writes of the Belgians' role:

While the high-ranking political advisers were in no way involved in the Lumumba affair, the same cannot be said for the Belgians in the Katangan *Gendarmerie* and police force. . . . They never interfered on their own initiative, they only had a secondary role, they were well-disciplined subordinates [of the Katangan ministers].[4]

It is far too easy to reduce Belgian responsibility for the crime to the part played by subordinates – Gat, Verscheure, Michels, Son and Soete. But the *Schreibtischtäter*, the shadowy figures giving orders from their desks in Brussels, Léopoldville and Élisabethville who sent Lumumba, Mpolo and Okito to their deaths, must under no circumstances be forgotten. Jean-Claude Marlair, an officer with a lot of experience in military co-operation with Mobutu's regime, indirectly acknowledges this in his comment that Tshombe alone cannot be accused of Lumumba's assassination, any more than Kalonji could have been if Lumumba had been sent to Bakwanga: "Everyone knew full well that this was a death sentence, with no possibility of remission. The rest is just hot air!" He does not want to point his finger solely at the subordinates:

And, if Captain Gat and a few others were named as the protagonists in those lunatic hours, they were only fulfilling the contract they had been paid for, and for which they were sent by their government! Naturally under the control of their superiors! And they too had their loyalty! Everything else is rubbish![5]

This is straight talking. Vandewalle writes that the Katangans "are incapable of measuring the consequences of the rabble army's brutality". But Vandewalle and his colleagues in the Bureau Conseil discussed *ad nauseam* with the Katangans the political consequences of a transfer and passed on their conclusions to Brussels and Léopoldville. And of course Vandewalle and his assistants were in command of the soldiers whose behaviour at the airport foretold what the three prisoners could expect in the Brouwez house.

Vandewalle ends his plea with the crucial role of those he calls "the official advisers, political or military", and concludes: "Even if they had wanted to, they could not have stopped the machinery set in motion in Léopoldville to remove Lumumba from the political scene." This is manifestly untrue.

Guy Weber says in his own book, *Le Katanga de Moïse Tshombe* (1983), that the assassination was a settling of scores among Africans: "I was in Elisabethville the day Lumumba died, so I can assure you it was a Bantu affair. A matter settled 'between them', in a fully independent country. . . . In Lumumba's case, the process was 'traditional', Bantu, African and primitive in every sense." His racist "explanation" is incredibly simple: "The African man does not look upon death as we, Europeans, do. His idea of a murder is different from ours. He thinks of himself as a natural dispenser of justice."[6] While Weber was working on his book *Comme je les ai connus* (As I Knew Them) (1991), he came across a 1981 article published in the Milan magazine *Storia* saying that Weber himself killed Lumumba: "Commander Weber, a Belgian officer, gave the *coup de grâce* by slowly pushing a bayonet into Lumumba's heart." Angry, Weber answered by referring to Brassinne's doctoral thesis which emphasised that he had played no role in the drama. Weber shares Brassinne's view that the Belgian government and its superior officers were innocent. But he does not share the belief that Verscheure, Gat, Michels and Son were innocent. Eric de Bellefroid, a journalist on *La Libre Belgique*, echoed Brassinne's conclusions when he wrote in an article with the subtitle "La Belgique dédouanée" (Belgium in the Clear) that the Belgians at the execution "could only obey orders. On loan to the Katangan authorities from the Belgian government, all they did was obey."

Weber's comment amounts to a confession: "I did not like the subtitle 'La Belgique dédouanée'. The Belgians at the execution could have prevented it. I know them all. I don't have to be their conscience." Weber's accusation says a lot about the responsibility of Gat, Verscheure, Michels and Son, but also a fortiori about the senior officers' culpability in the chain of command. Weber tries to protect himself by pretending that, for him, the matter was closed from the moment the prisoners were taken from the airport to the Brouwez house. From then on there is a total "black-out. The story becomes Bantu".[7] This book has disproved that assertion.

DANSE MACABRE IN GBADOLITE (1985)

Luc Putman was the Belgian ambassador in Kinshasa between1983 and 1986 and as such was a privileged observer of the improved relations between the two countries. Relations had been somewhat cool since the international crisis of 1973–74. The economic impasse and Mobutu's inability to repulse Angola-based rebels with his own forces aroused doubts about his ability to continue playing a stabilising role in the country and region's neo-colonial order. The root of the problem was that the Zaïrian elite was having difficulty becoming a relatively stable comprador bourgeoisie capable of securing the country's entry into the global market.

However, the IMF measures introduced in the early 1980s once again turned Zaïre into a favourite ground for exploitation. A long article published in *Le Soir* in 1985, on the eve of the 25th anniversary of independence, provides proof of the model pupil's good behaviour. In less than two years, the country was subjected to one of the most brutal electric shock treatments ever administered to a developing country. Under the benevolent eyes of the IMF, Prime Minister Kengo wa Dondo carried out a drastic devaluation, deregulation and general reorganisation on all levels.

"Zaire has had a thorough clear-out", says the article.

> Today it offers the main ingredients the business world requires: the country is safe for commerce again; banks have free access to currency markets; . . . inflation, still at 100 per cent in 1983, has been reduced by more than half; the budget deficit is back to a reasonable proportion of GDP; public finances are more transparent; and debt repayment is more regular. Impoverished, shaken and still gasping, it is now looking for investments, an increase in production, the boost which should follow austerity.

The message is clear: conditions were ripe for a rapid development of Zaïre through private initiatives.[8]

What *Le Soir*'s journalist describes as a "thorough clear-out" is a more practical matter for the population. Implementing the IMF measures caused deep social misery in poor areas. Kinshasa's inhabitants added a few expressions to their popular vocabulary, like "the single gong", the only meal of the day served at around 3 p.m., "a Banque Lambert loan", 50 per cent interest to be repaid the following month, and the famous "Article Fifteen" or "Making do". A few figures convey the burden the IMF and the government were making the people carry. Between 1982 and 1985, foreign debt repayment rose from 35 to 47 per cent of current expenditure. During the same period, the number of public employees fell from 285,000 to 126,000. Between 1983 and 1987, Zaïre paid out $2 billion to the West, but only $1.1 billion went back into the country. Between 1975 and 1985, the purchasing power of public employees was cut by 77 per cent, and of private sector employees by "only" 25 per cent.[9] This disaster in social terms led the *Le Soir* journalist to draw his readers' attention to a few "drawbacks". The vertiginous foreign debt, which represented 90 per cent of GDP, would force Zaïre to remit enormous sums to foreign banks until 1990: "The need to balance the domestic budget at the same time leads to real stalemate." If this policy did not quickly produce a positive result, there was a danger of agitation and popular resistance, even explosion. But during 1984–85, this discontent and poverty did not yet represent a threat to the regime, and, as long as this continued, Brussels was not worried.

Around the mid-1980s, there was still a solid basis for renewed co-operation. Employers, as well as politicians, kept the door wide open. About 250 Zaïrian enterprises were partially or wholly in Belgian hands at the time. These companies had a turnover of about 30 billion Belgian francs, represented an investment value of 74 billion Belgian francs, and employed 1,000 Belgians and 100,000 Zaïrians. The balance of trade was level in 1984, a record year in which exports and imports amounted to nearly 18.2 billion Belgian francs. In 1983, the development budget was worth 4 billion Belgian francs. At that time, 15,000 Belgians were living in Zaïre, among them 3,000 missionaries. The Belgian military presence in the country comprised 110 men and a budget of 500 million Belgian francs. According to Putman, military aid was "among the most convincing areas of co-operation. Belgian soldiers are motivated, their presence is generally effective, they get on well with the Zaïrian authorities and are appreciated by them."[10]

Thus, twenty years after Mobutu came to power Brussels was still enthusiastically working to back up the dictatorship. Poverty and the military regime's excesses were no obstacle to strengthening the links between the two countries. In January 1984, Prime Minister Kengo wa Dondo, the darling of the IMF and the regime's Western mentors, had "a very friendly meeting" with the Société Générale chairman, Jacques Groothaert. At the same time, the Belgian Ambassador Putman wrote a confidential letter to his Foreign Minister Leo Tindemans, suggesting inviting the dictator to Brussels. Such a visit

would be a matter of enormous prestige here, all the more so since the president will have his candidacy for a new mandate confirmed in March, ahead of the presidential elections in October. The situation is untenable if this visit cannot take place this year. I am thinking here of Belgo-Zaïrian relations and the enormous interests we still have here.

In March 1984, as René Lamy, a governor of the Société Générale, was visiting Mobutu, Putman received a telex from Brussels suggesting he invite Mobutu to Belgium for an official visit.[11]

Mobutu went to Belgium in July 1984, and during the visit the entrepreneur

André Leysen invited him to dinner at the Société Générale's head office. Putman was happy to see some very favourable articles from Henri Simonet in *La Libre Belgique* and Manu Ruys in *De Standaard*. The official visit to Belgium had the desired effect of raising the dictator's prestige in his own country:

> The unbelievable fuss the Zaïrian media made of the visit to Belgium was to me proof of the great political importance Kinshasa puts on the success of the visit. . . . long after my return on 21 July, . . . the film of this visit, which lasts for ages, is still being shown daily on television. The presidential elections for a third seven-year mandate, with Mobutu as sole candidate, were brought forward. Planned for November, they took place at the end of July. The success of the presidential visit to Belgium suddenly became . . . one of the main themes of the electoral campaign, so much so that I think – and I am not the only one – that the date for the presidential elections was partly chosen to coincide with the dates of the Belgian visit.[12]

A year later, on the twenty-fifth anniversary of the Congo-Zaïre's independence, relations between Brussels and Kinshasa were at their closest. Yet, there were some worrying signs. Etienne Tshisekedi and other important figures in the regime who had been criticising government policy for some years and had even founded an opposition party – the UDPS – had been condemned to long prison sentences and internal exile. In the east, in the Fizi-Baraka-Kabambare region, the guerrillas of Laurent Kabila's Popular Revolution Party had got a second wind. In 1984 Mobutu reacted with blind terror against the civilian population, executing (so-called) rebels and reducing villages to ashes. Amnesty International chronicled the crimes and denounced them, but Brussels turned a blind eye. After Mobutu invited the king and queen to the 30 June 1985 festivities Ambassador Putman noted:

> The main reason for the success was entirely due to the sympathy and amiability which the president and the Zaïrian people showed to the king and the queen. . . . This became . . . a celebration of Belgo-Zaïrian friendship. . . . I do not think such a celebration of friendship between a former colony and the former colonial power would be possible in any other country in Africa.

Mobutu invited about a hundred Belgian notables, the only foreigners on whom this honour was bestowed. They all accepted the dictator's invitation and were flown by Air Zaïre to Kinshasa and Gbadolite,[13] to attend the festivities and clasp the dictator to their bosom.[14]

They wrote what Putman describes as a collective "thank you letter" – really a paean of praise to the "Supreme Leader" – which all signed, except Guy Cudell, leader of the Belgian Socialist Party, who refused to subscribe to the eulogy. Who are these people, the pride of Belgium, who only have Brussels' strategic interests in their heads and pretend not to know about the tens of thousands of victims of the regime? Not to know about the bestial assassination of Pierre Mulele and his associate Théodore Bengila in 1968, about the crackdown on the student revolt of 1969 which killed dozens of students, about the repression of the popular uprising at Idiofa at the end of 1977 and beginning of 1978 when Mobutu's troops massacred hundreds of villagers, hanged a dozen village chiefs and publicly hacked Mulele's mother into pieces, about the massacre of diamond miners in Kasai in 1979, about the repression of the UDPS and its leaders. They purge their memories of these crimes and many others, look away from the misery in the poorer districts, wield the strict implementation of IMF rules as the sole criterion, and give Mobutu a certificate of Western respectability. Former prime ministers, former ministers, a former vice-governor of the Belgian Congo, former generals, Colonel Marlière, the governor of the Société Générale and the president of the Belgian Employers Association are among these VIPs. The gathering represented a cross-section of the Belgian ruling class which transformed Léopold II's legacy into a real colony. After independence, they destroyed the historic leadership of Congolese nationalism and brought a puppet to power. In 1985 this ruling class still thought of Mobutu as its best subcontractor, able to safeguard its interests in the former colony and the region as a whole.

The praise sung to Mobutu by these hundred eminent figures constitutes lasting proof that the Belgian ruling class has no moral right to lecture others on democracy or human rights. Here is the text:

Citizen President-Founder,

. . . the last twenty years have been of major importance for Zaïre. They have been years of progress inspired and stimulated by your energy, years shaped by you, and for which you have mustered all the necessary strength.

It has pleased you to invite us to witness the beginning of the next stage. . . . We hope that the few privileged Belgians you have received can contribute to the success of your efforts. Each of us will work with fervour and conviction to this end. We will dedicate this work not only to a beloved people, but above all to the leader responsible for this collective success. . . . In doing so, we express the words and even more the deep feelings of King Baudouin, his government and the vast majority of Belgians.[15]

On 30 June, the presidential couple gave a gala dinner in honour of their guests in Kinshasa's marble palace, the traditional residence for visiting heads of state. The guests gathered at night fall, to the sounds of a programme of classical music which, according to *Le Soir*, evoked "the great receptions in the days of the monarchs in Versailles". About a hundred guests, among them the Belgian royal couple and the Belgian ministers Tindemans and de Donnéa, enjoyed the dinner. Following this visit, the Belgian administration of the Co-operation in Development agency was instructed to open a line of credit in favour of Zaïre. The Société Générale did likewise, putting 1.8 billion Belgian francs at the disposal of the Belgo-Zaïrian (or Belgolaise) bank to finance Zaïrian government projects.[16]

Mobutu won the hearts of his guests. Foreign Minister Tindemans said straight out that he did not like the king's speech at the gala dinner: it was too reserved for Kinshasa. The Belgians who supported and maintained the colonial edifice and defended it with force of arms had succumbed to the field marshal's charm. For an article with the evocative title, "Old Belgians Won Over by Zaïre", E. Ugeux, a journalist on *Le Soir*, interviewed some of the Zaïrian head of state's elderly guests, of whom he knew several from the time when he was their comrade-in-arms in the battle against Lumumba's government. This eulogy of the dictator, sung by these hardened colonials, is like a *danse macabre* performed on the bodies of Lumumba, Mulele and tens of thousands of others. It is interesting to reproduce what some of them said about the dictator since during the 1990s a large number of articles were published claiming that the West had deserted Mobutu long ago. This claim followed the realisation by the Western troika of Brussels, Paris and Washington that Mobutu's chances of survival were diminishing due to successive recessions, austerity programmes and social unrest, at a time when the West, under the flag of democratisation and pluralism, was urging the regime to rejuvenate itself by accepting an opposition. In 1985, articles in *Le Soir* told a different story.

General Janssens, who led the fight against Africanising the Congolese army in July 1960, was the first to be interviewed by Ugeux:

> The military parade of 30 June was tremendous. It testified to the army's energy. The air force performance was remarkable. Mobutu has managed to fuse the army and the nation, which is driven by true patriotism. The friendship of the Zaïrian government is a reality which has lasted for twenty-five years. Many Zaïrians, particularly soldiers, have shown their affection for me.

Gilson, minister of defence at the time of the Congo crisis, was no less enthusiastic. He declared: "The meeting with the president was excellent. He is a man of swift decision. Zaïre is on the right track." Ganshof Van der Meersch, formerly minister-resident in the Belgian Congo, claimed to have met all the ministers and to have been struck by their maturity and sense of responsibility. "Prime Minister Kengo wa Dondo is first rate. . . . this maturity gives me confidence in the future." Leburton, a former prime minister dubbed "the big White chief", declared himself satisfied that at the same time as the festivities "the IMF has given Zaïre full marks for the economic upturn which will enable it to take its place on the international stage". Scheyven, a former minister of the Belgian Congo, perceived the event as a revenge on the Congolese nationalists:

"I suffered so much on Independence Day because of Lumumba's speech . . . today, I am glad to witness our sovereigns' happiness and the serenity that exists between the two countries". In the company of these notables were several comrades-in-arms from the old days: Bomboko, Nendaka and also Cardinal Malula.[17]

LUMUMBA'S NATIONALISM: A PROVISIONAL EVALUATION

Nearly forty years after his death, Patrice Lumumba is still largely unknown in Africa's political historiography. For most Africanists, Lumumba was a man who, without either a clear vision or a precise plan of action, and carried away by vehement anti-colonialism, declared war on the West and rapidly sank into the chaos of a Congo crisis he mostly created himself. In their approach to the Congo crisis, these Africanists reproduce the frame of reference of the Western rulers of the day. They have no critical view of UN intervention, underestimate the role of Western interference and describe Lumumba as stubborn, unrealistic, a man who made himself unacceptable to the nascent Congolese political class and its Western fulcra. Against this dominant current, a small group of writers has put forward a more qualified judgement on the murdered former prime minister and the West's role in the Congo crisis. For them, Lumumba was a man who did not really have a concrete policy and did not try to accomplish attainable goals. He dreamed of a better world, a world which, in 1960, was not yet viable. These writers see him as a martyr of independence, crucified by the West which did not want to part with its Congolese possessions. Their Lumumba is a tragic man, victim of a situation he did not control, he could never have controlled. These two currents (Jean-Claude Willame is spokesman for the first, Jean-Paul Sartre for the second) differ less than they would appear to at first sight. Both in fact highlight the role of the individual. Both emphasise Lumumba's weakness, his isolation, his ill-understood strategy. They begin with the premise that Lumumba had no chance of succeeding. Lumumba was the protagonist and the first victim of a crisis which tended to increase, rather than diminish, with his own intervention.[18]

These conceptions are seriously flawed, however. They do not answer crucial questions. If it is true that Lumumba was an isolated politician, why did Brussels, Washington and New York set up such a gigantic and long-lasting military operation, including the deployment of several thousand Belgian soldiers and Blue Berets, operations of destabilisation, murder and corruption, as well as a huge media campaign? Surely the Western powers which led these operations did not ignite one of the biggest crises since the Second World War solely to get rid of an isolated and unique political leader.

Access to the UN archives and the Belgian Foreign Ministry archives has certainly helped improve our understanding of the Congo crisis and of Lumumba's political actions. But the reason why his political legacy has not always been fully appreciated is in no way technical (lack of research material) but political. Lumumba's very short political career, his relatively easy over-throw, and finally his assassination which has taken decades to clarify, have had a very demoralising effect on African nationalism. The only event remembered is this revolting crime: the murder of a defenceless prisoner. That Lumumba's political memory remains linked to the exploits of an *individual* is due to the fact that, for the last few decades, there has been no Congolese movement capable of continuing his struggle and putting *into practice* the true importance of his con-victions and political stance. What has been lacking is a movement which could build on the experience of the Congo crisis and incorporate it into a new (polit-ical) project supported by a broad spectrum of the population.

To this day in the Congo there is still no popular movement incorporating Lumumba's political aims and putting the country's liberation from the burden of neo-colonialism high on the agenda. In these conditions, assimilating Lumumba's legacy remains a delicate enterprise. Until the process of national liberation has a higher profile, it is difficult to judge the true import of this legacy and to give it shape by integrating it into political lessons, structures and traditions. Consequently, the verdict given here is not univocal or definitive. The prevailing opinions about Lumumba can certainly be completely disregarded as non-scientific: the research material gathered here cannot possibly be refuted by those Africanists who interpret the crisis on the basis of clichés spread by Western propaganda of bygone days. Nevertheless, our verdict remains very provisional and tentative. Once the Congolese people really take control of their own country, they will be in a position to assess their own history, and this includes the political legacy of the father of Congolese independence.

When Lumumba was alive, the contours of his political *œuvre* were barely vis-ible. The man was a political meteor. Totally unknown in his country in 1955, by 1958 he had become a nationalist figurehead capable of leading the masses. In 1960 he was prime minister for ten weeks before his assassination in 1961. Lumumba was the product of a lightning transformation of political life in the Congo between 1958 and 1960. His tumultuous political evolution went hand in hand with the radicalisation of Congolese politics which, in turn was the expres-sion of the rapid collapse of the colonial order. After decades of artificial inertia during the colonial era, political life came into its own in dramatic fashion. *Le Congo, terre d'avenir, est-il menaçé?* (Is the Congo, Land of the Future, in Jeopardy?), written by Lumumba in 1956, demonstrates this development quite clearly. In this book he remains within the limits of what colonial paternalism prescribed for the "developed" Congolese: "the basic desire of the Congolese elite . . . is to be 'Belgians' and have access to the same affluence and rights, naturally taking into account individual merit." It reflects the aspirations of the Congolese *petite bour-geoisie* on the eve of the decolonisation process. This Congolese elite had obtained a relatively privileged position on the fringes of the colonial order. Its aim was not to liberate the country from its colonial yoke, but to eliminate the obstacles and discriminatory measures preventing the nascent bourgeoisie from achieving its ambitions. Since it was wary of the Congolese masses, it had limited its nationalistic ambitions and only wanted gradual independence under the supervision of the colonial powers to which it owed its status and position. In fact, this elite was nationalist despite itself. A year and a half after writing *Le Congo, terre d'avenir, est-il menaçé?*, Lumumba's views had changed radically. The Lumumba of 1956 had nothing in common with the Lumumba of 1958.

During these years of struggle against the colonial power, Patrice Lumumba totally broke away from the Congolese elite and its bourgeois ambitions. He resolutely decided on real decolonisation to benefit *the masses*. Over this period, Lumumba shaped a nationalism which rested on three political pillars: revolutionary and coherent nationalism, political action relying on a mass movement, and an internationalist perspective. Lumumba's speech on 30 June 1960 symbolised the victory of this progressive, forward-looking nationalism over the old order. Attempts were subsequently made to reverse this symbolic victory by characterising Lumumba's speech as a coup by a few disaffected European advisers in the Congolese leader's entourage. However, Jean Van Lierde, the Congolese prime minister's friend and adviser, is categorical:

> It was not difficult for me to persuade Patrice to break with etiquette and take the microphone before the crowd in the parliament building, to give his people's expectations a non-diplomatic vision. The reactionary press has accused me of having written this text – which is untrue – for the colonisers could not believe Patrice Lumumba could write and speak for hours. And it is this magnificent speech of 30 June 1960, before the king and diplomats from all over the world, that testified to the depth of his thinking.[19]

Lumumba's speech was impressive because his words reflected the mass-movement actions which had destroyed the colonial edifice. Each time Lumumba spoke, it was basically the masses speaking, taking the political stage and articulating the struggle for more and more rights, jeopardising what the West thought it could gain from an independant Congo.

To truly understand the Congo crisis and Lumumba's role in it, and also the meaning of his life and work, we need to study the power relationships between the social classes during the anti-colonial revolution. Only then can we understand why the West summoned an entire war machine to fight the first Congolese government. It is not enough to refer to the biographies of nationalist leaders who were formerly civil servants, teachers, employees or medical assistants. Lumumba and some of his comrades broke away from the Congolese elite and threw in their lot with the broad spectrum of the population who had decided to throw off colonisation.

An anecdote illustrates the difference of approach between Lumumba and this elite, and in some way is a mini-preview of what subsequently happened under Mobutu. Only a few days after independence, the appropriate parliamentary commission promised deputies a remuneration of 500,000 Belgian francs and a host of material benefits. The Belgian ambassador, as yet not "at war" with Lumumba, sent a telegram to Brussels describing the prime minister's reaction to this measure by the Congolese proto-bourgeoisie:

> The decision . . . caused feelings which rapidly spread beyond Congolese borders, and which the Belgian press has surely already picked up. I spent yesterday evening with the prime minister who opposed this decision in no uncertain terms. He thinks it would be damaging to the country's economy and could seriously undermine the prestige of the embryo state. The government is determined to fight these measures and reduce parliamentary remuneration to a level compatible with the Congo's national revenue. M. Lumumba sees this matter as an opposition manoeuvre. He seems determined to thwart it.[20]

Lumumba and his entourage were consistent radical nationalists. They fought all forms of colonial or neo-colonial domination, and wanted to build a unified nation within the borders of the Congolese state. The anti-colonial revolution was, in the light of these objectives, a bourgeois revolution. The national-democratic tasks were to free the country from the iron grip of imperialism and create an independent nation; to set up a democratic republic headed by a national assembly; and finally to develop a truly national economy to meet the needs of the population. The final objective was to build a unified nation state in which all peoples and regions considered themselves essential components of society.

The aims of this revolution were the same as those of the European and American revolutions which gave birth to modern nation states in the second half of the eighteenth and first half of the nineteenth centuries. Would the anti-colonial revolution in the Congo in turn produce a classical bourgeois state? This was not at all certain. The European and American revolutions had given power to the national bourgeoisies, even though it was often the lower classes that had led and fought for them. The situation in the Congo at the time made a repetition of this scenario unlikely. In order to exploit its colony, Brussels had created a large Congolese proletariat to work in the mines, factories and plantations. As this proletariat gradually grew in self-confidence and experience of the struggle, it, along with other popular classes, began to think of the fight for independence as a means of social transformation, as an instrument to improve their lot. Moreover, the coloniser had exploited the Congo to serve Belgian needs. It had not created a proper national economy or, therefore, a proper national bourgeoisie. Consequently there was no capitalist class to direct the nationalist movement towards an independence which did not affect neo-colonial domination. King Baudouin foresaw this danger. In November 1959, when pre-revolutionary developments in Lower Congo had Brussels with its back to the wall, he declared: "Events are moving at a speed nobody could have expected. Tumultuous forces have been set in motion, without sufficient numbers of wise and experienced elites to control and direct them."[21]

In this context, Lumumba represented a real threat to the West. The successful assault on the colonial structure gave the radical nationalists a whiff of oxygen and an important place within the Congolese government. Lumumba's anti-imperialism, his solidarity with the increasingly radicalised masses, his internationalism, and his disgust for bureaucratic and repressive methods favoured his politicising mission. All this meant he could incorporate all peoples and regions into his movement, and eventually raise it above purely bourgeois limitations. History has taught that the dynamic of post-colonial societies has led even moderate bourgeois-nationalist regimes, after their anti-colonial victory, to claim their national patrimony from the former colonial power. Examples include the nationalisation of the oil industry by Mossadegh (Iran, 1951) and of the Suez canal by Nasser (Egypt, 1956). If Mossadegh dared do it, why not Lumumba? If the Congolese masses had taken their destiny into their own hands and set up organisations to defend their interests (such as neighbourhood committees, trade unions, women's and youth organisations) and thought of themselves as the motors of social and political progress, not as passive spectators accepting measures taken by a state bureaucracy, there would have been a revolutionary situation. Lumumba's government would have been able to transcend the independence struggle, mobilise the people, and put a broader campaign on the agenda, including taking measures against the control of the nation's wealth by foreign capital.

The imminence of this process of radicalisation is the key to understanding why, as Sartre put it, "even though his economic programme was a very moderate one, the leader of the MNC was regarded as a brother-in-arms by [Frantz] Fanon the revolutionary, and a mortal enemy by the Société Générale".[22] It also explains why remarks by some authors that Lumumba did not have "a political programme" are not valid. Lumumba's Jacobinism (his absolute determination to achieve political power) met the demands of the anti-colonial revolution in the Congo of 1960. The nationalists had to take up the reins of state power: this was the *sine qua non* for progress, the lever for speeding up political mobilisation and, through the construction of a nation state, for stimulating the country's economic development.

The rationale behind the West's intervention in the Congo was its determination to nip this process of radicalisation in the bud. A few days after the 30 June 1960 speech, Lumumba put his words into action and sided with the Congolese soldiers who were fighting the reactionary Belgian officer caste. The disintegration of the colonial army and the unrest among public employees, who were encouraged by the soldiers' success to consolidate independence by making social demands, provoked an uncontrollable dynamic and forced the West to take radical counter-measures. They wanted at all costs to avoid the destruction of the pillars of neo-colonial society or, to quote Sartre, avoid "the radicalisation of Lumumba by the masses, and the unification of the masses by Lumumba". This fear was obvious in the messages Belgian Ambassador Van den Bosch sent to Brussels in mid-July 1960. His telegram of 18 July read:

> My telegrams underline the danger of situations which threaten not only the Belgian position in the Congo, but also the position of the West in central Africa as a whole. . . . One of Lumumba's creatures, appointed chief-of-staff, has been in command of Léo's garrison for 48 hours now. So far all UN troops are of African origin and probably would not be in a position to keep order if a large part of the civilian population, which currently numbers among it 40,000 unemployed, could be stirred up and joined the garrison. . . . It seems to me of the utmost importance that the Western powers involved consult each other.[23]

Western strategists were quick to recognise the potential danger stemming from developments in the spring of 1960. The dialectic between the revolutionary leader and the politicised masses could produce an explosive cocktail like the one undermining US interests in Cuba at the same time. This was the basis of the comparison some Western capitals made between Lumumba and Castro.

From 1 January 1959 onwards, when the Cuban revolution's victory was sealed by the fall of the dictator Batista, the radicalisation of the masses and their government far exceeded the initial nationalist programme of Fidel Castro's *barbudos*. During the first half of 1959, the representatives of the Cuban bourgeoisie were excluded from government due to pressure from the masses. A host of measures and counter-measures were taken in Havana and Washington which ended with the botched invasion of Playa Girón in April 1961 and the proclamation of the Cuban socialist revolution. The main planks in this process of radicalisation in Cuba were: the promulgation of the agrarian reform law by which large landowners were expropriated and parcels of land distributed to landless peasants (17 May 1959); the resignation of President Urrutia (July 1959); the nationalisation of Texaco, Shell and Esso which were refusing to refine Soviet oil (29 June–1 July 1960); the nationalisation of all large US enterprises in Cuba in response to Eisenhower's refusal to buy Cuban sugar (6 August 1960); the creation of committees of popular power to serve as pillars of the Cuban state in the prevention of sabotage (28 September 1960); the nationalisation of the whole of the banking sector and of about 400 Cuban companies (13 October 1960). The fear of facing an African variant of this process led the strategists in Brussels, Washington and New York to intervene militarily in the Congo.

It could be argued that the Congo was not Cuba and that Castro's 26 July Movement and rebel army were qualitatively different from Lumumba's Congolese National Movement. This is true. The Eyskens government accelerated the pace of decolonisation precisely to cut short any process of radicalising the Congolese masses. Eyskens wanted to curtail the period of politicisation as much as possible in order to avoid any escalation. Brussels thus hoped to put inexperienced and weak Congolese politicians in power and continue to pull the strings behind the scenes. This is why the Belgian government decided at the beginning of 1960 to grant independence on 30 June of that same year, when at the beginning of 1959 Brussels was still convinced that it could postpone the date for at least twenty years. This vertiginous transfer of power did not prevent Lumumba from leading the government, but it did not give nationalist leaders enough time to develop a properly structured movement with a solid leadership. The Congolese masses had snatched their independence with their own bare hands. They had begun their struggle without political parties, trade unions or other mass organisations worthy of the name. And Lumumba had neither the time nor the means to build a solid cadre within his movement: on Independence Day, very few nationalist leaders have any national vision and influence. What the Eyskens government's critics, in a rather misleading way, described as a *"politique du lâchez-tout"* (a let-it-all-go policy) nevertheless yielded a substantial result for Brussels: Lumumba took power without a well-organised nationalist movement at his disposal and that made it quite difficult for him to take an anti-colonial revolution to a higher level. However, it is important not to focus too narrowly on what the anti-colonial movement was in July 1960 but (as Western strategists did at the time) envisage what it could become, based on developments at the onset of independence.

Western fear of a Cuban-style evolution in the Congo was not without grounds. Suffice it to take a close look at revolutionary developments like those in Burkina Faso (1983–87), where the overthrow of the neo-colonial pro-French government was the work of a few hundred soldiers and armed civilians, under Captain Thomas Sankara. The class structure of this extremely poor Saharan country was even less favourable than in the Congo of 1960: the country had no working class, the traditional conveyor of progressive and socialist ideas. As in the Congo, the peasants who made up the majority of the population lived in archaic social conditions, with no proper organisations and no experience of fighting for land against a class of big capitalist or pre-capitalist landowners. Despite this, the Sankara government succeeded in directing the population's initial enthusiasm. Committees for the defence of the revolution and popular militias were formed. The literacy campaign, the involvement of the population in damming the Sourou river and irrigating its valley, the fight to stop deforestation and the setting up of village health clinics, all shaped the national-democratic revolution supported by broad sectors of the population. Twenty years after the Congo crisis, Patrice Lumumba was reincarnated in the person of Thomas Sankara.

The key to understanding this revolutionary process is the political mobilisation of the masses who gained experience of struggle and confidence in
themselves, put their stamp on the course of events and developed a national
consciousness. This consciousness was not strictly nationalist, but anti-imperialist. It was not specifically directed against the "French", "Whites" or other
"foreigners", but against imperialism and other enemies of the revolution's
social and political achievements like the local bourgeoisie which, as the collab-
orating elite of international capitalism and the political proxies of Paris, wanted
to perpetuate neo-colonialism. In 1987, counter-revolutionary soldiers murdered Thomas Sankara and halted the revolutionary process in Burkina Faso.[24]

Patrice Lumumba's attempt to introduce an authentic national-democratic
revolution to the Congo is enough to place him in the pantheon of universal
defenders of the emancipation of the people. But the political lessons of the
Congo crisis are also a substantial part of his legacy. Several authors stress that,
in the space of a few weeks, Lumumba succeeded in setting the international
establishment against him and was consequently soon driven from power. But
what many saw as the obstinacy of the Congolese prime minister was in fact the
expression of a much more fundamental phenomenon. The Congo crisis
revealed in one fell swoop the true nature of the powers which shaped large
parts of the post-war world. The crisis showed *in actual practice* the true nature,
not only of the former colonial powers, but also of the United Nations, of the
recently independent countries united in what was called the Afro-Asian bloc,
as well as of Moscow and finally, of the national elite in the Congo which bowed
its head to the Western offensive against the Congolese government. They all
betrayed their publicly professed principles and ideals as well as the Congolese
prime minister who had placed his trust in all of them at one stage or another.
It is this exceptional combination of circumstances, this stark choice under
Western pressure forcing them to take sides, that explains the outcome of the
Congo crisis.

Could Lumumba and his colleagues have "won" the Congo crisis? The
extremely critical situation of Kasa Vubu's and Tshombe's regimes in late 1960
and early 1961 shows that a nationalist victory would not have been impossible,
but only if Lumumba and the Congolese nationalists had avoided certain mistakes, and learned more quickly from those they did made. The political
weakness of Congolese nationalism, including the weakness of its central leader,
is therefore an integral part of the lessons to be drawn from the Congo crisis.

Lumumba deluded himself about his Afro-Asian allies, about Moscow and
about the tiny fraction of the Congolese elite which had sided with him at the
height of the anti-colonial revolution. Then, he badly misinterpreted the role of
the United Nations, mainly from mid-July to mid-August 1960, when he was
still hoping that it would put an end to Katanga's secession, and later, in October
and November 1960, when the UN was discussing whether to admit the Kasa
Vubu delegation or his own as the legitimate representative of the Congo, and

he thought the Third World would resist Western pressure and vote for him. Lumumba mistrusted the image of the UN as a neutral instrument of international law and order, as an instrument capable of defending the sovereignty of Third World countries. But he did hope that he could apply enough pressure, on the one hand on international public opinion, and on the other on the Afro-Asian heads of state, to neutralise Western influence within the UN and force the Blue Berets to carry out the mission for which the Congolese government had invited them. Sometimes this led him to make ambiguous statements. For instance, reacting to the UN resolution of 9 August, Lumumba said:

> The Security Council has decided . . . that UN troops should enter Katanga immediately to drive out Belgian troops. Today is a great victory for the Congolese people. . . . The imperialists have failed. The puppet Tshombe has also failed. The colonialist and imperialist Judases have failed. Today the Katangese people . . . are free.[25]

During this period, the Congolese people, who until independence had shown such initiative, courage and fighting spirit, were relegated to the role of spectator. Between mid-July and mid-August, Lumumba transferred the Congo's political arena to New York, Accra and Conakry. He hoped diplomatic pressure would make the Blue Berets take action against the secessionists. At that time, he counted on the support of (certain) UN contingents rather than on the ANC and the Congolese population inside and outside Katanga.

When by August 1960 it became clear that Nkrumah, Nasser and Nehru were putting the Congo crisis in the hands of the United Nations, despite the *de facto* protection Hammarskjöld was giving the Katangan secessionists, Lumumba changed his plans. He gave the green light to military action against the separatist provinces and went to Stanleyville to mobilise the population. But he had wasted a lot of precious time, while Washington, Brussels and New York relentlessly continued to reinforce their bridgeheads. Moreover, Congolese and African public opinion was confused by his ambiguous declarations of love for the United Nations. His hope, or rather his miscalculation, that the UN would be forced to thwart Western plans, was to be his downfall. The Belgians digging themselves in in Elisabethville and Bakwanga; the deployment of the Blue Berets in those provinces; the September coups and the UN diplomatic offensive at the 15th session of the General Assembly, all led to disarray among the nationalist forces, to Lumumba's assassination, and finally to an end to the momentum of the anti-colonial revolution in the Congo.

But in the end, important social change has more weight than historical defeats like those of 1960–61. Until the tasks of the national-democratic revolution in the Congo have been completed, the life and work of Lumumba will remain a source of inspiration for generations of Congolese, present and future. The red thread running through this political life is his transition from nationalist to revolutionary. Here is an example to illustrate this transition. During the colonial era, Patrice Lumumba championed mass but basically peaceful actions. In view of the military might of the Force Publique, such actions seemed the right way to demoralise the colonial power and neutralise its repressive forces. But developments after independence totally changed the rules of the game. The contradiction inherent in the relationship between coloniser and colonised turned into a struggle between an international neo-colonial coalition on one side and the nationalist Congo on the other.

In July and August 1960 when the balkanisation of the Congo became a reality, Lumumba did not hesitate. He resolutely chose military action to liberate the Congo from the neo-colonial stranglehold. His military campaign against the secession of South Kasai and Katanga (end of August, beginning of September); his intention, after his government was overthrown, to re-establish his legitimate power over the whole of the Congo from nationalist Stanleyville (September–November); then later on, in the death cell reserved for him by Mobutu, when he rejected any neo-colonial compromise (December–January 1961): these are all examples of the path followed by Lumumba during that short period between his election as prime minister and his death.

CONCLUSION: LUMUMBA'S POLITICAL TESTAMENT

Shortly before his death, Lumumba wrote a letter to Pauline from his cell. As his third and his fourth wives both had the same first name, which of the women it was meant for is not known. Lumumba was separated from his fourth wife Pauline Opango at the time of his dramatic arrest at Mweka, at the beginning of December 1960. Dressed up as a soldier, his third wife Pauline Kie visited him several times in his cell at Thysville. His letter is proof of his principled fight against neo-colonialism. It shows he was realistic: he knew his death was more than likely. But it also shows his unshakeable faith in the anti-colonial revolution's final victory. This letter can be seen as his political testament:

My beloved companion,

I write you these words not knowing whether you will receive them, when you will receive them, and whether I will still be alive when you read them. Throughout my struggle for the independence of my country, I have never doubted for a single instant that the sacred cause to which my comrades and I have dedicated our entire lives would triumph in the end. But what we wanted for our country — its right to an honorable life, to perfect dignity, to independence with no restrictions — was never wanted by Belgian colonialism and its Western allies, who found direct and indirect, intentional and unintentional support among certain senior officials of the United Nations, that body in which we placed all our trust when we called on it for help.

They have corrupted some of our countrymen; they have bought others; they have done their part to distort the truth and defile our independence. What else can I say? That whether dead or alive, free or in prison by orders of the colonialists, it is not my person that is important. What is important is the Congo, our poor people whose independence has been turned into a cage, with people looking at us from outside the bars, sometimes with charitable compassion, sometimes with glee and delight. But my faith will remain unshakeable. I know and feel in my heart of hearts that sooner or later my people will rid themselves of all their enemies, foreign and domestic, that they will rise up as one to say no to the shame and degradation of colonialism and regain their dignity in the pure light of day.

We are not alone. Africa, Asia, and the free and liberated peoples in every corner of the globe will ever remain at the side of the millions of Congolese who will not abandon the struggle until the day when there will be no more colonizers and no more of their mercenaries in our country. I want my children, whom I leave behind and perhaps will never see again, to be told that the future of the Congo is beautiful and that their country expects them, as it expects every Congolese, to fulfil the sacred task of rebuilding our independence, our sovereignty; for without justice there is no dignity and without independence there are no free men.

Neither brutal assaults, nor cruel mistreatment, nor torture have ever led me to beg for mercy, for I prefer to die with my head held high, unshakeable faith and the greatest confidence in the destiny of my country rather than live in slavery and contempt for sacred principles. History will one day have its say; it will not be the history taught in the United Nations, Washington, Paris, or Brussels, however, but the history taught in the countries that have rid themselves of colonialism and its puppets. Africa will write its own history, and both north and south of the Sahara it will be a history full of glory and dignity.

Do not weep for me, my companion, I know that my country, now suffering so much, will be able to defend its independence and its freedom. Long live the Congo! Long live Africa!

Patrice[1]

NOTES

PREFACE

1 Eisenhower's order is in M. Kalb, *The Congo Cables*, pp. 53–5, and "Did Ike Authorize a Murder?", in *The Washington Post*, 8 August 2000; memo of 19 September 1960, in *Foreign Relations of the United States, 1958–1960*, vol. XIV: Africa, p. 495; "Memorandum of Conference with the President", 28 January 1960, declassified US doc.; UK Foreign Office, H.F.T. Smith, A. Ross, M.B. Stevens and the Lord Privy Seal discuss "the possibilities of eliminating Mr. Lumumba from the political scene", FO JB1015/401, 28 and 29 September 1960, Public Record Office doc. H.F.T. Smith, who later became head of M15, wrote: "I see only two possible solutions to the problem. The first is the simple one of ensuring Lumumba's removal from the scene by killing him. This should in fact solve the problem since, so far as we can tell, Lumumba is not a leader of a movement within which there are potential successors of his quality and influence. His supporters are much less dangerous material. The other possible approach is for a constitution to be worked out which places far more power in the hands of the President [Kasa Vubu]." On the top secret CIA unit ZR/RIFLE, see R. Mahoney, *Sons and Brothers*, pp. 91–3, and "CIA Inspector General's Report on Plots to Assassinate Fidel Castro", 1967. The ZR/RIFLE agent recruited in Europe and sent to the Congo in November 1960 to eliminate Lumumba operated under the code name QJ/WIN. Richard Mahoney, who had access to very well informed Belgian and US sources on the Congo crisis, writes that QJ/WIN was Mozes Maschkivitzan. Our own research shows that Maschkivitzan was stateless, born 11 May 1910 in Antwerp (Belgium) of Jewish parents who had left Russia in 1907. In documents concerning CIA activities, one of the people considered to work under the code name QJ/WIN was a man born on 11 May 1910 in Antwerp . . . Moreover, information about Maschkivitzan's life allows us to reconstruct a general profile which does not contradict that of QJ/WIN, as he appears in the Church Report and declassified CIA documents. Mahoney also reveals that Maschkivitzan was sent to the Congo "after discussion through discreet intermediaries in Belgium". It is not impossible that Washington and Brussels acted in tandem in the elimination operation, or at least that Brussels was told about the US plan. This could explain why the Belgian commando operation was abandoned in October 1960 – more or less at the time the CIA gave the green light to ZR/RIFLE to take care of Lumumba.

2 L. Devlin, quoted by M. Kalb, *The Congo Cables*, p. 190; on the western contacts in January

1961 for the fight against the Lumumbists, see US State Department, "An Analytical Chronology of The Congo Crisis".

3 Krushchev, quoted by US ambassador to Moscow L. Thompson, in *Foreign Relations of the United States, 1961–1963*, Vol. V: Soviet Union, Documents 28 and 51; Timberlake, 6 Febuary 1961, quoted by R. Mahoney, "The Kennedy Policy in the Congo", p. 80.

4 Translators' note: We have left these two words from the crucial 5/6 October 1960 telegram in the original French to avoid confusion. See Translator's Note at p. xi for clarification.

5 B. Govaerts and K. Schoetens television documentary on Patrice Lumumba (VRT-Canvas, 21 and 28 October 1999); interviews with G. Soete, in *Humo*, 5 October 1999, and *Het Belang van Limburg*, 19 October 1999; L. Marlière, interviewed by VRT-Canvas for the programme *TerZake* of 15 December 1999 and the German television documentary *Mord im Kolonialstil* (Murder Colonial Style) by Thomas Giefer, ARD, 1 November 2000)

6 "Proposal to set up a parliamentary commission of inquiry charged with determining the exact circumstances surrounding the assassination of Patrice Lumumba and the possible involvement of Belgian officials in it", 9 December 1999, DOC 50 0312/005, Chambre des Représentants, Brussels, text adopted in plenary session, on 24 Febuary 2000; message 64, under sub-heading "d'Aspremont Lynden orders Lumumba's transfer to Katanga" in this book.

INTRODUCTION

1 *La Libre Belgique*, 14 February 1961.

2 A. Gizenga, declaration of 15 May 1961, in J. Ceulemans, *A. Gizenga,* p. 19.

3 B. Verhaegen, "Livres: Qui a tué Patrice Lumumba?", *Cahiers Marxistes,* March–April 1993, pp. 153–8.

4 J. Brassinne, "Enquête sur la mort de Patrice Lumumba", doctoral dissertation in social science and politics, ULB, Vol. II, pp. 597, 594. The examiners, who included famous experts like Professors Jean Stengers, Pierre Salmon and Paule Bouvier, gave the dissertation "la plus grande distinction". See *La Libre Belgique*, 19 February 1991 and 22 May 1991 for highly favourable comments on it.

5 M. Ruys, *Achter de maskerade,* p. 122; M. Ruys, "Leren uit de Afrikaanse crisis", *De Standaard,* 11 October 1996.

CHAPTER 1

1 Baudouin and Kasa Vubu's speeches, CRISP, *Congo 1960,* pp. 318–22; Lumumba's speech, J. Van Lierde, *La Pensée politique. . .,* pp. 197–201. On the events of 30 June, CRISP, *Congo 1960,* pp. 318–30, and J. Van Lierde, *Un insoumis,* pp. 7–11, 32–3.

2 F. Vandewalle, *Mille et quatre jours,* Vol. 1, pp. 1–2.

3 *Ibid.,* p. 3.

4 E. Grailly, in A. Closset, *Les Compagnons,* pp. 22–3; G. Weber, *Comme . . .,* p. 112; F. Vandewalle, *Mille . . .,* Vol. 1, p. 98.

5 J. Van Bilsen, *Congo 1945–1965,* p. 220; G. Moulin (Belgian Communist Party), Chamber of Representatives, 15 June 1960: see concerning this threat message 45 from Ganshof to De Schryver, 13 June 1960, and message 26114 from Schöller to De Schryver, 14 June 1960, Foreign Ministry archives.

6 P. Lumumba, in L.-F. Vanderstraeten, *De la Force Publique . . .,* p. 141; F. Vandewalle, *Mille . . .,* Vol. 3, p. 474.

7 Telex from Foreign Minister Wigny to Consul General Créner (E'ville), arrived 9 July 1960 at 13.35, L.-F Vanderstraeten, *De la Force Publique . . .*, pp. 281, 338; chronology of 9 and 10 July, *La Libre Belgique* (hereafter *LLB*), 11 July 1960 and J. Chomé, *La Crise congolaise,* pp. 171–2.

8 F. Vandewalle, *Mille . . .*, Vol. 3, p. 308, and "Face aux Mutins. Elisabethville, 8, 9 et 10 juillet 1960", *Bulletin du Craoca,* 4/1978, p. 28.

9 Telegram from Bunche (Léo) to Hammarskjöld, 12 July 1960, no. 48, UN archives; telegram 281 from Van den Bosch to Belext Brussels, 13 July 1960, Foreign Ministry archives. On Bomboko, also see telegrams 234 (9 July), 316 and 319 (15 July), and on the opposition to Lumumba in the Congolese government the unnumbered telegram of 24 July, all from Van den Bosch to Brussels, Foreign Ministry archives.

10 Telegram from Kasa Vubu and Lumumba to "H", 12 July 1960, and Security Council resolution of 14 July 1960, S/4382 and S/4383; telegram "H" to Bunche (Léo), 9 July 1960, no. 21, United Nations archives.

11 A. Gizenga, in CRISP, *Congo 1960*, p. 615.

12 Telegram "H" to Bunche and von Horn (Léo), 26 July 1960, No. 389, United Nations archives; M. Ruys, in *De Standaard,* 14 July 1960.

13 H. Rolin, 25 January 1961, Parliamentary records, Senate; Baudouin, in CRISP, *Congo 1960,* pp. 513–14.

14 G. Eyskens, 25 July, F. Vandewalle, *Mille . . .*, Vol. 2, p. 156; Cardinal Joseph E. Van Roey and the Belgian bishops, in *De Standaard*, 26 July 1960; P. Wigny, 26 July 1960, and M. Tshombe, 25 July 1960, in CRISP, *Congo 1960*, p. 740.

15 Letter from Baudouin of 28 July 1960, quoted in the telegram from "H" (Léo) to Cordier, 31 July, no. B-278, and the reply from "H" to the king, cited in his telegram to Cordier, 1 August, no. B-281, United Nations archives; Hammarskjöld, "Second Report", 6 August 1960, S/4417; M. Ruys, *De Standaard*, 12/8/60.

16 "Analysis of meeting on 12 August 1960 between the UN secretary general and the government of Katanga" and "Analysis of the second meeting between M. Hammarskjöld and the government of Katanga on 13 August 1960", F. Vandewalle, *Mille . . .*, vol. 2, pp. B23–32, pp. B37–47; Tshombe to general consuls and consuls of E'ville, 5 November 1960, in *ibid.* Vol. 3, p. B3.

17 P. Davister, *Katanga . . .*, pp. 154, 156; telegram "Aspremont/Rothschild" to Belext Brussels, no. 247, 13 August 1960, Foreign Ministry archives; P. Wigny, 17 August, in CPE, *La Crise . . .*, p. 847.

18 Bunche cited in telegram 778 from Misdiplobel to Belext Brussels, 6 August 1960, Foreign Ministry archives; telegram "H" to Bunche and von Horn, 26 July 1960, no. 389, and telegram "H" (Léo) to Cordier, 1 August 1960, no. B-282, United Nations archives.

19 F. Vandewalle, *Mille . . .*, Vol. 2, p. 196.

20 Communications between Hammarskjöld and Lumumba of 14 and 15 August, Doc. S/4417/Add., 15 August 1960.

21 Letter from Hammarskjöld to Kasa Vubu, 15 August 1960, United Nations archives; telegram from the US mission to the UN, 16 August 1960, M. Kalb, *The Congo Cables*, p. 51; "H", declaration at Security Council 21 August 1960, Doc. S/PV 887.

22 *Le Figaro,* in G. Dinant, *L'ONU . . .*, p. 65.

23 W. Okumu, *Lumumba's Congo,* pp. 204, 214.

24 A. Dulles, message of 26 August 1960, and Bissell, in M. Kalb, *The Congo Cables,* pp. 64–6; telegrams from Timberlake of 17 and 19 August 1960, in *ibid*, pp. 52, 61.

25 *Ibid.,* p. 68.

26 Telegram from Bunche to "H", 21 August 1960, no. B-580, United Nations archives.

27 Cordier, quoted respectively in C. Collins, "The Cold War Comes to Africa: Cordier and the 1960 Congo Crisis", p. 259, and in G. Abi-Saab, *The United Nations Operation in the Congo, 1960–1964,* pp. 59, 66.

28 "H", UN Advisory Committee on the Congo, 2 September 1960, United Nations archives; I.J. Rikhye, *Military Adviser to the Secretary General. UN Peacekeeping and the Congo Crisis,* p. 102; on the battles in Kasai, see CRISP, *Congo, 1960,* pp. 802–6.

29 Telegram 465 from Van den Bosch to Belext Brussels, 23 July 1960, Foreign Ministry archives; telegram 143 from Belsulat Brazza to Belext Brussels, 16 August 1960, Foreign Ministry archives; G. Eyskens, *De memoires*, p. 586; telegram 335 from "davwe" (probably Davignon/Westhof or Wendelen) (Belsulat Brazza) to Belext Brussels, 3 September 1960, Foreign Ministry archives.

30 F. Vandewalle, *Mille . . .,* vol. 2, p. 206; telegram 304 from Lahaye/Dupret (Brazza) to Belext Brussels, 31 August 1960, Foreign Ministry archives.

31 Telegram 330 from Dupret (Brazza) to Wigny, 3 September 1960, Foreign Ministry archives; "Un appel de Mgr. Malula aux élites congolaises", *LLB* 3 August 1960.

32 J. Van Bilsen, *Congo 1945–1965,* pp. 257–8; M. Kalb, *The Congo Cables,* pp. 73–4; State Department report No. 373A, Institut Africain archives; Lumumba, in J. Van Lierde, *La Pensée politique . . .,* p. 328.

33 C. von Horn, *Soldiering for Peace,* p. 208; telegrams "H" to Cordier (Léo) of 5 September 1960, nos 1552 and 1562, United Nations archives.

34 Telegram from Cordier to "H", 5 September 1960, no. B-797, United Nations archives; Timberlake, M. Kalb, *The Congo Cables,* p. 77; telegram from "H" to Cordier and Dayal, 7 September, no. 1598, United Nations archives.

35 Telegram from Cordier/von Horn (Léo) to Berendsen (E'ville), 7 September 1960, no. B-837; telegram "H" to Berendsen, 7 September, no. 37; telegram Byrne/Berendsen to "H", 8 September, no. 96; telegram "H" to Byrne/Berendsen, 8 September 1960, no. 40, United Nations archives; J. Gérard-Libois, *Sécession au Katanga,* p. 153, and J. Gérard-Libois, *L'Opération . . .,* p. 15.

36 F. Perin and R. Scheyven, quoted in CRISP, *Congo 1960,* pp. 104–35, 306; E. Luard, *A History of the United Nations*, Vol. 2: *The Age of Decolonisation,* p. 243.

37 On the proceedings in the House of Representatives, see telegram 378 from Belsulat Brazza to Belext, 7 September 1960, Foreign Ministry archives; Timberlake, State Department document, 27 January 1961, quoted by D.N. Gibbs, *The Political Economy of Third World Intervention . . .,* p. 95; telegram from Dayal to "H", 8 September 1960, no. B-861, United Nations archives; Lumumba's speech, in CRISP, *Congo 1960,* pp. 828–48.

38 CIA (Dulles and Gray), 8 September 1960, quoted by M. Kalb, *The Congo Cables,* pp. 77–8; telegrams 358, 365 and 367 of 6 September 1960, and 371 of 7 September 1960, from Dupret (Belsulat Brazza) to Belext Brussels, Foreign Ministry archives.

39 Telegram from Dayal to "H", 9 September 1960, no. B-874, United Nations archives; P. Wigny, quoted by G. Heinz and H. Donnay, *Lumumba Patrice,* p. 31, and F. Vandewalle, *Mille . . .,* Vol. 2, p. 267.

40 Telegram from Marlière (Brazza) to Minaf (Brussels), undated, unnumbered, with the stamp "received" 13 September 1960; telegrams from Marlière to Loos (Brussels) of 15 and 17 September 1960, unnumbered, and telegram 58316 from Loos to Marlière (Brazza), undated. All these messages are in the Foreign Ministry archives. On Dedeken, see F. Vandewalle, *Mille . . .*, Vol. 2, p. 242, and *Bulletin du Craoca,* no. 2, 1991.

41 Telegram 486 from Davignon/Dupret (Brazza) to Belext Brussels, 16 September 1960; telegrams from Marlière to Loos of 17 and 28 September 1960, unnumbered, and message 60826 from Loos to Marlière, 27 September 1960. All messages are in the Foreign Ministry archives.

42 Telegram from Dupret (Brazza) to Minaf and Caeymaex (Brussels), unnumbered, 3 October 1960, telegram Marlière (Brazza) to Minaf Brussels, unnumbered, 1 October 1960 and minute telex from Loos (Minaf) to Belsulat/Marlière, no. 65505, 5 October 1960, Foreign Ministry archives; Albert, Associated Press, *LLB* and *Le Peuple,* 3 October 1960.

CHAPTER 2

1 Telegram from "H" to Dayal/Cordier (Léo), 6 September 1960, no. 1593, United Nations archives; R. Dayal, *Mission for Hammarskjöld*, p.66; minute of telex Loos (Minaf) to Belsulat/Marlière, no. 60826, 27 September 1960; also see his telex no. 65505 of 5 October 1960, Foreign Ministry archives.

2 Telegram from Dayal/von Horn to "H", 14 September, no. B-965, United Nations archives; on the ANC offensive against Katanga, also see telegram 55209 from d'Aspremont Lynden (Brussels) to Consubel E'ville, 9 September 1960, Foreign Ministry archives.

3 Telegram from Rikhye (UN E'ville) to Dayal, 15 October 1960, unnumbered, United Nations archives; telegram 1349/54 from "Bloock/Créner" (E'ville) to Brussels, 20 October 1960, Foreign Ministry archives.

4 F. Vandewalle, *Mille . . .*, Vol. 2, p.261; telegram 680 from Lahaye/Dupret (Brazza) to Belext Brussels, 18 October 1960; see also telegram 699 from Dupret (Brazza) to Belext Brussels, 20 October 1960, Foreign Ministry archives.

5 Message from Marlière (Brazza) to Loos (Brussels) of 22 September 1960, unnumbered, and message Minaf to Marlière (Belsulat Brazza) of 28 September 1960, no. 61428, Foreign Ministry archives; letter from Lumumba, quoted by K. Nkrumah, *Challenge of the Congo,* pp. 61–3; letter from P. Dufour (UN Stanleyville) to B. Urquhart (UN Léo), 12 September 1960, United Nations archives.

6 Telegram from Timberlake of 13 October 1960 to Washington, quoted by M. Kalb, *The Congo Cables,* p.138; telegram from Dayal to "H", 19 October 1960, no. B-1275, United Nations archives; telegram from Belsulat Brazza to Loos (Minaf), unnumbered, 13 October 1960, Foreign Ministry archives.

7 F. Vandewalle, *L'Ommegang,* p.20; F. Vandewalle, *Mille . . .,* Vol. 3, p.482.

8 Conakat memo, 20 June 1959, in J. Chomé, *Moïse Tshombe . . .,* pp. 140–1; Mikolacjczak, quoted by A. Schöller, *Congo 1959–1960,* pp. 200–1; UN report, probably of 23 October 1960, in D.N. Gibbs, "Dag Hammarskjöld. . .", p.165; G. Weber, *Le Katanga de Moïse Tshombe . . .,* p. 193.

9 J. Brassinne, "Enquête sur la mort de Patrice Lumumba", Vol. 1, p. 46; F. Vandewalle, *Mille . . .,* Vol. 1, p.91; G. Weber, *Le Katanga . . .,* pp. 67–8.

10 F. Vandewalle, *Mille . . .,* Vol. 2, pp. 172, 186, 223, 217, 259, and Vol. 3, p. 359.

11 Minister for African Affairs, "Ordre de mission" (of G. Weber), 11 January 1961, in G. Weber, *Le Katanga . . .,* p.208.

12 F. Vandewalle, *Mille . . .,* Vol. 2, p. 166; telegram from "H" (Léo) to Cordier, 14 August, no. B-452, United Nations archives; M.G.R., *De Standaard,* 18 August 1960.

13 F. Vandewalle, *Mille . . .,* Vol. 3, p. 457.

14 M.G.R., *De Standaard,* 18 August 1960; E. Troch, "Op de uitkijk", *De Standaard,* 18 August 1960; letter from Tshombe to Eyskens, 8 October 1960, quoted by F. Vandewalle, *Mille . . .,* Vol. 3, p. A39.

15 W.J. Ganshof, *Fin de la Souveraineté belge au Congo,* pp.332, 338.

16 List established on the basis of H. Gaus (ed.), *Politiek-biografisch lexicon,* pp.190–5; *Biographie Belge d'Outre-Mer,* VII-a, pp.16 ff.; E.M., "Qui contrôle la Société Générale?", in CRISP, *Courrier Hebdomadaire,* 8 May 1959; P. Joye and R. Lewin, *Les Trusts au Congo,* pp. 284ff.; P. Joye and E. Glinne, in *L'Eglantine,* p.20.

17 Baudouin, in CRISP, *Congo 1960,* pp. 513–51; Tshombe, in F. Vandewalle, *Mille . . .,* Vol. 2, pp. A1–2.

18 Letter from Baudouin to Tshombe, 28 October 1960, in F. Vandewalle, *Mille . . .,* Vol. 3, pp.A53–A54; *ibid.,* pp.395–6.

19 Newspaper articles in J. Chomé, *Moïse Tshombe . . .,* pp.270ff.

20 Interview with Tshombe and comments by M.G.R., *De Standaard*, 9 December 1960; "Exposé de P. Wigny à une délégation de l'Union Minière" "Aide-mémoire concernant

l'indépendance du Katanga et l'attitude de la Belgique à cet égard", 5 December 1960, in "Cab 3722" – 168, Foreign Ministry archives.

21 Oldenhove, in a note from Weber to Vandewalle, 28 May 1961, in F. Vandewalle, *Mille . . .,* Vol. 5, pp. A29–32; letter from Baudouin to Tshombe, arrived in E'ville on 26 July 1961, in *ibid.,* p.536.

22 Letter from M. Dubuisson to F. Vandewalle, 26 October 1961, in F. Vandewalle, *Mille . . .,* Vol. 6, p. A73.

23 J. Stengers, *L'Action du Roi . . .,* p. 23.

24 Eyskens's statement of 14 July 1960 and Wigny's of 19 July 1960, in CPE, *La Crise . . .,* respectively p. 685 and pp. 714, 718 – on the Polish cargo, see telegram 350 from Van den Bosch to Belext Brussels, 18 July 1960, Foreign Ministry archives; comments by Vandewalle, in *Mille . . .,* Vol. 1, pp. 98 and 125.

25 H. d'Aspremont Lynden, "Note pour monsieur le premier ministre", notes 27 February, 2 March, 7 and 10 July 1960, in Vandewalle archives, "Dossiers VDW. Rapports – Notes 1959–1960"; Count J. Pirenne, "Note au sujet de l'indépendance du Congo", 12 February 1960, A.E. De Schryver archives.

26 G. Weber, *Comme . . .,* p. 107; *Pourquoi Pas?,* 9 September 1960; *LLB,* 5 September 1960.

27 On support for Mobutu, see telexes from Loos to Marlière of 27 September 1960, Nos 60826 and 60996, Foreign Ministry archives; on the coding system, dixit Verdickt, quoted by F. Vandewalle, *Mille . . .,* Vol. 3, p. 415.

28 F. Vandewalle, *Mille . . .,* Vol. 3, p. 416; message 364 from d'Aspremont Lynden (E'ville) to Wigny, Eyskens and De Schryver, 22 August 1960, Foreign Ministry archives.

29 Falsification, in F. Vandewalle, *Mille . . .,* Vol. 2, pp. 242, 273; telegram 286 of 23 February 1961 from Duprct to Belext/Minaf Brussels, Foreign Ministry archives.

CHAPTER 3

1 Telegram 491 from Denis/Dupret (Brazza) to Belext Brussels, 17 September 1960, Foreign Ministry archives; telegram "Aspremont" to Mistebel, E'ville, message 657, 6 October 1960, in F. Vandewalle, *Mille . . .,* Vol. 3, p. A28 – minute by d'Aspremont Lynden, with copy for Wigny, of 5 October, Foreign Ministry archives.

   Translators' note. We have left the last two words of the crucial 6 October telegram in the original French to avoid confusion. It can be translated into English as "to eliminate Lumumba once and for all" or "to dispose of Lumumba once and for all".

2 Devlin, Gottlieb and Dulles, in M. Kalb, *The Congo Cables,* pp. 100–2, 131–3, 151–2, 183; on Gottlieb and QJ/WIN, see *ibid.,* pp. 102, 130–1, 151–2, and R. Mahoney, *Sons & Brothers,* pp. 92–3.

3 J.-M. van der Dussen (Jean Kestergat), "La mort de Patrice Lumumba" (1989), in J. Brassinne, "Enquête", Vol. IV, testimony 51.1 – also see J. Kestergat, "Du Congo de Lumumba au Zaïre de Mobutu", *LLB,* 2–3 August 1986; General E. Janssens, quoted by W. Geerts, *Binza 10,* p. 116.

4 F. Vandewalle, *Mille . . .,* Vol. 3, p. 308; Prince Albert, Associated Press, quoted by *LLB,* 3 October 1960, and by *Le Peuple,* 3 October 1960; F. Vandewalle, *Mille . . .,* Vol. 3, p. 317.

5 On the missions to Pointe-Noire and Usumbura, see F. Vandewalle, *Mille . . .,* Vol. 3, p. 320.

6 F. Vandewalle, *Mille . . .* Vol. 3, pp. 333–4, telegram from Wigny (New York) to Dupret (Brazza), 8 October 1960, no. 298, in Vandewalle archives, "Boîte Mille et quatre jours. Documentations fascicules 1–2–3. Dossier Antoine".

7 Telegram 655 from Dupret/Westhof (Belsulat Brazza) to Belext Brussels, 13 October 1960, in Vandewalle archives "Boîte Mille et quatre jours. Documentations fascicules 1–2–3. Dossier Antoine", and in Foreign Ministry archives; telegram 664 from Westhof (Brazza) to

Belext Brussels, 14 October 1960, in Foreign Ministry archives; F. Vandewalle, *Mille . . .,* Vol. 3, pp. 323–4, handwritten "Top secret" (unnamed), "Rapport de mission à Usumbura le 8 septembre", 10 September 1960, addressed to Lt. Col. BEM Grandjean and to R. Rothschild, in Vandewalle archives, "Boîte Mille et quatre jours. Documentations fascicules 1–2–3. Dossier Antoine."

8 Conversation between L. Marlière, A. Lahaye and J. Brassinne, in J. Brassinne, "Enquête", Vol. IV, testimonies 35.1 and 36.2; telegram from L. Marlière (Brazza) to J. Loos (Minaf), unnumbered, 14 October 1960, Foreign Ministry archives; A. Verdickt, "Etat du Katanga. Forces katangaises. Etat-major Section G2, Très Secret, E'ville", 26 November 1960, in Vandewalle archives, "Boîte Mille et quatre jours. Documentations fascicules 1–2–3. Dossier Antoine".

9 C. Hoskyns, *The Congo . . .*, p. 264; R. Dayal, *Mission . . .* p. 119. See for this sub-chapter L. De Witte, *Crisis in Kongo*, pp. 352–60.

10 F. Vandewalle, *Mille . . .,* Vol. 3, p. 400.

11 F. Vandewalle, *Mille . . .,* Vol. 3, p. 401.

12 Telegrams from Dayal to "H" of 29 November 1960, B-1544 and B-1541, United Nations archives; C.H. Timberlake, *First Year . . .*, p. 128; statement "H" to Wadsworth, quoted by M. Kalb, *The Congo Cables*, p. 160.

13 Lumumba's statement to the press, 27 November 1960, in "Central Africa Project Collection 1920–1980", archives of the Schomburg Center for Research in Black Culture.

14 Telegram Dayal to "H" of 29 November 1960, No. B-1545, United Nations archives; G. Heinz and H. Donnay, *Lumumba Patrice,* pp. 47ff. (this book has been translated into English as *Lumumba: The Last Fifty Days*, but the citations here are translated from the original; Heinz and Donnay are the pseudonyms of J. Gérard-Libois and J. Brassinne respectively); telegrams from Belsulat/Ambabel Brazza to Brussels of 20 November 1960 (no. 834) and of 28 November 1960 (nos 864 and 866), Foreign Ministry archives.

15 G. Heinz and H. Donnay, *Lumumba Patrice*, pp. 47–8; telegrams 877 and 878 from Ambabel Brazza to Belext Brussels, 30 November 1960, Foreign Ministry archives.

16 G. Heinz and H. Donnay, *Lumumba Patrice,* p. 48; telegram 880 from Rothschild (Ambabel Brazza) to Belext Brussels, 1 December 1960, Foreign Ministry archives.

17 UNOC, "Summary of events leading to the arrest of Mr Patrice Lumumba at Mweka in Kasai Province on December 2 1960", United Nations archives; telegram from Dayal to "H" of 1 December 1960, B-1561, United Nations archives.

18 "H" statement of 15 February 1961, Press Release SG/1008.

19 G. Heinz and H. Donnay, *Lumumba Patrice,* p. 60; telegram 536 from Dupret (Consubel Brazza) to Belext Brussels, 23 September 1960 – also see telegram 553 from Dupret to Wigny of 26 September 1960, Foreign Ministry archives.

20 C. von Horn, *Soldiering for Peace*, p. 248; "H", quoted in a telegram from the US delegation to the UN, 2 December 1960, in M. Kalb, *The Congo Cables,* p. 163; Mobutu, quoted by *Pourquoi Pas?,* 9 December 1960.

21 Minutes of the College of Commissioners, in G. Heinz and H. Donnay, *Lumumba Patrice,* p. 61; telegram from Rothschild (Ambabel Brazza) to Brussels, 895, 3 December 1960, Foreign Ministry archives; UN observers, quoted by R. Dayal, report of 5 December 1960, Doc. S/4571.

22 G. Heinz and H. Donnay, *Lumumba Patrice,* p. 64.

23 A. Cahen, in J. Brassinne, "Enquête", Vol. 1, p. 103; telegram Ambabel Brazza, number unknown, to Brussels 3 December 1960, in F. Vandewalle, *Mille . . .* Vol. 3, p. 437 and in G. Heinz and H. Donnay, *Lumumba Patrice,* pp. 69–70.

24 Telegram from Timberlake (Léo) to Herter, 3 December 1960, Institut Africain archives.

25 Dayal, "Verbal protest to M. Bomboko", 3 December, and Hammarskjöld "Letter to Kasa Vubu", 3 December 1960, in Dayal Report of 5 December 1960, Doc. S/4571; "H" "First Report . . .", 18 July 1960, in Doc. S/4389; F. Vandewalle, *Mille . . .*, Vol. 3, p. 409.

26 On Lumumba's cell, see J. Brassinne, "Enquête", Vol. 1, p. 116.

27 R. Dayal, Report of 5 December 1960, Doc. S/4571; telegrams from Dayal to "H" of 5 and 22 December 1960, B-1603 and B-1744, United Nations archives.

28 Letter to Dayal of 4 January 1961, in J. Van Lierde, *Lumumba Speaks* . . ., pp. 424–6; letter to A. Onawelo of 4 January 1961 (underlined in the original), in B. Verhaegen, "Patrice Lumumba, martyr d'une Afrique nouvelle", *Jeune Afrique*, 1 September 1978, p. 87; Institut Africain, biographical file. On Lumumba's marriages, see J. Omasombo Tshonda and B. Verhaegen, *Patrice Lumumba* . . ., pp. 135–50; telex from d'Aspremont Lynden to Consubel Brazza of 22 September 1960, 59922, Foreign Ministry archives.

29 C. Kamitatu, *La Grande Mystification du Congo-Kinshasa*, pp. 83–4, R. Dayal, Second Report of 2 November 1960, Doc. A/4557; letter from Lumumba to Dayal, 4 January 1961, in J. Van Lierde, *Lumumba Speaks*, pp. 424–6; letter from Kamitatu to "H", 5 January 1961, United Nations archives.

30 Schoonbroodt, in J. Brassinne, "Enquête", Vol. 1, p. 115–16. On the political disputes between the soldiers in Thysville, also see telegram 65 from Ambabel Brazza to Brussels, 17 January 1961, in *ibid.*, Vol. III, annexe 12.2.

31 Lahaye, in J. Brassinne, "Enquête", Vol. 1, p. 116; L. López Alvarez, *Lumumba* . . ., p. 132.

32 Telegram 01404/cab from Minaf to Ambabel Brazza/Lahaye, 4 January 1961, and telegram 19 from Dupret/Crokart (Brazza) to Belext Brussels, 5 January 1961, Foreign Ministry archives; interview with F. Kazadi by J. Van Lierde (Léopoldville, 1966), Doc. Van Lierde; on Shinkakasa, see J. Brassinne, "Enquête", Vol. IV, testimony 46.1 from A.-H. Schoonbroodt; F. Vandewalle, *Mille* . . ., Vol. 4, p. 17.

33 J. Brassinne, "Enquête", Vol. IV, testimonies 36.2 from L. Marlière and 56.1 from A. Lahaye.

34 G. Heinz and H. Donnay, *Lumumba Patrice,* p. 93; biography of Lahaye in J. Brassinne, "Enquête", Vol. IV, testimony 56.1; telegram 32 from Dupret (Brazza) to Belext Brussels, 9 January 1961, Foreign Ministry archives.

35 F. Vandewalle, *Mille* . . ., Vol. 6, pp. A15–21; telegram from Rothschild (E'ville) to Belext Minaf (Brussels), 30 September 1960, in *ibid.*, Vol. 2, pp. C23–5.

36 Servais to UN officer Monahan, quoted by F. Vandewalle, *Mille* . . ., Vol. 2, p. 278; *ibid.*, Vol. 3, pp. 416–17; P. Davister, *Katanga* . . ., p. 254.

37 Weber, note of 28 May 1961, in F. Vandewalle, *Mille* . . ., Vol. 5, pp. A29–32.

38 F. Vandewalle, *Mille* . . ., Vol. 1, p. 132; note from Cumont, 14 July 1960, in *ibid.,* .pp. 99–100.

39 Rikhye, meeting of 15 October 1960, quoted by F. Vandewalle, *Mille* . . ., Vol. 3, pp. 339–40; F. Vandewalle, in *ibid.,* p. 351; intelligence officer R. Pire, "La Sécession katangaise . . .", p. 50.

40 General Assembly resolution of 20 September 1960, 1474 (ES-IV); note from "H" to Loridan, 8 October 1960 in Doc. A/4557, 2 November 1960; F. Vandewalle, *Mille* . . ., Vol. 3, p. 313 – also see the telegram from Scheyven (Ambabel Washington) to Belext Brussels, 313 of 18 October 1960, in F. Vandewalle, *Mille* . . ., p. A48.

41 F. Vandewalle, *Mille* . . ., Vol. 4, p. 2.

42 F. Vandewalle, *Mille* . . ., Vol. 4, p. 24.

43 "Top secret" memo from Vanden Bloock (E'ville), 12 December 1960, in F. Vandewalle, *Mille* . . ., Vol. 3, pp. C 9–16; memo from UNOC Elisabethville to Tshombe, 15 December 1960, in *ibid.,* pp. C 17–18.

44 F. Vandewalle, *Mille* . . ., Vol. 4, pp. 25–6.

CHAPTER 4

1 Document from H. d'Aspremont Lynden, quoted by F. Vandewalle, *Mille* . . ., Vol. 3, p. A55; F. Vandewalle, *L'Ommegang*, pp. 14, 16.

2 Rothschild (E'ville) to Belext/Minaf (Brussels), message no. 1208/55, 11 October 1960, Foreign Ministry archives; F. Vandewalle, *Mille* . . ., Vol. 4, p. 30; *La Relève,* 14 January 1961.

3 F. Vandewalle, *Mille . . .*, Vol. 4, pp. 19–22.

4 Telegram from Rothschild (Ambabel Brazza) to Brussels, no. 895, 3 December 1960, Foreign Ministry archives; on the meeting in Brazza, see F. Vandewalle, *Mille . . .*, Vol. 3, pp. 403–44, and G. Weber, quoted in telegram 965 from Dupret (Brazza) to Belext Brussels, 19 December 1960, Vandewalle archives, "Boîte Mille et quatre jours. Documentations fascicules 1–2–3. Dossier Antoine".

5 Message 49 from Brazza to the *Gendarmerie* (E'ville), 24 December 1960, and telegram 990 from Ambabel Brazza to Brussels, 24 December 1960, J. Brassinne, "Enquête", Vol. III, Annexes 4 and 7.2; telegram 4296/t486 from Vanden Bloock (E'ville) to Belext and Minaf (Brussels), 28 December 1960, Foreign Ministry archives – also see F. Vandewalle, *Mille . . .*, Vol. 3, p. 463.

6 G. Eyskens, *De memoires*, p. 587; report Brazza, F. Vandewalle, *Mille . . .*, Vol. 4, p. 12; telegram 14 from Brussels to Ambabel Brazza, 4 January 1961, J. Brassinne, "Enquête", Vol. I, p. 63 – draft from d'Aspremont Lynden to Lahaye, no. 01404, 3 January 1961, Foreign Ministry archives; Heinz and Donnay, *Lumumba Patrice*, p. 93.

7 On the missions of Mukamba (2 January 1961) and Delvaux and Adoula (8 January 1961) to E'ville, see F. Vandewalle, *Mille . . .*, Vol. 4, p. 17, and J. Brassinne, "Enquête", Vol. 1, pp. 85–6, 99; Wigny's instructions, 12 January 1961, "Enquête", Vol. III, Annexe 8.1; telegram 83 of 19 January 1961 from Ambabel Brazza to Brussels, Foreign Ministry archives.

8 J. Brassinne, "Enquête", Vol. IV, testimony 36.2 of L. Marlière; discussion L. De Witte/J. Gérard-Libois, Brussels, 11 May 1998.

9 Marliere, quoted by J. Brassinne, "Enquête", Vol. I, p. 74; Marlière at E'ville quoted in Dupret's (Brazza) message to Minaf and Minaffreta (Brussels) of 18 January 1961, F. Vandewalle, *Mille . . .*, Vol. 4, p. 53; F. Vandewalle, *Mille . . .*, Vol. 3, p. 438.

10 F. Vandewalle, *Mille . . .*, Vol. 4, p. 21; telegram 27 from Dupret (Ambabel Brazza) to Belext (Brussels), 7 January 1961, Foreign Ministry archives.

11 Unless otherwise indicated, for all information about the mutiny see J. Brassinne, "Enquête", Vol. IV, testimony 46.1 from A.-H. Schoonbroodt and testimony 53.1 from J. Cordy, and telegram 226 of 9 February 1961 from Ambabel Brazza to Belext Brussels, with testimony from Lt. Nicolai (Thysville), Foreign Ministry archives.

12 M. Kalb, *The Congo Cables,* p. 184. Also see telegram 51 from Dupret (Brazza) to Belext Brussels, 14 January 1961, J. Brassinne, "Enquête", Vol. III, annexe 8.3.

13 J. Brassinne, "Enquête", Vol. IV, testimony 53.1 from J. Cordy; telegram Dayal to "H", 15 January 1961, D-93, United Nations archives.

14 Telegrams Dayal to "H", 18 January 1961, no. D-120, United Nations archives; R. Dayal, *Mission for Hammarskjöld*, p. 190; L. Marlière, quoted by Cdt. Matthys, "Memorandum réunion de contact ANC/Gdkat", Elisabethville, 20 January 1961, F. Vandewalle, *Mille . . .*, Vol. 4, pp. 58–9, A15–17; telegrams Dupret (Brazza) to Belext (Brussels), 5 November 1960 (774) and 17 November 1960 (830), and 5 January 1961 (19) and 9 January 1961 (32, 37), Foreign Ministry archives.

15 Letter from Kasongo to "H", 4 January 1961, United Nations archives; Timberlake, 11 January 1961, quoted by M. Kalb, *The Congo Cables,* pp. 178–9.

16 Telegrams 43 of 11 January 1961, 50 of 13 January 1961 and 58 of 16 January 1961 from Ambabel Brazza to Brussels, Foreign Ministry archives.

17 Dulles, 22 July 1960, quoted by M. Kalb, *The Congo Cables*, p. 29; Eisenhower, 18 August 1960, according to the testimonies of Vice-Minister Dillon and National Security Council staff member Johnson, in *ibid.*, pp. 53–5; Devlin and Kalb, in *ibid.*, pp. 190, 207.

18 A telegram from CIA-Elisabethville of 19 January 1961 supports this argument: "Thanks for [sending] Patrice. If we had known he was coming we would have baked a snake." CIA chiefs L. Devlin and B. Tweedy confirm the CIA was not implicated: M. Kalb, *The Congo Cables*, p. 192. On the difficulties concerning Operation Barracuda, see telegrams from Marlière (Brazza) to Loos (Minaf military adviser) of 15, 17 and 28 September, all unnumbered, and telegrams from

Loos to Marlière no. 59020 of 20 September 1960, no. 58920 undated, no. 61828 of 26 September 1960, and unnumbered of 27 September, Foreign Ministry archives.

19 Draft from d'Aspremont Lynden to Lahaye and Marlière, no. 03610, 10 January 1961, Foreign Ministry archives; telegram 51 from Dupret (Brazza) to Belext (Brussels), 14 January 1961, J. Brassinne, "Enquête", Vol. III, annexe 8.3; J. Brassinne, *ibid.*, Vol. I, p. 72; J. Cordy, *ibid.* Vol. IV, testimony 57.1.

20 F. Vandewalle, *Mille . . .*, Vol. 4, pp. 42–3; L. Marlière, quoted by J. Brassinne, "Enquête", Vol. I, pp. 73, 127, and Vol. IV, testimony 36.2. – also see F. Vandewalle, *Mille . . .*, Vol. 4, pp. 43–4; J. Kestergat, quoted by J. Brassinne, "Enquête", Vol. I, p. 34.

21 J. Brassinne, "Enquête", Vol. I, pp. 89–90, 92.

22 J. Brassinne, "Enquête", Vol. III, annexe 9.1. (message from the Belgian embassy in Brazza to the chief-of-staff of the Katangan *Gendarmerie*, 14 January 1961) and annexe 10 (telegram 53 from the Belgian Embassy in Brazza to Brussels, 14 January 1961).

23 Message 64 from d'Aspremont Lynden to the General Consulate in E'ville, 16 January 1961, his message 66 to the Belgian Embassy in Brazza, 16 January 1961, and telegram 14 from Wigny to the General Consulate in E'ville, 18 January 1961, in J. Brassinne, "Enquête", Vol. III, annexes 11.1, 11.2 and 14.1; message 06616/cable from d'Aspremont Lynden to the Belgian Embassy in Brazza, 16 January 1961, and minutes of messages from d'Aspremont Lynden on 15 January 1961, nos 06416 and 06616, Foreign Ministry archives. F. Vandewalle compares Wigny's message of 18 January to "water after wine": *Mille . . .*, Vol. 4, p. 50.

24 J. Brassinne and Kestergat, *Qui a tué . . .*, p. 119.

25 J. Brassinne, "Enquête", Vol. 1, pp. 101–2.

26 F. Vandewalle, *Mille . . .*, Vol. 2, p. 201. On Lumumba's plans to go to Katanga in August 1960, see telegram 893 from Misdiplobel Léo to Belext Brussels, 13 August 1960, Foreign Ministry archives.

27 Bartelous, J. Brassinne, "Enquête", Vol. IV, testimony 12.2; Larock, 14 February 1961, Annales Parlementaires de Belgique, Chambre des Représentants, Session ordinaire 1960–1961; Munongo, quoted in "Meeting Jonas Mukamba-Jean Van Lierde", Brussels, 14 February 1961 (Doc. Van Lierde) – also see F. Vandewalle, *Mille . . .*, Vol. 4, p. 84.

28 Telegram 4296/t486 from Vanden Bloock (E'ville) to Belext and Minaf (Brussels) of 28 December 1960, Foreign Ministry archives.

29 A. Kalonji, quoted by C. Kamitatu, *La Grande Mystification . . .*, p. 87, and by Heinz and Donnay, *Lumumba Patrice,* p. 80; N. Dedeken, *Chimères baluba,* p. 132 – also see "Meeting Jonas Mukamba-Jean Van Lierde", Brussels, 14 February 1961 (Doc. Van Lierde).

30 J. Brassinne, "Enquête", Vol. I, p. 160; J. Brassinne, *ibid.* Vol. IV, testimony 28.1 of A. Belina.

31 On Devlin, see M. Kalb, *The Congo Cables,* pp. 190–1; on Gillet, see J. Brassinne, "Enquête", Vol. I, pp. 79, 90–1, 94–8, Marlière, quoted by Brassinne, "Enquête", Vol. I, p. 79.

32 J. Brassinne and J. Kestergat, *Qui a tué . . .*, p. 118; J. Brassinne, "Enquête", Vol. I, p. 96.

33 J. Brassinne and J. Kestergat, *Qui a tué . . .*, p. 120; J. Brassinne, "Enquête", Vol. I, p. 101.

34 See F. Vandewalle, *Mille . . .*, Vol. 4, pp. 41–2; J. Brassinne, "Enquête", Vol. I, pp. 84–5, and *Bulletin du Craoca,* 1/84, pp. 14–16.

35 J. Brassinne, "Enquête", Vol. I, p. 95 – also see *ibid.*, Vol. III, annexe 9.3.

36 J. Brassinne and J. Kestergat, *Qui a tué . . .*, p. 117; two memos from G. Weber, undated, Van Doal (F. Vandewalle), *Une ténébreuse affaire . . .* pp. 97–9 and 111–113.

37 J. Brassinne, "Enquête", Vol. I, pp. 94–5, 97; F. Vandewalle, *Mille . . .*, Vol. 4, p. 30.

38 F. Vandewalle, *Mille . . .*, Vol. 4, pp. 30, 32.

39 Letters from Tshombe to Kasa Vubu and Bomboko, 15 January 1961, ref. SR 20/35/TN and SR 20/36/TN; J. Brassinne, "Enquête", Vol. I, pp. 96–8 and Vol. III, annexe 13.1; "Conclusions" in *ibid.*, Vol. II, p. 593; testimony 6.1 from A. Cahen in *ibid.*, Vol. IV. See also J. Brassinne and J. Kestergat, *Qui a tué . . .*, pp. 118–20. On Servais, see J. Brassinne, "Enquête", Vol. IV, testimony 16.2 from A. Verdickt; J. Brassinne and J. Kestergat, *Qui a tué . . .*, p. 120.

40 On the telephone link Léo-E'ville, see J. Brassinne, "Enquête", Vol. I, p. 98; Delvaux, quote in *De Standaard,* 18 January 1961.

41 F. Vandewalle, *Mille . . .,* Vol. 4, p. 30; J. Brassinne, "Enquête", Vol. I, p. 98; Vol. IV, testimony 16.2 by A. Verdickt and testimony 57.1 by J. Cordy.

42 J. Brassinne and J. Kestergat, *Qui a tué . . .,* p. 119; conversation between L. Marlière, A. Lahaye and J. Brassinne, in J. Brassinne, "Enquête", Vol. IV, testimony 35.1.

43 J. Brassinne, "Enquête", Vol. I, p. 102.

44 F. Vandewalle, *Mille . . .,* Vol. 4, p. 38; telegram 64 from d'Aspremont Lynden to the consul general in E'ville of 16 January 1961 and his message 66 to the Belgian Embassy in Brazza of the same day, in J. Brassinne, "Enquête", Vol. III, annexes 11.1 and 11.2 – draft of 15 January, no. 06416, Foreign Ministry archives; J. Brassinne and J. Kestergat, *Qui a tué . . .,* pp. 118–19.

45 J. Brassinne, "Enquête", Vol. I, p. 177; telegram 52 from Consubel E'ville to Belext Brussels, 18 January 1961, Foreign Ministry archives.

46 F. Vandewalle, *Mille . . .* Vol. 4, pp. 30, 32; UN, *Report of the Events leading to the Death of Mr. Lumumba, Mr. Okito and Mr. Mpolo,* A/4964. According to Brassinne, Tignée was among the three Belgians heard by the UN Commission; J. Brassinne, "Enquête", Vol. II, p. 480.

47 J. Dumba, quoted by J. Brassinne and J. Kestergat, *Qui a tué . . .,* p. 121, on the conversation between Kasa Vubu and Longerstaey, see F. Vandewalle, *Mille . . .,* Vol. 4, p. 39.

48 On the meeting in the Sabena-Afrique office at Ndjili, see J. Brassinne, "Enquête", Vol. I, pp. 122–31, and minutes of the Sabena meeting of 20 August 1987, in *ibid.*, Vol. IV, testimony 30.1; on the situation at Luano, in *ibid.,* Vol. I, p. 175; on G. Dieu, see J. Van den Bosch, *Pré-Zaire,* pp. 99–100.

49 J. Brassinne and J. Kestergat, *Qui a tué . . .,* p. 113.

50 For these measures see J. Van Lierde, "Lettre à Jules Gérard-Libois. Rencontre avec Kazadi sur la mort de Patrice Lumumba", Kinshasa, 11 May 1966, and J. Brassinne, "Enquête", Vol. I, pp. 132ff. and Vol. IV, testimony 46 from d'A. H. Schoonbroodt.

CHAPTER 5

1 On the events in Thysville, see J. Brasssinne, "Enquête", Vol. I, pp. 144 ff., and Vol. IV, d'A.-H. Schoonbroodt's testimony 46. I. All times are local. Local time in the province of Léopoldville is the same as Belgium, Greenwich Mean Time + 1; for Katanga, GMT + 2.

2 On Mpolo and Okito, see J. Gérard-Libois, *Sécession . . .,* p. 165; on their arrest by the ANC, see Conférence Nationale Souveraine, *Commission des Assassinats . . .,* pp. 33–4.

3 UN, *Report of the Events leading to the Death of Mr. Lumumba, Mr. Okito and Mr. Mpolo,* A/4964; on the events in Lukala, see J. Brassinne, "Enquête", Vol. I, pp. 153ff.

4 J. Brassinne, "Enquête", Vol. IV, R. Linard's testimony 44.1.

5 On the events in Moanda and afterwards, see J. Brassinne, "Enquête", Vol. I, pp. 158, and Vol. IV, B. Watson's testimony 39.2, and G. Goblet's 43.1.

6 Telegram No. 64 from Dupret (Brazza) to Brussels, 17 January, in J. Brassinne, "Enquête", Vol. III, annexe 12.1.

7 J. Brassinne and J. Kestergat, *Qui a tué . . .,* p. 124.

8 On the flight Moanda-E'ville, see J. Brassinne, "Enquête", Vol. I, pp. 161, 166ff.; J. Van Lierde, "Interview de Ferdinand Kazadi", Léo, 27 April 1966 (Doc. Van Lierde); J. Dixon, quoted by *Durban Sunday Tribune,* 12 February 1961, in J. Brassinne, "Enquête", Vol. II, p. 461, Vol. IV, J. Michaux's testimony 42.1.

9 B. Watson, quoted by J. Brassinne, "Enquête", Vol. IV; testimony 39.2; C. Souris, "La vérité sur l'assassinat de Patrice Lumumba", *Pourquoi Pas?,* No. 3376, 10 August 1983, in *ibid.*, Vol. I, p. 170, and Vol. III, annexe 31.3. Souris's article was based on a report from

Police Commissioner Verscheure on the events. The report is taken up in J. Brassinne, "Enquête", Vol. III, annexe 31.1. Léva and Lindekens on J. Dixon's film activities at Luano, in J. Brassinne, "Enquête", Vol. I, p. 236. According to R. Jaspar, Radio Katanga's director, the journalist Albert Pirard was also in Luano with his cine-camera and camera, in J. Brassinne, "Enquête", Vol. IV, testimony 49.1, but we do not know the results of his work.

10　For E'ville's first reactions on Lumumba's arrival, see J. Brassinne, "Enquête", Vol. I, pp. 175ff.

11　J. Brassinne, "Enquête", Vol. IV, J. Gat's testimony 24.2; on the requisitioning of the Brouwez house, see F. Vandewalle, *Mille . . .*, Vol. 4, p. 46.

12　On Captain Gat, Camp Massart and preparations for receiving the prisoners, see J. Brassinne, "Enquête", Vol. I, pp. 188–200, and Vol. IV, C. Grandelet's testimony 17.2.

13　J. Brassinne, "Enquête", Vol. I, p. 197, and Vol. IV, J. Gat's testimonies 24.1 and 24.2.

14　*L'Essor du Katanga,* 19 January 1961; telegram Bomboko to the Comité consultatif sur le Congo, 21 January 1961, in CRISP, *Travaux Africains*, No. 30, p. 24; F. Vandewalle, *Mille . . .*, Vol. 4, p. 41.

15　Bio Segers, in J. Brassinne, "Enquête", Vol. I, p. 230, and Vol. IV, Segers's testimony 45.1; Verscheure's bio, in *ibid.*, Vol. II, p. 352; on Lumumba's arrival in Luano, see *ibid.*, Vol. I, pp. 203ff.

16　J. Brassinne, "Enquête", Vol. IV, P. Perrad's testimony 19.1; G. Weber, *Le Katanga . . .*, p. 178.

17　See, for instance, Tshombe's statement, quoted in *Pourquoi Pas?*, 31 January 1964.

18　Grandelet, Lindekens, Kazadi, Mumba and Smal testimonies, in J. Brassinne, "Enquête", Vol. I, pp. 227–31.

19　J. Brassinne, "Enquête", Vol. I, p. 237.

20　F. Vandewalle, *Mille . . .*, Vol. 4, p. 47; Verdickt, in *ibid.*, pp. 47–8; and J. Brassinne, "Enquête", Vol. III, testimonies 16.1 and 16.2; Blistein, in J. Brassinne, "Enquête", Vol. I, p. 250. For other testimonies on the arrival, see J. Brassinne, "Enquête", Vol. I, pp. 237ff.

21　Report Lindgren, in UN, *Report of the Events leading to the Death of Mr. Lumumba, Mr. Okito and Mr. Mpolo*, A/4964; Kibwe, quoted by F. Vandewalle, *Mille . . .*, Vol. 4, p. 47; J. Brassinne, "Enquête", Vol. IV, J. Gat's testimony 24.2.

22　P. Davister, in *Pourquoi Pas?*, 20 January 1961.

23　On the prisoners' transfer from Luano to the Brouwez house, and the first hours there, see J. Brassinne, "Enquête", Vol. I, pp. 260ff. On the requisition, see *ibid.*, Vol. I, pp. 281–2.

24　"Plan de la maison Brouwez" in J. Brassinne, "Enquête", Vol. I, p. 290; J. Gat, in *ibid.*, p. 285.

25　Léva and Gat, quoted by J. Brassinne, "Enquête", Vol. I, pp. 289, 292; F. Vandewalle, *Mille . . .*, Vol. 4, p. 49.

26　Gat and Huyghé, quoted in J. Brassinne, "Enquête", Vol. I, p. 291. Huyghé is wrong: there were no Ghanaian Blue Berets in E'ville, only Swedish, Irish and Tunisian.

27　J. Brassinne, "Enquête", Vol. I pp. 286, 291; J. Brassinne and J. Kestergat, *Qui a tué . . .*, p. 151; F. Vandewalle, *Mille . . .*, Vol. 4, p. 49.

28　Brassinne, Son, Grandelet, Verscheure, in J. Brassinne, "Enquête", Vol. I, pp. 291, 293, 296; *ibid.*, Vol. IV, F. Vandewalle's testimony 14.1, C. Grandelet's testimonies 17.1 and 17.2, and G. Segers's testimony 45.1.

29　Huyghé, quoted by J. Brassinne, "Enquête", Vol. I, pp. 301–2.

30　Bartelous, Rougefort, in J. Brassinne, "Enquête", Vol. I, pp. 313ff.

31　Report Verscheure, in J. Brassinne, "Enquête", Vol. III, annexe 31.1 and Verscheure's testimony 38.1; *ibid.*, Vol. IV, F. Vandewalle's testimony 14.1; C. Grandelet's testimonies 17.1, 17.2 and 17.3; C. Huyghé's testimonies 25.1 and 25.2.

32　J. Brassinne and J. Kestergat, *Qui a tué . . .*, p. 131; F. Vandewalle, *Mille . . .*, Vol. 4, p. 49.

33　On the meeting at the *Gendarmerie*'s headquarters and on the Bureau Conseil meeting, J. Brassinne, "Enquête", Vol. I, pp. 253–8; and Vol. IV, G. Weber's testimony 21.1.

34　J. Brassinne and J. Kestergat, *Qui a tué . . .*, p. 147; J. Brassinne, "Enquête", Vol. IV, G. Segers's testimony 45.1.

35　Smal, quoted by J. Brassinne, "Enquête", Vol. I, p. 255; W. Canup (E'ville), telegram 412,

18 January 1961, in M. Kalb, *The Congo Cables*, p. 186; *Bulletin de renseignements* (E'ville), No. 95, 23 January 1961, in J. Brassinne, "Enquête", Vol. III, annexe 44.

36 Document Verscheure, in J. Brassinne, "Enquête", Vol. III, annexe 31.1; G. Weber, in *ibid.*, Vol. IV, testimony 21.1.

37 G. Weber, quoted by J. Brassinne, "Enquête", Vol. I, p. 253. Weber writes in *Comme je les ai* . . ., p. 117, that Adam had said: "We must not have blood on our hands."

38 Perrad, quoted by J. Brassinne, "Enquête", Vol. I, p. 256; *ibid.*, Vol. IV, P. Perrad's testimony 19.1.

39 J. Brassinne, "Enquête", Vol. IV, A. Protin's testimony 18.1; Créner on the meeting Bartelous/Créner, and Vanden Bloock on the meetings Bloock/Créner, in *ibid.*, Vol. II, pp. 381–2; J. Brassinne and J. Kestergat, *Qui a tué* . . ., p. 174.

40 On Vandewalle, in J. Brassinne, "Enquête", Vol. I, p. 303; on Perrad, in *ibid.*, Vol. IV, testimony 19.1.

41 J. Brassinne, "Enquête", Vol. IV, J. Bartelous's testimony 12.2 and Charles (Carlo) Huyghé's testimony 25.1; P. Perrad, in *ibid.*, Vol. II, p. 323.

42 I. Berendsen, in UN, *Report of the Events leading to the Death of Mr. Lumumba, Mr. Okito and Mr. Mpolo*, A/4964.

43 On the activities at Tshombe's residence, J. Brassinne, "Enquête", Vol. I, pp. 305–6, 308ff.; *ibid.*, Vol. IV, J. Bartelous's testimonies 12.1 and 12.2, G. Lindekens's testimony 15.1, F. Verscheure's testimony 38.1 and M. Spandre's testimony 55.1; and J. Brassinne and J. Kestergat, *Qui a tué* . . ., pp. 155–6.

44 J. Brassinne and J. Kestergat, *Qui a tué* . . ., p. 156.

45 Testimony Munongo, in J. Brassinne, "Enquête", Vol. I, p. 309.

46 Breuer to Weber, in F. Vandewalle, *Mille* . . ., Vol. 4, p. 50; J. Brassinne, "Enquête", Vol. IV, J. Bartelous's testimonies 12.1 and 12.2.

47 J. Brassinne, "Enquête", Vol. I, p. 309.

48 J. Brassinne and J. Kestergat, *Qui a tué* . . ., p. 158; J. Brassinne, "Enquête", Vol. I, p. 312.

49 J. Brassinne, "Enquête", Vol. I, p. 313; J. Brassinne and Kestergat, *Qui a tué* . . ., p. 161.

50 J. Brassinne and J. Kestergat, *Qui a tué* . . ., p. 161; on the Katangans' last visit to the prisoners, see J. Brassinne, "Enquête", Vol. I, pp. 314ff., and Vol. IV, Bartelous's testimonies 12.1 and 12.2.

51 J. Brassinne, "Enquête", Vol. I, p. 318, and Vol. IV, X. Blistein's testimony 10.1; Vandewalle, quoted in *ibid.*, Vol. II, p. 357.

52 On Verscheure's role, see J. Brassinne, "Enquête", Vol. II, pp. 321–2.

53 F. Verscheure, quoted by J. Brassinne, "Enquête", Vol. I, p. 310; on the preparations, see *ibid.*, Vol. II, p. 335.

54 J. Brassinne, "Enquête", Vol. IV, C. Huyghé's testimony 25.1; Vanden Bloock, respectively in his note of 12 December 1960, in F. Vandewalle, *Mille* . . ., Vol. 3, pp. C. 9–16. and in telegram No. 329 from "Bloock/Créner" to Belext/Minaf (Brussels), 2 November 1960, Foreign Ministry archives; F. Vandewalle, in *Mille* . . ., Vol. 3, p. 456.

55 Vandewalle, quoted by J. Brassinne, "Enquête", Vol. I, p. 303; *ibid.*, Vol. IV, C. Huyghé's testimony 25.1, and F. Verscheure's testimony 38.1.

56 J. Brassinne, "Enquête", Vol. II, pp. 321–3.

57 On the prisoners' last hour, see J. Brassinne, "Enquête", Vol. II, pp. 321–50; *ibid.*, Vol. IV, J. Gat's testimonies 24.1, 24.2 and 24.3.

58 On the journey to the place of execution, see J. Gat, in J. Brassinne, "Enquête", Vol. II, p. 326; on the prisoners' arrival, preparations for the execution and a sketch of the execution spot, see *ibid.*, Vol. II, pp. 337ff., and *ibid.*, Vol. IV, F. Verscheure's testimony 38.1.

59 Lumumba, 11 October 1960, in *Remarques congolaises*, 17 February 1961, p. 65; F. Vandewalle, *Mille* . . ., Vol. 4, p. 55.

60 G. Soete on Verscheure, in J. Brassinne, "Enquête", Vol. IV, testimony 31.2; document-Verscheure, in *ibid.*, Vol. III, annexe 31.1.

61 J. Brassinne, "Enquête", Vol. IV, J. Gat's testimony 24.2; J. Van Lierde, "Lettre à Jules

Gérard-Libois. Rencontre avec Kazadi", Kinshasa, 11 May 1966; J. Brassinne and J. Kestergat, *Qui a tué . . .*, pp. 137–68.

62 J. Brassinne, "Enquête", Vol. II, pp. 340, 346–7; J. Brassinne and J. Kestergat, *Qui a tué . . .*, p. 167.

63 J. Brassinne and J. Kestergat, *Qui a tué . . .*, p. 167; J. Gat, in Brassinne, "Enquête", Vol. II, pp. 355–6, 360; Ugeux and Bartelous, in J. Brassinne, "Enquête", pp. 364–5, and Vol. IV, E. Ugeux's testimony 27.1.

64 Document-Verscheure and "La vérité sur l'assassinat de Patrice Lumumba", *Pourquoi Pas?* of 10 August 1983, in J. Brassinne, "Enquête", Vol. III, annexes 31.1 and 31.3; *ibid. . . .* Vol. IV, A. Verdickt's testimony 16.2; *ibid. . . .*, Vol. IV, X, Blistein's testimony 10.1.

65 J.C. Marlair, *Les Rêves des Noko*, pp. 111–12.

66 On Cornélis, see J. Brassinne and J. Kestergat, *Qui a tué . . .*, p. 179, and J. Brassinne, "Enquête", Vol. II, p. 401; F. Vandewalle, in J. Brassinne, "Enquête", Vol. IV, testimony 25.2; R. Jaspar, quoted by J. Brassinne, "Enquête", Vol. IV, testimony 49.1.

67 J. Brassinne, "Enquête", Vol. I, pp. 81–2.

CHAPTER 6

1 On the protagonists' activities after the assassination, during the night of 17 to 18 January, see J. Brassinne, "Enquête", Vol. II, pp. 350–61.

2 J. Brassinne, "Enquête", Vol. IV, Huyghé's testimony 25.1, Mumba's testimony 34.2; Breuer, quoted by G. Weber, *Le Katanga . . .*, p. 179.

3 According to F. Renard of the intelligence services, in F. Vandewalle, *Mille . . .*, Vol. 4, pp. 49–50.

4 On the Cercle d'Elisabethville (E'ville Circle), see J. Brassinne, "Enquête", Vol. II, p. 370 and J. Brassinne and J. Kestergat, *Qui a tué . . .*, p. 174.

5 F. Vandewalle, *Mille . . .*, Vol. 4, pp. 55, 58–60, and Commander Matthys, "Memorandum réunion de contact ANC/Gdkat", Elisabethville, 20 January 1961, *ibid.*, pp. A15–17.

6 F. Vandewalle, *Mille*, Vol. 4, p. 66. On Mobutu's promotion, see telegram 41 from Dupret (Brazza) to Belext (Brussels), 10 January 1961, Foreign Ministry archives.

7 "Passage à tabac?", *LLB*, 19 January 1961; "Tsjombe nu Loemoemba's cipier", *De Standaard*, 19 January 1961.

8 F. Vandewalle, *Mille . . .*, Vol. 4, pp. 52–3; Perrad, Grandelet, quoted by J. Brassinne, "Enquête", Vol. II, p. 387; Radio Katanga and Samalenge communiqué, 18 January, J. Brassinne and J. Kestergat, *Qui a tué . . .*, pp. 169, 172.

9 Testimony Verscheure, annotated by Huyghé, J. Brassinne, "Enquête", Vol. II, p. 393.

10 G. Soete, quoted by J. Brassinne, "Enquête", Vol. II, p. 395, and *ibid.*, Vol. IV, G. Soete's testimony 31.1.

11 Verscheure, quoted by J. Brassinne, "Enquête", Vol. II, p. 400. On the prisoners' pseudo-escape, see *ibid.*, Vol. II, pp. 416ff.

12 I. Berendsen, Verbal note to President Tshombe, 10 February 1961, J. Brassinne, "Enquête", Vol. II, p. 435; on Yumba, see F. Vandewalle, *Mille . . .*, Vol. 4, p. 128.

13 J. Gat, quoted in J. Brassinne, "Enquête", Vol. IV, testimony 24.1; G. Weber, *Le Katanga . . .*, p. 179.

14 Meeting Berendsen–Tshombe and communiqué Berendsen of 18 January 1961, quoted by J. Brassinne and J. Kestergat, *Qui a tué . . .*, pp. 172–3, UN, *Report of the Events leading to the Death of Mr. Lumumba, Mr. Okito and Mr. Mpolo*, A/4964, and telegram 56 from Consubel E'ville to Belext Brussels, 18 January 1961, Foreign Ministry archives; UN spokesman, quoted in *De Standaard*, 20 January 1961.

15 H. Wieschhoff, quoted in telegrams USUN, No. 1964, 19 January 1961, M. Kalb, *The Congo*

Cables, pp. 186–7; telegram "H" to Dayal, No. 388, 18 January 1961, United Nations archives; meeting Berendsen–Tshombe, 19 January, in UN, *Report of the Events leading to the Death of Mr. Lumumba, Mr. Okito and Mr. Mpolo*, A/4964; letter from "H" to Kasa Vubu, message from "H" to Tshombe, and message from "H" to Gizenga, Manzikala and Lundula, all of 19 January 1961, in CPE, *Evolution . . .,* pp. 1037–40.

16 Letter from "H" to Kasa Vubu, 5 December 1960, Doc. S/4571, (and answer from Kasa Vubu and Bomboko, 7 December 1960, in CPE, *Evolution . . .*, pp. 892–5.

17 Letter "H" to Iyassu, 13 February 1961, annexe to Berendsen's "Verbal Note" to Tshombe, in J. Brassinne, "Enquête", Vol. II, pp. 451–3; on RTB broadcast "Neuf millions", see F. Vandewalle, *Mille . . .,* Vol. 4, p. 149.

18 On the crackdown in north Katanga, see, for instance, P. Davister, *Katanga . . .*, p. 254, or J. Ziegler, *La Contre-révolution en Afrique*, pp. 85–6.

19 Telegram "H" to Cordier, 6 September 1960, No. 1582, United Nations archives.

20 On the journey of the Reconciliation Commission and the International Committee of the Red Cross, see UN, *Report of the Events leading to the Death of Mr. Lumumba, Mr. Okito and Mr. Mpolo*, A/4964, and telegram 79 from Consubel E'ville to Belext Brussels, 25 January 1961, Foreign Ministry archives.

21 "H" statements to the Security Council, 1 February 1961, Doc. S/PV928; Tshombe, press conference of 14 February 1961, in F. Vandewalle, *Mille . . .*, Vol. 4, p. 139.

22 Smal-Créner (Consubel E'ville) to Minaf Brussels, No. 457/d46, 18 January 1961, Foreign Ministry archives; telegram 52 from Bloock-Créner to Rothschild, 18 January, Foreign Ministry archives.

23 See J. Brassinne, "Enquête", Vol. II, pp. 363ff., 379, 384, and Vol. IV, J. Bartelous's testimony 12.2.

24 Message 10320 from d'Aspremont Lynden to Consubel E'ville, 20 January 1961 - also see message 12223/cab from d'Aspremont Lynden to E'ville, 23 January 1961, Foreign Ministry archives; telegram No. 568/t64 from Bloock-Créner (E'ville) to Belext and Minaf (Brussels), 20 January 1961, Foreign Ministry archives; telegram 106 of 23 January 1961 from Ambabel Brazza to Belext Brussels, Foreign Ministry archives; F. Vandewalle, *Mille . . .*, Vol. 4, p. 63.

25 Vanden Bloock, quoted by J. Brassinne and J. Kestergat, *Qui a tué . . .*, p. 175.

26 J. Brassinne, "Enquête", Vol. IV, Bartelous's testimony 12.2; F. Vandewalle, *Mille . . .*, Vol. 4, p. 56.

27 J. Brassinne and J. Kestergat, *Qui a tué . . .*, p. 175; F. Vandewalle, *Mille . . .*, Vol. 4, p. 51; telegram No. 56 from Créner (E'ville) to Belext (Brussels), 18 January 1961, in J. Brassinne, "Enquête", Vol. III, annexe 14.4.

28 F. Vandewalle, *Mille . . .,* Vol. 4, p. 63; telegram No. 568/t64 from Bloock/Créner (E'ville) to Belext and Minaf (Brussels), 20 January 1961, Foreign Ministry archives.

29 Telegram from the US State Department, No. 343, 18 January 1961, and from W. Canup, No. 420, 20 January 1961, quoted in M. Kalb, *The Congo Cables*, p. 187.

30 *LLB*, 19 January 1961 – also see "Loemoemba in E'stad toch mishandeld", *De Standaard*, 21–22 January 1961; E. Troch, "Voltooid verleden", *De Standaard*, 23 January 1961; " Une mise au point du ministère belge des affaires étrangères", *LLB*, 21–22 January 1961.

31 Declaration from the government, in *De Standaard*, 24 January 1961; Foreign Ministry archives, African archives (A61.2), Ministry for African Affairs archives, committees; Wigny and Pholien, quoted by *Annales Parlementaires de Belgique, Sénat, Session ordinaire 1960–1961*, meetings of 24 and 25 January 1961; Baron Poswick, note to Minister Wigny, "Le Vatican et le Congo", 27 January 1961, in Vandewalle archives, "Dossier VDW. Rapports – Notes 1959–1960"; J. Pholien, "De Patrice Lumumba à André Renard", *LLB*, 23 January 1961.

32 (Shangungu, in Rwanda, was an outpost in Léopoldville's war on the nationalists.) H. Rolin, 25 January 1961, quoted by *Annales Parlementaires de Belgique, Sénat, Session ordinaire 1960–1961*; Larock, 14 February 1961, quoted by *Annales Parlementaires de Belgique, Chambre, Session ordinaire 1960–1961*.

33 Note Wigny, 25 January 1961, in F. Vandewalle, *Mille . . .*, Vol. 4, pp. 73–4; telegram Wigny, 8 Febuary 1961, and Vandewalle, in *ibid.* p. 119 – also see telegram 213 of 8 February 1961 from Ambabel Brazza to Belext Brussels, Foreign Ministry archives; R. Dayal, quoted by *De Standaard,* 24 January 1961.

34 On Trinquier, F. Vandewalle, *Mille . . .*, Vol. 4, pp. 92–3, 100.

35 "L'Afrique démoniaque", *LLB*, 27 January 1961.

36 On the disappearance of the bodies, see J. Brassinne, *Enquête.*, Vol. II, pp. 399ff.

37 G. Soete's testimony, in the documentary of B. Govaerts and K. Schoetens on Patrice Lumumba (VRT-Canvas, 21 and 28 October 1999), and G. Soete's interview in *Humo*, 5 October 1999.

38 G. Soete, *De Arena,* pp. 137, 156–68; J. Brassinne, "Enquête", Vol. IV, A. Belina's testimony 28.1.

39 "L'attitude de Gerard Soete", in J. Brassinne, "Enquête", Vol. II, pp. 412–15; see also *ibid.*, Vol. IV, G. Soete's testimony 31.1.

40 Statement Munongo of 13 February 1961, Doc. S/4688, Add. 1.

41 F. Verscheure, quoted by J. Brassinne, "Enquête", Vol. III, annexe 31.1.

42 *LLB*, 14 February 1961; *De Standaard,* 14 February 1961; *L'Écho de la Bourse*, 14 February 1961; J. Brassinne at "Lundis du Centre Paul Huymans", 20 February 1961, Vandewalle archives, "Boîte Mille et quatre jours. Documentation. Dossiers VDW. Katanga janvier-avril 1961"; "Patrice Lumumba mort", *Pourquoi Pas?*, 17 February 1961.

43 H. d'Aspremont Lynden, Pierson and Wigny, 14 February 1961, *Annales Parlementaires de Belgique, Chambre, Session ordinaire 1960–1961*; Loos's and Wigny's messages, 14 February 1961, in F. Vandewalle, *Mille . . .,* Vol. 4, p. 139; telegram 146 from Consubel E'ville to Belext Brussels, 15 February 1961, Foreign Ministry archives.

44 "Cruel et sanglant", *LLB*, 14 February 1961; J. Van den Bosch, "Les journées dramatiques des 6 et 7 juillet à Léopoldville", *LLB,* 7 December 1960.

45 On the reactions after the announcement of Lumumba's death, see *De Standaard,* 15, 16 and 17 February 1961; *Le Monde*, 16 February 1961; speech Nkrumah, 14 February 1961, in K. Nkrumah, *Challenge of the Congo*, pp. 129–33; *The Observer*, 15 February 1961, in C. Hoskyns, *The Congo . . .,* p. 324.

46 "Madame Lumumba conduit une manifestation de deuil à travers Léopoldville", *Le Monde,* 16 February 1961; *Time*, 24 February 1961; exchange of letters Dayal/Tshombe in February 1961, UN, *Report of the Events leading to the Death of Mr. Lumumba, Mr. Okito and Mr. Mpolo*, A/4964, Annexe 17.

47 "Vlaamse arts bewaart Lumumba-geheim", *De Standaard,* 17 February 1961; Wigny's declaration on Belgian Radio and TV, 15 February 1961, in CPE, *Evolution . . .*, pp. 1084–85.

48 Declaration "H", 15 February 1961, Press Release SG/1008.

49 On Luluabourg, see telegram 249 of 15 February 1961 from Ambabel Brazza to Belext Brussels, Foreign Ministry archives; on reactions in the east of the Congo, see F. Vandewalle, *Mille . . .*, Vol. 4, pp. 137–58.

CHAPTER 7

1 For Finant's end, see J. Brassinne, "Enquête", Vol. II, pp. 375–7, and Vol. IV, testimony 42.1.; J. Mukamba, in "Meeting Jonas Mukamba-Jean Van Lierde", Brussels, 14 February 1961.

2 Katangan armed forces, "Notice sur l'action des Forces katangaises", July 1960–June 1961, in Vandewalle archives, "Boîte État du Katanga"; telegram from Bloock-Créner (E'ville) to Belext Brussels, No. 134, 13 February 1961, in Vandewalle archives, "Boîte Mille et quatre jours, Documentations Vol., 1–2–3. Dossier Antoine"; Report Dayal, 20 February 1961, Doc. S/4691, Add. 2; B. Verhaegen, *Rébellions au Congo I,* p. 142.

3 *De Standaard,* 14 February 1961, and F. Vandewalle, *Mille . . .*, Vol. 4, p. 144.

4 Security Council Resolution of 21 February 1961, Document S/4741; declaration "H", Security Council, 15 February 1961, press release SG/1008.

5 On the UN Commission of Inquiry, see UN, *Report of the Events leading to the Death of Mr. Lumumba, Mr. Okito and Mr. Mpolo*, A/4964.

6 "Verbal note from 'H' to the Permanent Representative of Belgium", 22 February 1961, Doc. S/4752. See also his "Letter to all Member States", 23 February 1961, Doc. S/4752, Annex III; "Mort de Lumumba", 13 February 1961, in P. Davister and Ph. Toussaint, *Croisettes et Casques bleus*, p. 218.

7 "H" in UN, *Report of the Events leading to the Death of Mr. Lumumba, Mr. Okito and Mr. Mpolo*, A/4964; Linner, Gardiner and Khiari, "Message de trois fonctionnaires de l'ONUC", in *ibid.*, p. 705; F. Vandewalle, *Mille . . .*, Vol. 5, p. 513.

8 Letter of 19 September 1961, in UN, *Report of the Events leading to the Death of Mr. Lumumba, Mr. Okito and Mr. Mpolo*, A/4964; Tshombe's attitude, in *ibid.*

9 On Moscow's role in the Congo crisis, see L. De Witte, *Crisis in Kongo*, pp. 416–19.

10 Many authors interpret the Congo crisis in the light of the East/West divide. They are victims of the Cold War rhetoric of the time, for Moscow's real role in the Congo crisis was very limited. Abstract notions like "Cold War" or " struggle against Soviet influence" are in fact code words in the propaganda war aiming to convince public opinion of the benefits of setting up stable neo-colonial regimes. In the 1950s and 1960s, this objective meant fighting the rise of nationalism, under the guise of fighting "communism"; nowadays the slogans for the same objectives are "democratic reform" and "human rights".

11 Security Council Resolution of 24 November 1961, Doc. S/5002.

12 J. Brassinne, "Enquête", Vol. III, annexe 29.2 ("Reçu d'une prime octroyée à un policier militaire katangais"); Testimony Verdickt, *ibid.*, Vol. II, p. 322; telegram from Lahaye (Brazza) to Brussels, unnumbered, 17 January, and telegram Marlière (Brazza) to Loos (Brussels), unnumbered, 18 January 1961, Foreign Ministry archives.

13 Letter from Baudouin to Tshombe, 13 March 1961, in F. Vandewalle, *Mille . . .*, Vol. 4, p. A60 – letter from Tshombe to Baudouin, quoted in telegram 170 from Consubel E'ville to Belext Brussels, 21 February 1961, Foreign Ministry archives.

14 Information in *État présent de la Noblesse belge*, 1983 directory. Collection "État Présent", Brussels, 1983, pp. 159–60, G. Eyskens, *De memoires*, pp. 940–1, and L. De Witte, *Crisis in Kongo*, p. 391.

15 Letter from d'Aspremont Lynden to Vandewalle, Brussels, 24 February 1961, F. Vandewalle, *Mille . . .*, Vol. 4, p. A43; on the conference of 28 February 1961, see *ibid.*, pp. 190–1; speech Vandewalle in *ibid.*, pp. A48–9.

16 Letter from d'Aspremont Lynden to Tshombe, 27 September 1961, in F. Vandewalle, *Mille . . .*, Vol. 6, pp. A41–3; F. Vandewalle and J. Brassinne, "Rapport sur la situation au Katanga", E'ville, 3 November 1961, in *ibid.*, Vol. 7, pp. 1–33.

17 G. Ball, declaration of 19 December 1961, quoted by E.W. Lefever, *Crisis . . .*, p. 72; P.H. Spaak, *Combats inachevés . . .*, p. 261.

18 Telegram Spaak, beginning of 1963, and Tshombe, quoted by Vandewalle, *L'Ommegang*, pp. 26, 30.

19 A. Closset, *Les Compagnons . . .*, pp. 13, 17; telegram from the US Embassy (Léo) to the State Department, 5 November 1964, quoted by D.N. Gibbs, *The Political Economy . . .*, pp. 153–5.

20 F. Vandewalle, *L'Ommegang*, p. 14; J.C. Marlair, *Les Rêves des Noko*, p. 144.

CHAPTER 8

1 Meanwhile, Mobutu did all he could to hide the truth about Lumumba's assassination. There was no mention of the assassination during the mockery of a trial the regime organised against Tshombe, sentenced in absentia. Munongo did not appear either.

2　E. Tshisekedi (Léo), "Lettre à Sa Majesté l'Empereur du Sud Kasai 'Le Mulopwe' à Bakwanga", 23 December 1960 (Doc. De Witte). On Tshisekedi and Lumumba's fate, see F. Vandewalle, *Mille . . .*, Vol. 2, p. 291, and Vol. 3, p. 436.

3　"Le dossier Lumumba rouvert", *Le Soir*, 7 July 1997, and "Geschiedenis is nieuwste wapen tegen Tshisekedi", *De Morgen*, 1 April 1998.

4　F. Vandewalle, *Mille . . .*, Vol. 4, pp. 41 and 143; J. Brassinne, "Enquête", Vol. II, p. 597.

5　J.C. Marlair, *Les Rêves des Noko*, pp. 121–2.

6　F. Vandewalle, *Mille . . .*, Vol. 4, p. 143; G. Weber, *Le Katanga . . .*, pp. 178, 180–1.

7　*Storia*, No. 279, February 1981, and Brassinne on the role of Weber, in J. Brassinne, "Enquête", Vol. II, p. 539; E. de Bellefroid, "Lumumba, maintenant on sait. L'énigme de l'assassinat de Patrice Lumumba est enfin élucidée trente ans plus tard", *LLB*, 19 February 1991; G. Weber, *Comme . . .*, pp. 114–15.

8　P. Lefèvre, "Assaini et libéral, le Zaïre attend les investissements", *Le Soir*, 28 June 1985.

9　C. Braeckman, "Petit lexique kinois", *Le Soir*, 27 June 1985; C. Braeckman, *Le Dinosaure,* pp. 236–7; G. de Villers, *De Mobutu à Mobutu*, pp. 151, 157.

10　L. Putman, *Van Kinshasa tot Moskou*, pp. 5–6, 35–7; G. de Villers, *De Mobutu à Mobutu*, p. 131.

11　L. Putman, *Van Kinshasa tot Moskou*, pp. 81, 14.

12　*Ibid.*, pp. 54, 56.

13　Translator's note: Gbadolite was Mobutu's native village in the north, where he had a palace built.

14　L. Putman, *Van Kinshasa tot Moskou,* pp. 119–20. On the festivities of 1985, see *LLB*, 27 June and 1 July 1985, *Le Soir*, 1 and 7 July 1985, *De Morgen*, 4 July 1985.

15　L. Putman, *Van Kinshasa tot Moskou*, pp. 121–3. *Le Soir,* 29–30 June 1985.

16　*Le Soir*, 1 and 3 July 1985.

17　E. Ugeux, "Les 'anciens Belges' conquis par le Zaïre", *Le Soir*, 6–7 July 1985.

18　J.C. Willame, *Patrice Lumumba*; J.P. Sartre, "Introduction", in J. Van Lierde, *Lumumba Speaks*.

19　P. Lumumba, *Le Congo . . .*, p. 29; J. Van Lierde, "Patrice Lumumba. La dimension d'un tribun", p. 3.

20　Message D.3201/3–4 No. 913 from Van den Bosch (Léo) to Belext Brussels, 5 July 1960, Foreign Ministry archives.

21　Baudouin, speech at the ULB (Brussels), 20 November 1959, in CRISP, *Congo 1959,* p. 245.

22　J.P. Sartre, "Introduction", in J. Van Lierde, *Lumumba Speaks,* p. 5.

23　Telegram 350 of 18 July 1960 from Van den Bosch (Léo) to Belext Brussels, Foreign Ministry archives.

24　See Th. Sankara, *Thomas Sankara Speaks*.

25　Lumumba's speech on the radio, 10 August 1960, in Min. de l'Information, Service de Presse, doc. No. 293, Institut Africain archives. See also Lumumba's kindly declarations on the UN and "H" of 13 October and 7 November in Commission de coordination, *La République du Congo . . .*, pp. 12, 27, or his message to the General Assembly's chairman and to "H" of 25 October, United Nations archives, and his letter to Dayal of 26 October 1960, in Central Africa Project Collection, 1920–1980.

CONCLUSION

1　"Letter to Pauline Lumumba", in J. Van Lierde, *Lumumba Speaks*, pp. 421–3.

BIBLIOGRAPHY

Apart from the United Nations documents and traditional literature about the Congo available in books, newspapers and weekly magazines, I have consulted several archives:

Foreign Ministry archives (Brussels): I was given authorisation by the Diplomatic Commission to consult the messages sent to Brussels from Belgian diplomatic missions in Léopoldville, Brazzaville and Elisabethville between July 1960 and February 1961. These documents are collected in the files No. 14558 and 18297 I/a-b-c-d (Brazzaville), files No. 18290 II(b) and 18290 III (a) (Elisabethville), and file No. 18288/I (Léopoldville, from 5/7 to 20/8/1960); and on microfilm DF 902 file AF1/56, with numbers P 1331 (from 4/5/1960 to 30/9/1960), P 1332 (from 1/10/1960 to 31/1/1961) and P 1333 (from 31/1/1961 to 22/8/1961). The messages from Minister of African Affairs Harold d'Aspremont Lynden and his deputy Jules Loos to Brazzaville and Elisabethville are on the three microfilms and in the files "Cab 3722" and "Cab 3684". The archives of the Foreign Affairs Minister Pierre Wigny's Cabinet are not kept in this department.

United Nations archives (New York): the documents on the UN operation in the Congo (ONUC) are under the following headings:
– DAG 1 (the Secretary General's office), Series 2.2.1, 2.3.9, 5.0.1.1. and 5.1.2;
– DAG 13 (Missions, and Commissions, United Nations Operations in the Congo 1960–1964), Series 1.6.1.1.

Frédéric Vandewalle archives (Musée Royal de l'Afrique centrale, Tervueren): these contain the former head of the colonial intelligence service's archives for the period 1960–64. Except where indicated to the contrary, all documents quoted are from "Boîte Mille et quatre jours [104 Days Box] – Documentations fascicules 1–2–3(-4) – Dossier Antoine" (Antoine File) or "Dossiers VDW".

Minister of State August E. De Schryver archives (1898–1991) (KADOC, Louvain): A.E. De Schryver was Minister of the Belgian Congo and Rwanda-Burundi (later Minister of African Affairs) from 3 September 1959 until the Eyskens government reshuffle on 3 September 1960. These archives contain internal documents and correspondence with some of the Belgian protagonists in the Congo's decolonisation process.

L'Institut Africain archives, Tervueren: these archives have different sources (M. Hockers, J. Van Lierde, Th. Turner, B. Verhaegen collections, etc.) and were placed there by CRISP. Among these collections are telegrams and notes exchanged between Léopoldville's Belgian diplomatic mission and Brussels in July–August 1960; also letters and documents on and from Patrice Lumumba.

Schomburg Center for Research in Black Culture archives (The New York Public Library, New York): these archives contain the "Ralph J. Bunche Papers" and the "Central Africa Project Collection, 1920–1980 (Unprocessed manuscript collection)". There are also a limited collection of telegrams from the United Nations, documents from and on Lumumba and the MNC, reports on Lumumba government's sessions and copies of Congolese nationalist magazines.

Grootaert archives (Université Libre de Bruxelles, Brussels): these contain the papers of Jozef E.A. Grootaert, assistant private secretary to Prime Minister Lumumba until mid-August 1960. These are mostly documents from the colonial era.

Fondation Joseph Jacquemotte archives (Brussels): these are the archives of the leaders of the then Belgian Communist Party (PCB). I consulted the archives of Albert De Coninck, Marcel Levaux, Gaston Moulin and Jean Terfve, as well as a collection of diverse materials. These archives contain PCB documents, memos on the Congo crisis and correspondence between party officials and several dozen Congolese, including nationalist leaders.

The notes and photocopies of the archive material on which this work relies have been deposited in the archives of the Université catholique de Louvain, Bibliothèque centrale, Mgr Ladeuzeplein 21, 3000 Louvain, Belgium.

This bibliography lists only the books and articles which are referred to in the text. For a complete list of works consulted, see Ludo De Witte, *Crisis in Kongo*, Van Halewyck, Louvain, 1996.

Abi-Saab, Georges, 1978, *The United Nations Operation in the Congo 1960–1964,* Oxford, Oxford University Press.
Artigue, Pierre, 1961, *Qui sont les leaders Congolais?*, Brussels, Editions Europe-Afrique.
Benot, Yves, 1989, *La Mort de Lumumba, ou la tragédie congolaise*, Paris, E. Chaka.
Blommaert, Jan, 1990, "Lumumba, Hammarskjöld, and the 1960 Congo Crisis: A Case of International Misunderstanding?", *Afrika Focus*, No. 2, pp. 97–118.
Bouveroux, Jos, 1993, *Koning Boudewijn. Macht en invloed van de monarchie in België*, Antwerp, Standaard Uitgeverij/BRTN/VAR.
Braeckman, Colette, 1992, *Le Dinosaure. Le Zaïre de Mobutu*, Paris, Fayard.
Brassinne, Jacques, 1990, "Enquête sur la mort de Patrice Lumumba", Political science doctoral dissertation (ULB), Brussels, unpublished.
Brassinne, Jacques and Kestergat, Jean, 1991, *Qui a tué Patrice Lumumba?,* Paris/Louvain-la-Neuve, Duculot.
Bulletin du Craoca, bulletin of the Royal Society of Former Officers in African Campaigns, Brussels.
Ceulemans, Jacques, 1964, *A. Gizenga*, Brussels, Ed. Remarques congolaises.
Chambre des Représentants (House of Representatives), 1960–61, Belgium's parliamentary annals, ordinary session 1960–61, Brussels.
Chomé, Jules, 1960, *La Crise Congolaise: de l'Indépendance à l'intervention militaire belge (30 juin–9 juillet),* Brussels, Ed. Remarques congolaises.
—— 1966, *Moïse Tshombe et l'escroquerie katangaise*, Brussels, Ed. Fond. Jacquemotte.
Chronique de Politique Etrangère (CPE), 1960, *La Crise congolaise: 1 janvier 1959–15 août 1960*, Brussels, IRRI, Nos 4–6, July–November.
—— 1961, *Evolution de la crise conglaise: de septembre 1960 à avril 1961,* Brussels, IRRI, Nos 4–6, September–November.
—— 1962, *l'Onu et le Congo: avril 1961 à octobre 1962,* Brussels, IRRI, Nos 4–6, July–November.
Closset, André, 1995, *Les Compagnons de l'Ommegang,* Avin-en-Hesbaye, Ed. de l'Aronde.
Collins, Carole J.L., 1993, "The Cold War comes to Africa: Cordier and the 1960 Congo Crisis", *Journal of International affairs*, Vol. 47, No. 1, summer, pp 243–69.

Commission de Coordination, 1960, *La République du Congo devant l'opinion mondiale. Chronologie des évènements et commentaires de presse*, Brussels, Comm. de Coord.

——1960, *Documents Congolais*, Brussels, Comm. de Coord.

Conférence Nationale Souveraine (Kabamba Mbwebwe and Kasusula Douma Lokali), 1992, *Commission des assassinats et des violations des droits de l'homme. 1ère Partie: 1ère République*, Kinshasa.

CONGO, weekly, 1960, editor-publisher: Philippe Kanza, Léopoldville.

CRISP (ed. J. Gérard-Libois), 1961, *Congo 1959*, Brussels.

CRISP (ed. J. Gérard-Libois and B. Verhaegen), *Congo 1960*, with Annexes and Biographies, Brussels.

CRISP (ed. B. Verhaegen), *Congo 1961,* Brussels.

CRISP (ed. J. Gérard-Libois and J. Van Lierde), 1965, *Congo 1964,* Brussels.

CRISP, 1959–61, *Courrier hebdomadaire,* Brussels.

CRISP, 1960, *Courrier Africain*, Brussels.

Dastier Philippe, 1964, "Qui est Albert Kalonji? Interview exclusive", *Le dossier du mois,* April-May, pp. 31–48

Davister Pierre, 1960, *Katanga: enjeu du monde*, Brussels, Editions Europe-Afrique.

Davister, Pierre and Toussaint, Philippe, 1962, *Croisettes et Casques bleus. Les envoyés spéciaux du "Pourquoi Pas?" au Congo. L'affaire katangaise,* Brussels, Editions Actuelles.

Dayal, Rajeshwar, 1976, *Mission for Hammarskjöld,* London, Oxford Unversity Press.

Dedeken, Noël C., 1978, *Chimères baluba. Le Sud-Kasaï 1960–1962 à feu et à sang,* Brussels, Dedeken (self-published).

De Heusch, Luc, 1962, "Plaidoyer à la mémoire de Patrice Lumumba", *Synthèses,* No. 189 (February), pp. 280–308.

De Villers, Gauthier, 1995, *De Mobutu à Mobutu. Trente ans de relations Belgique–Zaïre,* Brussels, De Boeck-Wesmael.

De Vos, Pierre, 1961, *Vie et mort de Lumumba,* Paris, Ed. Calmann-Lévy.

De Witte, Ludo, 1996, *Crisis in Kongo. De rol van de Verenigde Naties, de regering-Eyskens en het koningshuis in de omverwerping van Lumumba en de opkomst van Mobutu,* Louvain, Van Halewyck.

——1998, "De Lumumba à Mobutu: nouvelles clartés sur la crise congolaise", *Cahiers Marxistes,* January-February, Brussels, pp. 9–49.

——2000, "Dossier Lumumba. Pour le roi et la patrie", *Le Vif/L'Express,* 20 October.

Dinant, Georges, 1961, *L'ONU face à la crise congolaise. I: La politique d'Hammarskjöld,* Brussels, Ed. Remarques congolaises.

Durnez, Gaston, 1993, "Van Kolonie naar Kongostaat. De journalistieke opgang van Manu Ruys", in X, *De Standaard. Het levensverhaal van een Vlaamse krant, van 1948 tot de VUM*, Tielt, Lannoo, pp. 241–50.

L'Echo de Stan, daily newspaper of the Eastern Province, Stanleyville, 1958–59.

Eyskens, Gaston, 1993, *De memoires,* Tielt, Uitgeverij Lannoo.

Gálvez, William, 1997, *El sueño africano de Che. Qué sucedió en la guerrilla congolesa?*, Havana, Editorial Casa de las Américas.

Ganshof van der Meersch, W.J., 1963, *Fin de la souveraineté Belge au Congo. Documents et réflexions,* Brussels/Hague, IRRI & Martinus Nijhoff.

La Gauche. Organe de combat socialiste, weekly, Brussels, 1959–61.

Gaus, Helmut (ed.), 1989, *Politiek-biografisch lexicon. De Belgische Ministers en Staatssecretarissen 1960–1980,* Antwerp, Standaard Uitgeverij.

Geerts, Walter, 1970, *Binza 10. De eerste tien onafhankelijkheidsjaren van de Demokratische Republiek Kongo,* Gans/Louvain, E. Story-Scientia.

Gérard-Libois, Jules, 1963, *Sécession au Katanga,* Brussels/Léopoldville, CRISP/INEP.

——1965, *L'Opération des Nations unies au Congo (1960–1964) (Le rôle de la Belgique dans . . .),* Brussels, CRISP, *Travaux Africains,* Nos 68– 71.

Gibbs, David N., 1991, *The Political Economy of Third World Intervention. Mines, Money, and U.S. Policy in the Congo Crisis,* Chicago/London, The University of Chicago Press.

—— 1993, "Dag Hammarskjöld, the United Nations, and the Congo Crisis of 1960–1: a Reinterpretation", *Journal of Modern African Studies,* Vol. 31, No. 1, pp. 163–74.

Heinz, G. and Donnay, H., 1966, *Lumumba Patrice. Les cinquante derniers jours de sa vie,* Brussels/Paris, CRISP/Le Seuil.

Hippolyte, Mirlande, 1970, *Les Etats du Groupe de Brazzaville aux Nations Unies,* Paris, A. Colin.

Hoskyns, Catherine, 1965, *The Congo since Independence. January 1960–December 1961,* London/New York, Oxford University Press.

Infor Congo, 1958, *Congo belge et Ruanda-Urundi. Guide du voyageur,* Brussels, Office de l'Information et des Relations publiques pour le Congo belge et le Ruanda-Urundi.

Institut Africain, Fichier biographique (Biographic index), Brussels/Tervueren.

Jacques, Gérard, 1995, *Lualaba. Histoires de l'Afrique profonde,* Brussels, Editions Racine.

Joye, Pierre and Lewin, Rosine, 1961, *Les Trusts au Congo,* Brussels, Société Populaire d'Editions.

Kalb, Madeleine, G., 1982, *The Congo Cables. The Cold War in Africa – From Eisenhower to Kennedy,* New York, Macmillan.

Kamitatu, Cléophas, 1971, *La Grande Mystification du Congo-Kinshasa,* Brussels, Complexe/Maspero.

Kingalu, Kilashi, 1970, *Lumumba vivant,* Brussels, Editions La Taupe.

Lefever, Ernest W., 1965, *Crisis in the Congo. A United Nations Force in Action,* Washington, DC, The Brookings Institution.

López Alvarez, Luis, 1964, *Lumumba ou l'Afrique frustrée,* Paris, Ed. Cujas.

Luard, Evan, 1989, *A History of the United Nations.* Vol. 2: *The Age of Decolonisation, 1955–1965,* London, Macmillan.

Lumumba, François, 1988, "L'assassinat de Patrice Lumumba", *Solidaire,* 3 August.

Lumumba, Patrice, 1958, "Summary of the Lecture given on 13 April 1958 by M. Patrice Lumumba to the members of the Batetela Federation", unpublished, Bibliothèque africaine, Brussels.

—— 1960, *Les Incidents de Stanleyville,* Ed. Jacques Yerna, *et al.* 11 January.

—— 1960, "Man Grüsst Sich mit Uhuru. Gespräch mit dem Kongo-Politiker Patrice Lumumba", *Der Spiegel,* No. 26.

—— 1960, "1960 doit être la fin du colonialisme et de l'impérialisme en Afrique, 19/4/1960", *Le Courrier d'Afrique,* 20 April.

—— 1960, "S'entendre pour sauver l'avenir du Congo", *Le Stanleyvillois,* 11 May.

—— 1960, *Propos de M. Patrice Lumumba, Premier ministre de la République du Congo, 1/6/60–9/8/60,* Brussels, Commission de Coordination, August 10.

—— 1961, *Le Congo, terre d'avenir est-il menacé?,* Brussels, Office de la Publicité.

—— 1961, *La Vérité sur les crimes odieux des colonialistes,* Moscow, Editions en Langues Etrangères.

—— 1962, "Lettres de la prison de Stanleyville", *Europe,* No. 393, January, pp. 19–26.

See also Van Lierde, Jean.

Luykx, Theo, 1973, *Koninklijke toespraken,* Brussels, Uitgeverij Labor.

Mahoney, Richard D., 1979, "The Kennedy Policy in the Congo 1961–1963", Doctoral dissertation, Johns Hopkins University School of Advanced International Studies, Washington, DC.

—— 1999, *Sons and Brothers. The Days of Jack and Bobby Kennedy,* New York, Arcade Publishing.

Manya K'Omalowete, A. Djonga, 1985, *Patrice Lumumba, le Sankuru et l'Afrique,* Lausanne, Les Editions Jean-Marie Bouchain.

Marlair, Jean-Claude, 1993, *Les Rêves des Noko. Présence militaire belge au Congo-Zaïre,* Jalhay, Foxmaster and Pozit Press.

Maurel, Auguste, 1992, *Le Congo: de la colonisation belge à l'indépendance,* Paris. L'Harmattan (originally published under the pseudonym of Merlier Michel, *Le Congo: de la colonisation . . .*).

Michel, Serge, 1962, *Uhuru Lumumba,* Paris, René Julliard.

Monheim, Francis, 1962, *Mobutu, l'homme seul,*Brussels, Ed. Actuelles.

Mutamba Makombo, Jean-Marie, 1993, *Patrice Lumumba, correspondant de presse (1948–1956),* Brussels, Institut Africain.

Ndaywel, è Nziem Isidore, 1997, *Histoire du Zaïre. De l'héritage ancien à l'âge contemporain,* Louvain-la-Neuve, Duculot/Afrique-Editions.

Nendaka, Victor, 1998, "Memorandum adressé à Monsieur Kabila Laurent-Désiré, Président de la République du Congo", Rome, November.

Nkrumah, Kwame, 1967, *Challenge of the Congo,* London/Edinburgh, Nelson.

Okumu, Washington, 1963, *Lumumba's Congo: Roots of Conflict,* New York, Ivan Obolensky.

Olela Odimba, Raphaël, 1995, "Qui sont responsables de l'assassinat de P. Lumumba?", *Mashindano,* January–March, pp. 11–13.

Omasombo Tshonda, J. and Verhaegen, B., 1998, *Patrice Lumumba, Jeunesse et apprentissage politique 1925–1956,* Tervueren/Paris, Institut Africain–L'Harmattan.

Peemans, Jean-Philippe, 1975, "Capital Accumulation in the Congo under Colonialism: the Role of the State", in Peter Duignan and L.M. Gann (eds) *Colonialism in Africa 1870–1960,* Vol. 4, Cambridge University Press, pp. 165–212.

—— 1980, "Imperial Hangovers: Belgium – The Economics of Decolonisation", *Journal of Contemporary History,* pp. 257–86.

Piniau, Bernard, 1992, *Congo-Zaïre 1874–1981. La perception du lointain,* Paris, L'Harmattan.

Pire, René, 1996, "La Sécession katangaise: Impressions à chaud . . . ", *Bulletin du Craoca,* No. 4, Spring, pp. 45–61.

Pourquoi Pas?, weekly, Brussels, 1960–61.

Putman, L. 1994, *Van Kinshasa tot Moskou. Herinneringen van een ambassadeur,* St Martens-Latem, Aurelia Books.

Réchetniak, Nikolai, 1990, *Patrice Lumumba,* Moscow, Novosti.

Rikhye Indar, Jit, 1993, *Military Adviser to the Secretary General. UN Peacekeeping and the Congo Crisis,* London/New York, Hurst/St Martin's Press.

Rivele, Stephen, J., 1987, "Death of a double man", *The National Reporter,* Spring, pp. 44–50.

Ruys, Manu, 1985, *Vijfentwintig jaar Kongo-Zaïre,* Brussels, Uitgeverij Grammens.

—— 1996, Achter de maskerade. Over macht, schijnmacht en onmacht, Kapellen, Uitgeverij Pelckmans.

Salmon, Pierre, 1974, "Une correspondance en partie inédite de Patrice Lumumba", *Bulletin des séances, Académie Royale des Sciences d'Outre-Mer,* pp. 359–68.

Sankara, Thomas, 1988, *Thomas Sankara Speaks. The Burkina Faso Revolution 1983–87,* New York, Pathfinder.

—— 1991, *Oser inventer l'avenir,* Paris, Pathfinder-L'Harmattan.

Schöller, André, 1982, *Congo 1959–1960. Mission au Katanga. Intérim à Léopoldville.* Paris/Gembloux, Ed. Duculot.

Scott, Ian, 1969, *Tumbled House. The Congo at Independence,* London, Oxford University Press.

Sénat, 1960–1961, *Annales Parlementaires de Belgique. Session ordinaire 1960–1961,* Brussels.

Smith, Hempstone, 1963, *Rebels, Mercenaries and Dividends: the Katanga Story*, New York: Praeger.

Soete, Gerard, 1978, *De Arena. Het verhaal van de moord op Lumumba,* Bruges, Uitgeverij Raaklijn.

Spaak, Paul-Henri, 1969, *Combats inachevés. De l'espoir aux déceptions,* Paris, Fayard.

Stengers, Jean, 1992, *L'Action du Roi en Belgique depuis 1831. Pouvoir et influence,* Paris/Louvain-la-Neuve, Duculot.

Stenmans, A., *Les premiers mois de la République du Congo (1er juillet–22 novembre 1960),* Académie Royale des Sciences d'Outre-Mer, Brussels, Ed. Duculot.

Stockwell, John, 1978, *In Search of Enemies. A CIA Story.* New York, W.W. Norton.

Timberlake, Clare Hayes, 1963, "First Year of Independence in the Congo" (Master's thesis), George Washington University.

Tshisekedi, Etienne, 1960, "Lettre à sa Majesté l'Empereur du Sud-Kasaï 'Le Mulopwe' à Bakwanga", 23 December (doc. LDW).

Turner, Thomas, 1969, "L'ethnie tetela et le MNC-Lumumba", *Études congolaises*, No. 4, pp. 36–57.

—— 1973, *A Century of Political Conflict in Sankuru (Congo-Zaïre)*, Michigan, University of Michigan Press.

UK Foreign Office, African Department, 1960, H.F.T. Smith, A. Ross, M.B. Stevens and the Lord Privy Seal discuss the "possibilities of eliminating Mr Lumumba from the political scene", 28 and 29 September 1960, FO JB1015/401, Public Record Office, London.

United Nations, 1961, Report of the Commission of Investigation established under the terms of General Assembly Resolution 1601 (XV) of 15 April 1961. *Report of the Events leading to the Death of Mr. Lumumba, Mr Okito and Mr. Mpolo*, 11 November 1961, A/4964, New York.

Urquhart, Brian, 1994 (1972), *Hammarskjöld,* New York-London, W.W. Norton and Co.

US, 1975, United States Senate, Senate Select Committee to Study Governmental Operations With Respect to Intelligence activities, *Alleged Assassination Plots Involving Foreign Leaders. An Interim Report*, 94th Congress, 1st Session, Washington, DC (the Church Report).

—— 1992, *Foreign Relations of the United States, 1958–1960*, Vol. XIV: *Africa*, Washington, DC, United States Government Printing Office.

—— 1994, *Foreign Relations of the United States, 1961–1963*, Vol. XX: *Congo Crisis*, Washington, United States Government Printing Office.

—— 1997, *Foreign Relations of the United States, 1961–1963, Microfiche Supplements*, Vols. XVII/XVIII/XX/XXI, *Near East; Congo; Africa*, Washington, DC, United States Government Printing Office.

—— 1998, *Foreign Relations of the United States, 1961–1963*, Vol. V: *Soviet Union*, Washington, DC, United States Government Printing Office.

US State Department, 1961, "An Analytical Chronology of the Congo Crisis", declassified document.

Van Bilsen, A.A.J., 1962, *L'Indépendance du Congo,* Doornik, Casterman.

—— 1977, *Vers l'indépendance du Congo et du Ruanda-Urundi*, Kinshasa, Presses Universitaires du Zaïre (2nd edn) (1958).

Van Bilsen, Jef, 1993, *Kongo 1945–1965. Het einde van een kolonie,* Louvain, Davidsfonds.

—— 1994, *Congo 1945–1965. La fin d'une colonie* (preface by J. Gérard-Libois, with annexes), Brussels, Editions du CRISP.

Van den Bosch, Jean, 1986, *Pré-Zaïre. Le cordon mal coupé,* Brussels, Le Cri.

Vanderstraeten, Louis-François, 1993, *De la Force Publique à l'Armée Nationale Congolaise. Histoire d'une mutinerie (juillet 1960),* Académie Royale de Belgique, Gembloux, Duculot.

Vandewalle, Frédéric, 1970, *L'Ommegang. Odyssée et reconquête de Stanleyville 1964,* Brussels, Ed. F. Vandewalle (self-published, in collaboration with Le Livre Africain).

—— 1974–77, *Mille et quatre jours. Contes du Zaïre et du Shaba,* Brussels, Ed. F. Vandewalle (self-published), 13 fascicules.

—— 1978, "Face aux Mutins. Élisabethville, 8, 9 et 10 juillet 1960", *Bulletin du Craoca,* No. 3, pp. 15–28, No. 4, pp. 22–8.

—— 1983, "Katanga Atawina", *Bulletin du Craoca,* No. 3, pp. 77–97.

—— 1987, "A propos de la *Gendarmerie* katangaise (I–XVII)", *Bulletin du Craoca,* 1987, No. 4, to 1991 No. 4.

—— 1991, "Il y a trente ans Lumumba, Okito et Mpolo mouraient au Katanga", *Bulletin du Craoca,* No. 2, pp. 63–4.

Van Doal (Vandewalle, Frédéric), 1979, *Une ténébreuse affaire ou Roger Trinquier au Katanga,* Brussels, Editions de Tam Tam Ommegang.

Van Grieken, M., 1972, "Afrikaans Archief: inventaris" (unpublished), Brussels, Ministry of Foreign Affairs.

Van Lierde, Jean, 1961, "Rencontre Jonas Mukamba–Jean van Lierde", 14 February, Brussels, Doc. Van Lierde.

—— 1963, *La Pensée politique de Patrice Lumumba,* Paris, Présence Africaine.

—— 1966, Letters to Jules Gérard-Libois, Léo-Kinshasa, 27 April, 9 May, 11 May, Brussels, Doc. Van Lierde.

—— 1972, *Lumumba Speaks. The Speeches and Writings of Patrice Lumumba, 1958–1961,* Boston/Toronto, Little, Brown.

—— 1988, *Patrice Lumumba. La dimension d'un tribun,* Charleroi, Editions du Fusil Brisé.

—— 1998, *Un insoumis,* Brussels, Labor.

Verhaegen, Benoît, 1966, *Rébellions au Congo I,* Brussels, CRISP.

—— 1978, "Patrice Lumumba, martyr d'une Afrique nouvelle", *Jeune Afrique,* 1 September, pp. 69–96.

—— 1993, "Livres: Qui a tué Patrice Lumumba?", *Cahiers Marxistes,* March–April, pp. 153–8.

Volodine, Lev, n.d., *Patrice Lumumba, champion de la liberté africaine,* Moscow, Ed. du Progrès.

von Horn Carl, 1967, *Soldiering for Peace,* New York, David McKay.

Weber Guy, 1982, *Ces coloniaux . . . Histoires du Zaïre,* Brussels, Ed. Louis Musin.

—— 1983, *Le Katanga de Moïse Tshombe, ou le drame de la loyauté,* Brussels, Ed. Louis Musin.

—— 1991, *Comme je les ai connus,* Dinant, L. Bourdeaux-Capelle.

Weissman, Stephen R., 1974, *American Foreign Policy in the Congo 1960–1964,* Ithaca/London, Cornell University Press.

Willame, Jean-Claude, 1990, *Patrice Lumumba. La crise congolaise revisitée,* Paris, Karthala.

X, *Les Namurois au Congo Belge,* Brussels, L'Etoile belge.

—— 1988, *Etat présent de la Noblesse belge. Annuaire de 1988,* Collection "État Présent", Brussels.

Ziegler, Jean, 1963, *La Contre-révolution en Afrique,* Paris, Payot.

CHRONOLOGY

1959

4–7 January: Uprising in Léopoldville; hundreds of Congolese are killed in the post-rebellion repression.

13 January: King Baudouin states he is in favour of the Congo's independence, "without harmful procrastination, but without ill-considered haste".

End of October/beginning of November: Anti-colonial demonstrations end in bloody confrontation with the armed forces. Patrice Lumumba, leader of the Congolese National Movement (MNC), is jailed.

End of 1959: Pre-revolutionary chaos in large parts of Léopoldville province, controlled by Kasa Vubu (Abako party) and Gizenga (Parti Solidaire Africain).

1960

27 January: Round table in Brussels. The Belgian government gives in to the anti-colonial movement: independence will be granted to the Congo on June 30. Lumumba is freed and transferred to Brussels.

11–25 May: Elections in the Congo.

31 May: Lumumba and the MNC claim electoral victory and the right to form a government.

15 June: The Belgian parliament unilaterally modifies the provisional Basic Law relating to the structure of the Congo. Thus Tshombe, the colonial power's man of straw, can form a homogeneous government in Katanga.

23–24 June: Vote of confidence in Lumumba's government by the Congolese Chamber and Senate. Kasa Vubu is elected president.

30 June: Declaration of Congolese independence.

5 July: Uprising in army camps in Léopoldville and Thysville, after General Janssens declares he is against admitting Congolese into the Congolese army's Belgian officer corps.

6–8 July: The Congolese government Africanises the army. Lundula becomes commander-in-chief; Mobutu is appointed colonel and chief-of-staff. Rumours about the rape of European women by mutinous soldiers cause a mass exodus of Europeans. Meanwhile, calm returns to Léopoldville and Thysville.

9 July: Belgian officers in Katanga oppose Africanisation. Congolese soldiers in Camp Massart (Elisabethville) revolt against their officers.

10 July: Belgian troops intervene in Elisabethville; interventions follow in Luluabourg (10 July), Matadi (11 July), Léopoldville (13 July) and other strategic areas of the Congo.

11 July: Supported by Belgian troops, Tshombe proclaims Katanga's secession.

12 July: President Kasa Vubu and Prime Minister Lumumba call on the UN to act "against the present external aggression".

14 July: The UN Security Council decides to intervene in the Congo and calls on the Belgian government "to withdraw its troops from the territory of the Republic of the Congo". Barely forty-eight hours after this decision, the first Blue Berets arrive in the Congo.

22 July: The Security Council calls on Brussels to "speedily" implement the 14 July resolution.

23 July: Departure of the last Belgian soldiers in Léopoldville. Contingents of UN troops establish themselves throughout the Congo, except in Katanga where Belgian troops keep Tshombe in the saddle.

5 August: Following Tshombe's vehement protests, UN Secretary General Dag Hammarskjöld abandons the idea, which had been publicly announced, of sending Blue Berets to Katanga.

8–9 August: The Security Council demands that Brussels withdraw its troops from Katanga "immediately". The Security Council states that the UN "will not be a party" to the conflict between Léopoldville and Elisabethville. Encouraged by these developments, Kalonji proclaims the secession of South Kasai.

12–13 August: Negotiations between Hammarskjöld and Tshombe in Elisabethville. UN troops will go to Katanga, but guarantees are given to Tshombe that they will not intervene in the secession.

14–15 August: Relations between Hammarskjöld and Lumumba break down.

18 August: During a National Security Council meeting in Washington, US President Eisenhower makes clear that he favours Lumumba's elimination.

21–22 August: The Security Council sides with the secretary general.

26 August: Allen Dulles, head of the CIA, sends a telegram to the CIA in Léopoldville: "the removal [of Lumumba] must be an urgent and prime objective . . . this should be a high priority of our covert action".

27 August: Congolese government troops take Bakwanga, the South Kasai "capital". A few days later, other nationalist units progress towards the north of Katanga.

5 September: President Kasa Vubu dismisses Prime Minister Lumumba and six other ministers from their duties. Behind the scenes, the UN, helped by Washington, gives Kasa Vubu decisive support.

7–8 September: The Congolese Chamber and the Senate reject Kasa Vubu's coup.

10 September: Pierre Wigny, the Belgian foreign minister, writes to his assistants in Brazzaville: "the constituted authorities have the duty to render Lumumba harmless."

11–12 September: Belgian Colonel Louis Marlière starts preparing for a Belgian plan to eliminate Lumumba, called Operation Barracuda. In a message, Brussels says that the African affairs minister will judge the moment to act, unless an emergency arises, in which case the minister will cover up an immediate assassination initiated in Africa.

13 September: A joint meeting of both Chambers gives full powers to Lumumba's government.

14 September: Kasa Vubu dissolves parliament. That same evening, Colonel Mobutu proclaims his first coup. During this time, Kasa Vubu, Mobutu and the UN leaders move heaven and earth to stop Lumumba's offensive against South Kasai and Katanga.

6 October: the Belgian Minister of African Affairs d'Aspremont Lynden demands that "Lumumba be eliminated once and for all".

10 October: Patrice Lumumba is a *de facto* prisoner in his house in Léopoldville. Soon afterwards, Operation Barracuda which aims to eliminate the former prime minister is cancelled.

24 November: Under massive pressure from the West, the UN General Assembly recognises Kasa Vubu's delegation as the Republic of the Congo's legal representative.

27 November: Lumumba escapes from his residence and tries to reach Stanleyville where Antoine Gizenga is regrouping the nationalists.

2 December: The UN leadership orders its troops not to protect Lumumba, who is being pursued by Mobutu's soldiers. Ghanaian Blue Berets refuse to protect the hunted Lumumba. The former prime minister is arrested and imprisoned in Thysville. The CIA stops its operation to kill Lumumba.

End of December/ beginning of January: nationalist offensive from Stanleyville: Bukavu (Kivu) falls on 25 December; Manono (north Katanga) on 7 January.

1961

1 January: Mobutu's attempt to reconquer Bukavu ends in fiasco.

4 January: Brussels sends a telegram to Brazza, where Léo's "special attention" is drawn to "the disastrous consequences of releasing Lumumba".

12–13 January: Revolt in the army camp of Thysville, where Lumumba is a prisoner.

13 January: The CIA in Léo writes to Washington: "[The CIA] station and embassy believe current government may fall within few days. Result would almost certainly be chaos and [Lumumba's] return to power. . . . Refusal to take drastic steps at this time will lead to defeat of [US] policy in Congo."

14 January: The mutiny extends to the army camp in the capital. Lumumba's political return seems imminent.

14–17 January: Brussels is relentless in its attempt to have Lumumba sent to Tshombe (Katanga) or Kalonji (South Kasai).

17 January: Patrice Lumumba, Maurice Mpolo and Joseph Okito are transferred to Elisabethville. While Belgian prime movers and UN leaders look away, the prisoners are murdered. Their deaths are not made public.

1–2 February: New US President John F. Kennedy defines his policy on the Congo. He favours a strengthened UN mandate in the Congo and the constitution of "a middle-of-the-road government under Ileo as prime minister". Kennedy opposes Lumumba's return to power: he can only be released from prison (in Katanga, where he is thought to be) after the establishment of a new Congolese national government. Ghanaian President Nkrumah and Indian Prime Minister Nehru are informed of Kennedy's policy.

13 February: Katanga announces the deaths of Lumumba, Mpolo and Okito.

21 February: New Security Council resolution authorising the United Nations to use force if necessary in order to "prevent the occurrence of civil war in the Congo". The Council recognises "the imperative necessity of the restoration of parliamentary institutions in the Congo."

2 August: Under UN auspices, a vote of confidence in the Adoula government is passed by the Congolese Chamber and the Senate. The nationalists support the regime; Tshombe maintains Katanga's secession.

1963

17 January: Military confrontations between Blue Berets and Katangan *Gendarmerie* lead to an agreement between Tshombe and the UN. Katangan secession is overturned; Tshombe and his followers keep the political mandates they held before the secession.

29 September: Kasa Vubu dissolves parliament.

1964

January: Pierre Mulele who has been preparing a network of resistance in Kwilu since July 1963 launches an uprising against Kasa Vubu and Mobutu's regime.

May: Soumialot, Gbenye and Nicolas Olenga open a second front in the East.

July: Rebels' blitzkrieg offensive: Mobutu's units capitulate in Albertville and Stanleyville; Kindu falls on 21 July; Stanleyville on 4 August. Nationalist positions are 100 kilometres away from Léopoldville. Mobutu rescues Tshombe: together they recruit a large number of mercenaries.

24 November: Belgo-American intervention. Belgian para-commandos are dropped in Stanleyville and Paulis. An armoured brigade, with hundreds of mercenaries and led by Belgian army officers, starts a bloody counter-attack.

1965

24 November: Mobutu's second coup. The general proclaims the Second Republic, and invests all powers in himself.

INDEX

Adam, Pierre 110
Adoula, Cyrille 41, 62, 72, 161–2, 163
  Bakwanga rebellion 159
  new prime minister 157
Akunda, L. 52
Albert, Prince of Belgium 25, 49
Allard, Jules 50, 129
Annez de Taboada, Jean 91
The Arena: The Story of Lumumba's Assassination
    (Soete) 141
Aronstein, George 154
Aspremont Lynden, Charles d' xviii, 43
Aspremont Lynden, Gobert d' 37, 43
Aspremont Lynden, Count Harold d' 12
  appointed to African affairs 19
  background and roles 37
  Belgian complicity 137
  on danger of releasing Lumumba 70
  direction of blame 145
  elimination of Lumumba 46–7, 49
  government role 43–5
  in Katanga 9
  military strategies 64
  Operation Barracuda 25
  orders tight guard for safety 134
  pleased with Vandewalle 160
  sets the tone 113, 114
  telegram urges transfer 81–3, 86, 90,
      92, 108, 109
  warns against Gizenga 161

Ball, George 162
Baluba (Nendaka's soldier) 93

Bartelous, Jacques xviii, 83, 86–7, 106
  advice 110–11
  Bakwanga rebellion 159
  cover-up 134
  distraught over execution 122
  gives the message 90
  Lumumba's arrival 98, 113
Bauchau, Pierre 64
Baudouin, King of Belgium xxii
  appeals to UN 11–12
  decision to intervene 7
  foresees revolution 178
  independence celebration 1–2
  proposed transitional head of Congo
      44
  protests against in India 147
  publicly condemns Lumumba 48–9
  rewards and gratitude 159–60
  role in the crisis 36–42
  support for Tshombe 10, 159
Beaumont, François 95
Behind the Masquerade (Ruys) xxiii–xxiv
Belina, Alexandre 128–9, 142, 144
  Bakwanga rebellion 159
Bellefroid, Eric de 168
Ben Bella, Ahmed xxv
Berendsen, Ian 21, 112
  Lumumba's arrival in Elisabethville
      130
Bintu, Raphaël 159
Bissell, Richard 17
Blistein, Captain Xavier 99, 117
Bobozo, Lieutenant-Colonel Louis 59

personal guard 61
  releases Lumumba to Nendaka 93–4
  Thysville mutiny 73–5
Bolikango, Jean 63
  Brazzaville conference 69
Bombeko, Justin
  in College of Commissioners 27
Bomboko, Justin 8, 21, 72, 174
  aware of public opinion 29
  Brazzaville conference 69
  to Camp Hardy 74
  Ileo's provisional government 153
  ill-treatment of Lumumba 58
  Lumumba's transfer 71, 79
  protests to UN 153
  on safety of prisoners 100
  UN protection 130
Brassinne, Jacques xviii, 62–3
  Belgian complicity 85–7, 87–8, 89,
        107–12, 167, 168
  on the execution 122–3
  ill-treatment of prisoners 103
  'Inquiry into the death of Patrice
        Lumumba' xxii–xxv, 82–3, 85, 167
  on Katanga 33
  Lumumba: The Last Fifty Days of His Life
        (with Gérard-Libois) 53, 55, 56
  Lumumba's transfer 70, 79, 80
  reward 160
  Soete's job 140–43
  on threat of Lumumba 145–6
  on treatment at Brouwez house 105–6
  on Tshombe's "cabinet meeting" 113–14,
        115
  Who Killed Patrice Lumumba? (with
        Kestergat) xxiii, 82
Brecht, Bertolt
  The Threepenny Opera xxv
Breuer (butler) 115, 117, 126
Brouwez, Lucien 104
Bunche, Ralph 8
  on overthrow 17
  on Tshombe 13–14
Byrne, H. 66

Cahen, Alfred 57
Canup, William 109
Capiot, Second Lieutenant Raymond 64
Cardoso, Mario 27
Castro, Fidel xviii, xxiv, 179–80
Central Intelligence Agency

  responsibility xxiv
Clémens, Professor René 34, 64, 86, 108,
        163
  civilian authority 118
  complicity 110
  cover-up 139
  favours trial 116
Conakat Party 32
Le Congo, terre d'avenir, est-il menaçé?
        (Lumumba) 175–6
Congolese National Army (ANC)
  Africanisation 6–7, 8
  UN pays wages 28
  see also Mobutu, Joseph-Désiré
Congolese National Movement (MNC) 5
Conrad, Joseph
  Heart of Darkness 147
Cordier, Andrew 17, 19–20
Cordy, Jacques 74
Cordy, Jean xviii, 50
  Lumumba's transfer 79
Cornélis, Joseph 132
Cornet, Jules 31
Corte, Marcel de 11, 82
Le Courrier d'Afrique (newspaper) 29
Cousin, Jules 155
Créner, Henri 89–90, 110–11, 135, 147
Crèvecoeur, Jean-Marie 33, 64, 66
  Lumumba's arrival 101
Crisis in the Congo (De Witte) xxii
Crokart, Jean-Baptiste 54
Cudell, Guy 171
Cumont, Commander-in-chief Belgian army
        64

Davignon, Viscount Etienne 24
Davister, Pierre 12, 63, 103, 156
Dayal, Rajeshwar 23, 27–8
  assures protection to all foreigners 139
  Lumumba in prison 59, 75
  Lumumba's escape and capture 52, 53,
        55
  protests violence 58
  request for body 150
  on Tshombe's repression 154
De Corte, Professor 48
De Witte, Ludo
  Crisis in the Congo xxii
Dedeken, Guy 98
Dedeken, Noël 24, 98
  reaction to execution 132

Delvaux, Albert 62, 126
Denis, Georges 50
    on eliminating Lumumba 46
    Lumumba's transfer 79
Devlin, Lawrence xvi, 47–8, 77–8, 85
Diaka, Bernardin Mungu 52
Diem, Ngo Dihn xxiv
Dieu, Gaston 92
Diomi, Gaston 25
Disase, Jérome 99
Dixon, Jack 95
    film of beatings lost 97–8
Donnay, H. *see* Brassinne, Jacques
Doutreloux, Michel 91
Drugmand, Jean-Louis 95, 96
    sickened by torture 97
Dubuisson, Marcel 41–2
Dulles, Allen 78
    on overthrow of Lumumba 16–17
    plans to eliminate Lumumba 47–8
Dumba, Jacqueline 91
Dupret, Marcel 18, 23, 25, 50
    on Lumumba's escape 53–4
    on mutiny 76–8
    on prisoner transfers 69
    on support for Lumumba 75–6
Duray, Louis 86

Eisenhower, Dwight D. xv, xvi, xxii, 47, 179
    favours assassination 78
Elengesa, Pierre 166
Eyskens, Gaston xxii
    Belgian complicity 137, 139
    conspiracy theory 4
    decision to intervene 7
    decolonisation 180
    government grants independence 5
    Katanga 34
    king's reward 160
    Lumumba's independence speech 2
    Lumumba's transfer 81
    prepared for Congo crisis 42–3
    pressures Kasa Vubu 18
    responsibility xxiv
    soothes king 36
    treatment of Lumumba in prison 70

Fanon, Frantz xxv
Fataki, Major Jacques 73
    murder 153
Fau, Robert 95

Finant, Jean-Pierre 73, 166
    murder 153
Forminière, République de la 12

Gat, Captain Julien 103
    background 99
    at Brouwez house 104–5
    cover-up 129
    execution of prisoners 119–21
    homicide 112
    later consequences 129
    Lumumba's arrival 98–100, 101
    ordered to carry out assassinations
        117–19
    post-execution 122–3, 125
    responsibility 167, 168
    rumour about interview 147
    takes charge of prisoners 108
    tries to stop beatings 102
Gbenye, Christophe 5, 52
Gérard-Libois, Jules 21, 62, 70, 72
Gilbert, O. P.
    "empire of silence" 2
Gillet, Colonel Jean 85, 159
Gizenga, Antoine xxii, 5, 30
    d'Aspremont Lynden warns against 161
    gathers nationalist forces 52
    on intervention 9
    Kasa Vubu requests 56–7
    recognized by international leaders 154
    successes 76, 77
    transfer to Elisabethville 69
Goblet, Guy 96, 97
Goffin, Léon 154
Goffinet, Police Chief 64
Gottlieb, Sidney 17, 47
Grandelet, Lieutenant Claude 99, 100, 102
    at Brouwez house 103, 105
    cover up 127
Grandjean, Lieutentant-Colonel 64
Grenfell, Georges 59
Groothaert, Jacques 170

Hammarskjöld, Dag xv, xvi, xxii, 25, 144
    briefed on capture 56
    embarrassment 60–61
    international reaction to news 147, 150
    intervention 8, 9
    on Katangan army 34
    Kremlin blames 158
    offers troops 52

overthrow of Lumumba 14–15, 17
passivity 130–31, 131–2
Hammarskjöld, Dag *continued*
  protests violence 58
  request for information 155–6
  statement on Lumumba's death 151
  supports Tshombe 12–14
  US financial aid 27
  worried about support 66
Heart of Darkness (Conrad) 147
Heinz, G. *see* Gérard-Libois, Jules
Hellemans, J. 34
Hemptinne, Monsignor Jean-Félix de 32
Horn, General Carl von 20, 55–6
Huyghé, Carlo 101, 103
  at Brouwez house 105
  complicity 111
  Lumumba's arrival 126
  Verscheure's visit after execution 125

Ileo, Joseph 17, 23
  Bakwanga rebellion 159
  Brazzaville conference 69
  to Camp Hardy 74
  Lumumba's transfer 79
  provisional government 153
Illunga, Valentin 34
"Inquiry into the death of Patrice Lumumba"
    (Brassinne) xxii–xxv, 82–3, 85

Jacquemain, Betty 101
Janssens, General E. 6, 48, 173
Janssens, Major Paul 64
  promotion 65
Jaspar, Roger 132
Jonniaux, Jean 91

Kabeya, André 159
Kabila, Laurent xxvi, 171
  calls for punishment 166
Kalb, Madeleine 74
  on Lumumba's position 77, 78
Kalonji, Albert 12, 16, 17–18, 159
  desire to kill Lumumba 83, 84
Kamishanga, Mathias 54
Kamitatu 61
Kandolo, Damien 62, 79
  children safe in Belgium 159
  transfer operation 91
Kasa Vubu, Joseph xxv
  and Lumumba

agreement about soldiers 7
  army co-operation 26
  coup against Lumumba 19–22
  coup voted against 22–3
  didn't want elimination 51
  ill-treatment of Lumumba 58
  negotiates with Lumumba 74
  notified of Tshombe's acceptance 87,
      88–9
  political strength against Lumumba
      181
  under pressure 15, 17, 18
  transfer 79, 83
  UN passivity about prisoners 131, 133
politics and career
  asks for Gizenga and Mpolo 56
  Brazzaville conference 69
  democratic façade 153, 157
  gathers demonstrators 30
  independence celebration 1–2
  kicked out by Mobutu 164
  later years 161–2
  network 72–3
  plane denied access to Katanga 8
  as president 5
  promotes Mobutu 127
  relations with Tshombe 71, 90–91
  Tshombe's direction of blame 145
  UN support shifts to 51–2
Kashamura, Anicet 5, 52
Kasongo, Joseph 2, 76
Le Katanga de Moïse Tshombe (Weber) 167
Kazadi, Ferdinand 62
  "cabinet meeting" 113–15
  to Elisabethville 92
  flight from Camp Hardy 95
  Lumumba's transfer 79, 91, 101–2
  negotiates with dissatisfied soldiers 75
  watches beatings 97
Kengo wa Dondo 169, 170, 173
Kennedy, John F. 77, 161
Kestergat, Jean 48, 62–3
  on Belgian advice about transfer 85–7
  Belgian political advisers 107–12
  Lumumba's transfer 80, 81, 82
  on Belgian complicity 87–8, 89
  Who Killed Patrice Lumumba? (with
      Brassinne) xxiii, 82
Khrushchev, Nikita xvi, xvii, 158
Kibwe, Jean-Baptiste 35, 101
  attends execution 119–20

Belgian complicity 110
"cabinet meeting" 113–15
visits Brouwez house 105, 106–7, 117–19
Kie, Pauline 60, 184
Kimba, Evariste 35, 159
  attends execution 119–20
  visits Brouwez house 117–19
Kini, Emmanuel 96
Kinsch, Monsignor 151
Kisolokele, Charles 159
Kitenge, Gabriel 101
  attends execution 119–20
  "cabinet meeting" 113–15
  visits Brouwez house 105, 117–19

Lahaye, André 50, 62
  Belgian observer 70
  Lumumba's transfer 79, 80, 89
  transfer operation 91, 92
Lamy, René 170
Larock, Victor 83, 139
Lebrun, A. 135
Leburton, Edmond 173
Léopold II xvii, 1, 6, 37, 73
Léva, Second Lieutenant Roger 99, 101
  at Brouwez house 103, 105, 117
Leysen, André 170–71
Lihau, Marcel 27, 159
Lilian, Princess of Retie 160
Lindekens, Gerard 98, 101
Lindgren, UN NCO 102–3, 112
Longerstaey, E. 91
López Alvarez, Luis 62
Loos, Major Jules xviii, 139
  appoints Vandewalle 67
  on interview with Gat 147
  mission to eliminate 49
  Operation Barracuda 24–5
  rewards 159
  sphere of influence 44–5
Lubuma, Valentin 54
Lumumba, François 150
Lumumba, Léonie 21
Lumumba, Patrice Emery
  aftermath
    halts revolutionary momentum 164
    Mobutu and Kabila's political use of
      165–6
  arrest
    Belgian determination to eliminate
      46–51

loses UN support 51–52
Mobutu surrounds house 30–31
temporary escape 48
colonial days
  arrests and imprisonment 100–101
  Le Congo, terre d'avenir, est-il menaçé?
    175–6
cover-up
  conjectures about plots 146–7
  escape story released to world 143–5
  UN Commission conclusions 157–8
death
  Belgian involvement 121–2, 123–4
  Belgian political advisors 107–13
  cover-up 128–9, 133–40
  execution 112, 119–24
  exhumed, dismembered and dissolved
    in acid 140–43
  funeral service 150, 151–2
  impact in Belgium 133–40
  Kalonji eager to kill 83, 84–5
  national and international reactions to
    147–52, 154–8
  rumours spread of 126–8
  Tshombe and ministers condemn
    113–15, 117–18
  UN passivity 130–33
escape
  capture outside Stanleyville 55–7
  defends political project 53
  evades house guard 52–3
  journey to Stanleyville 52–4
execution
  later reflections on 166–7
family
  denied Léonie's funeral 21
government
  agreement about soldiers 7
  CIA hit list xxiv
  foreign portrayal as madman 48–9
  before independence 4–6
  Independence Day speech 2, 6, 176
  international forces against 14–22
  Kasa Vubu's *coup* against 19–23
  Marlière's Operation Barracuda 23–6
  media attacks 11, 12
  misunderstood UN 181–2
  nicknamed "Satan" 45
  plane denied access to Katanga 8
  public support for 29–31
  upsets king 36–42

Lumumba, Patrice Emery *continued*
  historiography xxi–xxv, 174–83
  imprisonment
    arrival in Katanga 100–107
    beaten in transit to Katanga 97–8,
      101–2
    Belgian advice 82–7
    Brouwez house beatings 104–7, 117
    in Camp Hardy 59–63
    code named "Satan" 81
    decision to eliminate 80, 82–3
    effect of possible release 77–8
    fetched from Camp Hardy 93–100
    letters from prison 59–60, 184–5
    official indecision 70–72
    possibility of a trial 108–9
    publicly ill-treated 57–9
    refuses government post 74
    Thysville mutiny 75–9
    transfer to Katanga 69–71, 89–92
  personal
    dignity through beatings 102, 106,
      136
    Verscheure calls 'brave' 125
Lumumba, Patrice (son) 150
Lumumba, Roland 52, 150
Lumumba: The Last Fifty Days of His Life
  (Brassinne and Kestergat) 53, 55, 56,
  62–3
Lundula, Victor
  becomes commander-in-chief 6–7
Lutula, Joseph 150
Luxemburg, Rosa xxv

Macmillan, Harold xv
Malcolm X xxv
Malula, Bishop 19, 174
Manzikala, Jean 151
Marlair, Jean-Claude 164, 167
Marlière, Colonel Louis xviii, 18
  ANC crisis 75
  anti-Lumumba network 72–3
  arrives in Elisabethville 126
  assassination as "public health" 112
  complains about Lumumba's freedom
    30
  disappointing arrest 50–51
  later career 172
  Lumumba's transfer 79–81, 85, 88
  measures against Lumumba 23–6
  Operation Barracuda 31

  practicalities of transfer 92
  reaction to execution 132
  rewards 159
Massart, A. 34
Masuba, Alphonsine 150
Matthys, Major J.
  offensive against nationalists 153–4
Mbungu, Joseph 19
Mbuyi, Joseph 52, 166
Mezo, André 95
Michels, Lieutenant Gabriel 99
  at Brouwez house 103
  conditions for killing 107
  execution of prisoners 119–21, 123
  homicide 112
  military police escort 119
  post-execution 125
  responsibility 167, 168
Mikolacjczak, Marc 33
Mille et quatre jours see Vandewalle, Colonel
  Frédéric
Mobutu, Joseph-Désiré xxi, xxvi
  beating of prisoners 57, 103
  Brazzaville conference 69
  to Camp Hardy 74–5
  captures Lumumba outside Stanleyville
    54
  College of Commissioners 76
  in Kasai 16
  Lumumba's transfer 79, 83
  negotiates with dissatisfied soldiers 75
  network 72–3
  rabble army 61, 77
  support for xxiv, 25, 26, 27–8, 50
  surrounds Lumumba's house 30
  later career
    Ileo's provisional government 153
    Mulele's rebellion 163
    rehabilitates Lumumba 165–6
    repressive regime 171–2
    takes power 164
    Zaïrian economics and Belgian visit
      169–74
Mohammed V of Morocco 148
Mossadegh, Mohammed 178
Moulin, Gaston 6
Moumié, Félix xxv
Mpolo, Maurice 30, 52
  arrival in Katanga 101–3
  Belgian complicity 111, 112
  at Brouwez house 103–4

escape story released to world 143–5
execution 119–21
exhumed, dismembered and dissolved in
 acid 140–43
fate decided at 'cabinet meeting' 116
international reaction to death 148, 151,
 154–8
Kasa Vubu requests 56
taken from Camp Hardy 93, 97–8
transfer to Elisabethville 69
Tshombe and ministers condemn 118–19
UN Commission conclusions 157–8
UN passivity 130
Muhona, Paul 35, 159
Mujanay, Barthélemy 52
Mukamba, Jonas 95, 97
 to Elisabethville 92
 Lumumba's arrival in Katanga 101
Muke, Major Norbert 99, 105
 execution of prisoners 119–21
 military police escort 119
Mukeba, Cléophas 113
Mulele, Pierre xxvi, 5, 30
 escape with Lumumba 52, 54
 hacked to pieces by Mobutu 163, 172
 mother hacked to pieces 172
 rebellion 163
Mumba, Raphaël 99, 101
 at Brouwez house 103–4
 cover-up 128
Munongo, Antoine 140
Munongo, Godefroid 12, 35, 101
 attends execution 119–20
 Bakwanga rebellion 159
 "cabinet meeting" 114–15
 cover-up 128, 129, 136
 "honour" to kill Lumumba 83–4
 Lumumba's transfer 90, 91
 releases cover story 143–4
 visits Brouwez house 105, 106–7,
 117–19
Muzungu, Christophe 166

Nasser, Gamal Abdel xviii, 147, 178, 182
Ndele, Albert 27, 72
Nehru, Jawaharlal 182
Nendaka, Victor 50, 57, 174
 arrives in Elisabethville 126
 background 94
 to Camp Hardy 74
 children safe in Belgium 159

fetches Lumumba from Camp Hardy 93–7
Ileo's provisional government 153
leadership 72
Lumumba's transfer 79, 91, 92
and the UN 133
Nkrumah, Kwame 17, 182
 eulogy 148
Nussbaumer, José 79
Nzuzi, Emmanuel 166

Okito, Joseph 52
 arrival in Katanga 101–3
 Belgian complicity 111, 112
 at Brouwez house 103–4
 at Camp Hardy 93, 97–8
 disposal of body 140–43
 escape story released to world 143–5
 execution 119–21
 fate decided at 'cabinet meeting' 116
 imprisoned with Lumumba 59, 60
 international reaction to death 148, 151,
 154–8
 Tshombe and ministers condemn 118–19
 UN Commission conclusions 157–8
 UN passivity 130
Oldenhove, Jean 41
Onawelo, Albert 60, 150
Opango, Pauline 52, 60, 150
 letter from Lumumba 184–5

Perin, François 22
Perrad, Paul 86–7, 98
 at Brouwez house 107
 complicity 110, 111
 cover-up 127, 129
 favours trial 116
Pholien, Joseph 138
Pieters, Dr Guy 143–4, 151
Pilaet, E. 24
Pirenne, Jacques 42
Pongo, Gilbert 55, 56, 57
 begs for Lumumba's freedom 73
Protin, Captain 101, 110
Puati, Commandant 126, 159
Putman, Luc 169, 170, 171

Renard, André 138
Renard, F. 86
Renous, Maurice 95
Rikhye, Indar Jit 18
 protecting Tshombe 65, 66

Rolin, Henri   10, 138
Rothschild, Robert   12, 44
    on fragility of Tshombe's government
        67–8
    on Lumumba's mistreatment   57, 58
    Lumumba's transfer   68–9, 71
Rougefort, René   106
    at Brouwez house   117
Ruys, Manu   171
    attacks on Lumumba   11, 12
    Behind the Masquerade   xxiii–xxiv
    defence of Belgians   9–10
    on Katanga   35
    on Tshombe's visit to king   40

Sakela, Warrant Officer   105, 119
Samalenge, Lucas
    boasts of Lumumba's death   126
    visits Brouwez house   117
Sankara, Thomas   180–1
Sapwe, Pius   99, 102, 103
    attends execution   119–20
    at Brouwez house   118, 119
    cover-up   128, 129
    disposal of the bodies   140
Sartre, Jean-Paul   xxiv, 174, 178
Scheyven   173–4
Schöller, André   33
Schoonbroodt, Second Lieutenant   61, 73, 94
Segers, Georges   99, 100, 101, 102
    at Brouwez house   103–4, 106
Sendwe, Jason
    political elimination   86, 87
Servais (Tshombe's secretary)   87–8, 115
Smal, *Major* René   101, 108, 111
    celebrations   126
Smets, Lieutenant Walter   64
Soete, Gerard   xviii
    *The Arena. The Story of Lumumba's
        Assassination*   141
    cover-up   128
    exhumes, dismembers and dissolves
        bodies   140–3
    responsibility   167
Son, Sergeant François   103, 104, 105
    at Brouwez house   117
    execution of prisoners   119–21, 122
    homicide   112
    military police escort   119
    post-execution   122–3, 125
    responsibility   167, 168

Soumialot, Gaston   163
Souris, Christian   98
Spaak, Paul-Henri   161, 162, 163
Spandre, Mario
    favours trial   116
Stalin, Joseph   157
Stengers, J.   42

Thomas, François   86–7, 98, 113
A Thousand and Four Days (Vandewalle)
        3–4
The Threepenny Opera (Brecht)   xxv
Tignée, Victor   86–7, 103, 111
    arrival of prisoners   98–9
    Bakwanga rebellion   159
    cover-up   128
    crucial role   118–19
    Lumumba's arrival   101
Timberlake, Ambassador Clare H.   17, 52
    on Lumumba's isolation   30
    stops disturbing images   58
Tindemans, Leo   170
    charmed by Mobutu   172–3
Toussaint, Philippe   156
Trinquier, Colonel   139
Troch, E.   35, 136–7
Trujillo, Rafael   xxiv
Tshisekedi, Etienne   27, 166, 171
Tshombe, Marie   116
Tshombe, Moïse   xxv, 4
    career
        strength against Lumumba   181
    cover-up   134
        refers to beatings on plane   144–5
        refuses body or grave to widow
            150
    death of prisoners
        accepts Lumumba   81–2, 87–9
        attends execution   119–20
        on beatings in transit   101
        Belgian support   9–11, 110
        celebrates Lumumba's arrival
            113–16
        deal includes Sendwe   86–7
        determined for execution   107–8
        responsibility   167
        transfer decided   89–92
        UN passivity about prisoners
            130–3
        visits Brouwez house   105, 106, 115,
            117–19

later career
  Bakwanga rebellion 160–3
  esteem from King Badouin 159
  misses Vandewalle 162
  Mulele's rebellion 163
politics
  allegiances 35–6
  Belgian advisors 85–6
  Brazzaville conference 69
  king's support for 37–42
  "'legal *coup d'état*" 6
  military repression 153–4
  nicknamed "the Jew" 45
  overthrow of Lumumba 14–15, 19
  party and allegiances 32, 33–4
  relations with Kasa Vubu 71, 90–1
  supports Belgian officers 7
  UN support 12–14, 28, 64–8
Tshungu, Michel 60

Ugeux, E. 122, 173
  cover-up 134
Urbain, Sergeant 139

Van Bilsen, Jef
  "'legal *coup d'état*" 6
  pressure on Kasa Vubu 18
Van den Bosch, Ambassador Jean 8, 179
Van der Meersch, Captain Piet 91–2, 95,
    100
  sees abuse of prisoners 97, 98
Van der Meersch, Ganshof 44, 173
Van Gorp, J. 24
Van Lierde, Jean 97, 176
Van Roey, Cardinal 11
Van Zeeland, Paul 44
Vandamme, Commandant René 68
Vanden Bloock, Jan 28, 84
  arrives in Elisabethville 126
  cover-up 134, 135, 139
  discussion about prisoners 111
  on Katanga 66
  on prisoner transfers 69–70
Vandewalle, Colonel Frédéric
  career and views
    on Africanisation of army 7
    appointed secret military chief
      67–8
    attends meetings 86
    becomes Belgian chargé d'affaires 41
    on Belgian support for Katenga 11

  on Belgophobia and Lumumbaphobia
    49
  independence day 3–4
  on Katanga 14, 32, 33, 34
  king's support for Katanga 39
  later years 160–64
  Loos brings to Katanga 45
  on opposition 23
  on Polish arms cargo 43
cover-up
  on Belgian role 166–8
  UN investigation 156
executions
  celebrations 126
  complicity 108–10
  cover-up 121, 127, 134, 135–6
  planned elimination 100
Mille et quatre jours (A Thousand and Four
    Days) 3–4, 166–8
the prisoners
  on bloodthirsty actions 63
  at Brouwez house 107–8, 117
  Lumumba's arrival 101
  Lumumba's transfer 79, 87
  plans commando action 50
  on torture 105
Verdickt, Armand 'Joe' xviii, 98, 163
  at Brouwez house 107
  complicity 110
  intelligence operation 45
  Lumumba's arrival 101
  Lumumba's transfer 81
  pays executioners 158–9
  silence to colleagues 87–8
  witnesses beating 102
Verhaegen, Benoît xxiii
Verscheure, Commissioner Frans 99, 101
  after assassination 111
  Brouwez house 103, 106–7, 117–19
  cover-up 144
  death only solution 109
  execution of prisoners 119–23
  homicide 112
  keeps souvenir from bodies 140
  on ministers' decision 115
  payment for execution 158
  post-execution 125–6
  responsibility 167, 168
von Horn, Carl 66

Watson, Bob 91, 95–6, 98

Weber, Major Guy 4, 33, 34, 86–7
  Bakwanga rebellion 159
  Belgian military presences 63–4
  on Belgians and Africans 167
  at Brouwez house 107–8
  complicity 109–10, 112
  on Gat's harrassment 129
  Le Katanga de Moïse Tshombe 167
  king's support 41
  Lumumba's arrival 101, 113–14
  reward 160
Westhof J. 50
Who Killed Patrice Lumumba? (Brassinne and
    Kestergat) xxiii, 82
  Tshombe's reaction to Lumumba's arrival
    113–14
Wieschhoff, Heinrich 130
Wigny, Pierre
  Belgian intervention 137–9, 146–7,
    150–51

  cover-up 135–6, 137
  direction of blame 145
  instructions on transfer 96
  Lumumba's overthrow 11, 15, 18, 23
  Lumumba's transfer 71, 79, 81–3
  prepared for war 43
  preventing Lumumba's return 49–50
  on putting Lumumba out of harm 47
  reward 160
Willame, Jean-Claude 174
Wingudi, V. 52

Yav, Colonel Joseph 65
  appointed defence minister 63
Youlou, Fulburt 19, 69
  political balancing 75
Yumba, Jean 129

Zuzu, Lieutenant 93
  "cabinet meeting" 113–15